THE CLASSICS
OF WESTERN
SPIRITUALITY

THE CLASSICS OF WESTERN SPIRITUALITY
A Library of the Great Spiritual Masters

THE PURSUIT OF WISDOM

and other works, by the author of The Cloud of Unknowing

TRANSLATED, EDITED, AND ANNOTATED BY

JAMES A. WALSH, S.J.

PREFACE BY

GEORGE A. MALONEY, S.J.

PAULIST PRESS

NEW YORK ● MAHWAH

Cover Art: Frank Sabatté, C.S.P., received his B.A. in art from U.C.L.A. in 1973, studying under James Valerio, Lee Mullican and others. He has been a campus minister since 1979, and an illustrator for Paulist Press since 1977. In 1986–87 he served as vice-president of the Liturgical Arts Guild of Ohio.

Library of Congress Cataloging-in-Publication Data

Author of the Cloud of unknowing.
    The pursuit of wisdom and other works / by the author of the Cloud of unknowing; translated and edited by James Walsh.
        p.   cm.—(Classics of Western spirituality)
    Bibliography: p.
    Includes index.
    ISBN 0-8091-0404-0: $17.95   ISBN 0-8091-2972-8 (pbk.):
$14.95
    1. Spiritual life—Catholic authors—Early works to 1800.   I. Walsh, James,
1920-   . II. Title.   III. Series.
BX2349.A84   1988
248—dc19

Published by Paulist Press
997 Macarthur Boulevard
Mahwah, New Jersey 07430

Printed and bound in the United States of America

Contents

CONTENTS

Editor of this Volume

The late JAMES WALSH, S.J. was born in Lancashire in 1920, and was educated at the Catholic College, Preston, Lancashire. He joined the Society of Jesus in 1938, took an honors degree in the Classical Languages and Literature at Oxford University, and was ordained a priest in 1952. He received a doctorate in Ascetical and Mystical Theology at the Gregorian University, Rome, in 1957. He was Vice-Postulator for the Cause of the English and Welsh Martyrs, and for the Cause of Mother Cornelia Connelly, Foundress of the Society of the Holy Child Jesus.

Father Walsh's special study was fourteenth-century English spirituality. With Edmund Colledge, O.S.A. he co-edited *Julian of Norwich, Showings*, in the Classics of Western Spirituality series. He published numerous articles on medieval spirituality, and contributed to *The Month*, and *The Way*. Father Walsh also edited and introduced the book *Pre-Reformation English Spirituality*.

Author of the Preface

REV. GEORGE A. MALONEY, S.J., was ordained in Rome as a priest of the Russian Byzantine Rite, April 18, 1957. He earned a doctorate in Oriental Theology, summa cum laude in 1962 from the Pontifical Oriental Institute.

Father Maloney began an ecumenical journal, *Diakonia*, to promote dialogue between Orthodox Christians and Roman Catholics. He has served as editor of all the Eastern Rite articles for the *New Catholic Encyclopedia*.

Father Maloney is the founder of the John XXIII Institute for Eastern Christian Studies at Fordham University, and teaches Oriental philosophy and spirituality on the master and doctoral levels. He has established himself as an outstanding author on works on prayer and Eastern Christian Spirituality as applied to the daily life of Western Christians. Some of his works include *The Cosmic Darkness; Listen Prophets; Theology of Uncreated Energies;* and *Nesting in the Rock*.

This simple and delightful work (which)
is in fact the high wisdom of the Godhead
descending through grace into man's soul,
knitting it and uniting it to himself
in spiritual wisdom and discernment.

—*A Letter of Private Direction*, V

Foreword

From the Council of Trent to Vatican II—with Vatican I making scarcely a ripple on the surface of the controversy—spiritual theology in the modern schools was primarily concerned with distinctions between "infused" and "acquired" contemplation, and with the question whether high sanctity could be achieved without the regular conferral of those special infused graces of contemplative prayer. The controversy was, of course, related to the traditional division between the "lives" of monastic contemplation and apostolic action. It was generally accepted, following the teaching in the sixteenth century of St. John of the Cross—the heritage labeled Western Mysticism by Cuthbert Butler—that a long and painful apprenticeship in the ascetical life was a necessary prerequisite for the achievement of the spiritual and psychological state of readiness to receive these graces. The asceticism proper to the apostolic life and its purposes would, it was taken for granted, be less drawn-out and severe.

The focus of the controversy has shifted dramatically in our day. Though the subject of contemplation and contemplative prayer looms large in the spiritual reflections of the modern religious and theologians, consequent on the teaching of Vatican II, the idea that God should withhold his gifts to suit the categorizations of ascetic and mystical scholars now seems faintly ridiculous. We have passed through a short period in which the horizontal dominated over the vertical—when serious attempts were made to divorce the apostolic and pastoral from the *ex professo* cenobitic and eremitical; and the

1

present preoccupation is the search for the appropriate interpenetration of contemplation and action. What has to be avoided is any serious entanglement of ephemeral monastic custom and life-style belonging to an agrarian and civic environment, which not only antedates the modern technological future shock but even the European industrial revolution, with the evangelical following of Christ, the type of a truly human life. This is the simple principle that sustains those who embark on the pursuit of perfect Christian charity for life, irrespective of "state." It is the only one that defeats the ephemeral and accepts passion and resurrection as permanent. It demands that "we keep our eyes fixed on Jesus, who leads us forth in faith and will bring it to its perfection. It is he who for the sake of the joy to come endured the cross and made light of its shame" (Heb. 12:2).

So it is, then, that we follow as we watch the Father presenting us with the living Christ from Incarnation to the Descent of the Spirit, instructing us in the ways of Gospel contemplation, the descent of the heavenly wisdom. Though the author of the *Cloud* will draw his distinctions between salvation and perfection in terms of intellectual and anagogical contemplation; and though he will insist that meditation—properly understood, of course—is proper to the active life, which is synonymous with the lower branch of the contemplative, he believes that there is a consistency about the Christian pilgrimage, in which one stage merges into the other. He is confident that the contemplative virtues of humility and charity embrace the whole of the Christian life, and that the discretion governing them all will confer the openness of heart that alone is ready to receive the gifts of heavenly wisdom—the love poured out by the Spirit of God who is given to us.

There is then a quality about the six short treatises in this volume, constituting the extant *corpus* of the author of *The Cloud of Unknowing*, that succeeds in transcending times, circumstances, and the very categorizations he himself offers. In his version of Richard of St. Victor's On the Pursuit of Wisdom, which has for subtitle "the spirit's preparation for contemplation" *(De preparatione animi ad contemplationem)*, he is at pains to underline the distinction between spiritual discernment and contemplation, in the broad sense of being a contemplative human being, or an *alter Christus*, to use an old phrase. The homogeneity of the six pieces both among themselves and with the *Cloud* itself will, I think, be found to be eminently satisfying and, one hopes, instructive.

FOREWORD

Acknowledgements

This book has been long in the making. John Farina of Paulist Press, editor of the Classics of Western Spirituality, has waited long and patiently. I am grateful to my fellow Jesuits at St. Beuno's in North Wales for refusing to be bored with me when I rambled on about English Mediaeval Spirituality, and to my provincial, Fr. Jock Earle, for encouraging me to live again amid the beauties of Hopkins's Vale of Clwyd. This, of course, is rivaled by Bethany in Highland Hills, New York, where Mother Catherine and her community have treated me as one of their own. I have nothing but admiration and affection for my cryptographers, as I continue to live in primitive ignorance of wordprocessors and their like: Elizabeth Cooper, Sr. Emmanuel Orchard IBVM, and never least, Sr. Janice Farnham R.J.M.; and I remember with affectionate gratitude Denise Critchley, who believed in this book.

Preface

What we see in contemporary society, magnified by the communications media, is a burst of consciousness development. In the sixties a great social and political concern erupted, especially among the young. Americans marched, demonstrated, and lay down in the streets for peace, racial equality, the right to life. They also tripped on "acid" or played in the Dionysian hills of sexual freedom. Behind all this turmoil, we find a frenetic thirst for expanded consciousness, a defiant rebellion against being a statistic or a digit, a dehumanized "cog" in the modern industrial wheel.

The seventies rolled in with a powerful *Drang am Osten* with the journey inward and eastward. The Far-Eastern religions, Yoga, Zen, the Tibetan Book of the Dead, Gurdjieff, occultism, Edgar Cayce, were common bits of conversation. Not merely students, but middle-class businessmen, housewives and professional women, Catholic nuns, priests and ministers, were into meditation and "blowing the mind" out of stagnation by TM, Silva Mind Control, hypnosis, Arica, EST, process meditation, and transactional analysis.

They found that such disciplines not only relieved anxieties but opened up areas of the unconscious that they never suspected, except in their wildest dreams or nightmares. Creative powers were being unleashed: clairvoyance, telepathy, psychokinesis, and Theta experiences out of the body. Communing with the dead became a favorite activity. From human potential movements to spooks, the "spiritual" life was in vogue.

PREFACE

During this period lay persons began experimenting with expansion of consciousness. No doubt the rise in anxieties and stresses in daily living, the inability to cope with the speed of urban life, and the meaninglessness of it all pushed most "seekers" into the area of transcendent, psychic experiences as a way to avoid mental breakdown.

The eighties burst upon us with a spreading hunger among all classes of human society for mystical, religious experiences. No doubt this desire to encounter the living God of Abraham, Jacob, and Isaac rose up because the traditional views presented by Western Christianity and based largely on an exhausted Scholastic philosophy and theology no longer seemed adequate.

To Experience the Living God

Spiritual seekers find that Western organized religions, which tend toward teachings and dogmas, hierarchical structures of authority, and liturgical ritualism, are in a desperate need of revitalization. The faithful are desperate to experience God, not as an objective "being" outside them, but as a Divine Love, intimately and immanently present within them at all times, as well as in their creative work in the world.

The heavy rationalistic framework of Western Christianity is in need of a complementary vision. Such a "new" vision is not really so new. The God of the Old and New Testament is a God of mystery, met in wonder. Knowledge of him is grounded in intuition rather than in rational ideas The Judeo-Christian God takes man's eyes away from himself as the exploiting center of the universe and demands a humble response to God's invitation to share his divine life.

Christianity was born as the flowering of Judaism. Moses was the model of Semitic mysticism: one who in awe and trembling dared not to look upon the face of Yahweh but rather listened to the Word of God. Moses met God on top of Mount Sinai in the cloud of darkness amid thundering and lightning. The accent is on the existential encounter with the Absolute, not in images or concepts, or through a reasoning process alone, but through a reverent, silent listening.

As St. John's Gospel portrays the incarnate Word of God, God is life, to be experienced, received, to be the new force to make us into children of God. Christ is the Life of God and is our true, full life. The early Christian documents, therefore, transmit faith, the Gospel, and the sacraments under the aspect of life. Faith is the germ of life. To preach the Gospel is to sow the word of life. This new life is given in baptism. In the immersion of the Christian into the waters of baptism, the total Christian is submerged in death to selfish sinning in order that the same total person may put on the new life brought to us through Christ. Salvation is a new life in Christ that has to grow and possess our consciousness more and more.

Neoplatonic Christianity

Gradually there appeared in Christianity a shift from the existential approach to one that is more intellectual. Origen developed the Platonic concept of life assimilating light. Evagrius of Pontus of the fourth century, who has been described by Hans von Balthasar as a Christian Buddhist, defined prayer in terms of the mind: "The State of prayer is a passionless state in which supreme love transports on high a wisdom-loving spiritual mind" *(On Prayer)*.

God was now to be seen by the human intellect turned within. We see the basis for the Eastern Christian spirituality of *hesychasm* that would soon develop around this inner light. God is now experienced as light in an intellectual vision. This is the doctrine of the Alexandrian School, developed largely in the mysticism of Clement of Alexandria, Origen, and Evagrius of Pontus.

The more Semitic influence, with its accent on the total, existential encounter with God in the "heart," continued chiefly in the Antiochene School of Ignatius of Antioch, Polycarp, Irenaeus, Pseudo-Macarius, and Anthony of the desert and the whole school of mystics that placed the accent on an affective encounter in the heart with Jesus as Lord. It is the heart, not the mind, where God is encountered as the source of life. The Jesus Prayer would develop from the affective-heart spirituality of intellectualism. By reverently pronouncing the name of Jesus the Christian mystic in the desert was immersed in the presence of the risen Lord. Here we encounter an existential spirituality built around a mysticism of darkness, not light. It is considered temerity to approach God by any human reasoning. It is by purification of the heart that man disposes himself, and then God reveals himself as the Life-giver, not by means of any intellectual experience, but in the darkening of man's intellect.

PREFACE

Apophatic Theology

The author of the *Cloud of Unknowing* stands strongly in a synthesis, through the evident influence in his writings of the Pseudo-Diony-sius corpus, of the Neoplatonic traditions of the Alexandrian theologians of the early Church, but also of the apophatic, affective school of the Antiochene tradition. *Apophatic* is usually translated as negative, but this is to misunderstand the nuanced mysticism of the early Christian mystics of the East and of our *Cloud* author. The accent is entirely on God doing the revealing, giving the Gift of himself in complete freedom. No longer are men and women and their personal activities the place of emphasis except in the *praxis* or ascetical purification and illumination levels as preparatory to God's gift of infused contemplation.

Thus the early Fathers and the author of these six works plus his classic, *The Cloud of Unknowing*, unanimously agree on the importance of a *cataphatic* or positive, deductive, affirming approach to theology. They see such an approach as yielding a certain positive knowledge about God, man, and the world. Such an approach is, however, an imperfect way and must be complemented by the apophatic approach.

Thus the author in his translation, *Denis's Hidden Theology*, writes out of a long apophatic tradition:

> But in our denyings we begin with the least noble and climb up to the most noble, and then from the highest to the lowest by way of the middle, and then from the lowest to the highest again. So we fold them all up together and do away with them, that we may clearly know this unknowing which in all these existing things is walled round and hid from all intelligible powers; that we might see that darkness, the Substance beyond all substances, secretly hid from all light in these existing things.

The positive approach to theology is a descent from the superior degrees of being to the inferior. It is to speak of God through his causality upon the material effects of his created order, including man/woman and the entire material world. But the apophatic approach of true and immediate knowledge given by God's Spirit to the humble and pure of heart comes through a "luminous darkness," to quote St. Gregory of Nyssa of the fourth century.

Through Pseudo-Dionysius this mysticism of darkness reached the West mainly through the medieval Dionysians in their commen-

8

taries and through the Rhenish mystics of the fourteenth century as Meister Eckhart, Tauler and Suso, and the Flemish mystic Jan Ruysbroeck. We must place our author of the *Cloud* and these six essays as one of the main fourteenth-century mystics who developed in his writings this affective darkness of knowing by not knowing. From such sources, St. John of the Cross in his apophatic mystical theology of the sixteenth century drew heavily for his insights.

The Anonymous Author of the *Cloud*

James Walsh, S.J., the editor and commentator of the other extant works of the anonymous author presented in this present volume, has earlier traced the influence of Pseudo-Dionysius on Western spiritual writers, including the fourteenth-century author of *The Cloud of Unknowing* (see *The Cloud of Unknowing*, The Classics of Western Spirituality, Paulist Press, 1981).

In these seven works of the unknown author, whom Walsh thinks was most likely a Carthusian recluse of the fourteenth century in East Midlands, England, we now possess the complete translations from the Middle English texts into modern English. First is *The Cloud of Unknowing*. This present volume contains six works: "The Pursuit of Wisdom" (the author's translation of Richard of St. Victor [+ 1173] of his treatise *Benjamin Minor*); his translation of Pseudo-Dionysius's Mystical Theology, entitled "Denis's Hidden Theology"; his translation—or, better, paraphrase and free development—of St. Bernard's homilies, "The Discernment of Spirits"; the author's treatise "The Assessment of Inward Stirrings"; "A Letter on Prayer" (evidently directed to the same person beginning the contemplative life in a Carthusian monastery to whom the author also directed his *Cloud*); and "A Letter of Private Direction" (often entitled *The Book of Privy Counseling*).

As more Western Christians seek to discover God as immanently present as indwelling presence to be experienced immediately and personally and not merely through conceptual knowledge, the writings presented in this volume of the anonymous author of fourteenth-century England will serve as a safe, spiritual guide into deeper, more transcendent-immanent prayer.

We will be assured through the learned and exhaustive scholarly notes and commentaries given by the translator and editor, James Walsh, S.J., that this mysterious author of the *Cloud* is firmly rooted within the long tradition of both Eastern and Western mystical theologians. He gives us very balanced and prudent guidelines to discern the fruits of such affective-speculative prayer. Walsh takes pains to highlight, not only how the author purifies his writings of the pagan Neoplatonic influences, especially of Proclus coming out of the Pseudo-Dionysius corpus, but how trinitarian and christocentric he is in his personal stress on Johannine and Pauline mystical oneness with the historical and gloriously risen Jesus Christ.

This volume's six treatises can serve as a commentary to *The Cloud*. Walsh with exhaustive scholarship shows conclusively the homogeneity of *The Cloud's* teaching and that found in these six essays. We can be assured that these teachings are of one piece with the best and most orthodox teachings among the medieval mystical theologians of the Carthusian, Victorine, and Cistercian schools. Above all, as Walsh points out, these medieval Dionysian theologians, chief among whom must be ranked the anonymous Midland mystic of the fourteenth century, the *Cloud* author, invested the apophatic, Neoplatonic writings of earlier writers of the East with Christian "devotion."

In the unknown author's works presented in this volume we are treated to an apophatic "dark" exercise that externally in technique might find a similarity with techniques used in transcendental meditation found among Hindus, Buddhists, and, especially, Sufis. Yet it is in the burning love of the author for Jesus Christ as indwelling and risen that techniques are seen always as subservient to the essential Christian teaching of mystical union with Christ and through him with the indwelling Trinity. The fruit of such "darkness" spirituality is seen as an outward movement toward active service on behalf of other human beings to co-create a better world through a loving synergy with the indwelling Trinity.

The editors of the Paulist Press are to be thanked, as well as James Walsh, S.J., for giving us this present volume to stimulate us all to encounter God as a "consuming fire" (Heb 12:29). It will be a faithful guide to help us to become a fire of love toward others in loving service to transform this world through contemplation-action into the fullness of the total Christ.

The Pursuit of Wisdom

Editor's Note

James Walsh had virtually completed this work before his death in the spring of 1986. Notes to the General Introduction for the *Pursuit of Wisdom* were not completed. However, I felt that this small omission would not diminish the quality of this work or detract in any significant way from Walsh's first-rate scholarship. I am pleased to offer this volume as one more testimony to the genius of the unknown author of *The Cloud*, and of the most perceptive student he has had in our times.

Translator's Introduction

Richard of St. Victor (†A.D. 1173)

"A greet clerk that men clepyn Richard of St. Victore," says the Middle English translator. We learn from John of Toulouse, himself a Canon Regular of the Abbey of St. Victor in Paris in the seventeenth century, that Richard was a Scotsman (*natione Scotus*); or possibly an Irishman, since the epithet "Scot" traditionally meant a person of either Scots or Irish nationality. But we are told nothing of his antecedents nor of how he came to seek entry into St. Victor. We know that he was received by the second Abbot Guilduin and professed before the latter's death in A.D. 1155, that he was the abbey's subprior in 1159, and was elected its prior in 1162, an office he retained until his death in 1173. These last ten years of his life were bedevilled by the laxity of the Abbot Ernisius and the divisive nature of his government: "It was Richard's endeavour to show a steadfast spirit in the face of difficulties; but these years were not without heartbreak and interior suffering. His Abbot Ernisius was wholly unpredictable in his government and was wont to relax the discipline of regular observance under the pretext of the lack of obedience and the indifferent counsel offered him by the elder canons." Ernisius resigned his abbacy in 1172 by order of the pope. However, Richard died less than a year later.

St. Victor had been founded almost by accident early in the twelfth century, its charter being granted in A.D. 1113. Its first abbot was William of Champeaux, who, after years of teaching at Notre Dame, retired to a hermitage called St. Victor with some of his erst-

13

while pupils and friends, to lead a life of study and prayer. They adopted the rule of St. Augustine, though William was soon persuaded to resume his public teaching of theology. When Richard came to the abbey, probably between thirty and forty years after its foundation, and attracted no doubt by its reputation for scholarship as well as for its contemplative spirit, its first fervor was not yet exhausted. The great Hugh—he died in A.D. 1141—was still alive, and his vast erudition and genuine piety still animated the community. It was only with the election of Ernisius as abbot in A.D. 1163 that the regular observance began to suffer. One of Richard's longest and most sternly ascetical works, his *Instruction of the Interior Man*, seems to say as much. There he writes: "Let those in authority over us learn what they ought to do. Let them learn to correct undisciplined behaviour and advance an honest life-style. . . . How often have I witnessed the impious inflated and elevated above the upright Cedars of Lebanon!" Pope Alexander III was in agreement. He called Ernisius "another Caesar," one who disposed of everything according to his own caprices, and against the statutes of the order. Even in a well-ordered religious community, there would always be the need for those virtues typified by the sons of Jacob and Lia: fear of God, sorrow and hatred for sin.

The English author calls Richard a great theologian. Yet his name is by no means universally remembered in the history of Western theology. It would have been remarked in an earlier generation that his was an ascetical and mystical theology; and in fact he is one of those in whose works such a distinction seems justified. His *Benjamin Minor* could be designated ascetical and the *Benjamin Major* mystical. Such neat categories, however, would hardly be familiar to a fourteenth-century English Carthusian. Even in the *Benjamin Minor* the subject is the pursuit of heavenly or contemplative wisdom, achieved through the knowledge of the powers of one's soul and their proper use and control: powers that are infused theological and cardinal virtues and their adjuncts, coming down from God under the dynamic impulse and in the presence of his Spirit.

There is a third work that makes a triad with the other two already named, the *De Trinitate*. For Richard's disciple, Thomas of St. Victor (known variously as Thomas Gallus or *Commentator Vercellensis*), this treatise deals with the *culmen*, the heights of contemplation, though for the modern theologian it ranks as Richard's only dogmatic work of any weight. Gallus also began his religious life in the Abbey of St. Victor, and he considers himself Richard's pupil, though the latter was dead probably thirty years and more by the time Thomas was professed. *Prior Richardus* he always calls him, and repeats that the *Benjamin Minor* is the prelude to the *Major*, just as this latter is the prelude to the third work, the *De Trinitate*. It is Gallus perhaps who offers us the most laudatory observation on Richard's stature as a theologian of medieval times, when in his Commentary on four verses of Isaiah (6:1–4), he writes: "At last someone came to light who, faithfully multiplying the talent of his spiritual intelligence, founded a new art on his affective experience, and discovered reason enough to cry out with the Seraphim of his mind, 'Holy, holy, holy.' This was Prior Richard in his book, *Justus Meus.*" Thomas goes on to explain what he means: "For often the spirit is especially illuminated and strengthened in such a way that the propositions concerning the Trinity, previously apprehended only by a slender grasp of faith, are now understood to be in a manner that could not or should not be otherwise, though the understanding is still partial." As for Richard, so for Thomas and indeed for the English translator: "What the fruit of love is, you may learn from the lips of truth itself. For that manifestation is from love, and contemplation is from manifestation, as knowledge is from contemplation." Gallus, writing in the first decades of the thirteenth century, looks back with satisfaction on the hundred years of existence of the Abbey of St. Victor, with its constant study—*lectio divina*—and its practice of contemplation as recorded in the theological and exegetical writings of Hugh and Richard. This is the contemplative prayer—and its theology—of which the *Cloud* author considers himself to be the legitimate heir.

There are two other rather surprising witnesses to the quality of Richard's mystical theology whom we would like to notice briefly alongside the *Commentator Vercellensis*. The first is the medieval epic poet Dante, who, in his *Divina Commedia*, identifies Richard among the figures of the Western Fathers in Paradise:

> See, farther onward, flame the burning breath
> Of Isidore, of Beda and of Richard
> Who was in contemplation more than man.

In the *Purgatorio*, too, Dante elaborates on Richard's first distinction in the *Benjamin Minor* between Rachel and Lia, the figures respectively of Contemplation and Affection. The former is depicted as gazing at the reflection of her own beautiful eyes, for in love is the power of seeing—*amare videre est*. The other is adorning herself with garlands that she herself has woven, for affection is the source of all virtue—*ex affectione omnis virtus*. More recently, the poet Ezra Pound

15

has made a special study of Richard's works, compiling a series of his epigrams, and introducing them into one of his *Cantos:*

Out of heaviness where no mind moves at all
"birds for the mind," said Richardus,
"beasts as to body for know-how,"
Not love but that love flows from it
ex animo
and cannot *ergo* delight in itself
but only in the love flowing from it
Ubi amor, ibi oculus.

The Translation

The English translator draws immediate attention to the allegorical form of the *Benjamin Minor* with his diagrammatic illustration. In this, as in all his writing, the *Cloud* author is not only at home with what Henri de Lubac has classified as Medieval Exegesis; he could hardly conceive of any other approach to Scripture or theology. Allegory is these days alleged to be a bore if not a difficulty for modern readers of patristic and medieval theology, who are unwilling or unable, apparently, to follow the advice of Chaucer's Nun's priest in his tale of the cock, the fox, and the hen: "Taketh the moralité, good men. . . . /Taketh the fruyt and lat the chaffe be still." The "moralité"—the tropological or moral sense—has endured not only in fable and nursery story as well as in Sacred Scripture; it is the enduring feature of so many distinguished novels of high seriousness. Most modern scriptural exegetes cannot rouse much enthusiasm for it, possibly because it appears to trivialize the word of God. Here, however, at least, we may reasonably ask what Christian value can the "history," the dubious origins, the etymology and the genealogy of the twelve tribes possibly have, when separated from allegory, as Paul taught it to his Galatians. As Richard says: "The moral sense deals with questions which anyone can easily understand. For what is tropology except the science of human behavior? Moral principles are written by nature on the human heart. But it would be rash to presume to separate the profundities of the mysteries from their own proper sense." The English translator has been brought up on these traditional hermeneutics. It is noticeable that the naming of the various powers, affections, and virtues of the mind is so often no more than the rhetorical figure of personification, helping to make more

16

concrete what might become too abstract and boring. Dante called allegory the beautiful mantle that not only covers but adorns the truth, and Francis of Assisi immortalized Lady Poverty.

The English author's introduction to his paraphrase of Benjamin is a brief description of the powers of the soul, two principal and two secondary, which he will describe in seven chapters of the *Cloud*, with never a glance at the personification here. There he speaks of the "sotil condicions of the myghts of thi soule and theire worchynges in goostly thinges, as ben vices or vertewes of thi self": the intricacies of the soul's powers and the way in which they operate. These seven chapters, then, turn out to be extended translations from the Latin text of the *Benjamin Minor*, providing yet another indication of the unity of authorship of the *Cloud* and this version of *Benjamin*, which the author calls the *Pursuit of Wisdom*. In the English preface, the translator selects four sentences from Richard's third chapter and slightly longer extracts from Chapter 5: "Imagination is subject to the reason, sensuality to the affection"; and from Chapter 6: "The vices of the imagination and the sensuality."

Audiant adolescentuli sermonem de adolescente, evigilent ad vocem prophetae: "The youthful must now listen to a sermon about a young man; they must awaken to the voice of the prophet." Richard's opening words, with the apparent allusion to the story of the young Samuel and his temple-apprenticeship to the prophet Eli, strengthen the impression that the work is intended primarily for novices. The English synopsis imparts the same flavor, especially in the careful definitions of terms, and the simple descriptions of fear, with the "answering look of compassion, seen of God"; of sorrow, with "tears of compunction; of hope of forgiveness, which comes to the heart humbled in fear and contrite in sorrow"; and of the first kindling of love at the sight, the experience of God "so sweet, so merciful, so good, so courteous, so true and so kind, so loving and so homely." The translation involves us in the same way of purification mapped out by Richard; and yet the precision of the translator's style allows him to indicate that this purgation is achieved through the sighs of love—*per suspirium amoris*.

The English author here introduces the distinction between salvation and perfection, in order to mark for himself the first transition from purification to illumination, from the lower part of the active life to the higher, which is also the first part of the contemplative life. For the illuminative way first consists in the imaginative contemplation of "the passion of Christ . . . the kindness of God . . . and the joys of heaven." So the reason enables us "to focus the mind on God and spiritual things through the imagination." The first objects in this preparation of the heart for contemplation are the pains of hell and the joys of heaven, the one enabling us "to put down every sinful suggestion, the other to stimulate our will to work good and to kindle our desire."

At the beginning of the *Benjamin Major*, for which this present treatise serves as introduction, Richard defines cogitations as "an improvident looking around which makes the soul prone to wandering distraction" (*improvidus animi respectus, ad evagationem pronus*). He makes the same point here about the sensuality and "uncontrolled thinking." The English author, however, uses images of gossiping and chattering common to a more popular contemplative tradition. The *Ancrene Riwle* contrasts the serpent's garrulity with Mary's silence. Julian of Norwich describes her diabolic temptation as being like two people both talking at once, and those who "chatter in church" belong to the devil's crew. At the same time the translator obviously relishes Richard's protracted image of the city of conscience (chs. 31–33) and reproduces it with gusto: "Now here we must notice how the city of conscience is wonderfully protected from all temptations by the four sons of these two maids."

Chapter 7 of the translation, though it follows the structure of the Latin (chs. 36–39) and its tropology, is quite different from it. The Latin proceeds by way of commentary on a number of scriptural texts. After an initial citation from Philippians (4:7), which the translator adapts, Richard proceeds to quote and comment on a variety of texts containing the word *joy* (Ps 30:20, 4:7; Mt 25:21; Phil 4:1; Ps 31:11; etc.). The English author, who has rendered Richard's *gaudium verum* as "the joy of inward sweetness," ignores his original's Scripture and hermeneutics. By way of summary, he introduces two Pauline texts of his own, to illustrate his point that this joy is compounded of unfulfilled desire.

The Latin disquisition on the aversion from sin and the sense of shame occupies fourteen columns of the Migne edition (chs. 40–59). The English summary is six paragraphs long and deals with just two points: first, the hatred of sin is proportionate to a person's appreciation of the harm sin does to the soul, and yet this hatred is not contrary to charity, since we can hate the sin and love the sinner. Second, we always need the sense of shame, since we can never root out our propensity to sin. Also we are speaking of an ordered sense of shame, which is concerned only about what God and his angels and saints think of us. When he comes to deal, equally shortly, with the virtue of discretion, he has only three points to make. Discretion is the mistress of all the other virtues, and it can be acquired only by a long experience of excess and defect in ourselves of the various virtues, which is why Joseph is born late. Second, according to Richard (ch. 81), the ultimate principle for discretion or discriminatory judgment is the testimony of scripture. For the English author it is, of course, spiritual counsel: "After many fallings and failures, and the consequent shame, a man learns by experience that there is nothing better than to be directed by counsel. This is the quickest way of acquiring discretion." The translation never mentions the Scriptures, and Richard says nothing about spiritual direction. Third (and the English author is here faithful to his original), discretion leads to self-knowledge.

In his closing section (chs. 69–87), Richard is concerned to show how close are discretion and contemplation, how one depends on the other. This is in no way a preoccupation of the English author. He does not, however, introduce any new material. Rather, by a judicious selection—the greater part of chapters 71–73 of his original— he sketches in outline how a person shall come to contemplation. As our annotations to the text illustrate (nn. 131–42), there are common points of doctrine with Walter Hilton here, in the later chapters of Book II of the *Scale of Perfection*. It would appear that Richard is their common source rather than that Hilton should have borrowed from the English translation. The emphasis on the growth in self-knowledge, the images of the mirror and the light to see both "by" and "in," all indicate the presentation of a like doctrine—though it is Hilton alone who draws the distinction between reform in faith and in feeling. The English Carthusian simply states that "his grace refashions us in his image, which has been disfigured by the darkness of sin," whereas the Latin reads: *Ubi, quaeso, quam in eius imagine cognitionis vestigia expressius impressa reperiuntur, hominem secundum animam ad Dei similitudinem factum?*

The last paragraph of the translation is extremely important for the light it casts on the devotional bent of the *Cloud* author. It is often alleged that he is wholly taken up with the "work," the method of dark contemplative prayer, the apophatic mysticism described at such length, with such intensity and such loving care, in the *Cloud* and Privy *Counselling*. Yet as the *Letter on Prayer* and various aspects of his teaching in the *Cloud* indicate, he is in no sense a single-minded fanatic, teaching one only contemplative way to God, to the exclusion of all others. This would indeed be a harsh and even untrue criticism of one who shows such breadth of vision and admirable prudence as a spiritual counselor; but it is one that is frequently made.

Here, also, he brings to his text his own deep devotion to the Holy Name of Jesus. He gives strong hints of the personal importance to him of this contemporary and traditional devotion in the Church: "Love only this good word 'Jesus' . . . love Jesus alone . . . in thoughts and desires of the love of Jesus . . . all your thoughts and desires, all your meditations and aspirations are directed alone to the love and praise of this Lord Jesus." Once again it is the affective reminiscence of the Incarnate Savior, particularly the imaginative contemplation of the mysteries of his Passion, which are the direct way to and preparation for unitive contemplation.

The Pursuit of Wisdom[1]

A great theologian called Richard of St. Victor, in his book on the pursuit of wisdom,[2] argues that there are two powers in man's soul, the gifts of the Father of heaven from whom all good things come.[3] One is reason and the other affection, or will. Through reason we know, and through affection we feel or love. From reason springs right judgment and the intellectual faculties; from the affection, spiritual desires and well-ordered feelings.[4] And just as Rachel and Lia were the two wives of Jacob, so man's soul is married to God by the light of knowing in his reason and by the sweetness of love in his affection. Jacob stands for God, Rachel for reason and Lia for affection.[5]

Each of the two wives, Rachel and Lia, employed a maid. Rachel had Bala, and Lia had Zelpha. Bala was a great chatterbox, and Zelpha was a drunkard and always thirsty. Bala stands for the imagination, which is the servant of reason, as Bala was of Rachel. Zelpha stands for the sensuality,[6] which is the servant of the affection, as Zelpha was of Lia. These maids are so necessary to their ladies[7] that without them all this world would be of no use to them. And why? Because of all these outward bodily things, without imagination reason can have no knowledge, nor without sensuality can affection experience them.[8]

Yet Imagination chatters so ignorantly in the ears of our hearts, that no matter what her lady Reason may do, she cannot quieten her. And so it is that oftentimes when we should be praying, the many and varied fantasies which accompany evil thoughts make clamor in our hearts,[9] so that no matter what we do we cannot by our own power[10] drive them away. Thus it is well proven[11] that Bala is a fearful chatterbox.

21

Again, Sensuality is always so thirsty that, no matter what her lady Affection experiences, her thirst is never slaked. The drink she desires is the pleasure of natural, fleshly, and worldly delights; and the more she drinks of these, the greater her thirst; because the whole world is not enough to satisfy the appetite of the sensuality.[12] So it is that oftentimes when we are praying, or meditating on God and spiritual things,[13] we would fain experience the sweetness of love in our affection, and yet we cannot, because we are so busy satisfying the uncontrolled desires of our sensuality.[14] For in its greed, it never stops demanding, and we have a fleshly sympathy with it. So it is well proven that Zelpha is a drunkard and always thirsty.[15]

Lia, then, conceived and had of Jacob seven children; Zelpha conceived and had of Jacob two children; Bala conceived and had of Jacob two children; and Rachel conceived and had of Jacob two children. So the affection conceives and has of God's grace seven virtues; the sensuality conceives and has of God's grace two virtues; the imagination conceives and has of God's grace two virtues or two sights; and also the reason conceives and has of God's grace two virtues. The names of these children and of their virtues are shown in the following diagram:[16]

Husband
Jacob—God

Wife
Lia—Affection

Wife
Rachel—Reason

Maid
Zelpha—Sensuality

Maid
Bala—Imagination

Jacob's sons by Lia
Ruben—Fear of God
Simeon—Sorrow for sin
Levi—Hope of forgiveness
Judas—Love of the good God
Issachar—Joy in inward sweetness
Zabulon—Perfect hatred of sin
Dinah—True shame for sin

Jacob's sons by Rachel
Joseph—Discretion
Benjamin—Contemplation

Jacob's sons by Bala
Dan—Sight of sufferings to come
Nephthalim—Sight of joys to come

Jacob's sons by Zelpha
Gad—Abstinence
Asser—Patience

This diagram shows us something of Jacob, his wives, their maids and all their children. Now we must show the manner of their begetting and in what order. First we must speak of the children of Lia, for we read that she was the first to conceive. Jacob's sons born of Lia signify nothing else than well-ordered affections or feelings in a man's soul; for if they were disorderly, they would not be his sons. So the seven children of Lia are seven virtues, for virtue is nothing else but a well-ordered and well-measured affection in a man's soul. An affection of soul is well ordered when it is what it should be. It is well measured when it is as much as it should be. These affections in a man's soul may be sometimes well ordered and well measured, and sometimes disorderly and unmeasured. When they are well ordered and well measured, then they are counted among Jacob's sons.[17]

I. How the Virtue of Fear Arises in the Affection

The first child that Lia conceived by Jacob was Ruben, that is, fear. And therefore it is written in the Psalm: "The beginning of wisdom is fear of our Lord God!"[18] This is the first virtue experienced in man's affection, and without it one can have no other.[19] And therefore whoever desires to have such a son must diligently and frequently look upon the evil he has done. Here he shall think on the greatness of his trespass, and, on the other hand, on the power of the Judge. From such consideration comes fear; that is to say, Ruben, who is rightly called "the son of sight."[20] For he is truly blind who does not see the punishment that is to come and is not afraid to sin. This Ruben is indeed well named the son of sight, for when he was born his mother cried out and said: "God has looked upon my lowliness."[21] In the consideration of his past sin and of the power of his Judge, man's soul truly begins to see God by the affection of fear; and also to be seen of God, by the answering look of compassion.

II. How Sorrow Arises in the Affection

While Ruben is growing up, Simeon is born; for sorrow must surely follow hard on fear. The more a man fears the punishment he has deserved, the more bitter his sorrow for the sin he has committed. At the birth of Simeon, Lia cried out and said: "Our Lord has heard that I was despised."[22] And therefore Simeon is called "hearing";[23]

for when a man has bitter sorrow and despises his past sins, he begins to be heard by God and also to hear this blessed judgment from God's own lips:[24] "Blessed are they that sorrow, for they shall be comforted."[25] For in the moment when a sinner has sorrow and turns from his sin, he shall be safe.[26] This is the witness of Holy Scripture. And thus by Ruben he becomes meek, and by Simeon he is contrite and has tears of compunction.[27] And as David bears witness in the Psalm, "God shall not despise the humble and contrite heart;" so without doubt such sorrow brings true comfort.[28]

III. How Hope Arises in the Affection

And now I pray you, what comfort will be afforded to those who have true fear and bitter sorrow for their past sins, if not true hope of forgiveness, which is the third son of Jacob? This is Levi, who is called in the story "adding to."[29] For when the other two children, fear and sorrow, have been given of God to a man's soul, this third, hope, shall not long be delayed,[30] but shall be added to them. So the story of Levi bears witness: that when his two brothers were given to their mother Lia, he, Levi, was added to them.

Notice what Scripture says, that he was added to them, not just given. Therefore it is said that a man shall not presume to hope for forgiveness until such time as his heart is humbled in fear and contrite in sorrow.[31] Without these two, hope is presumption. But where these two are present, hope is added to them. And thus comfort follows hard on sorrow, as David says in the Psalm—that "after the multitude of sorrows in my heart," he tells our Lord that his comforts have gladdened his soul.[32] And so it is that the Holy Spirit is called Paraclete, that is, Comforter;[33] for he often graciously brings comfort to a sorrowful soul.[34]

IV. How Love Arises in the Affection

And now a manner of homeliness[35] begins to grow up between God and man's soul, and a certain kindling of love; so much so that a man is oftentimes aware that he is being visited by God and is also greatly comforted by his coming.[36] Lia was first aware of this homeliness and this kindling of love when, after Levi was born, she cried out with great joy and said: "Now my husband will be joined to me."[37] The true husband of our soul is God.[38] And we are truly joined to him when we draw near to him in hope and steadfast love.[39] And just as love follows hard on hope, so, after Levi, Judas was born, the fourth son of Lia.

At his birth Lia cried out and said: "Now shall I confess to our Lord." And therefore in the story Judas is called "confession."[40] Further, in this state of love, man's soul offers itself wholly to God, and says: "Now shall I confess to our Lord." For before a man has this feeling of love in his soul, all that he does is done more out of fear than love.[41] But in this state a man knows by experience that God is so sweet, so merciful, so good, so courteous, so true and so kind, so faithful, so loving and so homely, that there is left nothing in him, neither power nor understanding nor wit nor will, which he does not offer plainly, freely, and in homely fashion to God. This is a confession not only of sin, but also of God's goodness.[42] It is a great sign of love when man declares to God that he is good. David speaks very often of this confession in the Psalms, when he says: "Make it known to the Lord that he is good."[43]

So then, we have told the story of four sons of Lia. And after this, she ceased to bear children for a time.[44] Similarly, a man considers that it is enough for him when he is aware that he loves true goods.[45] And indeed this is enough for salvation; but not for perfection.[46] It belongs to a perfect soul not only to be on fire with love in the affection, but also to be illumined with the light of understanding in the reason.[47]

V. How the Twofold Sight of Pain and Joy Arises in the Imagination

So when Judas was born, that is, when love and desire of true goods, things unseen,[48] arise and grow in man's affection, then Rachel has a great desire to bear children. That is, Reason desires to know the things that Affection experiences. For as it belongs to Lia, the Affection, to love, so it belongs to Rachel, the Reason, to know. From Lia, the Affection, come well-measured and orderly affections; and from Rachel, the Reason, come true knowledge and clear understanding.[49] And the more Judas, that is, Love, grows, the greater is Rachel's desire to bear children—that is, Reason's desire to know.

But who is there that does not know how difficult it is, and wellnigh impossible for a soul living in this flesh,[50] one still untaught in spiritual pursuits,[51] to come to the knowledge of invisible things, and to fix the eye of contemplation on spiritual things?[52] The reason is that a soul that is carnal and untaught knows only bodily things, and nothing comes into its mind but visible things.[53] But still it turns its gaze inward as far as it can, and what it cannot yet see clearly by spiritual understanding, it considers in the imagination.[54]

This is the reason why Rachel first had children of her maid rather than of herself. For although a man cannot straightaway acquire the light of spiritual understanding in the reason, he still considers it sweet to focus the mind on God and spiritual things through the imagination.[55] By Rachel we understand reason; by her maid Bala, Imagination. Hence Reason shows that it is more profitable to think about spiritual things in any way at all—even if this merely means exciting the desire with some pleasant image—than to think about the vanities and allurements of this world.[56] And therefore these two, Dan and Nepthalim, were born of Bala. Dan means the sight of sufferings to come, Nepthalim the sight of joys to come.

These two children are very necessary and also profitable for the soul engaged on spiritual exercises,[57] the first for the putting down of every sinful suggestion, and the other for stimulating our will to work good and to kindle our desire. For just as it belongs to Dan to put down evil suggestions of sin through the sight of sufferings to come, so it belongs to the other brother, Nepthalim, to stimulate our will to the working of good, and to kindle our desires by the sight of joys to come.[58] And therefore when holy men are tempted to anything unlawful through the occurrence of any evil thought, straightaway they set before their minds the pains that are to come; and thus they extinguish the temptation in its beginnings, before it results in any evil delight in their souls.[59] And whenever their devotion and liking for God and spiritual things ceases and grows cold (which often happens in this life because of the flesh's frailty and many other reasons), they set before their minds the joys that are to come.[60] And thus they rekindle their will with holy desires, and destroy their temptation in its beginnings before it results in the weariness or heaviness of sloth.[61]

Because, then, with Dan we condemn all unlawful thoughts, in the story he is rightly called "judgment." Also, his father Jacob spoke of him thus: "Dan shall judge his people."[62] And it is further told in the story that when Bala brought forth Dan, Rachel said: "Our Lord has judged me." That is to say: "Our Lord has made me equal to my sister Lia".[63] And so Reason might say, when Imagination has received the sight of pains to come, that our Lord has made her equal to her sister, Affection; because in her imagination she had sight of those pains to come of which she had fear and sorrow in her affection.[64] Next came Nepthalim, that is, the sight of joys to come. At his birth Rachel spoke and said: "I am made like to my sister Lia."[65] And so in the story Nepthalim is called "likeness." Reason says that she is like to her sister Affection, because there she had hope and love of joys to come in her affection, and now she has begotten the sight of joys to come in her imagination. Jacob said of Nepthalim that he was a hart let loose, giving forth words of beauty.[66] Even so, when we imagine the joys of heaven we say that it is fair in heaven.[67] For Nepthalim wondrously enkindles our souls with holy desires, whenever we set ourselves to imagine the true worth and the beauty of the joys of heaven.[68]

VI. How the Virtues of Abstinence and Patience Arise in the Sensuality

When Lia saw that her sister Rachel had great joy in these two children born of her maid Bala, she called her own maid, Zelpha, and sent her in to her husband, that she too might rejoice as did her sister Rachel, by having two more bastard children born of her maid Zelpha. Even so should it be in a man's soul. Once Reason has controlled the constant chattering of Imagination and made her docile to God[69] and to bear fruit in assisting the understanding; then Affection should control the desires and thirst of Sensuality, and make her docile to God and bear fruit in assisting the feelings. But what fruit can Sensuality bear, except to live temperately with regard to bodily comforts, and patiently with discomfort? These then are the children of Zelpha: Gad and Asser. Gad is Abstinence and Asser is Patience. Gad is the older child, and Asser the younger. For first we must become temperate interiorly by a rightly measured abstinence; and then to bear exterior hardship with the strength of patience.[70] These are the children that Zelpha brought forth in sorrow; for by abstinence and patience the sensuality suffers greatly in the body.

But what is sorrow to Sensuality becomes great joy and bliss to Affection.[71] So it is that when Gad was born, Lia cried out, saying: "Happily." And thus in the story Gad is called happiness or blessedness, whichever you prefer. Hence it is well said that abstinence in the sensuality is bliss in the affection: because the less pleasure that Sensuality takes in her desires, the more sweetness Affection experiences in her love. After Asser was born, Lia said: "This shall be for my bliss." And therefore in the story Asser was called blessed.[72] Thus it is well said that patience in the sensuality is bliss in the af-

27

fection; because the more discomfort the sensuality endures, the happier the soul is in her affection.[73]

By abstinence and patience we should understand not only temperance in food and drink, and endurance in the tribulations that come from without, but in every kind of earthly, natural, and worldly delight, and every kind of bodily and spiritual discomfort whether from within or without, whether rational or irrational, which torments or delights the sensuality through any of our five senses.[74] In this way Sensuality is fruitful in helping her mistress, Affection. There is great peace and rest in the soul which is not immersed in the lust of the sensuality nor rebellious because of the suffering experienced by it.[75] The first peace is got by Gad, the other by Asser.

Here we must notice that Rachel's maid went in to the husband before Lia's. And this is the reason why: for truly, unless the chattering of the imagination, that is to say, the crowding in of idle thoughts,[76] is first of all restrained, then the concupiscence of the sensuality will doubtless remain uncontrolled. And therefore whoever wishes to abstain from fleshly and worldly desires must seldom or never indulge in idle thoughts.[77] Hence it is not possible in this life for anyone perfectly to despise bodily comfort and not to be afraid of discomfort, unless he earnestly contemplates beforehand the joys and the torments of the world to come.[78]

Now here we must notice how the city of our conscience is wonderfully protected from all temptations by the four sons of these two maids. For every temptation comes either by thought from within, or from without through one of our five senses.[79] But within, Dan shall judge and condemn evil thoughts by contemplating the pains, and Gad shall put away the false delights which come from without, by use of abstinence. Dan is vigilant within, and Gad without. And their other two brethren help them very much: Nepthalim with Dan makes peace within and Asser bids Gad have no fear of his enemies. Dan puts fear into the heart with the horror of hell, while Nepthalim comforts it with the promise of heavenly bliss. Further, Asser helps his brother without; so that through them both the city walls are not breached. Gad repels bodily comfort and Asser pursues spiritual discomfort. Asser takes the enemy by stratagem as soon as he brings to mind his own patience, and the promise of Nepthalim. And thus the more enemies he has and as often, the more opportunities he has for victory. And it is then, when he has overcome his enemies—that is, the adversities of this world—that he immediately comes to stand by his brother Gad to help destroy his enemies. And as soon as he ar-

28

rives, without fail they turn and fly. The enemies of Gad are fleshly delights. And truly, as soon as a man gains patience under the pains of abstinence, false delights find no lasting dwelling in him.[80]

VII.   How the Joy of Inward Sweetness Arises in the Affection

When, then, the enemies are fled and the city is at peace, a man comes to know what is the high peace of God that is beyond all human understanding.[81] And so it is that Lia ceased to bear children until Gad and Asser were born of her maid Zelpha. For truly, unless a man has gained control, by abstinence and patience, over the pleasure and pain experienced in the sensuality through his five senses, he shall never experience inward sweetness and true joy in God and spiritual things in the affection.[82] This sweetness is Issachar, the fifth son of Lia, who in the story is called reward. This joy of inward sweetness is rightly called reward, for this joy is a taste of heavenly bliss, which is the endless reward of the devout soul, and begins here.[83] At the birth of this child Lia said: "God has given me my reward, because I gave my maid to my husband for the bearing of children."[84] And so it is good when we make our sensuality bear fruit by its abstinence from every kind of bodily and worldly comfort and by its fruitful endurance in all bodily and worldly discomfort;[85] because our Lord, of his great mercy, gives us ineffable joy and inward sweetness in our affection, as an earnest of the supreme joy and reward of the high kingdom of heaven.[86]

Jacob said of Issachar that he was a strong ass, dwelling on the borders.[87] And so it is that a man who dwells in this state, and experiences this earnest of everlasting joy in his affection, is like a strong ass which dwells on the borders.[88] For no matter how full his soul may be of spiritual gladness and joy in God, yet because in this mortal life the body is corruptible, he must put up with his mortal body, with its hunger, thirst, and cold, and many other discomforts.[89] And for this reason he is likened in his body to an ass; but in his soul he is strong enough to destroy all the passions and lusts of the flesh, by patience and abstinence in his sensuality, and the abundance of spiritual joy and sweetness in his affection.

Again, a soul in this state lives between the extremes of mortal and immortal life. He who lives thus has almost, but not quite, forsaken mortality; and has almost, but not quite, achieved immortality. For while he has need of this world's goods, such as food, drink, and clothing, as is the lot of every living man, yet he has but one foot in this mortal life. For his other foot is in immortal life through the great abundance of the spiritual joy and sweetness which not rarely but often he experiences in God.[90] Such, I suppose, was St. Paul's experience when he said, with great desire: "Who shall deliver me from this mortal body?"[91] And again when he said: "I wish to be set free and to be with Christ."[92] This is the desire of the soul that experiences Issachar in its affection: that is, the joy of inward sweetness, which is the meaning of the name Issachar. This drives on the soul to forsake this wretched life; but it cannot. It desires to enter the blessed life, but it cannot.[93] It does what it can, but it still lives between these extremes.

VIII.   How Perfect Hatred of Sin Arises in the Affection

Hence it is that Zabulon is born after Issachar: that is to say, hatred of sin.[94] Here we must notice why hatred of sin is never experienced perfectly in man's affection until the time that spiritual joy of inward sweetness is also experienced in the affection.[95] The reason is this: Before this time the true cause of this hatred was never experienced in the affection. For the experience of spiritual joy teaches a man what harm sin does to a soul; and the hatred of sin is proportionate to a man's greater or lesser appreciation of this harm in the soul. But when by the grace of God and after long striving a man comes to the experience of spiritual joy in God, then he appreciates that sin has been the cause of this delay.[96] And when he also appreciates that he cannot continue to experience that spiritual joy because of the corruptible nature of the flesh, of which sin is the cause, then there arises in him a strong hatred of all sin and of every sinful quality. David taught us to have this appreciation when he said in the Psalm: "Be angry and refuse to sin"; or "be angry and do not sin":[97] which means, be angry against the sin, but not with your mortal nature.[98] For nature is the source of action, but not of sin.[99]

Here we must notice that this anger and hatred are not contrary to charity. Charity teaches how a man must regard this anger and hatred in respect of himself and of his fellow-Christians.[100] For a man must hate sin in his own nature; and with regard to our fellow-Christians, we must hate sin in them, and yet love them.[101] David speaks of this hatred in the Psalm, where he says: "I hated them with a perfect hatred."[102] And in another Psalm he says that he held in hatred every wicked way.[103]

Thus it is clearly shown that Judas and Issachar were both born before Zabulon. For unless a man first have charity and spiritual joy in his affection, he can in no way experience this perfect hatred of sin. For Judas, that is to say, charity, teaches us how we must hate sin in ourselves and in our brethren. And Issachar, that is to say, spiritual awareness of joy in God, teaches us why we must hate sin. Judas bids us hate sin and love humankind; Issachar bids us destroy the sin and preserve humankind. And so it happens that human nature is made strong with regard to God and spiritual things by the perfect hatred and destruction of sin.[104]

Hence Zabulon is called in the story a dwelling-place of strength.[105] At his birth Lia said: "My husband shall dwell with me."[106] And so it is that God, the true husband of our soul, is dwelling in that soul, strengthening it in its affection by spiritual joy and sweetness in his love; this it is that works diligently in destroying sin in itself and in others by the perfect hatred of sin—even the whole of sinfulness.[107] Thus is it shown how Zabulon is born.

IX.　How True Shame Arises and Develops in the Affection

But even though a soul should experience within itself perfect hatred of sin, is it possible for it to live without sinning? Not by any means. So let no man be so presumptuous, when the Apostle says: "If we say we have no sin, we deceive ourselves, and the truth is not in us."[108] And also St. Augustine says that he daresay that there is no man living without sin.[109] And who is there, I pray you, that does not sin in ignorance?[110] Yes, and it often happens that God permits those men to fall very grievously to whom he has given the charge of correcting others, that they may learn by their own falling how merciful they should be in leading others to amend. And because men often fall grieviously into those very sins that they hate most, true shame arises in a man's soul after hatred of sin.

So it is that after Zabulon Dinah was born;[111] by Zabulon is understood hatred of sin, and by Dinah, a well-ordered shame of sin. But notice that he who never experienced Zabulon, never experienced Dinah. An evil man has a kind of shame, but it is not this true shame. Because if such people had perfect shame of sin, they would not commit it so readily with deliberation and consent. Such men are more ashamed of dirty clothes on their body than of dirty thoughts in their souls.[112] But whoever you are who think you have got Dinah, consider whether you would be as ashamed of a foul thought in your heart as you would be if you were made to stand naked before the king and all the realm.[113] Otherwise take it for certain that you have not yet got true shame in your affection: if, that is, you are less ashamed of a filthy heart than a filthy body; or if you are more ashamed of your filthy body in the sight of men than you are of your filthy heart in the sight of the King of heaven and of all his angels and holy saints in heaven.[114]

The story has now been told of the seven children of Lia, by which is understood seven kinds of affection in a man's soul.[115] These are sometimes orderly, sometimes disordered, sometimes rightly measured, sometimes unmeasured. When they are orderly and rightly measured, then they are virtues; and when they are disordered and ill-measured, then they are vices. So a man must take care that they be not only orderly, but also rightly measured. They are orderly when they are what they should be; and they are disorderly when they are what they should not be. They are rightly measured when they are as much as they should be, and they are unmeasured when they are more than they should be,[116] because too much fear brings despair; too much sorrow brings a man to bitterness and weariness of nature, which makes him unfit for spiritual comfort; too much hope is presumption; excessive love is flattery and blandishment; excessive gladness is dissipation and wantonness; untempered hatred of sin is a frenzy.[117] In this way virtues become disordered and unmeasured, and are turned into vices. Thus they lose the name of virtues and cannot be counted among the sons of Jacob: that is, of God. For by Jacob is understood God, as is shown in the diagram above.[118]

X. How Discretion and Contemplation Arise in the Reason

So it would appear that the virtue of discretion is necessary, by which all the rest must be governed;[119] for without it, all virtues are turned into vices. This is he, Joseph, a child born late. And yet his father loves him more than all the others;[120] because truly, goodness can neither be got nor kept without discretion.[121] It is no wonder that the virtue without which no other can be received or regulated should be specially loved.

32

What wonder, then, if this virtue is late in coming, when we cannot achieve the perfection of discretion except by habitual exercise and through much labor in these other affections? For first we must acquire the habit of each virtue individually and make progress in them all separately, before we may have full knowledge of them all, and can form a sufficient judgment of them all. And when we exercise ourselves diligently in these affections and the perception of them, frequently we fall and as frequently rise again. Then, by our frequent falling, we can learn how much awareness we need to have if we are to acquire and keep these virtues.[122] Thus finally, after long exercise, a soul is brought to full discretion[123] and it can at last rejoice in the birth of Joseph.

But before this virtue is conceived in a man's soul, everything that these other virtues effect is without discretion. Because in proportion as a man rashly presumes and exerts himself in any of these affections beyond his strength and to excess, the more grievously he falls and fails in his purpose. And so it is that after them all Dinah, the last, is born; for shame follows hard upon grievous falling and failure. After many fallings and failures, with the consequent shame, a man learns by experience that there is nothing better than to be directed by counsel; this is the quickest way of acquiring discretion.[124] For he who always acts according to direction will never regret it. A skillful man is better than a strong man, even as skill is better than brute strength.[125] And the sagacious man shall speak of victories.[126]

Here is the obvious reason why neither Lia nor Zelpha nor Bala could bear such a child, but Rachel alone. For, as was said above, from reason comes right counsel which is true discretion—understood by Joseph, Rachel's first son. We first bring forth Joseph in our reason when in all that we are moved to do we do under direction.[127] For this Joseph not only knows what sins we are most inclined to commit; he also knows the weakness of our nature. And we shall take the remedy which he prescribes for both, seeking counsel from those who are wiser than we and following their direction.[128] Otherwise we are not Joseph, Jacob's son, born of Rachel.

Also by this same Joseph a man is not only taught to avoid the deceits of his enemies; he is also frequently led by him to the perfect knowing of himself. And a man makes progress in the knowledge of God, of whom he is the image and likeness, in proportion as he knows himself.[129] And so it is that Benjamin is born after Joseph; for as by Joseph, we mean discretion, by Benjamin we mean contemplation. They are both born of the same mother and father. For through the illumination of our reason by the grace of God we come to the perfect knowledge of ourselves and of God, as far as is possible in this life.[130]

But Benjamin is born long after Joseph; because, unless we exercise ourselves diligently and for a long while in those spiritual works by means of which we are taught to know ourselves,[131] we cannot be lifted up to the knowledge and contemplation of God. He who is not yet able to see himself, and lifts up his eyes to see God, is wasting his time. For I would prefer that a man first learn to understand the invisible things of his own spirit, before he presume to comprehend the invisible things of the spirit of God. I have no doubt that he who does not yet know himself, and thinks that he has acquired some knowledge of the invisible things of God, is deceiving himself. And so I counsel that a man should first seek earnestly to know himself; for in his soul he is made to the image and likeness of God.[132]

Notice, too, that he who desires to see God must purify his soul; for it is like a mirror in which, when it is clean, everything can be seen clearly. But when the mirror is dirty, you can see nothing clearly in it.[133] It is just the same with your soul; when it is dirty, you know neither yourself nor God. When a candle is burning, you can see the candle itself by its own light, and other things also.[134] In the same way, when your soul is aflame with the love of God—that is, when you feel a constant desire in your heart for God's love—then you may hope to see both your unworthiness and his great goodness by the light of the grace which he sends to your reason.[135] And therefore cleanse your mirror and hold out your candle to the flame; so that when it is purified and aflame and you steadfastly behold it, a certain brightness of God's light begins to shine in your soul, and a kind of spiritual sunbeam becomes visible to your spiritual sight, which is the eye of your soul;[136] and it is opened to behold God and Godly things, heaven and heavenly things, and every kind of spiritual object.[137]

But such sight is a rare occurrence while the soul is fighting the battle of this mortal life, whenever God graciously wills to give it to the soul that labors for it.[138] But after this life it will be everlasting. This light shone in David's soul when he said in the Psalm: "Lord, the light of thy face is stamped upon us. Thou hast given gladness within my heart."[139] The light of God's face is the shining of his grace. It refashions in us his image, which has been disfigured with the darkness of sin.[140] And therefore a soul that is aflame with the desire of his light and hopes to attain to what it desires: know well that such a soul has conceived Benjamin.[141] What is more conducive to salvation than the sweetness of this sight, what more delightful experience? Truly, none. Rachel knew this very well; because reason says that, compared with this sweetness, every other sweetness is as sour and bitter as is gall compared to honey.[142]

Nevertheless, a man cannot attain to such a grace by his own skill, because it is the gift of God which a man can never deserve.[143] Equally, no one is ready to receive such a grace except after deep meditation and ardent desire: which Rachel knew very well.[144] For she multiplied her meditations and sharpened her appetites, desire on desire; until at the last, with great abundance of burning desires and of sorrow in the postponement of fruition, Benjamin was born, and his mother Rachel died.[145] For whenever a soul is ravished above itself, in the abundance of desire and the great fulness of love, and is aflame with the light of the Godhead, then indeed all man's reason dies.[146]

Whoever you are, then, who desire to come to the contemplation of God: that is to say, to bring forth the child who in the story is called Benjamin, the sight of God, you must exercise yourself in this way. You must gather together your thoughts and your desires and make of them a church; and there learn to love only this good word Jesus, so that all your desires and thoughts are directed to love Jesus alone; and that unceasingly, insofar as it may be here.[147] So you will fulfill what is said in the Psalm: "Lord, I will bless thee in churches":[148] that is, in thoughts and desires of the love of Jesus. And then, in this church of thoughts and desires, in this union of meditations and aspirations, see to it that all your thoughts and desires, all your meditations and aspirations, are directed alone to the love and praise of this Lord Jesus. And do not fail in this mindfulness, insofar as is possible by grace, and your frailty will permit, humbling yourself more and more in prayer and in taking counsel,[149] patiently waiting on the will of the Lord; until the mind is ravished above itself to be fed with the sweet food of angels in the beholding of God and godly things.[150] Thus will come true of you what is written in the Psalm: "Here is Benjamin, a young child, in ecstasy of mind."[151]
Amen.

Notes

The Pursuit of Wisdom

1. The title of the English version, "A tretyse of the stodye of wysdom that men clepen *Beniamyn*," occurs in eight MSS.

2. The Latin title of the work is *De praeparatione animi ad contemplationem*—"the preparation of the soul [or spirit] for contemplation"; and the title of its first chapter, *De studio sapientiae et eius commendatione*—"the pursuit of wisdom and its praise."

3. "Every best gift and every perfect gift is from above, coming down from the Father of lights" (Jas 1:17). The Latin cites the Vulgate accurately.

4. The English author's first borrowing from Richard is these three sentences from Chapter 3: "Richard argues that . . . ; One is reason . . . ; well-ordered feelings."

5. Nowhere does Richard say that "Jacob stands for God." The English is concerned to classify and simplify the allegory.

6. For the English author's disquisition on those principal and secondary powers of the soul, cf. the *Cloud, ed. cit.*, chs. 63–66, pp. 244ff. Perhaps Julian of Norwich is the clearest-eyed theologically in her understanding of the sensuality; cf. her *Revelations, ed. cit.*, pp. 28ff.

7. A literal translation from the Latin, which reads: *In tantum unaquaeque ancillarum dominae suae necessaria ut sine illis totus mundus nil eis posse conferre videretur.*

8. Richard develops this epistemological reflection specifically in order to consider the relationship of the imaginative faculty with invisible things, citing Rom 1:20: "His invisible things are clearly seen from the creation of the world." The English author is not concerned with this, but simply with the effect of a disordered imagination on the mind engaged in mental prayer.

9. ME: diuerse fantasies of yuel thoughtes crien in our hertes. A more vivid and direct image than the Latin, which does not speak of *bad* thoughts.

10. Cf. 2 Cor 11:3. The English author is more insistent than Richard on our own powerlessness: cf. the *Cloud, ed. cit.*, ch. 65, p. 246.

11. Well proven: i.e., by witness of Scripture, theology, and experience.

12. Julian of Norwich reminds us that the Incarnate Word has taken our sensuality, and the work of mercy and grace is to restore its failing. Cf. *Revelations*, ch. 57.

13. ME: thinkyn on God and goostly thinges: a short description of meditation. Cf. the *Cloud, ed. cit.*, chs. 35 and 36.

14. The English balances the operation of the sensuality against that of the imagination in a more summary and ordinary fashion than the Latin, which speaks of "the vices of imagination and sensuality" (*De vitio imaginationis et sensualitatis*—ch. vi).

15. The English improves on the Latin in offering the rhetorical device of the *argumentatio perfectissima: Proposition:* "Sensuality is always so thirsty . . . "; *reason:* "The drink that she desires . . . "; *confirmation of the reason:* "Because the whole world is not enough . . . "; *adornment (exornatio):* "So it is that oftentimes . . . "; *conclusion (complexio):* "So it is well proven. . . . "

16. The diagram is the English author's invention, and the scribes of several MSS have obviously felt that they could improve on the efforts of their own particular exemplar. Cf. P.H., p. 15. The critical edition also has a frontispiece that reproduces the actual figure of MS Harleian 674.

17. Richard (ch. vii) is less didactic and more descriptive than the *Cloud* author. He names the seven principal affections (hope and fear, joy and sorrow, hate, love and shame), and offers scriptural proof of how they become virtues.

18. Ps 110:10 (Vulgate): *Initium sapientiae timor Domini*. Richard also cites Ps 13:5 and 18:10: "The fear of the Lord is holy."

19. The author instructs us how we are to practice the virtue at the beginning of the contemplative effort.

20. Both authors blithely ignore the game of sexual deceit that Laban plays with Jacob, with his two daughters as pawns. Cf. Gn 29:21–31. The Hebrew name Ruben means "Behold, a son." The English is a literal translation of Richard's *filius visionis*.

21. "And she conceived and bore a son, and called his name Ruben, saying, The Lord saw my affliction." The Latin reproduces the Vulgate (Gn 29:32)—*Deus vidit humilitatem meam*. The *Cloud* author seems to be influenced in his translation by the Magnificat, Lk 2:48.

22. "And again she conceived and bore a son, and said: Because the Lord heard that I was despised, he hath given this also to me."

23. Latin *exauditio*. The English *Leryng* is obviously an early usage—God gives a hearing—as does the judge in a law court. Cf. 2 Paralipomenon 33:19 (of the Acts of Manasses): "His prayer also, and his being heard [*exauditio*] and all his sins . . . are written in the words of Hozai"—a *hapax legomenon* in the Vulgate.

24. The English author reveals his strong feeling for Trinitarian doctrine, which is particularly in evidence in *Private Direction*.

25. ME: "This blessid sentence of Goddes owne mouthe: Blessed be they that sorowen for their scholen be coumforted"—Mt 5:5.

26. Probably an allusion to Ez 18:21: " . . . if the wicked does penance for all his sins which he has committed . . . and turns away from all his iniquities, he shall live and not die."

27. Latin: *in fletu compungitur*. The translator may be influenced by the liturgical prayer in the Gregorian Sacramentary for the gift of tears: "Draw forth from our stony hearts tears of compunction, that we may bewail our sins."

28. ME: Hert contrite and meek, God schal not dispise—Ps 50:19.

29. ME: doying to, Latin *additus vel additio*: a popular etymology in the Hebrew also. "Do to" in the sense of "join to" or "add to" is now obsolete.

30. The author, in his "Letter on Prayer," advises that hope should be knit to the first thought, which is fear.

31. Richard writes: "The divine word names this son 'added,' not 'given,' lest any man should presume of hope of forgiveness before fear and a sorrow which matches penitence" (*ante timorem et condignum poenitentiae dolorem*). The English "it is seyde" thus refers to the Latin text.

32. Ps 93:19 (Vulgate): "According to the multitude of sorrows in my heart, your consolations have gladdened my soul."

33. Cf. Jn 14:16.26;15,26,34. Cf. the Pentecost Sequence "Veni Sancte Spiritus" thought to have been composed by Stephen Langton, Archbishop of Canterbury and founder of the Cistercians, and introduced into the liturgy at the end of the twelfth century: *Consolator optime, dulcis hospes animae, dulce refrigerium . . . in fletu solatium.*

34. The translator simply ignores here the rhetoric of his original in the same way as he introduced his own in the previous chapter.

35. ME: homlynes, Latin *familiaritas inter Deum et animam*. The technical word in English for contemplative union. The first example in O.E.D. is from Richard Rolle's *Psalter* (1340): "Fosterand barnes (bairns) with hamlynes." It is one of the key words in the vocabulary of Julian of Norwich. Cf. J. Walsh, "God's Homely Loving," *The Month* 19 (1958): 164–72.

36. ME: ofttymes be felith hym not only be visited of God, but greetly coumfortyd in his comyng. The Latin has the more dramatic *immo aliquoties quodam ineffabili gaudio repleri* (sometimes, even, filled with an ineffable joy).

37. Gn 29:34: "Now also my husband will be joined to me, because I have borne him three sons."

38. Richard and his translator use the technical sponse (*sponsus*), bridegroom. Julian of Norwich says that "God enjoyeth that he is our spouse and our soule his loyal wyfe."

39. Cf. Ps 72:28 (Vulgate): "It is good for me to cling to my God, to put my hope in the Lord"; Dt 30:20. " . . . Love the Lord your God and cling to him, for he is truly your life . . . " ME: sothfast love. The early usages of the word given in O.E.D. are from devotional works.

40. Gn 29:35: "The fourth time she conceived and bore a son, and said: now will I praise the Lord: and for this she called him Juda." In the popular etymology, the Hebrew word is said to mean praise. Richard, whose Latin is *confitens*, avers that its primary meaning is *laudatio*, praise. The English "schrift," however, was coined to mean all that had to do with sacramental confession, which is the first sense in which the translator uses it—it means for him at once perfect contrition, as distinct from attrition—"for drede," auricular confession, and satisfaction in the offering of self. Finally (as the O.E.D. notices), it translates the Vulgate *confitens*, in the sense of discharging the prime Christian duty of praising God.

41. The reference to fear is introduced by the English author.

42. Richard separates the two: "All that we have said so far is about the confession which is praise. What of the confession of sin?"

43. There are some fifty or so examples in the Vulgate of the Psalmist's exhortation to confess to—i.e., to praise—the Lord. The observation is the English translator's.

44. Gn 29:35. Not in the Latin.

45. Latin: *Sufficere enim sibi posse existimat, cum se vera bona veraciter amare considerat.*

46. The distinction between salvation and perfection is drawn in the "Letter on Prayer," where the context is "loving God for himself and not for his goods"; and in "Private Direction," where those called to the "work" of the *Cloud* are called to perfection: otherwise, to salvation. Here the English author introduces it to summarize Richard's teaching on the superiority of the intellect over the affection in the work of contemplation. Cf. Introduction.

47. The translator here paraphrases, among other utterances, the aphorism of his original, *ubi amor ibi oculus*, which Ezra Pound rendered "Where love is, there is the power to see."

48. ME: desire of unseen trewe goodes; Latin: *bonorum invisibilium desiderio.* There is an allusion to the description of faith in Heb 11:1: "Faith is the substance of things to be hoped for, the evidence of things that appear not." Richard Rolle in the *Pricke of Conscience* uses the epithet "invisible" of God, so that it was unlikely that the English author was ignorant of it. He seems often to choose a word of native origin as against one derived from the Latin.

49. Latin: "From Lia comes ordered affections, from Rachel pure understanding." In the *Cloud*, the author speaks of the thought of Christ's Passion (meditation proper to the lower part of contemplation) as "a well-defined and clear sight of your natural intelligence imprinted upon your reason . . . a ray of God's likeness" (*ed. cit.*, ch. 8, p. 135).

50. 1 Cor 3:1: "I could not speak to you as spiritual, but only as fleshly; as babes in Christ, I gave you milk, you could not take solid food; nor can you now, for you are still fleshly." The distinction is made much of in ch. 45 of the *Cloud*, where the author is warning beginners in the contemplative exercise against a particular form of illusion.

51. ME: ruyde in goostly studies; Latin: *in studiis spiritualibus rudem;* i.e., the quest for God's truth and heavenly wisdom.

52. In the *Cloud* (*ed. cit.*, ch. 5, p. 129), the author says: "The eye of your soul is opened at it [sc. the object of meditation] and fixed upon it, like the eye of the bowman upon the eye of the target that he is shooting at."

53. ME: bodely thinges . . . seable thinges; Latin: *corporalia . . . visibilia.* Again the author avoids the Latin derivation "visible." "Seeable," according to O.E.D., though rare, was used by Richard Rolle. There is no phrase in the Latin that corresponds to this clear and summary statement on the act of introversion. Cf. C. Butler, *Western Mysticism, passim.*

54. In the *Cloud* it is said that only before the fall was imagination properly the servant of the reason—*ed. cit.*, ch. 65, p. 246.

55. Such activity is carefully described in the *Cloud:* "Perhaps the thought will bring to your mind a variety of excellent and wonderful instances of his kindness; it will say that he is most sweet and most loving, gracious and merciful" (*ed. cit.*, ch. 7, p. 132).

56. "The lower part of the contemplative life consists in good spiritual meditations . . . of the wonderful gifts, kindness, and works of God in all his creatures, corporal and spiritual"—the *Cloud, ed. cit.*, ch. 8, p. 137. It seems that a further distinction is being employed here. Richard is lucid on the precise way in which the imagination is to be used to increase the soul's fervor.

57. ME: ful needful and also speedful unto a worcking soule. The phrase is introduced, characteristically, by the English author, who expatiates on the work of treading down evil thoughts in ch. 10 of the *Cloud.*

58. The *Cloud* author, writing of the distinction between action and contemplation, in the contemplative life, makes the point that the two must be kept distinct. "It would be a wrong thing for a man engaged on meditation, and a hindrance to him, to turn his mind to the outward corporal works which he had done or should do, even though in themselves they are very holy works"—*ed. cit.*, ch. 8, p. 138.

59. The same point is made in the *Cloud*, where the "holy men" are those "who have, with a sincere will, forsaken the world and have bound themselves in any way, privately or openly, to the devout life in holy Church"— *ed. cit.*, ch. 10, p. 142.

60. This acute observation is the English author's. It reflects his peculiarly modern psychological acumen and balance as a spiritual director. Cf. his image of the "sely schyp" in *Inward Stirrings.*

61. In the *Cloud*, sloth is defined as "a weariness and a repugnance for any good occupation, bodily or spiritual"—*ed. cit.*, ch. 10, p. 143. The English author is similarly aware here of one of the occupational hazards of the solitary.

62. This is not the only or primary reason why, for Richard, Dan is called judgment: Gn 49:16—"Dan shall judge his people like another tribe in Israel." Popular etymology derived the name from the Hebrew *Dîn*, to judge.

63. Gn 30:6: "And Rachel said: The Lord hath judged for me, and has heard my voice, giving me a son. And therefore she called his name Dan." Neither the quotation nor the interpretation (made me equal to) is in the Latin.

64. For the use of the imagination in the contemplation of pains to come, cf. Ignatius Loyola's application of the (interior) senses to the pains of hell, where the Second Prelude is illustrative of the English author's teaching: "To ask for what I desire. It will be here to ask for an interior sense of the pain which the lost suffer, in order that if through my faults I forget the love of the Eternal Lord, at least the fear of punishment may enable me not to give way to sin" (*Exx* 65).

65. Gn 30:8: "Rachel said: God has compared me with my sister, and I have prevailed: and she called him Naphtali." The Latin says that Nepthalim means comparison or conversion (*comparatio, conversio*). The Hebrew etymology looks to the word "prevailed" and "prevailed by ruse."

66. Gn 49:21: "Naphtali, a hart let loose, and giving words of beauty." Richard follows this citation with others, on the allegory of divine love, from the Canticle of Canticles, which the translator ignores.

67. "The [sight of] joys to come" means, for the English author, simply heaven; the English word *feyre* translates the Latin *pulchritudo*.

68. J. LeClercq cites an anonymous monk of the twelfth century: "He who would deserve to come to the threshold of eternal life, God asks of him only a holy desire. Even if we are unable to make the efforts which merit eternity, in spite of being so base and so slow, because of our desire for eternal realities, we are already hastening towards it . . . it is by virtue of holy desire that we search for Christ, that we are united with him, and love him" (*The Love of Learning and the Desire for God*, ed. cit., p. 86).

69. Richard says that the wandering (*evagatio*) of the imagination is caused by useless thoughts. Here and in the *Cloud*, the author implies that the imagination out of hand is very difficult to control. It serves up a variety of disordered fancies and images (ch. 10, pp. 246–47).

70. The English author has much to say elsewhere about temperance—cf. *Inward Stirrings, infra*.

71. Gn 30:8–13: "Lia, perceiving that she had left off bearing, gave Zelpha her handmaid to her husband. And when she had conceived and brought forth a son, she said, Happily. And therefore called his name Gad." (The Hebrew *gad* means good fortune.)

72. Gn 30:12–13: "Zelph also bore another. And Lia said: this is for my happiness, for women will call me blessed. Therefore she called him Aser."

73. Cf. Rom 5:3: "We glory also in tribulations, knowing that tribulation brings patience, and patience, testing, and testing hope. And hope does not confound, because the love of God is poured out in our heart."

74. John of the Cross will stress the need for spiritual temperance in the preparation for contemplation. Cf., e.g., the *Ascent of Mount Carmel*.

75. The allusion is to the behavior of the Israelites in the desert as they rebelled against the hardships of hunger and thirst. Cf. Heb 3 and 4.

76. ME: the jangelying of the ymaginacioun, that is to sey, the inrennyng of veyne thoughtes. Cf. the *Cloud, ed. cit.*, ch. 7, p. 132. "It (the thought) will increase its chattering more and more" (ME: will thus jangle ever more and more).

77. After pointing out that the sudden and vain impulse that causes pleasure or resentment will, for the contemplative, be no more than venially sinful—the *Cloud, ed. cit.*, ch. 10, p. 142—the English author adds that carelessness in venial sin should always be avoided by "all true disciples of perfection" (ch. 11, p. 144).

78. ME: bot he have before besyli beholden. . . . The *Cloud* author is at pains to add that this gazing on the rewards and torments of the next world is antecedent contemplation, since for the *ex professo* contemplative the temptations are avoided by the exercise of dark contemplation (ch. 12, p. 145). Richard proceeds with an elaborate allegory of the biblical story of Ruben and the mandrakes (chs. 28–30), which is ignored by the English author.

79. The same advice is given in the *Cloud* to the one who is preparing for the contemplative exercise. The image used there for the senses is the door and windows of the house, which are to be kept against the inroads of flies— the bad thoughts from without. For the rest, we are to "avoid thinking of anything but God himself" (chs. 2 and 3, p. 119).

80. The paragraph reproduces the highly praised chs. 31–33 of the original, notable for the stylistic use of dissimilarity, a unique combination of *oppositio* or *contrarietas* defined by the rhetoricians as "combining a litotes with a corresponding positive affirmation," and of *contentio* ("a statement built on contraries"), in order to reinforce the affirmation. The English author also makes forceful use of alliteration.

81. The city of conscience becomes the city of peace—Jerusalem with Zion its high citadel. The immediate reference is Phil 4:7: "The peace of God which surpasses all understanding guard your hearts and minds in Christ Jesus." However, the English author introduces the epithet *high*, so that the passage becomes redolent of another in "Discernment of Spirits": "He who would have God dwelling in him constantly, and live in love and in the vision of the high peace of the Godhead, which is the highest and best part of contemplation that may be had in this life, such a man must be vigilant night and day to put down the spirit of the flesh and the spirit of the world."

82. "Sweet" and "sweetness" are the key words in the medieval monastic vocabulary of contemplation, particularly in the Psalter and the sapiential books. Cf. Vulgate, Ps 20:4, 30:20, 24:8, 118:103, 18:11; Prv 16:24; Wis 16:21, etc. In his chs. 36–37, Richard cites Ps 30:20, 4:7, 31:11, 33:91.

83. The allusion here would appear to be to the traditional Eucharistic text in Wis 16:20.

84. Cf. Gn 30:18: "And Lia said, God has given me a reward, because I gave my handmaid to my husband. And she called his name Issachar."

85. Cf. Rom 8:13: "If you put to death the deeds of the body, you will live . . . I consider that the sufferings of the present time are not worth com-

paring with the glory that is to be revealed in us . . . creation, and we ourselves grown inwardly as we wait for . . . the redemption of our bodies."

86. ME: erles; Latin: arrham. Richard says here: "Every time we enter into that interior joy of our Lord, we receive the first fruits as it were, the pledge (*arrham*), a taste of some portion of it." Hugh of St. Victor, Richard's master, has a short soliloquy on charity that he calls *De arrha animae*—the pledge of the soul.

87. Gn 49:14: "Issachar shall be a strong ass, lying down between the borders. He saw rest that it was good; and the land, that it was excellent."

88. Richard's immediate comment on "dwelling on the borders" is: "If we wish to know by experience true inward joy, we must travel from country to country, from an alien land to our own, from exile to the fatherland, from the country of the dying to that of the living" (ch. 38).

89. The "borders" or "extremes" are a common spiritual theme in twelfth-century monastic writing. St. Bernard speaks of joy in the Holy Spirit with mind of the blessings to come, and the necessary tolerance of present tribulation; Alcuin and Aquinas, of the need for the persevering prayer of petition; William of St. Thierry, of steadfast belief in the divine promise through the illumination of the Word. Cf. F. Chatillon, "Hic, ibi, interim," *RAM* 25 (1949): 194–99.

90. The image of standing over the border line is the English author's. Richard of St. Victor prefers the pun *pene sed non plene*—almost entirely, but not quite, a traditional eschatological expression.

91. The citation from Rom 7:24:—"Unhappy man that I am, who shall deliver me from the body of this death?"—is inserted by the translator.

92. The English author achieves his contrast by a short citation from Philippians, where Paul declares himself to be in this precise position: "For me to live is Christ, and to die is gain. And if to live in the flesh, this is the fruit of labor, and what I shall choose, I know not. I am straitened between the two, having a desire to be dissolved and to be with Christ . . . but to abide still in the flesh is needful" (1:21–24).

93. This state of mind and heart the English author describes most graphically in the *Cloud*, when he elaborates on the sorrow of the contemplative (*ed. cit.*, ch. 44, p. 204).

94. Gn 30:20: "Lia conceived again and bore the sixth son, and said, God hath endowed me with a good dowry." The Latin text says: "After Issachar, is born Zabulon, which means dwelling-place of strength. For what else do we understand by Zabulon but hatred of vices?" (40).

95. "Sweetness in the affection" has now become a catch phrase for the translator. It is the title of his previous chapter (VII) and he has used it there six times, though Richard never once links the two words. Mary Magdalen is pictured in the *Cloud* as striving for it (*ed. cit.*, ch. 15, p. 155). It is the equivalent of the reverent affection of the "Letter on Prayer," *infra*, and its beginnings are simultaneous with the entry to the higher part of contemplation. In the *Cloud*, this sweetness and the perfect hatred of sin constitute the perfection of the work of dark contemplation.

96. For the *Cloud* author, we have here the two sides of the coin of compunction: the perfect hatred of one's own sin, and that desire for heaven which he has called an earnest.

97. Ps 4:5.

98. For the *Cloud* author, the "lump of sin" that turns out to be "no other than yourself" tempts the contemplative to an irrational hatred of the self. However, "in all this sorrow . . . he is very glad to be" (*ed. cit.*, ch. 44, pp. 204–05).

99. This philosophical observation is the English translator's. Richard writes: "What does it mean, not to sin when in anger, and to grow angry when not sinning? It means to love people for their good and not for their attractiveness, and to be angry at their sins."

100. The commonplace doctrine here is introduced by the English author.

101. "You shall love the man, be he never so sinful, and you shall hate sin in every man, no matter what he is" (Hilton, *Scale of Perfection I*, ch. 64). "To love his fellow-Christian in charity and hate his sin—no man can do this but only good men" (ibid., ch. 65).

102. Ps 138:22.

103. Ps 118:104 (Vulgate): "By your commandments I have understanding; therefore I have had in hatred every way of iniquity."

104. The paragraph summarizes chs. 40 and 41 of the Latin text.

105. Latin: *habitaculum fortitudinis*. The name appears to mean simply "gift."

106. Gn 30:20: "This turn also my husband will be with me, because I have borne him six sons."

107. For the *Cloud* author, the exercise of love in dark contemplation— the perfection of charity—destroys not only sin but the root and ground of sin. Cf. ch. 12.

108. Cf 1 Jn 1:8.

109. This allusion to St. Augustine is not in the Latin text. *In epistolam Joannis ad Parthos* 1, 6, we have: "It is not possible for anyone, as long as he is in the flesh, not to be guilty of at least venial sins."

110. Cf. 24:7: "The sins of my youth and my ignorances do not remember".

111. Gn 30:21.

112. The English author in the *Cloud* writes of those who "care more and sorrow more for a disordered gesture, or an unseemly and unfitting word spoken before men, than they do for a thousand idle thoughts on foul stirrings of sin" (*ed. cit.*, ch. 54, p. 225).

113. The echo of a courtly love theme. Ignatius Loyola in his *Spiritual Exercises* recommends that "I bring myself to confusion for my many sins, proposing examples to myself, as if a knight were to stand before his king and all his court, covered with shame and confusion" (*Exx* 74).

114. A like phrase, "in the sight of God and of the saints and angels of heaven," is used in the similar context of ch. 54 of the *Cloud.*

115. Apart from two short chapters (60–61), the translator ignores chs. 47–70 of his original. This paragraph follows Richard's own list of the seven principal affections, though they are not named in the translation—sc.: fear, pain, hope and love, joy and anger, shame. Julien of Norwich says: "I felt within me five affections working; they are: rejoicing, mourning, desire, fear, and true hope" (*Showings*, ch. 47).

116. A repetition of what is said initially as a general comment of the allegory of Jacob and his sons: cf. *supra*. A similar general comment is made when the *Cloud* author introduces his disquisitions on humility—ch. 12, p. 147.

117. Again the translator summarizes his text over 6 chapters (60–65), with short descriptions of how the virtues or affections become vices through excess.

118. This forms an *inclusio* with the last sentence of the translator's Introduction.

119. The common doctrine of the Western tradition. Cassian says of discretion that it is the mother (*generatrix*), the guardian (*custos*) of all virtues (Coll. I, 23).

120. Gn 37:3: "Now Israel loved Joseph above all his sons, because he had him in his old age."

121. The Rule of St. Benedict (ch. 64) directs the abbot to keep in mind "the discretion of holy Jacob" in the instructions he gives concerning both temporalities and God's affairs: "If I course my flocks to be overdriven, they will all die in one day" (Gn 33:12).

122. These two sentences are inserted into the text (ch. 67) by the translator. They express one of his most cherished beliefs. Cf. "Inward Stirrings," with its famous image of the ship, the "Letter on Prayer," "Private Direction,"

123. Elsewhere, Richard distinguishes three degrees of discretion—childhood, adolescence, and maturity: a perfection that is the fruit of experience and the practice of all the virtues. Cf. Dsp. "Discretion," III, 1323.

124. The prime quality of a good spiritual director is discretion, a charism, says St. Bernard, that enables us to distinguish what is given us for our own good and for the direction of others. Cf. *Serm. de diversis* 88, 2: P.L. 183, 706.

125. Latin: *Melior est vir prudens viro forti*, a citation from Prv 16:32, where the Vulgate reads *patiens* for *prudens*. The second sentence is not in the Latin, and is a favorite adage of the English author. It occurs both in the *Cloud, ed. cit.*, ch. 64, p. 208, and in the "Letter on Prayer."

126. Prv 21:28: "The obedient man shall speak victory." The ME has *sley*.

127. The Cellarer of the Monastery is to be a man of mature character. "He is to have charge of all affairs, but he is not to act without the Abbot's approval" (*Rule of St. Benedict*, ch. 31).

128. St. Thomas Aquinas tends to equiparate discretion with the cardinal virtue of prudence; here it is *prudentia regnativa*: cf. *Summa Theol.* 2–2

ae, 50, 1. Richard, however, speaks of the gifts of the Spirit: wisdom and counsel.

129. The consistent doctrine of the Fathers, East and West. Gregory of Nyssa writes that "the soul is indeed the image of that Nature which reaches beyond all understanding, the imprint of the Deity, the tabernacle of life, the looking-glass of the true Light. How could the soul come to the knowledge of herself and fail to know her Creator?" (P.G. 44, 806–07).

130. This doctrinal statement is not in the Latin. We find a similar one in Hilton: "Your reason, that is properly the image of God through the grace of the Holy Ghost, shall be clothed in a new light of soothfastness, holiness and righteousness; and then it is reformed in feeling. For when the soul has perfect knowing of God, then it is reformed in feeling" (*Scale of Perfection* II, ch. 31, p. 368).

131. Hilton describes these spiritual works: "Think of the kind of a reasonable soul ghostly . . . think that a soul is a life deathless and unseeable and hath might in itself for to see and know . . . and love the sovereign goodness that is God . . . seek thyself in none other place" (ibid., ch. 30, p. 357).

132. The translator makes the same point in the *Cloud*, in distinguishing between imperfect and perfect humility (*ed. cit.*, ch. 14, p. 150).

133. So Hilton: "For thy soul is but a mirror, in which thou shalt see God ghostly. And therefore thou shalt first find thy mirror and keep it bright and clean from fleshly filth . . . that thou mayst see it, and our Lord therein also" (*loc. cit.*, ch. 30, p. 358).

134. The candle image is not in the Latin. Hilton offers the same teaching, but substitutes the sun for the candle: "Right as the sun shows to the bodily eyes itself and all bodily being by it; right so soothfastness, which is God, showeth to the reason of the soul itself first, and by itself all other ghostly thing that needeth to be known of a soul" (*loc. cit.*, ch. 33, p. 377).

135. The chapter following in *Scale of Perfection* shows "why a soul cometh to this sight and to this knowing"; and "the love that our Lord hath to a sinful soul that cannot love him right is the cause why this soul cometh to this knowing and to this love that cometh out of it" (*ibid.*, p. 380).

136. Hilton speaks of "this ghostly opening of the inward eye into the knowing of the Godhead" (*loc. cit.*, ch. 33, p. 378). The translator has elsewhere: "Then perhaps it will be his will to send out a ray of spiritual light . . . and he will show you some of his secrets. . . . Then you shall feel your affection all aflame with the fire of this love" (*Cloud, ed. cit.*, ch. 26, pp. 174–75).

137. Cf. *supra*, n. 134.

138. (Ed. note: this citation was not included in the mss.)

139. Ps 4:7.

140. "Fed and filled with clear sight and burning love of our Lord Jesus . . . the same grace that turneth first them from sin and maketh them beginning and profiting by gifts of virtues . . . reformed in feeling, made able and ready to contemplation" (Hilton, *Scale of Perfection*, pp. 423–26).

141. Richard here cites Prv 13:12: "Hope that is deferred afflicts the

soul." The translation reflects the second half of the verse: "desire when it comes in the tree of life."

142. Ecclus 24:26: "Come over to me all you that desire me [wisdom] . . . for my spirit is sweet above honey."

143. "Another soul that hath not yet received this fulness of grace, if her desire for to come to this ghostly knowing of Jesus . . . he must learn for to die to the world, and forsake the love of it truly" (Hilton, *Scale of Perfection* II, ch. 24, pp. 337–38).

144. Jer 31:15: "A voice was heard on high of lamentation, of mourning and weeping, of Rachel weeping for her children and refusing to be comforted. . . . Let thy voice cease from weeping and thy eyes from tears, for there is a reward for thy work, says the Lord."

145. Gn 35:16–18: "When Rachel was in travail, by reason of her hard labor she began to be in danger. . . . And when her soul was departing for pain, and death was now at hand, she called the name of her son Benoni, that is, the son of my pain. But his father called him Benjamin, that is, the son of the right hand: So Rachel died."

146. "As soon as Benjamin was born, his mother Rachel died. Benjamin stands for contemplation, Rachel for reason. As soon as a soul is touched by true contemplation, as it is in this royal reduction of itself to nothing and this high extolling of God as all, it is certain and true that all a man's reason dies in that moment" "Private Direction."

147. Another of "the voluntary captives of the name of Jesus," Aelred of Rielvaux, writing in the same vein as our English translator, says: "A certain sweetness begins to flow from the honeycomb of the Holy Scriptures, and the honey-sweet name of Christ insinuates itself in my affection" (P.L. 185, 662; cf. P. Dumontier, *S. Bernard et la Bible*, p. 104).

148. Ps 25:12 (Vulgate). Richard here cites Ps 67:27: "Bless God in the churches."

149. The English author, in both the *Cloud* and *Private Direction*, never tires of insisting on the crucial need the *ex professo* contemplative has for spiritual direction, especially if he is an apprentice.

150. Wis 16:20: "You fed your people with the food of angels, and gave them bread from heaven prepared without labor having in it all that is delicious, and the sweetness of every taste."

151. Ps 67:28.

Denis's Hidden Theology

Translator's Introduction

The Mystical Theology *and its author*

Apart from the Gospels and some of the Pauline Epistles, there is no single short work in the whole body of Western religious literature that has had so profound a theological influence and so extraordinary a spiritual impact as the anonymous *Mystical Theology*. Within our own theological and spiritual time span, the works of the Areopagite have commanded the veneration of the greatest of the Scholastic theologians, and won them as commentators. We have already had occasion to glance at the father of them all, John Scotus Erigena. Summoned to the Frankish Court, he succeeded in shaping the literary and philosophical direction of Western civilization in the new life given to Europe after the destruction of Rome by the barbarian.[1] Aquinas, in the Epilogue to his *Commentary on the Divine Names*, writes that his own intellectual powers are far inferior to those of the Blessed Denis, and he beseeches that his readers will correct whatever is *non recte dictum*. But it is Hugh of St. Victor who stands at the head of all the Scholastic admirers of Denis with his *chef-d'oeuvre*, the commentary on the *Ecclesiastical Hierarchy*. Richard's contributions are well enough known to the *Cloud* author's readers, while the extensive glosses of Albert the Great on the whole Dionysian corpus speak for themselves. When we come to the spiritual tradition known now as Western mysticism, we find a long line of monastic theologians thoroughly conversant with at least the *Mystical Theology* and using it to expound their doctrine of the contemplative ascent. Among the Cistercian spirituals, William of St. Thierry bases much

51

of his Christian anthropology on the Dionysian corpus. The Rhine-land mystics, Eckhart, Tauler, and Ruysbroeck, follow Denis reli-giously. The Carthusians, Guigo the Angelic and Guigues du Pont, Hugh de Balma, and the synthesizer Denis the Carthusian, are all his followers. The Franciscans, beginning with the great Bonaven-ture himself and down to Benet Canfield, the English exile, accept him as taught by St. Paul himself. Augustine Baker, the Benedictine who maintains the tradition of the English mystics in the contem-plative convents of English ladies in the Flanders and Paris of the seventeenth century, writes his commentary for them on the *Mystical Theology*; while the Flemish Jesuit theologian, Leonard Lessius, fights for the authentic apostolic identity of its author against in-creasing historical odds. It is the Carmelite doctor, however, who finally sets the seal on the spiritual preeminence of the Areopagite in the history of Western spirituality, and justifies the title by which he is now universally acknowledged, "The Father of Christian Mys-ticism."[2] St. John of the Cross takes it for granted that the Dionysian ascent is analogous to the complete passivity symbolized by his own three nights, and writes: "This dark night is the inflowing of God into the soul . . . which is called by contemplatives infused contem-plation and mystical theology. . . . When this divine light of con-templation assails the soul which is not enlightened, it causes spiritual darkness in it. . . . For this reason St. Denis and other mys-tical theologians call this infused contemplation a ray of darkness."[3] An apposite illustration of the nature of this spiritual paternity is in-deed the *Cloud* author's Middle English paraphrase, *Deonise hid divin-ite*. It betrays not the slightest indication that the Englishman even suspected his original to have been written in sixth-century Greek: and this in spite of his knowing—though he nowhere says so explic-itly—that Denis was an Athenian.[4] However, it is worth recalling that the Greek author himself does not reveal any autobiographical detail or anything else to sustain the fiction that he was the convert of St. Paul, save for his naming Paul's disciple, Timothy, as the re-cipient of the *Divine Names* and the *Mystical Theology*.[5] He does indeed cite the famous sentence from Galatians, "I live now, it is not I, but Christ who lives in me";[6] but he does so simply as an exemplifying expression of the ecstatic love that is the point of union in the neg-ative ascent. In fact, there is nothing in the context of the *Divine Names* that might indicate that the "divine Paul" is the author's mas-ter and guide, and the one who imposed hands on Timothy. It must be remarked that this is the only quotation that could be considered as even loosely relevant to any specific Dionysian thesis; his writings as a whole, and especially his mystical theology, are singularly free of Pauline influence. In fine, there would seem to be no doubt that it is the story in the Acts of the Apostles of the altar on the Athenian Areopagus dedicated to the unknown God that has determined the pseudonym of the anonymous author.[7]

But whatever we, of a very different age and outlook, may make of his arrogating to himself the identity of a saint and of an apostle chosen by the great Paul himself, it remains that the Pseudo-Dionysius was a theologian of vast energy and talent. His treatise *The Heavenly Hierarchy* and its *Ecclesiastical* and earthly counterpart present us with a world and a whole divine economy that René Roques had no hesitation in calling *L'Univers Dionysien*.[8] Yet none of it enters into the consideration of the *Cloud* author, whether or not any of it was ever known to him. In none of his works, apart from the brief mention of the ministration of angels in *Private Direction*,[9] does he refer to the hierarchical operations so essential to the thought and system of Denis. He is concerned only with the latter's theology in the sense in which it is used in the title of this little treatise,[10] and more generally with the knowledge and notion of being as the Areopagite reflects on it in the *Divine Names*.[11]

In the history of Christian thought, it is generally accepted that the Pseudo-Dionysius[12] is concerned to reconcile the revealed certitude of Christian life and doctrine with the pale cast of Neoplatonic thought. With the great patristic figures who had preceded him, Ignatius of Antioch, Origen, or Gregory of Nyssa, the marriage between their theology and the inherited philosophy of Plato and the eminent figures who followed him was uneasy enough. But in the works of a sixth-century scholar like the Areopagite we are dealing with a Neoplatonism already exposed to centuries of Christian influence.[13] This said, Denis's immediate philosophical source is not so much Christian revelation as the pagan Neoplatonism of Proclus.[14] Nor can his constant, multiple, and random citation from Scripture disguise the truth of this. What is undeniable is that two thinkers, a thousand years apart, embrace a Christianity of completely different sources, cultures, and orders. The English Carthusian would take it for granted that he and Denis shared the same substantial faith: that when the Deity is addressed as Trinity in the opening prayer of the *Mystical Theology*,[15] they are worshiping the same God. They are together addressing the Father revealed in the Son, who has mysteriously humbled himself in order to save sinful humankind.[16] What seems to be far more important to the Areopagite's religious system is the unicity of a transcendent God, the universal Cause from whom everything flows and to whom everything returns. It is thus that in God we have unity and plurality, the finite and the infinite, rest and movement, inexhaustible riches and continuous gift: in other words, the apparent contraries of transcendence and causality. According to the Western tradition it would be sacrilegious to assume that Denis has not resolved in the most perfect manner the wonderful tension between the divine and the human, between revelation and the sublimities of ancient Greek thought. Certainly for the author of the *Cloud*, Denis was one of those chosen few who saw eternity in the dazzling darkness of night.

The Mystical Doctrine of Denis

Substantially, the *Mystical Theology* begins from the truth that because God is transcendent, he is unknowable. This is an absolute principle for Denis: No one can know what God is in himself. This is God's secret, his hiding place, where he is above all and over all.[17] Denis summons his disciple and friend Timothy to embark on the ascent of the mind to God, which has three moments: (1) the abandonment of human sensations and intellectual operations, (2) and this by the way of unknowing, (3) so as to be lifted up to union with him who transcends all being and knowledge. The abandonment is itself a positive attempt to attain the Transcendent: an attempt that, at its ultimate point, will be rewarded by unknowing, itself implying union with the Transcendent.[18] The first moment corresponds with the Platonic catharsis—purification;[19] but for Denis this is rather an intellectual than a moral purgation. For the abandonment of all sense-knowledge and intellectual knowing, Denis uses as symbol the ascent of Moses on Mount Sinai; and he simply accommodates the text to suit his own purposes: "There he [Moses] does not encounter God nor contemplate him; only the place where he dwells." We must note that the abandonment concerns only the knowledge of God by affirmations, such as we have it in the various attributes analyzed in his *Divine Names*. That which makes God positively known as Cause is the first and most venerable name of the Good. After this is Being, and then the One; for the outstanding characteristic of the Transcendent is Unity. To explain the knowing that leads to this Unity, and that is conditional on initiation,[20] we are given Plotinus's image of the sculptor. This example takes the fancy of the English author and is drawn out by him in fine style.[21] What the Areopagite is concerned with is a philosophical exercise: to deny or to remove all the divine attributes by means of successive negations. However, this is also a spiritual activity, as Denis insists. Negative theology and mystical theology are identical.

Abandonment (aphairesis), Unknowing, and the Divine Darkness

For Denis, the term *aphairesis*[22] indicates the movement to total negation, the entry into the absolute of the Divine Darkness "which is all-light." The ascent by negations, cataloged in the last two chapters of the *Mystical Theology*, is equally to penetrate into the Darkness; it is the substance of prayer, and the dark cloud in which Moses was seen to lose himself—the prophet's own ascent by negations. John of the Cross believed that it was the total passivity of his "nights," which he describes as follows: "This dark night is the influence of God on the soul which purifies it of its ignorance and its habitual imperfections. This contemplatives call infused contemplation or mystical theology. . . . When this divine light of contemplation shines in the soul which is not yet wholly illumined, it brings to it spiritual darkness."[23] We must note, however, that with the Areopagite the darkness in no way describes the mystical state that is the result of God's extraordinary graced action on the soul. Rather the Dionysian mystique is a striving to penetrate the darkness, where the point at issue is not the psychological state of the soul but union with the God who dwells in the darkness of his inaccessible transcendence. It is God who is the unknowable object. But though the Dionysian meaning of the term covers at once ignorance, unknowing, and unknowability, what is central to the meaning and movement here is unknowing, and the *aphairesis*, the abandonment, that achieves it: unknowing of that Essence above all essences which surpasses every word, understanding, and essence. It is to the not-knowing of God's transcendence that we must attribute the science that surpasses the knowing and the being.[24] It follows then that we know God but not by a direct knowledge of his nature, for that is unknowable and surpasses all reason and understanding. Knowledge through knowing is in fact gained by affirmations, but knowledge by unknowing is realized by *aphairesis*, the series of successive negations. One does not attain to the comprehension of God by means of the understanding, or by speaking him or naming him. As the *Cloud* author will insist: "The most divine knowing that we have of God is that which is obtained by unknowing."[25]

With regard to the "content" of the unknowing, Denis speaks in his prayer of the highest peak of the Scriptures where there is revealed to him a darkness that envelops the mysteries of theology, and the biblical image of darkness serves to explain the reality of the unknown. So, after he has passed above the heights of intelligible things, he comes to a knowing beyond knowing, and this by not knowing. The statement follows that the Transcendent really shows himself to those—but only to those—who enter the Darkness of unknowability (*gnophon tēs agnōsias*).[26] The more perfect union with the One who is totally unknowable takes place in a passivity without knowledge. It is thus that the essential element of this goal of the ascent by negations is established: to know nothing and to know in a way that is above knowledge.

Denis, in his fifth letter, explains the Divine Darkness thus:

> All who penetrate it deserve to know and to see God. It is by not-seeing and not-knowing that one at last arrives there, above all that is seen and known, where one knows well that this is beyond all sense-knowledge and all understanding.[27]

In the history of Christian mysticism, the concept of darkness and its antinomy have always had their special place, as the symbols that express the conflicting, constant, and dominating aspects of mystical experience. In the West, as we have said, this is largely due to the influence of the Areopagite and his *Mystical Theology*. Denis employs the symbol of light for the emanations of the universal Cause, and of darkness for the ineffable divine Transcendence. It is, however, not simply a question of two contrasting realities, the luminous and the obscure. Each of them carries a preeminent significance whose purpose is to express an over-reaching reality. The Transcendent is described by obscurity insofar as it is understood as negation, and by the luminous insofar as it is understood as supereminence. In this sense light and darkness are both expressive of the one transcendent reality: Transcendent Darkness and Supereminent Light coincide. So Denis in his exhortation to Timothy will speak of "the superessential ray of darkness,"[28] which is in fact the brilliance of transcendent light. Finally, it is the darkness that imparts supereminent luminosity to the One who shines above the brilliance of all light, filling beyond all measure those whose intelligence has ceased to see, with a transcendent and astonishing beauty.[29] Again it is the fifth letter that carries a more simple explanation: "The Divine Darkness is the inaccessible light where God is said to dwell. It is invisible because of its transcendent clarity, and inaccessible because of its supereminent effusion of light."[30]

Union and Unity

The goal of abandonment and knowing by unknowing is *henōsis*, union. The word does not occur in either the Old or the New Testament. It appears to have been first used in a Christian context by Ignatius of Antioch, whom Denis cites in his *Divine Names.*[31]

In the Areopagite's ontology, *henōsis* appears to have three meanings, each of which seems to derive from his epigram "God does not permit any being to destroy its own unity." So *henōsis* is first a unification of a triple flowing forth, the consequence of the reduction of plurality to unity in the moment of conversion. Though achieved by the Good, it is more directly attributed to the intelligible light, but above all to love. Its second meaning is union proper: union with God that all being attains in the flowing forth from and conversion to him—a return that is the first consequence of the operation of the Good. Lastly, *henōsis* is imitative of the Divine Transcendence by participation in the form of the One, which with us at least is the result of the unification of plurality. It is the goal and final term of the mystical theology. As unknowing (*agnōsia*) indicates both incognoscibility as a divine attribute and the unknowing by means of which we know him, so *henōsis*, one of his transcendent attributes, also expresses union achieved with the Transcendent God; and as it goes beyond every form of created unity, it is unknowable to every affirmative activity of the understanding. This unity, as we have reiterated, is the result of the dynamism of the Dionysian abandonment; and to help us to understand the efficacy of the movement of *aphairesis*, Denis uses a synonym for union, the verb *sunaptō*, "to attach." So it is, then, that our intelligence, besides having the faculty of knowing and the vision of intelligible forms, also possesses a union (*henōsis*) that overpasses the nature of the intelligence and binds it (*sunaptei*) to the Transcendent.

We have said that the third moment of the Dionysian ascent is the inevitable consequence of the Areopagite's conception of the Divine Transcendence. The human intelligence, carried along by its desire to find true union with him, has no other goal than to search for the image of this "Being-in-him" by an entire unknowing (*agnōsia*). It is this abandon whose task it is to drive on the understanding by the negation of every affirmation toward the absolute simplicity of the transcendent One.

The Dionysian Ecstasy

"The doctrine of ecstasy," writes J. Lemaitre, "that is to say, an intellectual going outside or beside oneself in order to enter with God into a contact or a union which surpasses the natural faculties, at least with regard to the vocabulary employed and the characteristics by which it tends to be identified, does not come from the Christian tradition, but explicitly from neo-Platonic philosophy."[32] The Pseudo-Dionysius has said very little directly about the nature of the human spirit or the psychological makeup of the soul, nor has he used the very expressive Proclean phrase "the flower of the intelligence" (*anthos tou nou*) to indicate a faculty that is above intelligence. However, out of the many senses in which Denis uses the word *henōsis*, there is the prominent meaning of a faculty of knowing by unknowing: The soul or the understanding or whatever knows by means of "the union that surpasses understanding" (*henōsis huper noûn*). So in the key-text from the seventh chapter of the *Divine Names:* "We must notice that our understanding has the faculty of knowing, by means of which it can see intelligible forms. But it also possesses a union (*henōsis*) which reaches beyond the nature of the understanding. By this unity it is joined to that which is above itself."[33] It is by this faculty that the divine is to be comprehended.

Denis pushes the meaning of *henōsis* even further when he is arguing for the use of the Greek word for human love (*erōs*) to be employed in the mystical context. He insists that "the faculties of the understanding in fact are to be declared superfluous when the soul, approximating to the form of God, tends towards the rays of inaccessible light with those blind glances, by means of a union that is unknowable (*di' henōseōs agnōstou*)."[34] So for Denis there is a faculty that can have knowing of the Transcendent, which he calls union (*henōsis*) and which outreaches the understanding; and this in spite of the fact that the Transcendent is inaccessible to every kind of affirmative knowing of the human understanding. Whoever succeeds in knowing nothing at all by unknowing, which is the result of abandonment (*aphairesis*), will succeed in knowing above all understanding. Thus, by this act of knowing through the mysterious union that outreaches the understanding, union with God (*henōsis pros Theon*) as he is in himself will be achieved.

Here then is the meaning of ecstasy, of going out of oneself, of being beside oneself in the Dionysian sense. By abandonment, the successive negations, which are *aphairesis*, negative theology proceeds by way of denying all beings and all forms of the intelligible world, including those of the Christian mysteries, until it reaches total unknowing. In this way it achieves the end and goal of its journey, union with God—which is what Denis says to Timothy at the beginning of the first chapter of *Mystical Theology:*

> My friend Timothy . . . be intent on abandoning both your bodily senses . . . and your intellectual operations . . . and be intent on ascending in a way in which you could never understand to union with him who is above every substance and every kind of knowledge. For it is by passing beyond yourself and all other things, and so purifying yourself . . . of everything . . . you shall be carried up . . . to the substance beyond all substances, to the radiance of the divine darkness.

It follows that there would seem to be little room for the divine love in the Dionysian *ascensio mentis in Deum* (ascent of the mind to God), in any accepted Christian sense; nor can Denis's negative theology give any account of a love that is truly consonant with the Gospel. In what has been called *la sécheresse metaphysique*, he is seen to prefer the Platonic *erōs* to the Christian *agapē*; nor does the term retain for him anything of the original satyric sense, even figurative. In the *Divine Names*, God's love is one of the attributes subjected to analysis, and human love is seen as a reflection, an imitation of this divine power of loving. It is this *erōs*, this power, that drives God outside himself, without in any sense lessening the perfection of his inner being. "This God," says Denis, "who is universal cause and whose amorous desire (*erōs*) is equally good and beautiful, reaches out to the totality of beings by the superabundance of its amorous goodness, and goes out of itself when it exercises its Providence in respect of all beings."[35] Denis will even categorize the effects of ecstasy:

> It is a power of unification and of bringing together.
> It emanates from the Beautiful-and-Good, thanks to the Beautiful-and-Good.
> It unites beings of the same rank one to another.
> It drives superior beings to exercise their providence over their inferiors.
> It converts inferior beings and attaches them to the superior.[36]

The Middle English Translation

In spite of the apparent dependence of the fourteenth-century English author on Denis's *Divine Names*, especially in *Private Direction*,[37] he sits very lightly, whether he intends this or not, both to the Dionysian Neoplatonism and to the specific Christian theology professed by the Areopagite. He has nothing to say, directly or indirectly, about the intelligible Forms or Ideas that are the exemplary causes of all that participate in the Divine Being.[38] He speaks only of "the qualitees of the beyng of thi-self. For ther is no name, no felyng, ne beholdyng more ne so moche, acordyng to ever-lastynges, the whiche is God, as is that the whiche may be had, seen and felt in the blinde and lovely beholdyng of this worde *is*."[39] When Denis writes of the divine love in the seventh chapter of the *Divine Names*, he is concerned only with a force that creates and draws all things to itself, and in no sense with the everlastingly benevolent love (St. Bernard says, *Deus movet desiderans*—"God moves by his longing"[40]) of the Father, which recreates and restores all things to itself through the only-begotten Son in the Spirit. For the author of the *Cloud*, "the love which achieves ecstasy" is at one and the same time love for man equal to the love of oneself for God's sake. Nonetheless, the *Cloud* author expects that his version of Denis's obscure and enigmatic treatise, with a certain elucidation and addition in the first three of its five short chapters, will be both intelligible and reassuring to those readers for whom he has written the *Cloud* and *Private Direction*.

The Middle English translator follows the Areopagite in suggesting that Timothy, his fellow-presbyter, should embark on the mystical ascent to the divine, to that highest summit of the godly and mysterious darkness where God has his hiding-place.[41] The journey involves, he says, (1) a leaving behind of human sensations and intellectual operations, (2) the pilgrimage along a road from which no traveler returns unscathed, and (3) a being raised to him who transcends all substance and knowledge. It is a secret journey and one that is not to be divulged to the uninitiated, an ascent the map of which is drawn by the teachings of the Gospel and the elucidations of theology. It appears that the typical pilgrim was Moses when he ascended Mount Sinai. He had to be purified, and to leave behind divine lights and sounds and words, so that he might enter into the *Cloud of Unknowing*,[42] and be united in a better way to him who is totally unknowable.[43] Here we have the three ways or moments the Western Tradition has inherited from Denis: purification, illumination, union. The first of these is wider in its scope than, say, the night of the senses of John of the Cross, for it involves the mortification of every human mode of knowing. It is an ascesis adopted by all Western spiritual writers, and for those whose language is English, influenced since the fifteenth century by the *Cloud of Unknowing*. No one has ever dared to contradict the *Cloud* author's claim that Denis's words corroborate his own. No matter how their theological presuppositions and their ascetical and mystical teaching may differ, the purpose is the same: as Christians to ascend to the transcendent God, who, in some way or another, reveals himself.

The second moment, the unknowing, is that which advances to the union with God. The third moment follows from the first two. It is union with the Superessential, the Transcendent, which of itself implies ecstatic experience. Denis never uses the word *love*, but the translator speaks of *affeccioun* five times in the first chapter.[44]

The prayer to the Blessed Trinity, with which the treatise begins, revolves round the theme of darkness. "I beseech you to lift us up," translates our author, "to those utterly unknown and sovereign-shining heights of your mysterious, inspired utterances, where all the secrets of divine knowledge are concealed and hidden under the sovereign-shining darkness of wisest silence, making what dazzles beyond compare to shine forth secretly."[45] This is the dark night of Moses' ascent of Mount Sinai; and for the medieval Dionysians it is the analogue of the receptivity that is the result of perfect active and passive mortification. This is the view of Thomas of St. Victor, and of the *Cloud* author who follows the former's basic intuitions. It would appear to be the Areopagite's own position—at least in the *Ecclesiastical Hierarchy* (ch. III), where he emphasizes the difference between those who, receiving the Eucharist, have been purified from their sensual fantasies and those who have not. That such a view is envisaged by Denis in the *Mystical Theology* is highly unlikely, no matter how Gallus approaches it in his *Extractio*. Denis, here and also in the *Divine Names*, certainly goes no further than to restrict his purifications to the chain of affirmations and negations:

> We mount upwards, so far as our feet can tread that ordered path, advancing through the negation and transcendence of all things and through a conception of a universal cause, towards that which is beyond all things. Hence God is known through knowledge and through unknowing; and on the one hand he is reached by intuition, reason, understanding, perception and so on; and yet on the other hand he cannot be grasped by intuition, language or name, and he is not anything in the world, nor is he known in anything. He is all things, in all things and nothing in any.[46]

Hid Divinite and Peri Mustikès Theologías

There does not appear to be any other ascent to God than by those apparent contraries that have been felicitously called *La Mystique de la Lumière* and *La Mystique de la Ténèbre*. All will admit that with Denis and the Christian writers who followed him—notwithstanding the many attempts to link the two "ways", and among these theologians we must certainly number the *Cloud* author[47] and the other Carthusian Guigues du Pont[48]—the Mystique of Darkness has tended to prevail, at least up to the time of St. John of the Cross. We would find it hard to put our finger on any Christian writer of note who ever argued otherwise; and Meister Eckhart would seem to speak for all when he writes:

> Man has to seek God in error and forgetfulness and foolishness. For Deity has in it the power of all things, and no thing has the like. The sovereign light of the indivisible essence illumines all things. St. Dionysius says that beauty is good order with pre-eminent lucidity. Thus God is an arrangement of three Persons. And the soul's lower power should be ordered to her higher, and her higher ones to God; her outward senses to her inward and her inward ones to reasons; and thought to intuition, to the will and all to unity, so that the soul may be alone with nothing flowing into her but sheer divinity, flowing here into itself.[49]

This mélange of Augustinianism and Dionysianism can scarcely be said to form a harmonious whole, and its very obscurity would lead us to sympathize with the Churchmen who urged the condemnation of certain propositions of the saintly Dominican contemporary of Dante. The Middle English translator, with his own considerable erudition, has no truck with such psychological and theological subtleties as these. He will use what passes for Denis—his *Mystical Theology* and *Divine Names*—with every freedom, but with one single acknowledgement. He never names his other mentors and translators numbered among the medieval Dionysians—Hugo de Balma, John Sarracenus, and in all probability Guigues du Pont. At the same time, for all the early medieval Spirituals, plagiarism was in no sense considered disreputable. Perhaps, in our modern considerations and overpossessiveness, we might recall again Dante's words: "This is why the Saints never envy one another, because each one attains the goal of his longing, which is equal to the nature of his excellence."[50]

The English Translator and His Sources

We have noticed more than once that the Latin version of John Sarracenus was accepted by the *Cloud* author as the original text of
Denis. Sarracenus, a friend of Thomas à Becket's secretary, John of
Salisbury, to whom he dedicated the translation of the two *Hierarchies*, concludes his translation of the *Mystical Theology* in 1167, ded-
icating it to Odo, abbot of the Benedictine monastery of St. Denys
in Paris. *Denis's Hidden Theology* is in no sense an accurate or exact
translation of Sarracenus—even in the first three chapters, where
Sarracenus is certainly his starting point. The English author considers that he enjoys total freedom in the treatment of his text, usually by way of expansion of obscure phraseology, and of explanatory
addition. To illustrate more precisely his *modus operandi*, I have pro-
vided a precise translation of the Latin words and phrases of chapter
one (left-hand column) and of the author's Middle English rendering
(right-hand column):[51]

94.10	These things are what I ask for in my prayer.	2.25	And for all thees thinges ben aboven minde, therfore with affeccyon aboven mynde as I may I desire to purchase hem to me with this preier.
94.10	The proper way of investigating true wisdom.	2.29	How a man schal rise in this hid deuinite bi doing awey of alle thinges on this side God.
94.12	by a strong contrition		by the steryng of grace with a strong and a sleigh and listi contricyon
94.13	sensible things	3.2	(as heryng, seying, smelling, taasting, and touching)
94.14	intelligible things	3.3	the whiche ben clepid thin understondable workynges
94.13	and all nonexistent and existent things	3.5	and alle thoo thinges, any of thi fyve bodely wittes without-forthe; and alle thoo thinges whiche mow be knowen by thi goostly wittes withinne-forth; and all thoo thinges that ben now, or yit mow be in tyme for to come, thogh thei be not now

95.1 And insofar as is possible, ascend unknowingly to his union who is above all substance and knowledge

3.9 And, as it is possible to me for to speke and to thee to understonde, loke that thou rise with me in this grace, in a maner that is thou woste never how, to be onid with him that is aboven alle substaunces and al maner knowyng.

95.2–5 For by passing above yourself and purified of all that might impede (you), you will be raised up to the sovereign-substantial ray of the divine darkness, denuded of all and set free from all.

3.13 For whi, thorou the overpassyng of thiself and all other things and thus makyng thiself clene from all worldly, fleshly and kyndely likyng in thin affeccioun, and fro al thing that may be knowen by the propre fourme in thi knowyng, thou schalt be drawen up aboven mynde in affeccioun to the sovereyn-substancyal beme of the godliche derknes, alle thinges thus done away.

95.6 See to it that none of the unlettered hear these things.

3.19 Yit wonyng in here wittys.

95.7 . . . those who are trained in things existing . . .

3.21 thoo that ben fastnyd in knowing and in loving of these things

95.10 If the divine teachings of the mysteries are above such men

3.25 by the witnes of the prophete

95.11 What can one say of even those less wise, who manufacture the cause which is above all things, from things in the past and things in the future?

3.27 . . . wonyng yit not only in heer ghostly wittes of natureel philosophy, bot lowe downe benythe in here bodely wittes, the whiche thei haven bot in comoun with only beestes?

3.30 For thees men kun not come
to the knowing of the first
cause, the whiche is sover-
eynliche set aboven alle
thinges, bot bi making of figures of last and the least worthi thinges of the thees beyng
visible thinges, as stockes or
stones, and seyen that it hath
nothing aboven thoo wickyd
and manyfolde formatiouns
maad of hemself in here fan-
tastik ymagynatyve wittes.

95.16

4.3 . . . in hym that is aboven al
knowyng and mynde, as hym
being the cause of all thees
thynges

95.17

4.8 Bot fortliche for to holde in
syght of byleve, him for to be
aboven alle doyng awey.

95.19 Bartholomew

4.12 Bertelmewe, the Apostle of
Christ seith in his writyng

95.20 says its theology is much
and minimal, and its Gos-
pel broad and great, and
yet constricted

4.13 . . . that Cristes devinitee, it
is moche . . .

95.30 Moyses . . .

4.27 Moyses, mildest of men . . .

96.10 passing above and exceeding . . .

5.7 . . . passyng aboven and havyng in subjeccioun all men's
resons, as the lady hath hir
maydens.

96.11 . . . ab ipsis absolvitur . . .

5.15 . . . Moyses in singulertere
of affeccioun was departyd

96.14 And he becomes in an entirely impalpable and un-
seeing manner the entire
existence who is above all
things, and also of nothing,
neither of himself nor of
anything else.

5.19 . . . and algates he is maad in
a maner that is invisible and
ungropable for to fele in experience the presence of hym
that is aboven alle thinges,
not having felyng ne thynking
of no beyng thing, ne yet of
himself.

Vercellensis: A Noble and Worthi Expositour

"Therfor, in translacioun of it [*Mistica Theologia*] I have not onliche folowed the nakid lettre of the text, bot for to declare the hardnes of it, I have moche folowed the sentence of the Abbot of Sainte Victore." In the prologue to his translation,[52] the author refers to his claims there that the Areopagite and he himself are at one concerning the "work" of the *Cloud* and of all that is to be said about its process and structure.[53] He adds, however, that his purpose is not simply to translate and leave it at that, but to clarify and elucidate a very difficult Latin text. This is why, he says, he leans so hard on the interpretations of Thomas Gallus. It was pointed out sixty years ago that Chapter 4 of the Middle English is a fairly close translation of the first version of Thomas Gallus written at the Victorine Abbey of Vercelli in 1238, to which he gave the Latin name *Extractio*—"the drawing forth of the meaning." The fifth chapter likewise might have been based on the *Extractio*; but equally, Gallus could have followed the Latin text, the translation of Sarracenus. The obvious reason is that by and large these two chapters are typical examples of the Dionysian "metaphysical dryness": They are for the most part simply lists of abstract and concrete attributes and qualities that cannot properly be Divine Names. Gallus gave to his great commentary on the *Mystical Theology*, as on the other extant works of the Pseudo-Dionysius, the description *Explanatio*, a phrase-by-phrase commentary, with the full text of the translation of Sarracenus given at the head of each section.[54] It is highly probable that the *Explanatio* is the main source of the ME translation, as the annotations to our text will show; and it is only rarely that the *Extractio* is pressed into service by the *Cloud* author. Indeed, it is not a question of textual similarity, but of the handling—one might almost say manipulation—of its substance.[55]

First of all, at the end of the invocation to the Holy Trinity with which the treatise begins, the translator makes an important addition to his text in identifying the power that attains to the mysteries of Holy Writ: "affection above mind." This is a laconic reference to a special faculty that Gallus calls variously "the high point of the synderesis" (*summum apicem synderesis*), "the high point of the affect at the head of the mind" (*apicem affectionis principalis*), "the head of the affection, itself the spark of the affective mental power which alone is capable of union with the Divine Spirit."[56] Then, the Latin text has *forti contritione*—"by a strong contrition," and the *Cloud* author,

66

"with an intense, sagacious and loving contrition." Gallus notes that this contrition demands not only a vigorous mental effort, but also a great grace from God.[57] The *Cloud* author is more specific than this: He associates the beginnings of the contemplative effort with the deep sorrow proper to sacramental confession.[58] The affection, which is at the head of the mind—Cassian calls it the *principale cordis*, and William of St. Thierry the *principale mentis*[59]—is the *synderesis*, the affective equivalent of that intuitive grasp of the moral conscience, where right ever triumphs over wrong.[60] So, when it comes to Moses going out of himself and entering the dark cloud, the English author, like Gallus, focuses on God's presence to the ecstatic: "He is united with God above mind . . . through his going out of himself and being separated from everything in so far as the intellectual presence of knowledge is concerned. It is the Divine essential presence which lifts one above intellect, and descends upon these essences."[61]

However, the evidence does not permit us to estimate with any exactitude the influence of Gallus on the ME translator. We find no reference to the fact that the Victorine abbot of Vercelli had his foothold and friends in thirteenth-century England,[62] nor to the other details of his career. He died in "exile" in the north Italian town of Ivrea, caught up willy-nilly in the quarrels between the imperial and papal powers, and sentenced to excommunication for allegiance to one who would have sacked the monastery of which Gallus was abbot had he not insisted on fleeing to Ivrea. There he died in peace, receiving the last rites as any contemplative Christian should. One hundred and fifty years later, the mystical terminology of the Victorine was well known to the *Cloud* author, as is clear from his terse additions to their common text, the translation of Sarracenus. As we know, for example, from the history of the Carthusian Priory of Mount Grace in North Yorkshire and the two monks, Richard Methley[63] and John Norton,[64] the vocabulary of Denis was still common parlance among the English Carthusians at the end of the fifteenth century; and not only this, but the Dionysian *Cloud* was itself translated back into a new Latin version, on similar terms to those in which its Carthusian author had rendered them into his own excellent and immortal English. If Phyllis Hodgson is right in giving credence to the alleged popularity of the *Cloud* in early sixteenth-century England,[65] there would certainly have been other *ex professo* contemplatives besides Carthusians who continued to profit by the works of the *Cloud* author. Once more, it was the tragedy of the dissolution of the monasteries that brought an end to this dark contemplation and in so doing altered the direction of the development of English prose.[66]

Hugo de Balma and the Middle English translator

We know that de Balma, prior of the Charterhouse of Méyriat in Bresse at the end of the thirteenth century, wrote the Commentary on the Dionysian *Mystical Theology*, attributed to St. Bonaventure until the last century.[67] Entitled variously *Viae Syon lugent*, from the *incipit* of its prologue,[68] and *De triplici via ad sapientiam*, which succinctly describes its content, its third and culminating section concerns the unitive way. This, for Hugo, is synonymous with the anagogical contemplation, which, the Carthusian claims, is the sole topic of Denis's work—the instruction to Timothy on the ascent of the mind to God. "This wisdom is called the *Mystical Theology*, first taught by Paul the Apostle, and handed on by Denis the Areopagite to his disciple in a written instruction. It is the reaching out in love to God, impelled by the desire of love."[69] In fact, in his third chapter on anagogical contemplation, he restricts himself to the first paragraph of the first chapter of Denis's little book,[70] and describes his whole treatise as follows:

This is the *Mystical Theology*, that is, the hidden word of God whereby the mind, prompted by ardent zeal, speaks secretly in the language of the affections to Christ the beloved. The arrangement of this mystical treatise is as follows: First, the Purgative Way is dealt with in three points: how the soul is to be purified, how abundance of grace is to be sought in true prayer, and how the sinner is to beseech plenary pardon for his sins. The second area to be considered concerns the Illuminative Way, where it is first explained how the mind ascends to the divine love by meditation, as a rule on the Lord's Prayer; and then it is shown, by an explanation of the Lord's Prayer, how the entire Scripture takes on a spiritual meaning when the whole is turned to God anagogically. The third part deals with the Unitive Way. There it is shown how sublime life can be, what a perfection of virtue can be attained through this hidden wisdom.[71]

The Carthusian is at pains to demonstrate the inferiority of speculative to anagogical contemplation, and to establish that there is an elevation of the loving power,[72] in which God alone acts interiorly (*solo Deo interius operante*), whereby the divine truth is experimentally

68

perceived. The spirit is taught by this wisdom, he says, how it is to be united to God in the supreme point of its loving power;[73] and there it will find experimentally—*experimentaliter*—the origin of all wisdom.[74] When the soul enters on the Unitive Way toward the super-intellectual union that takes place in the loving power, its contemplative effort is to reject all the intellectual knowledge that might prevent it from raising itself to God. Finally, these attempts of the loving power become so spontaneous that it can lift itself freely toward God without the help of any concomitant thought, and God accords it that hidden wisdom which accompanies the love proper to the Unitive Way.

For Hugh, and for the author of the *Cloud*, the address to Timothy at the head of the first chapter of the *Mystical Theology* is crucial: "Insofar as possible, be intent on ascending with me, *ignote*, by unknowing."[75] This elevation is not only without speculative knowledge, but without any reflexive consideration of the understanding. The greatest obstacle to overcome is the collusion between the knowing and loving powers. The eye of the intellect has to be blinded.[76] The soul's part in the exercise is the complete silencing of the understanding, so that God may communicate his efficacious illumination to the soul that draws near to him. Thus this perfect elevation of the affection brings about that supreme knowledge of the divine incomprehensibility: the true knowledge that infinitely surpasses whatever reason and understanding could ever achieve. There is, moreover, a further divine proffer of an even more sublime and comprehensive knowledge—"to be carried up in one's affections higher still": the rapture proper to union. As will be repeated by the *Cloud* author, the nature of mystical contemplation proper to the way of love is one in which the soul first exercises herself painfully in the elevation of pure affection toward God[77] until the moment when he puts his hand to the work. Then she sees herself truly purified and made capable of being raised to him in a manner more passive than active and without any antecedent or concomitant thought. From this union comes the rapture[78] that embraces the knowledge of the divine incomprehensibility.

The Carthusian Connection

Though in general Carthusian writers are reluctant to reveal the names of the brethren who have gone before them, as well as their own, Guigues du Pont does name de Balma's treatise of the *Mystical Theology* and gives high praise to its author:

> The kind of contemplation which we call anagogical makes its effort to reach out to God by a different way (*nititur aliter pertingere ad Deum*). It is the contemplation which is treated so well in the little book which begins *Viae Syon lugent;* and those who wish to come to this contemplation must study it with all diligence. Its author is a good priest and a very profound contemplative.[79]

This is the way in which the *Cloud* author speaks when he writes of "the threefold occupation of the contemplative apprentice: reading, reflecting, and praying." "You will find," he says, "a much better treatment of these three than I can manage in the book of another author."[80] He is none other than Guigo the Angelic, ninth prior of the Grande Chartreuse, whose book is the *Scala Claustralium.*[81] This is a different matter from our author's stated preference for not citing any authorities to support his views.[82] He expects his source here to be readily recognizable.

Ludolph of Saxony, successively prior of the charterhouses of Coblenz and of Strasbourg, where he was first professed as a Carthusian and died in 1377,[83] is even more reticent in the long citation at the very beginning of his *Vita Christi* from Guigues du Pont, monk of the Grande Chartreuse, where he died in 1297.[84] Ludolph's work, as we have had occasion to notice elsewhere,[85] is a series of meditations—or more properly, imaginative contemplations—on the mysteries of the life, passion, death, and resurrection of the Lord as recounted in the Gospels and elaborated by the Fathers and Scholastic theologians. Ludolph neither identifies Guigues, nor gives any indication that his own extended introduction on the nature of imaginative contemplation, and on the person of Christ as the Gospel reveals him, is not his own composition. However, there is no doubt that what Ludolph borrows from his brother Carthusian is highly characteristic of the *Life of Christ* in its entirety, as the following passage shows:

> Draw near to him then with a loving heart as he comes down from the bosom of his Father into the Virgin's womb; be another witness along with the Angel of this holy conception in luminous faith; give praise to the Virgin Mother who has conceived her child for your sake. Be present at his birth and assist at his circumcision with Joseph, like a good nurse. Go with the Magi to Bethlehem and in their company adore the infant King. . . . and if with a humble, devout and loving

heart you follow along with him on earth, he will raise you up to be with him on the Father's right hand in heaven, according to the promise he made to the faithful sinner who clings to him: "Anyone who ministers to me, let him follow me; and where I am there shall my minister be."[86]

These meditations of the life of Christ constitute the second step on the way to union in the *mystique de la lumière*, where Christ himself is the focal point of the contemplative effort. This life of Christ, says Guigues, and Ludolph repeats him word for word, "makes of the sinners who cling to him fellow-citizens with the Saints and familiars of God's household." It is the life of Christ's mother and of his Apostles. "This life is the best part, namely to sit at his feet and listen to his words. . . . It shall not be taken away from those who welcome the graces of the possession of it. . . . No tongue is eloquent enough to sing its praises.[87] It is so good and holy, so worthy as to be the beginning of a higher contemplation, and of that angelic and eternal life which we hope for in heaven."[88] These words are close enough to those of the *Cloud* author as to persuade us that he had read them. It constitutes "the second degree of the active life and the first degree of the contemplative life";[89] or, as Guigues names it, speculative or affirmative contemplation. As we have seen, however, the contemplation of the divine perfections is Guigues's third step to this affirmative kind of contemplation, and its culmination. The grace required for it is the humble devotion of filial love (*humilis devotio pietatis*)—"when the one who gazes upon God in the sovereign and secret point of a mind at rest (*speculator Dei in secretiori tranquillae mentis acie*) takes up one word divinely given, and through his holy desire and with all the devotion he can muster becomes wholly intent on experiencing God in wisdom, in goodness and simplicity of heart, and on seeking within his capacities but along the way of sweetness and love what God is, in the heavenly dew of the Holy Spirit."[90] The language of the ME translator is nearly always more sober than this, but the vocabulary has the same Dionysian ring, and it applies not to affirmative, but to negative or anagogical contemplation. Again Guigues provides the resolution to what appear to be contrary contemplations. Though he insists that in speculative contemplation one should always be ready to return to meditation if God withdraws the light of consolation, he also says that once one has arrived at the point of union, "he must diligently strive to submit himself to receive anagogical blessings, impulses and extensions."[91]

These Carthusians are witnesses to a marked and common contemplative background, shared by the Victorines and the Cistercian Spirituals, yet with its own distinctive flavor and emphasis. They illustrate one another's attempts to articulate the spirituality of the Carthusian cloister. The word that appears to summarize it best is *pietas*—the love of the son for the loving father, the son who is also the *fidelis peccator*—the converted, devoted, and repentant sinner. The ME translator offers as the English equivalent of *pietas* and *devotio*, "affeccioun," which occurs frequently in *Denis's Hidden Theology*,[92] the gift of the Holy Spirit that crowns the virtues of Wisdom, Understanding, Counsel, Fortitude, and Knowledge.[93] Guigues tells us why the Carthusians, and any devout soul who ponders their writings, will prefer the dark or anagogical contemplation:

> My belief is that when the good Lord has given you both kinds of contemplation, you will exercise yourself oftener and more preferably in the anagogical way, which neither sees nor understands but keeps its eyes closed and its own face veiled before the face of the Lord. It experiences, in its various efforts and reachings out with humble desires, the face of its Creator; and it strives with an ever increasing confidence in him to cling to him by clasping his feet. For by the other way it simply cannot see what it sees.[94]

The *Cloud* author has occasion to say that the contemplatives for whom he is writing yield place to none in their conscientious devotion to the prayer of the Church. In fact, the Carthusian day is divided up according to the hours of the *Opus Dei*, the Divine Office. The *Cloud* author tells us that not merely their personal prayers but even their meditations are sudden and unadvised: "sudden intuitions and obscure feelings learned from God more quickly than from man," full of mercy and compassion.[95] The "work" of the *Cloud* is that described by de Balma as being "impelled directly by the ardour of love, without any mediate knowledge through creatures, without any thought going before, without any accompanying impulse of the understanding."[96] Guigues speaks of anagogical exercises that imprint on the heart a spiritual quality,[97] and the loving soul begins to convert all its impulses into those sharp darts of longing love (*acutas sagittas piarum affeccionum*) of which the ME translator speaks so often and so fervently in the *Cloud*.[98] The first Guigo spoke of these ejaculatory prayers in the book of Carthusian customs:

> From terce to sext in the winter months, and from prime to terce in the summer time there will be manual works, which we recommend should be interrupted by short prayers. . . . And during the works

from none to vespers we should constantly have recourse to these short prayers which are fired like arrows.[99]

Finally, one of the cardinal points in the devotional life of the Carthusian was love of the name of Jesus, *toto cordis ac mentis affectu*. Ludolph bears eloquent witness to this, for example in his meditations on the Holy Name in the mysteries of the annunciation and the circumcision. One might say that the ME translator's use of the name of Jesus in the *Cloud* and in the final words of the *Pursuit of Wisdom* underline his deep personal reverence, and strengthen not a little the argument that he was a follower of St. Bruno. Despite, then, the Latinized vocabulary of the Pseudo-Denis, which is reproduced in the Middle English translation of *Mystica Theologia*, and of its author's conviction that he is reproducing faithfully the theological and psychological thought of St. Denis the Areopagite, it becomes clear that the medieval Dionysians, particularly the Carthusians and most precisely the *Cloud* author, achieved what earlier spiritual writers never succeeded in doing: investing an apophatic Neoplatonism with Christian devotion.

Denis's Hidden Theology

The Prologue to the Translation of Denis's Hidden Theology[1]

The treatise that follows is the English of a book that St. Denis wrote to Timothy,[2] whose title in the Latin is *Mystica Theologia*. It was mentioned in Chapter 70 of a book written before, called *The Cloud of Unknowing*.[3] There it was said that Denis's argument will clearly substantiate all that is written in that same book.[4] Hence in translating it I have given not just the literal meaning of the text, but, in order to clarify its difficulties,[5] I have followed to a great extent the renderings of the Abbot of St. Victor,[6] a noted and erudite commentator on this same book.[7]

St. Denis's Prayer

O Wisdom everlasting and without beginning, beyond all substance and yourself its first Source,[8] Godhead above all that is Godly, Good beyond all good, the one who sees within and above[9] the divinely created wisdom of Christian men;[10] I beseech you to lift us up, in proportion to our powers, to those utterly unknown and sovereign-shining heights of your mysterious, inspired utterances,[11] where all the secrets of divine knowledge are concealed and hidden under the sovereign-shining darkness of wisest silence,[12] making what dazzles beyond compare to shine forth in total splendor, secretly in utter darkness,[13] and filling, beyond all fulfilling, with the fairest brightness and in a way that is always invisible and intangible, all those souls who no longer

74

have the eyes of their minds.[14] For since all these things are beyond the reach of mind,[15] therefore with affection[16] above mind, insofar as I can, I desire to win them to me by this prayer.

Chapter I.   How a man must ascend in this hidden theology by doing away with all things other than God.

My friend Timothy, whenever you set yourself, by the stirring of grace,[17] for the practical[18] exercise of your dark contemplation,[19] be intent on abandoning, with an intense, sagacious, and loving contrition,[20] both your bodily senses[21] of hearing, seeing, smelling, tasting, and touching, and your spiritual faculties also—those which are called your intellectual operations; all those things outside yourself which can be known by any of your five bodily senses; all those things within you which can be known by your spiritual faculties; all the things that now exist, or have existed in the past, though they now exist no longer; and all those things which do not exist now, yet which must exist in time to come, though they are not in existence now.[22] And insofar as it is possible for me to speak of this and for you to understand,[23] be intent on ascending with me[24] in this grace, in a manner such as you could never understand,[25] to be made one with him who is above every substance and every kind of knowledge. For it is by passing beyond yourself[26] and all other things, and so purifying yourself of all worldly, carnal, and natural love in your affection,[27] and of everything that can be known according to its own proper form in your intellect;[28] it is in this way, when all things are done away with, that you shall be carried up in your affection and above your understanding to the Substance beyond all substances, the radiance of the divine darkness.[29]

Take care that none of these who are unwise, though sensible enough,[30] hear of these things. I call all those unwise who are still tied to the knowledge and love of things comprehensible and temporal; those, that is, who think that there is nothing sovereignly substantial above these existing things.[31] Indeed, they think that they can know him who "has made darkness his hiding-place"[32] by the knowledge which belongs to their own selves.[33] And if, as the Prophet testifies, the divine revelation of these secrets is beyond the grasp of these men,[34] what are we then to say of those still more unwise, who do not even stay within their spiritual faculties of natural philosophy,[35] but descend further below, living within their bodily senses which they have in common with the beasts?[36] These men do not know how to come to the knowledge of the first Cause which far transcends all things,[37] except by making images out of the lowest and least noble of existing material things, such as wood or stone, and saying that he is nothing more than those wicked and manifold images created by themselves, the products of their fantasies and imaginations.[38]

It is nothing at all like that. This is how it must be.[39] We must attribute to him and acknowledge and affirm of him all that is to be affirmed, and the essences of all existing things as existing in him who is above all knowledge and intellect; for he is the Cause of all these things.[40] And we must also, more properly and with greater emphasis, deny all these things of him as of one whose being transcends them all, most high in himself, separated off from them all. Nor must it be our opinion that such denyings contradict any previous affirmation of them. Rather we must steadfastly maintain what we see in faith,[41] that he is above all the doing away, in his regard, of these actual or possible beings: He is in himself above all, above all that is done away with or affirmed in his regard.

It is for this reason that the godly Bartholomew,[42] the Apostle of Christ,[43] writes that Christ's divine teaching[44] is extensive and is also very restricted;[45] and that the Gospel is large and great, but then (he adds) it is narrow and small. It seems to me that there where he says that the good Cause of all things expresses itself both in many words and in short sayings, he was ravished in contemplation above nature,[46] since neither by reason nor intellect could he come to him who is the Substance beyond all substance, set above all these existing things. And yet he is not hidden, but appears truly, clearly and openly;[47] not however to all, but only to those who rise above all things, clean and unclean alike, who mount above all the ascending grades and sacred ranks allotted to men or angels,[48] who leave behind all the divine illuminations and all heavenly sounds and locutions, to enter by affection[49] into the darkness where he truly is who, as the Scripture shows,[50] is above all.

You have an example of this in the story of the godly Moses,[51] humblest of men.[52] First he is told that he must be purified, both in himself and in his people; then he must be set apart from every occasion of defilement.[53] Next, after all this purification of himself and his people, he heard the sound of many trumpets, and saw many lights shining and sending out great wide shafts of pure light.[54] Then he was separated from the multitude of his people, and in the company of chosen priests he gained the highest point of that ascent to

76

the divine which is the limit and the boundary of man's understanding, no matter how well supported it may be by grace.[55]

Yet in all this he was not with God, insofar as this means the perfection of the Godhead.[56] The object of his contemplation was not God himself, for he cannot be seen by the eye of contemplation;[57] but the object of his sight was the place where God was. This place typifies the loftiest objects of divine contemplation,[58] which are as far above and have control of all man's rational activity[59] as the mistress has of her handmaids.[60] By these objects of divine contemplation the presence of him who is above all thought is revealed to man's understanding,[61] but transcendently, in a way that sets a man above the limits of his nature.[62] Then he is detached from the intelligible active powers of his soul and from the objects of those powers: that is to say, from all those things upon which these powers are exercised.[63] It was at this point that Moses, exercising his affection alone, was separated from those chosen priests, and entered by himself into the darkness of unknowing, the darkness which is truly hidden.[64] Here God shuts fast all knowledge—all that is intelligible; here, man is made to feel by experience in a way that is invisible and intangible, the presence of him who is above all things, without any feeling or thought of any other being, not even of himself.[65] Rather, in the emptying out of all knowing, he is united in the best way to him who is wholly unknown.[66] And inasmuch as he knows nothing he is enabled to know, in a way that is above mind.[67]

II.   How we are to be united to the Cause of all, who exists above all.[68]

We pray to be lifted up in this sovereign-radiant darkness,[69] and by seeing nothing and knowing nothing, to see and to know him who is above all seeing and all knowing, and in him neither to see nor to know;[70] and by the doing away of all these things that be,[71] transcendently to praise him who is in himself the Substance beyond all substances.[72] The method of this doing away may be understood by the following example.[73]

Suppose a man to have an enormous block of solid wood[74] lying before him, and in his mind the intention and the skill to make the smallest possible image out of that part of the wood which, by the measurement of a plumb line,[75] lies at the exact center of that block. First of all your common sense tells you that before he can succeed in seeing that image clearly by the physical sight of his exterior eye, or in making visible to others what he sees in his own mind by the visual power of his imagination, for the block is still whole and entire, he must by his skill and his tools cut away all the outward parts of the wood which surround the image and prevent it from being seen.[76]

In the same way we must conduct ourselves in this exalted work of theology[77]—insofar as it is possible to arrive at the understanding of it by such a crude example of so contrarious a kind.[78] We must behave in this exercise as if we were men making an image of his simple, uncreated, timeless nature;[79] which, though it always remains untrammeled in itself and to itself—within all creatures yet not closed in, outside all creatures yet not shut out, above all creatures yet not lifted up, beneath all creatures yet not forced down, behind all creatures yet not put back, in front of all creatures yet not driven forth—yet he is never clearly revealed to man's intellect (as long as this is joined to the corruptible body).[80] But he is, as it were, a thing covered up, wrapped around, overlaid with innumerable material bodies and intelligible essences, with many extraordinary images of the imagination,[81] solidified as it were in a dense mass[82] which is all around him; just as the image in our previous illustration was hidden in the thick, enormous, solid block of wood. It is this dense mass, all this innumerable variety of things solidified,[83] that we must skillfully cut away—with the skill conferred by grace[84]—in this exercise of theology, as being a great hindrance, blocking out this pure and hidden sight.[85] And thus by doing away with all these things, which is the skillful work of grace, we can praise the divine Beauty in itself unambiguously and transcendently,[86] the simple, uncreated, timeless nature, in a way that is unknown to all except to those that experience it; and unknown even to them, except in the moment of their experience.[87]

It is necessary for all of us who practice this theology to make our denyings in a manner opposite to our affirmings.[88] Because when we affirm, we begin with the noblest of existing things, and proceeding through the middle ranks, we descend to the least noble. But in our denyings we begin with the least noble and climb up to the most noble, and then from the highest to the lowest by way of the middle, and then from the lowest to the highest again. So we fold them all up together and do away with them,[89] that we may clearly know this unknowing which in all these existing things is walled round[90] and hid from all intelligible powers; that we might see that darkness, the Substance beyond all substances, secretly hid from all light in these existing things.[91]

III.   The Books of Positive and of Negative Theology

For this reason, in our other works on theology, and particularly those on positive theology (these are: first the *Hierarchies of Heaven*, and secondly the *Hierarchies of the Church Militant*),[92] in both of them we have celebrated the truth that the high, divine, unique nature, which is God, is one; and also how it is three, which according to its nature is termed Fatherhood, Sonship, and "Holy Spiritship";[93] and how the rays of goodness[94] dwelling in the heart of the Immaterial, the only Good, burgeoned forth in himself and from himself;[95] and how in this dwelling in himself by oneness of substance,[96] and in themselves by trinity of persons, they dwell in each other, all together, in an everlasting burgeoning,[97] without going out of themselves;[98] how Jesus who is Substance beyond all substances is become substance according to the truths of human nature;[99] and all other such things as are set forth in Scripture are also celebrated in a positive manner in these two works.

Further, it is positively set forth in the book of the Divine Names, and celebrated there, how he is called Good, Being, Life, Wisdom, Virtue, and all the other intelligible names of God, whatever they may be. But in the *Compendium of Divine Symbols*,[100] I have set forth and celebrated all the names that are applied to God from things perceivable by the senses: what are the forms and figures of God, his parts and his instruments, his places and his adornments, his frenzies and his sadnesses, his furies and his drunkenness, his gluttonies, his oaths and his cursings, his sleepings and his awakenings, and any other quality perceivable by the senses that is applied in any way to God in Holy Scripture.[101]

I think that you have seen in all this how these last things have more words to them than the first things. For it must surely be that the first two works, the *Hierarchies*, and the exposition of the Divine Names in the third, should contain fewer words than the *Compendium of Divine Symbols*, mentioned last. For in proportion as the things that we are considering are the highest, in that proportion the words spoken of them to correspond with our considerations show the limits of our understanding. So it is now, in this book; when we enter into the darkness that is above mind,[102] we shall find not merely a shortening of words,[103] but as it were a madness and an absolute irrationality in all that we say.[104] In writing all our other books, we descended from the highest things to the lowest; and we spread out to cover a great multitude, according to the length of our descent. But now in this book we ascend from the lowest things to the highest;

and according to the length of the ascent, which will be shorter at one time than another, the multitude is contracted. And when the ascent is complete, there will be no words at all, but all will be made one with the Ineffable.[105]

But perhaps you wish to ask:[106] What is the reason why in positive theology we begin with the noblest things, and in negative theology with the least noble? This is the reason. When we designate God by affirming all intelligible things of him who is himself above all affirmation and understanding, it is most fitting that we first affirm the things that are noblest and nearest to him. And if we wish to designate him by doing away with all intelligible things, it is most fitting that we first do away with those things which are seen to be furthest from him. For example: "life" or "goodness" is nearer and more fitting to him than "air" or a "stone"; and it is more obviously fitting that we should put away from him gluttony and madness than speaking or understanding—even though he in himself is above all speaking and all understanding.

IV.   He who is the Cause of all sensible things is himself none of them.[107]

Beginning with the remotest things, we first put away from God whatever is without substance and everything that does not exist; for that thing is further away than the things that merely exist and do not live: further, that is, than that which has being and lives.[108] And next we put away things that have being and live but lack feeling, for they are more remote than those which possess feeling.[109] And next we put away those that have sensation but lack reason and understanding, for they are more remote than those which have reason and understanding.[110] And along with all these things we remove from him all bodily things or all that belongs to the body or to bodily things: such as shape, form, quality, quantity, weight, place, visibility, sensibility, both active and passive; all the disorder of fleshly concupiscence,[111] all troubles of temperament arising from the bodily passions, all weakness affected by sensible change, all need of light; all generation and corruption, all division and passibility, all temporal succession by process of time. For he is none of these things, nor does he possess any of these or any other sensible things.

V. He who is the Cause of all intelligible things is himself none of them.

And now we ascend and begin our denyings and removals with the highest of intelligible things. We say that he is neither soul nor angel;[112] that he has neither imaginative faculty, nor apprehension,[113] nor reason, nor intellect; nor is he reason nor intellect; nor is he spoken nor understood. And, that we may pass from these high things by the middle to the lowest, we say that he is neither number, nor order, nor greatness, nor littleness, nor equality, nor likeness, nor unlikeness; he neither stands nor moves, nor keeps silence nor speaks.[114] And, that we may return to the highest things by the middle, and end our denyings at the highest, we say that he has no virtue, nor is he virtue nor light; he does not live, nor is he life, nor substance, nor age,[115] nor time; there is no intelligible contact with him;[116] he is neither knowledge, nor truth, nor kingship,[117] nor wisdom, nor one, nor unity, nor Godhead, nor goodness; neither is he spirit as we understand spirit, nor sonship, nor fatherhood, nor any other thing known by us or by any other being;[118] nor does he belong to nonbeing, nor to anything that is being; nor do any of these things that are [known] know him as he is;[119] nor does he know anything that is, according as they are in themselves, but as they are in him;[120] nor is there any way by which reason or understanding may attain to him;[121] there is no name, no knowing of him; nor is he darkness, nor is he light,[122] nor is he error, nor is he truth; nor, to sum up, is there either affirmation or negation of him. But when we attribute by affirming or remove by denying all or any of those things that are not he, we cannot posit him or remove him, nor in any intelligible way affirm him or deny him. For the perfect and unique Cause of all must necessarily be, without comparison, the highest height, above all affirmation and negation alike. And his unintelligible transcendence is, in an unintelligible way, above all affirmation and negation.

Notes

Introduction

1. Cf. *The Cloud of Unknowing*, Introduction, pp. 47–48.
2. M-D. Chénu, *Introduction à l'étude de Saint Thomas d'Aquin* (Paris: Vrin, 1950), p. 193.
3. John of the Cross, "Dark Night of the Soul," in *Complete Works of John of the Cross*, ed. and trans. Alison Peers (London: Burns Oates, 1935), Vol. I, Bk. II, ch. V, 1, pp. 405–06.
4. The *Cloud* author never gives him the title Areopagite. He simply calls him "Seynte Denis"—twice: once in the *Cloud* itself and once here, in *Hidden Theology*—and speaks of "Denis' bookes" and "Denis' sentence."
5. Cf. *Mystical Theology* I, 1; *Divine Names* I, 1.
6. Gal 2:20. *Divine Names* 7.
7. Acts 17:23.
8. René Roques, *L'Univers dionysien* (Paris: Aubier, 1954).
9. Cf. *infra*, and P.H., 144/28.
10. *Hidden Theology*, i.e., "dark," "obscure." Cf. *infra*, note 1.
11. What precisely the English author's acquaintance with the work was, he never tells us, nor even names it. *Private Direction*, however, indicates the extent to which he has mastered it; and his only explicit citation from Denis is *Divine Names* 7: "The truly divine knowledge of God is that which is known by unknowing." Cf. *The Cloud, ed. cit.*, ch. 70, p. 256.
12. Candidates are still offered for the assumption of Denis's mantle. It is accepted that he was a Christian and probably a Syrian monk and/or a priest. Severus of Antioch, Ammonius Sakkas, St. Basil even, have been seriously suggested.
13. Cf. the notion of Faith (*pistis*) in Proclus: L. J. Rosan, *The Philosophy of Proclus* (New York: Cosmos, 1949), p. 214, n. 152.

14. E. R. Dodds, *Proclus: The Elements of Theology* (Oxford: Clarendon Press, 1933). Proclus taught in Athens, and died in A.D. 485.

15. *Infra.*

16. There are only two words in the opening prayer that give it a Christian coloring, sc. *Trinity* and *Christian.* Cf. *infra.*

17. Ps 17:11; Eph 4:6.

18. On this union, *henōsis,* cf. *infra.*

19. J. Daniélou, *Platonisme et Théologie Mystique* (Paris: Aubier, 1944), p. 25.

20. Cf. the end of the prologue, *infra.*

21. Cf. *infra.*

22. ME: loke thou forsake with a stronge and a sleigh and a listi contricyon. The English author is as successful as most in translating *aphairesis, derelictio.*

23. John of the Cross, *loc. cit.,* II, v, 5.

24. Sc. in chs. 4 and 5.

25. Cf. *supra,* n. 11.

26. ME finds the phrase difficult and paraphrases ". . . entrid by hymself the darkness of unknowyng, the whiche darknes is vereliche hid; in the whiche he schittith a knowable knowyng."

27. The literal translation of the Latin of John Sarracenus might read as follows: "Everyone who is considered worthy to know and see God is established in it, lifted up in him who is truly above sight and knowledge through not seeing him and not knowing him, knowing indeed that this is beyond sensible and intelligible things."

28. ME: the sovereyn substancyal beme of the goodliche darknes. The Latin of Sarracenus has *supersubstantialem divinarum tenebrarum radium.*

29. So our modern translation, three removes as it is from the original Greek: ". . . making what dazzles beyond compare to shine forth in total splendor, secretly in utter darkness, and filling beyond all fulfilling, with the fairest brightness" (*infra*).

30. John Sarracenus's Latin has: *Divina caligo est inaccessibile lumen in quo habitare Deus dicitur. Et invisibilis quidem existens propter excedentem claritatem et inaccessibilis idem propter excessum supra-substantialis luminis effusionis.*

31. The Latin phrase and its English translation are equally well known: "My love is crucified"—*Amor meus crucifixus est.* Ignatius's *Letter to the Romans* 7; *Divine Names* 4, 12. It finds its last echo in the burden of the Victorian hymn: "O Come and Mourn with Me Awhile"—"Jesus our love is crucified."

32. Cf. "Contemplation" (*chez les Orientaux Chrétiens*), *Dsp,* xiv–xv, 1864–68.

33. *Divine Names* 7, 1.

34. *Divine Names* 4, 12.

35. *Divine Names* 4, 13.

36. *Ibid.,* 4, 12.

37. "Private Direction," *infra.* Cf. P.H. lix.

38. De Balma has a list of divine Attributes in ch. 1 of the Purgative Way. It is the same as that in "Private Direction," *infra*, and n. 58.

39. P.H., 143/19.

40. Cf. P. Dumontier, *S. Bernard et la Bible* (Paris: Desclée, 1953), p. 147.

41. Cf. Vulgate Ps 17:12: *Et posuit tenebras latibulum suum.*

42. Cf. Ex, 19:9, 10, 14, 16; 24:1–2; Ps 96:2, 9.

43. The *Cloud* author uses the English word *ungropable*—"impossible to be felt."

44. The entire ascent, in the petitionary prayer, is to be made "with affecyon aboven mynde."

45. The paradox of darkness and light, of which the Easter Vigil's *Praeconium Paschale* sings: "Darkness shall be light to you, and night my delight."

46. E. Rolt, trans. *The Divine Names* (London, 1920), ch. 7, 3, p. 152.

47. For the English translator, the second part of the Active Life and the first part of the Contemplative consists both of sweet and satisfying meditations and the "work" of this book. Cf. *The Cloud of Unknowing*, ch. 8, pp. 137–39.

48. *The Cloud, ed. cit.*, pp. 23–26.

49. Pfeiffer, ed., *Meister Eckhart*, tr. Evans (London: Evans, 1924), pp. 39–40.

50. Cf. "The Christian Life," in *The Legacy of the Middle Ages* (Oxford: Clarendon Press, 1925), citing Dante's *Il Convitto* iii, 15, p. 40.

51. The numbering refers to the page and line of P.H. *Deonise Hid Divinite*, Appendix A, *The Latin Sources*, and the critical text.

52. The ME translator in his prologue makes the following points: (1) The author of the book is St. Denis; (2) Timothy is the recipient; (3) the original is in Latin; (4) he had spoken of it in the *Cloud* as providing an apologia for the teaching offered there; (5) he has linked his literal translation with the "exposition" of the abbot of St. Victor. The prologue of John Sarracenus is addressed to his abbot, Odo. In the Dionysian corpus, the *Symbolic Theology* was intended to precede the *Mystical Theology;* but in those regions of Greece that Sarracenus had visited, his researches had not turned up this work. He asks Odo to be on the lookout for it. Meantime, he has translated the *Mystical Theology*, remarking that it is so called because of its hidden and closed nature (*quasi occulta et clausa*). Its method is the ascent to the knowledge of God by abstraction, and the question of what God is, is left closed and hid. Cf. *infra.*

53. *Infra.*

54. Cf. G. Théry, O.P., ed., *Thomas Gallus: Grand Commentaire sur la Théologie Mystique* (Paris: Haloua, 1934).

55. It has often been argued that the glosses on the *Mystical Theology* attributed to Erigena and printed in P.L. 122, 267–84, were also the work of Vercellensis. Cf. P.H. xl. This conjecture is now rejected.

56. Cf. Théry, *Thomas Gallus*, pp. 34; 15, n. 17; 14, n. 13.

57. Ibid., p. 14.

58. Both the *Cloud* author and Gallus employ the *double-entendre* here: the

exercise of dark contemplation and the sorrow associated with sacramental confession. Cf. *The Cloud of Unknowing, ed. cit.*, p. 72 and *passim.*

59. Ibid., p. 92.

60. "The principal affection, which is the *scintilla synderesis,* itself alone capable of union with the Divine Spirit." Cf. Théry, *Thomas Gallus,* p. 14.

61. The *Cloud* author will use these notions of presence, hovering, and descending in "Private Direction," to describe the moment of union.

62. Cf. *The Cloud of Unknowing, ed. cit.*, pp. 45–46.

63. Ibid., pp. 14–19.

64. Cf. A.G. Dickens, *Clifford Letters of the Sixteenth Century* (Surtees Society 172, 1957), p. 34.

65. Phyllis Hodgson argues for the widespread popularity of the *Cloud* and its author's minor treatises, from the fifteenth-century observation that they "walked up and down at deer-rates" (in D. M. McIntyre, "The Cloud of Unknowing," *The Expositor* 7, no. 22 [October 1907]: 373). Cf. P. H. p. lxxxii. Her view is recently corroborated by P. H. Jolliffe, *A Check-list of Middle English Prose Writings* (Toronto: IMS, 1974).

66. This is not to belittle efforts of directors like Augustine Baker and Benet Canfield for the contemplative English exiles in seventeenth-century Flanders. Cf. J. McCann, *The Cloud of Unknowing* (London, 1936), pp. 287ff.

67. Cf. *The Cloud, ed. cit.*, pp. 19–23.

68. Cf. Vulgate, Jeremiah, Lam 1:4.

69. For the *Cloud* author's spiritual exegesis of the verse of the Canticle "You have wounded me . . . in one of my eyes," cf. "Discretion of Impulses."

70. Cf. *infra.*

71. Cf. *Mystica Theologia, Prologus,* in *S. Bonaventurae, Opera Omnia* (Parisiis, 1866), tomus octavus, p. 3.

72. Ibid.

73. Ibid., p. 4.

74. Ibid.

75. Cf. *infra.*

76. Cf. *Ascent to Contemplative Wisdom,* Appendix, *infra.*

77. Cf. *The Cloud, ed. cit.*, ch. 26, p. 173.

78. Ibid., ch. 71, p. 257.

79. P. DuBourg, "La Date de la Theologia Mystica," in *Rêvue d'Ascétique et de Mystique (RAM)* 8 (1927): 158.

80. *The Cloud of Unknowing, ed. cit.*, ch. 35, pp. 187ff.

81. Cf. E. Colledge, and J. Walsh, *A Ladder of Monks* (New York and London: Doubleday/S.P.C.K., 1978).

82. Cf. *The Cloud of Unknowing, ed. cit.*, ch. 70, p. 256.

83. Cf. Sr. M. Immaculate Bodenstedt, *The* Vita Christi *of Ludolphus the Carthusian* (Washington, D.C.: C. U. Press, 1944).

84. Cf. L. M. Rigolot, ed., *Ludolphus de Saxonia: Vita Jesu Christi* (Parisiis et Roma, 1870), pars primus, pp. 1–10.

85. Cf. J. Walsh, "Application of the Senses," *The Way*, Supplement No. 27, Spring 1976, pp. 58–68.
86. Ludolph, *Vita Christi, ed. cit.*, p. 4.
87. Ibid., p. 3, citing Lk 10:38–42—Mary of Bethany at the Lord's feet.
88. Ibid.—*initium cuiuslibet altioris contemplationis.*
89. *The Cloud of Unknowing, ed. cit.*, ch. 21, p. 164.
90. J. P. Grausem, "Le *De Contemplatione* de Guigues du Pont," *RAM* 10 (1929): 273; and cf. *The Cloud, ed. cit.*, p. 24.
91. Ibid., p. 275.
92. Four times in the first chapter. Cf. *infra.*
93. Cf. Is 11:2.
94. Grausem, "Le *De Contemplatione*," p. 276.
95. Cf. *The Cloud, ed. cit.*, pp. 193–97.
96. *Mystica Theologia*, p. 39. Cf. Appendix, *infra.*
97. Grausem, "Le *De Contemplatione*," p. 274.
98. Ibid., p. 275.
99. Cf. *Consuetudines Carthusianae*, P.L. 153, 699.

Denis's Hidden Theology

1. John Sarracenus, in the prologue to his Latin translation, explains: "It seems to be entitled 'Mystical Theology,' as 'hidden' or 'enclosed'; because when one ascends to the knowledge of God through this removing, ultimately what God is, is left closed and hidden. It can also be called 'mystical' as belonging to the body of teaching about God. The word *mio*, from which 'mystical' is derived, means 'I close off' and 'I learn' and 'I teach' " (Théry, p. 8).

2. Thomas Gallus, in the prologue to his exposition on Denis's first letter to Gaius, sums up the medieval legend for us: "There were many disciples in the primitive Church, well-instructed in the mystical and moral interpretation of the Scriptures, from whom the apostle concealed the superintellectual wisdom of Christians, which he spoke amongst the perfect (1 Cor 2:6–7). These included Hierotheus, and Dionysius the Areopagite. . . . The latter, at the instance of Timothy, Paul's disciple, wrote four books for him; the Angelic Hierarchy, the book of Divine and the Mystical Theology" (cf. J. Walsh, S.J., "The Expositions of Thomas Gallus on the Pseudo-Dionysian letters," *ADHLMA* (1963): 202–03.

3. Cf. the *Cloud, ed. cit.*, p. 256.

4. " . . . whoever cares to examine the works of Denis, he will find that his words clearly corroborate all that I have said or am going to say" (the *Cloud, ed. cit.*, ch. 70).

5. Thomas Aquinas, in the prologue to his *Commentary on the Divine Names*, says that the difficulty arises from the fact that "the blessed Denis uses the style and way of speaking of the Platonists." Gallus speaks of the double difficulty—of style and interpretation.

6. This title is rather vague. Thomas Gallus was a monk at the Abbey of St. Victor in Paris. In A.D. 1218, at the instance of Cardinal Guala Bicchieri, he became founder and first abbot of St. Andrew's monastery in Vercelli, Italy. There he published his paraphrase of (1238) and his commentary on (1244) *The Mystical Theology*. Cf. the *Cloud, ed. cit.*, pp. 43–46.

7. ME: "a noble and a worthy expositour of this same book" (*H. Deonise*, p. 1/11); noted and erudite, able to explain the meaning. Our author is not alluding to the quality of the English translation (Introduction, *supra*).

8. The invocatory Latin here reads: *Trinitas supersubstancialis et superdea et superbona*. Sarracenus has coined the adjective *superdea*, implicitly denying its substantive nature. The *Cloud* author makes each adjective refer to the successive persons of the Trinity, perhaps following Gallus's gloss, which reads:

supersubstancialis: "incomparably overpassing every substance and every being"; and this can be attributed to the person of the Father, to whom is appropriated both being and power [*esse et posse*]; *superdea:* "that is, incomparably overpassing all knowledge and science or wisdom, which is specially attributed to the Son"; and *superbona:* "that is, incomparably overpassing all goodness, which is specially attributed to the Holy Spirit"—Théry, p. 24.

Perhaps he deliberately addresses the triune God as "Wisdom" since the Mystical Theology is concerned entirely with the divine knowledge.

"First Source:" ME: *Firstheed*. Wisdom is spoken of as having the *primatus* in the Vulgate (Ecclus 24:10), which Wyckleff translated as firstheed.

9. ME: the inliche beholder; Latin: *inspectrix*. Gallus adds that this inspecting is with approbation. *Behold*, in the English author's terminology means to contemplate; and the adjective *inliche* adds the immanent to the transcendent dimension of the eternal Trinitarian activity.

10. The purpose of the Mystical Theology, says Gallus, is to build up the true wisdom of Christians, the highest perfection of the soul that is achieved in this life through its union with God and the superintellectual knowledge of God, "the wisdom by which God is known": Théry, pp. 19–20. The *Cloud* author is careful to distinguish between the "unbigonne" wisdom of the initial invocation, and the "made" wisdom that constitutes the perfection of Christian existence.

11. Latin: *misticorum eloquiorum superignotum et supersplendentem et summum verticem*. The summit, says the Commentary, is our point of union with the Eternal Word, himself the fount and origin of all the words of Scripture in which are hidden its truths—i.e., mystical. This summit is transcendently unknown—*superignotum*—as is God himself, "not because of any defect of light but by an inaccessible excellence and an incomprehensible abundance" (Théry, pp. 25–26).

12. The key texts here for Gallus are Mt 13:11, "To you it has been given to know the secrets of the Kingdom of heaven," and Mt 11:25–27, "I thank you Father Lord of heaven and earth, for hiding these things from the wise and the clever and revealing them to little ones." The sovereign-shining

darkness of wisest silence is "the Eternal Word, which the Father utters eternally."

13. When Moses asks to see the splendor of the Lord, he is put in a cleft of the rock and covered with God's hand, "whilst my glory passes by" (Ex 33:18–23).

14. Denis's fifth letter, answering the question "How can it be said that God exists or dwells in darkness?," begins as follows: "The divine darkness is the inaccessible light in which God is said to dwell. He is invisible because of the surpassing brightness (*excedentem claritatem*), and inaccessible through the excessive effusion of transcendent light." Thomas Gallus assembles the illustrative texts from O.T. and N.T.: Ex 24:16; 2 Par 6:1; 1 Tm 6:16; Gn 32:30; Num 12:8; Is 6:1; Col 1:1–5; Heb 11:27; Ex 33:20; Jn 1:18. Cf. J. Walsh, "Thomas Gallus on the Dionysian Letters," pp. 215–16.

15. ME: "fulfillyng with ful fayre cleertees all thoo soules that ben not havyng eyen of myude." The Latin has *claritatibus superimplentem non habentes oculos menties*—an awkward construction. The English may be a misconstruction.

16. "For since . . . as I can be" is the translator's addition. It appears to be a simplification of the Commentary's gloss on the previous phrase. The soul is illuminated in the supreme point of the affection, where the mind has no eyes; it is there that the divine mysteries are grasped. They cannot be found by reason or contemplated by the understanding (Théry, p. 34).

17. "by the stirring of grace" is not found in Sarracenus. The paraphrase reads: "In order that you be made able for mystical contemplations which it is my purpose to teach in this book, and thus to co-operate with the divine light (*radio divino*)" (*Extractio*). The Commentary: "This cannot happen save by a great grace of God and a powerful effort of the spirit" (Théry, p. 38).

18. ME: "actueel exercise." The adjective is the translator's. Gallus frequently remarks that the Mystical Theology expounds the theory of dark contemplation, while the allegorical sense of the Song of Songs illustrates its practice.

19. ME: blynde beholdyngs; Latin: *mysticas visiones*; the contemplations of wisdom taught in the Mystical Theology.

20. Latin: *forti contritione*. The noun signifies the figurative action of "treading down," which is so integral a part of the exercise of dark contemplation described at such length in the *Cloud* itself. The adjectives qualifying it are teased out in ch. 31: "Dispose yourself earnestly for the labor of this exercise . . . any new thought or impulse . . . bravely step above it with a fervent impulse of love and tread it down under your feet . . . look for tricks and devices and secret subtleties of spiritual tactics . . . " (*Cloud, ed. cit.*, pp. 180–181).

21. "bodily senses." Latin: *sensus derelinque*. Only the English translator names them all. The Commentary says, "Ascend above the bodily senses and their use" (Théry, p. 38). The paraphrase has *sensus et sensibilia*.

22. The Latin simply has *omnia non existentia et existentia*—all things nonexistent and existent. The Commentary's gloss has: "Non-existent are those

which subsist only in the superessential Word, yet can be contemplated in that Word. How this might be he explains by the phrase 'insofar as it is possible' (*sicut est possibile*)" (Théry, p. 40).

23. The gloss on "possible" is the translator's.

24. "with me." As in the *Cloud*, the author associates himself with his addressee. This highly personal note in a translation is an indication that he has a specific individual in mind—at least at this point.

25. Latin: *ignote*—unknowingly. This ascent of the spirit to God is the reverse of an intellectual process. The ME translation—"in a maner that is thou woste never how"—alludes to the basic distinction between knowing by a rational process and "to know the love of Christ which surpasses knowledge" (Eph 3:19).

26. Latin: *excessu tui ipsius et omnium*. "That is, when you pass beyond your own nature and every other creature in contemplation" (Théry, p. 43).

27. Latin: *irretentibili et absoluto munde*—purified from all that might impede or limit you. The translator specifies, adding the objects of the purification. The paraphrase speaks of "being purified and set free from all concupiscence and care." Our text is more akin to the Commentary of Hugo de Balma, who writes: ". . . by this excess of burning love the mind is much more easily set free from all that holds it back, that is, from all worldly pleasure, and is purified from all extraneous affections" ("The Ascent to Contemplative Wisdom," p. 147).

28. "according to its own proper form." De Balma's commentary has this very phrase—*Absolutum enim dicitur omne quod sua propria forma cognoscitur habens esse distinctum*: "the term 'limited' is applied to every thing which is known as having its own distinct being according to its own proper form" (ibid.).

29. The Commentary reads: "Radiance (*radius*) here refers to the Word of the Father. . . . It is called radiance of darkness because it is superlatively invisible to us by reason of its subtlety and incomprehensibility" (Théry, p. 44).

30. ME: "yit still wonyng [dwelling] in their wittes." An addition of the translator, whose play on the word *indocti* is inspired by Rom 8:6: "natural wisdom is hostile to God," as well as the antinomy wisdom/folly in 1 Cor 2—God's foolishness is wiser than the wisdom of this world, in particular of the pagan philosophers.

31. ME: "the whiche han opinion that nothing is sovereyn substancyaly aboven thees forseide beying thinges."

32. Ps 17:12 (Vulgate): "He made darkness his covert"—*Et posuit tenebras latibulum suum*.

33. Thomas Gallus glosses: "that is by the natural and liberal sciences" (Théry, p. 49).

34. A likely reference is Wis 9:17: "But the things that are in heaven, who shall search out, and who shall know thy thought except thou give wisdom, and send thy Holy Spirit from above?"

35. "Who do not even stay . . . with the beast?" An addition of the trans-

lator. The Commentary explains it rather differently: "If this Wisdom is hidden from the philosophers of the world, because it transcends their own wisdom, so that they cannot take it in, how much further must it be hidden from simple yokels and idolators who have scarcely more than sense-knowledge?" (Théry, p. 51).

36. The unbaptized living in the darkness of original sin and its concupiscence. The Commentary cites Rom 1:20ff. (Théry, p. 50), with its Jewish emphasis on the relationship between idolatry and sexual perversity; and this allusion is clear in the translation, though not in the original.

37. Not in the author's original, but the Commentary reads, "They cannot come to Wisdom through their own lack of wisdom" (Théry, p. 50).

38. The translator is interpreting his original to suit the distinction drawn in the *Cloud*, e.g., in ch. 51 (*ed. cit.*), where the language is strikingly similar: "Take care that you do not construe in a material way what is to be understood spiritually . . . the material and sensual interpretations of those who go in for elaborate whims and fancies are the cause of much error" (p. 218).

39. Not in the original. The Latin of the Commentary has: "This is how they think perversely; but the truth of the matter is (*veritas sic se habet*)" (Théry, p. 55).

40. The author tries to clarify his very difficult original, which Gallus bypasses, both in the paraphrase and the Commentary. All the qualities that are seen to be in anything that exists are to be affirmed as existing in God principally, in virtue of the fact that he is their cause.

41. The reference to faith is the translator's; none of his possible sources have it. It represents the most direct Christianization of the pseudo-Dionysian Neoplatonism.

42. The Commentary notices that "the Apostles wrote much that is no longer extant" (Théry, pp. 56–57). He is called *divinus*, "godlike," says the Commentary, because conformed to God by wisdom, virtue, and imitation.

43. Part of the attempt of the Pseudo-Denys to give his writings Christian credibility. The only evangelical reference to Bartholomew is his call in Jn 1:45–51, which could be considered to have a Neoplatonic ring.

44. "Christ's" is the translator's addition; his source simply read *theologia*.

45. Gregory the Great speaks of Scripture as shallow enough for a fly to bathe in and deep enough to drown an elephant.

46. The Latin reads *illud supernaturaliter intendens*, as does the paraphrase; the Commentary explains the Latin, "that is, by means of truly supernatural and superintellectual wisdom," where *supernatural* is used in its literal meaning of "above nature." The author chooses to render this in the special "dionysian" sense of the contemplative effort.

47. The Commentary says, with an allusion to 1 Cor 13:12, *idest non aenigmatice*, "not in a dark manner," and adds: "but in the true sweetness to the taste and gentleness to the touch which the affection experiences when united to God (*quas experitur affectio Deo unita*)" (Théry, p. 59). This is the classical medieval exegesis of phrases like "taste and see how sweet the Lord

is"—Ps 33:9, 1 Pet 2:3; the contemplative experience by means of the spiritual senses, which impart an experiential as opposed to an abstract knowledge of God.

48. Gallus says that the unclean are the *sensibilia*, the clean the *intelligibilia*. In Dionysian terminology, what is sensible and imaginable is inferior to the purely intelligible. The affection has its blemishes—vices and sins, the intellect earthly and inordinate thought; even the angels can be considered to have impurities in respect of the purity of the more exalted in the angelic hierarchy (Théry, pp. 59–60).

49. The heavenly illuminations, sounds and words, says the Commentary (Théry, p. 61), revelations and inspirations—e.g., that made to the Blessed Virgin (Lk 1:33). "By affection" is the translator's addition.

50. "Clouds and darkness are round about him. . . . Thou art the most high Lord over all the earth; thou art exalted exceedingly above all Gods" (Ps 96:2, 9). The Commentary also cites the various passages from Ex and 3 Kgs 8:12—the Shekinah, "the Lord dwelling in the Cloud," and all its scriptural reminiscences.

51. Godly—Latin *divinus*. The text, says the Commentary (Théry, p. 63), is probably corrupt here. Our author turns it into a story, a medieval exemplum; Moses is the simple but profound archetype of the soul called to dark contemplation. The translator's method is to show by means of the scriptural source, the contemplative process: its main structure of purification, illumination, and union, and its consequences ("first . . . next . . . then . . . at this point . . . here . . . ").

52. An addition of the translator. Cf. Num 12:3: "For Moses was a man exceeding meek above all men that dwell upon earth."

53. "And Moses told the words of the people to the Lord. And he said to him: Go to the people and sanctify them today and tomorrow and let them wash their garments . . . And Moses came down from the mount to the people and sanctified them. And when they had washed their garments, he said to them: Be ready against the third day and come not near your wives" (Ex 19:9, 10, 14, 15).

54. "And behold thunders begun to be heard . . . and the noise of the trumpet sounded exceeding loud. . . . And all Mount Sinai was as a smoke, because the Lord was come down on it in fire . . . and the sound of the trumpet" (Ex 19:16–19). The "many lights shining" is an elaboration of the author's text on the scriptural passage.

55. "And he said to Moses: Come up to the Lord, thou and Aaron, Nadab and Abiu, and seventy of the ancients of Israel, and you shall adore far off. And Moses alone shall come up to the Lord, but they shall not come nigh; neither shall the people come up with him. . . . Then Moses and Aaron, Nadab and Abiu and seventy of the ancients of Israel went up: and they saw the God of Israel. . . . And the sight of the glory of the Lord was like a burning fire upon the top of the Mount" (Ex 24:1–2, 9–10, 17). "By grace" is a Thomistic interjection of the translator. Cf. *Cloud, ed. cit.*, ch. 26.

91

56. " . . . insofar as this accords with the perfection of the Godhead" is inserted by the translator. The allusion is to 1 Cor 6:17—"He who is joined to the Lord is one spirit with him." Cf. *Cloud, ed. cit.*, ch. 67: "You are made a God in grace united with him in spirit without any division between you . . . though you are one with him in grace you are yet far, far beneath him in nature" (p. 250). Cf. also the "Letter on Prayer," *supra*.

57. "The eye of contemplation." The sources, though they use the verb *contemplari*, say simply "he is invisible." The translator uses the image—from the Song of Songs 4:9—in "Inward Stirrings," *supra*. It is one developed at length by Richard of St. Victor in his treatise on the grace of contemplation. Cf. Kirchberger, *Richard of St. Victor*, p. 137.

58. ME: "The highest godliche beholdynges." Both the paraphrase and the Commentary explain these as the Platonic ideas, the *rationes aeternae* of Augustine and the archetypes of Dionysius—"the exemplars, the intelligible bases of all creatures which exist in the Word" (Théry, p. 66).

59. "Dionysius considers that the place of God also signifies the most sublime dignities of the heavenly spirits . . . which are beheld in intellectual contemplation" (Théry, p. 65).

60. ME: "as the lady hath her maydens," an addition. Though the translator does not attempt to describe the "godly beholdings," and mentions neither the eternal exemplar nor the heavenly hierarchies, he does allude to Ps 122 "as the eyes of the handmaid are on the hands of her mistress." The same allusion occurs in "Private Direction," where the context is the "ministration of angels" in the work of contemplation (cf. *infra*.).

61. ME: "By the whiche godliche beholdynges." The translator resolves the ambiguity of his original—the divine presence is shown in contemplation. He omits all reference to the divine exemplars and the heavenly intelligences of his Latin, or indeed to the elucidations of Vercellensis. Cf. Théry, p. 66.

62. Again the translator simplifies his text. As the Commentary points out, Denis is saying that God becomes cognitively present through the manifestation of the divine exemplars (Théry, p. 67). The translator simply says that to have God's presence revealed raises a man "above the natureel teermes of hymself."

63. The author first translates and interprets the Latin, which refers directly to Moses and the narrative of Ex 24:12–18: *Tunc et ab ipsis absolvitur visis et videntibus* (Then he is separated from both what was seen and those who saw). The *videntibus* are "the intelligible active powers of man's soul," the *visis*, "the objects of those powers." He then rejoins his text by naming again Moses, whom he has made an allegorical figure typifying the soul in contemplation.

64. "And Moses, going up into the mount of God, said to the ancients, wait you here till we return to you. . . . And Moses entering into the midst of the cloud, went up into the mount of God" (Ex 24:13–14, 18). ME: "the whiche derknes is vereliche hid"; Latin: *quae caligo vere est mystica*. The sen-

tence following, which the author carefully translates, word for word, from the Latin, explains the meaning of the word *mystica*.

65. The translator tries to put this experience into words in "Private Direction"; cf. *infra*.

66. The author translates the latin *vacatio* by the ME "avoiding," which means emptying. His allusion is almost certainly the Christological hymn of Phil 2:7—"He emptied himself." Vercellensis in his Commentary inevitably refers to ch. 7 of *The Divine Names*. Cf. Introduction, *supra*.

67. In this last paragraph the translator gives his own slant to the whole chapter by introducing the phrase, of Moses, "in his affection"—ME: in singulertee of affeccioun. It is in ch. 4 of the *Cloud* that the author speaks most eloquently of the power of the affection and its work in contemplation. Vercellensis in his Commentary summarizes the chapter thus: "The two knowings which we have described as intellectual, through the exemplars of the Word (*per rationes Verbi*) and superintellectual through union (*unicionem*), are constantly to be found in this chapter" (Théry, p. 71).

68. Mal 2:10; Eph 4:6; 1 Cor 8:6.

69. Cf. the Dionysian letter to Dorotheus, which begins: "The divine darkness (*divina caligo*) is the inaccessible light in which God is said to dwell: invisibly on account of the exceeding brightness; inaccessible on account of the excessive effusion of sovereign-substantial (*suprasubstantialis*) light" (cf. Walsh, "Expositions of Thomas Gallus," pp. 215ff.).

70. Gallus adds to the phrase "in him neither to see nor to know," *per mentis excessum*, i.e., through rapture when the mind is taken above itself. He glosses "to see and to know him" as "to know him *presentialiter;*" there is no exact English equivalent for this adverb. He means that the creator is immediately present to the creature, as is a material object to the five senses (Théry, p. 75).

71. "Doing away" translates the technical term of medieval philosophical logic *ablatio* (Sarracenus). In his *Extractio* Vercellensis prefers *remotio*.

72. "transcendently to praise"; the Latin has *supersubstantialiter laudare*. No human substantial quality can be worthily predicated of God, since he is the "substance beyond all substances." As Aquinas writes of the Eucharist:

> Dare all thou canst, thou hast no song (Quantum potes tantum aude)
> Worthy his praises to prolong (*Quia maior omni laude*),
> So far surpassing powers like thine (*Nec laudare sufficis*).— (*Lauda Sion: Corpus Christi* Sequence)

73. It is written of Michelangelo that he first drew outlines on the block, then cut away the marble to free the figure, which emerged complete. His poems interpret this procedure as an allegory of divine creativity and human salvation (NCE 9:801). Whether Michelangelo knew Plotinus's development of the image (*De Pulchritudine* VII) is disputed; our translator certainly did not. The development of the *exemplum* is his own.

74. Vercellensis refers to Scotus Erigena's transliteration of the Greek *agalma*—block of marble. Cf. Théry, p. 76. Our translator opts for wood.

75. The image of the plumb-line is the translator's.

76. The author's careful and yet highly imaginative translation is reflected in the balanced "cola" in the ME of this passage; each phrase has the same number of syllables.

First thou wost well by natureel wit
that ere he may com to for to see that ymage
bi cleer bodely sight of his outward eye,
or for to showe it to be seen unto other . . .
the stok yit beyng hole on euerich a side
he most algates by craft and by instrumentes
voide awey alle the outwerd partyes of that wode
being about and lettyng the sight of that same ymage.

77. The example illustrates vividly what the translator calls, in the *Cloud*, the *work* of his book, and here "this high devyne werk."

78. ME: "boistous ensaumple of so contrary a kind." The *captatio benevolentiae* is the translator's.

79. The translator seems to become suddenly aware that the one who contemplates begins by trying to make an image of God, and the way of doing it is seen as secondary.

80. The translator has used this analogy of space in the last chapters of the *Cloud*, chs. 68–70, in which he finally identifies Dionysius as his main source.

81. The *Cloud* says that "young presumptuous disciples in their fantastic imaginations . . . would fashion a God according to their own fancy" (*ed. cit.*, ch. 57, p. 230).

82. ME: conielid as it were in a kumbros clog abouten him. In this lengthy interpolation ("In the same way we must conduct ourselves . . . except in the moment of their experience"), the translator restates his teaching on the nature of the cloud of unknowing. It is original sin, it is the result of original sin (ch. 28), it is the sinful self "conielyd in a lumpe" (ch. 36); in fact, it is every kind of darkness that separates the soul from the dynamic union with God that is the purpose of the exercise. His source is Vercellensis: in the Explanation on *The Divine Names*, not the *Extractio* or the Commentary on the *Mystical Theology*. Cf. Introduction, *supra*.

83. Thomas Gallus speaks of this "dense mass" as being not around God but the soul, from which we are cleansed by the divine light. It surrounds us like a heavy body or a cloud; it is made up of original sin, actual sins, negligences, and the oppression of bodily inhabitation—"the body of this death" of St. Paul, Rom 7:24.

84. As Richard of St. Victor has it, this ascent to contemplation is by way of *industria et gratia*.

85. One of the few phrases in this section that is a translation of Sarracenus's Latin. It reads: *auferentes prohibitiones officientes mundae occultae visioni, et ipsam in se ipsa, ablatione sola occultam manifestantes pulchritudinem* (We must take away the hindrances to the clean hidden sight; by simple taking away revealing the hidden Beauty in itself).

86. The contemplative soul, by its own exercise aided by grace, reveals the divine beauty. This is the praise of the hidden God. Cf. Is 45:15.

87. The translator seems to withhold the names of God to the end of this imaginative description of the contemplative process—ME: the self fairheed in the selfe nakid, unmaad, unbigonne kynde.

88. "for all of us." Again the translator introduces himself and the contemplatives for whom he is writing into his text.

89. ME: We foulden alle togeders and done hem away—a clear indication that "treading underfoot" (the *Cloud*, e.g., ch. 7) is only a metaphor; it does not refer to the mental vigor with which the exercise must be prosecuted.

90. ME: Wallid aboute. The Latin of Sarracenus and Gallus is *circumvelatam*—"veiled around," but clearly the translator's MS read *circumvallatam*. The citadel image is used by Richard of St. Victor, and is thus familiar to this translator in the contemplative context. Cf. "Pursuit of Wisdom," *supra*.

91. The translator adheres to a literal rendering of Sarracenus. Gallus, reading *circumvelatam*, refers us to the capital contemplative text of 2 Cor 3:18: "But we all, beholding the glory of the Lord with unveiled face, are transformed into the same image." Cf. Théry, p. 78.

92. Neither Sarracenus nor Vercellensis mentions the *Heavenly* or *Ecclesiastical Hierarchies*. The identification by the translator indicates his ignorance of these works, and perhaps also of *The Divine Names*, since chs. 1, 12, and 13 of this work deal with the unity and trinity of God. Whether the unknown author, Pseudo-Dionysius, wrote this book of positive theology "on *Hypotyposes*, that is, the hypostases or appropriations of the Person," is a matter for doubt.

93. ME: Fatherheed and Sonheed and the Holi Ghostheed; Latin: *paternitas et filiatio, quid vult monstrare Spiritus theologia*. The translator follows Sarracenus faithfully in the whole of this third chapter.

94. The allusion is to Jas 1:17: "Every best gift and every perfect gift is from above, coming down from the Father of Lights with whom there is no change nor shadow of alteration."

95. The quality of the translation is vividly illustrated by this smooth change of image from light to life, and to growth that does not involve change.

96. Sarracenus uses the Johannine (vulgate) term for the indwelling, *mansio*, and the author likewise in English—"dwelling." Cf. Jn 14:23.

97. The *circumincessio*. Julian of Norwich coins the word "forthspredyng" to deal with the Scholastic description of the relations within the Trinity. Maybe this short paraphrase—"everlasting borionyng"—is superior.

98. Latin: *inegressibilia*; ME: unpassyngliche. St. Thomas in the Corpus Christi hymn sings of "the Supernal Word coming forth, without leaving the Father's side"—*Verbum supernum prodiens, nec Patris linquens dexteram*.

99. The Pseudo-Dionysius was suspected of the monophysite heresy. The text is anxious to assert that Jesus, who is in his Godhead "sovereynsubstancyal"—*supersubstancialis*—has a true human nature. The fourth

Dionysian letter deals with the question. Cf. Walsh, "Expositions of Thomas Gallus," pp. 211ff.

100. ME: Gadering of Devine Sentence, which translates *Symbolica Theologia.*

101. This description summarily coincides with the final chapter of the *Heavenly Hierarchies.* Vercellensis lists the following scriptural references: *forms,* Phil 2:6; Ps 44:3; Sg 5:10, 2:14; *figures:* Hos 13:7; Sg 5:11; Is 6:1; *instruments:* Amos 7:7; *places:* Ez 3:12; Is 6:1; *adornments:* Dn 7:9; Apoc 1:13; *frenzies:* Ps 6:1; *sadnesses:* Gn 6:6; *furies:* Hos 9:7; Mk 3:21; 1 Cor 1:25; *drunkenness and gluttonies:* Ps 77:65; *oaths:* Ps 109:4; *cursings:* Gn 3:17; *sleepings:* Ps 43:23, 3:6; *awakenings:* Jer 1:12 (Théry, pp. 87–88).

102. Vercellensis is never tired of reminding his readers that "the cloud and the darkness," according to Denis, is the divine light; in his first letter he says, "the darkness is hidden by the light, and the more light, the more it is hidden" (ADHLMA *art. cit.,* p. 203).

103. The context is always that of prayer and praise, so that "the shortness of words" corresponds with the intensity of the feeling, as the translator expresses it in the *Cloud,* chs. 37–39.

104. Again, as Vercellensis notices, sanity and reason do not fail; they are exceeded (Théry, pp. 90–91). So the translator writes in the *Cloud* that discretion applies to all other exercises but not to this; *ed. cit.,* chs. 41–44.

105. ME: And al it shal be knittid to a thing that is unspekable. The theory is turned into practice in "Private Direction," where the author exchanges all the names of God for "this little word *is,*" and concludes: "and thus schalt thou knittingly, and in a maner that is marvelous, worschip God with himself" (cf. *infra*).

106. The author here begins to translate from the *Extractio* of Thomas Gallus.

107. In the final two chapters, the author translates not from the version of Sarracenus, but from the *Extractio* of Vercellensis. However the latter omits chapter numbers and titles. Sarracenus's title for ch. IV reads: *Quod nihil sensibilium est, qui est omnis sensibilis causa secundum excessum.*

108. The text makes sense, though it does not have the same balance without the addition mentioned below.

109. H. Decuise and McCann (*Cloud of Unknowing,* p. 276), insert the following phrase, which occurs in neither of the two MSS: "And then we put away poo thinges that bot only ben and liven not." This is certainly needed by the sense and explicable. Both editors also make another insertion into the Latin text of the *Extractio,* which reads: *Et non sentiens quod remotius est his quae sunt [et] vivunt et sentiunt.* This, though not strictly needed by the sense, is suggested, not by the Latin text itself, but by the English of our author: "and after that we put away thoo that ben and levyn and lackyn felyng." Happily, it finds justification in the Commentary of Vercellensis, who lists "three degrees of inferior creature, sc., those which only exist and neither live nor feel; those which are and live but do not feel; those which live, feel and do not reason or understand" (Théry, pp. 96–97).

110. Presumably the "three degrees" are mineral, vegetable, animal.

111. The original text, as noted, does not carry this direct reference to original sin, the *fomes peccati;* it is Vercellensis's insertion and essential to the medieval understanding of Denis. Cf. the *Cloud, ed. cit.*, ch. 28, p. 176.

112. ME: Aungel. The Latin of Vercellensis and Sarracenus has *mens*. In the Commentary, the former simply notices: "He begins from the more worthy rational creature." *Mens* is a traditional word for the graced intellect, also a synonym for "spirit" in Western spiritual vocabulary.

113. ME: ne he hath fantasie, ne opinion. "Fantasie" is rather the imaginative impression, and opinion the thought-impression.

114. ME: ne he holdeth no silence, ne he spekith. Not in the Latin of Vercellensis' *Extractio*. Sarracenus has *neque silentium agit*, which the translator follows, adding his own reference to its contrary, speech.

115. ME: eelde, which the author uses to translate Gallus's *aevum*, the Scholastic designation of angelic duration, midway between time and eternity.

116. ME: ne ther is any understandable touchyng of him. Vercellensis's Latin reads *neque etiam intelligibiliter tangibilis secundum essentiam suam*. Sarracenus has ambiguously *neque tactus est eius intelligibilis*. There can be no direct intellectual experience of God as he is, essentially.

117. ME: Kyngdom. The original Greek—*Basileia*—is abstract, meaning kingship, royalty; and all the translators offer *regnum*. At the same time, the ME Kyngdom also has an early meaning of kingship.

118. The translator omits Vercellensis's addition to Sarracenus's *scilicet homine puro vel angelo*—"that is, by man purified or by angel." The *Extractio* offers no explanation for this qualification of *aliquo existente*—any other being—which may be why the translator omits it. Vercellensis argues at length in his commentary why the qualification is important (Théry, pp. 102–03).

119. ME: ne of any of poo thinges that ben knowen, knowen hym after that he is. The Latin of Vercellensis reads *neque existentia ipsam cognoscunt secundum quod ipse est;* Sarracenus has *neque existentia ipsam cognoscunt secundum quod ipsa est*. The Ms reading has suffered from dittography: probably the scribe did not immediately recognize "ben" as third person plural present indicative of "to be."

120. Latin *secundum quod sunt in Verbo*. The translator ignores the reference to the Word in Vercellensis. Sarracenus has *neque ipsa cognoscit ea que sunt existentia secundum quod existentia sunt*. Again less definite and more ambiguous than Gallus, who wants his text to speak Scholastic language: "The knowledge which God has of existing things is not drawn from the matter or the form of these things, but he knows all things by knowing himself eternally as the eternal cause of all things" (Théry, p. 103).

121. Vercellensis reads *neque est ipsius rationalis investigatio;* Sarracenus *neque ratio ipsius est*. The translator removes any ambiguity.

122. Vercellensis interprets: "Nor is he darkness lacking light nor intelligible light. Here Sarracenus is translated: nor is he darkness, nor is he light."

The Discernment of Spirits

Translator's Introduction

St. Bernard and the Discernment of Spirits

Discernment of Spirits, though it has distinct affinities with Bernard's sermon *De discretione spirituum*, is the most expert and original of the *Cloud* author's trilogy of "translations." It is very different in scope and texture from *A Study of Wisdom*, which is by and large a rather arbitrary and sometimes jejune synopsis of the *Benjamin Minor*, and from *Denis's Hidden Theology*, a reasonably faithful version of the Latin of John Sarracenus and Thomas Gallus. Nor did the *Cloud* author feel called upon either to claim or to acknowledge St. Bernard or this sermon as his source, as indeed did that other Middle English translator of the same sermon, who begins his extract with the words, "Seynt Bernard techith and seieth thus."[1]

St. Bernard's many references to discretion stress two different aspects of the spiritual tradition concerning the virtue and practice of discretion. He is most often quoted as coining aphorisms such as "Discretion is not so much a virtue as a governor and charioteer of the virtues: one who sets the affections in order and is the mistress of human behavior."[2] Here as elsewhere, the key to Bernard's teaching is the Pauline doctrine: Discernment of spirits is a gift of the Holy Spirit for spiritual government and right order in the Church. After commenting on the text in 1 Corinthians (12:8) concerning the distribution of gifts, and making the distinction between charisms given us for our own profit and those given for others, he concludes: "If the other gifts, that is, wisdom and knowledge, do increase in us, let us make sure that they are distributed to our neighbors. Thus indeed we shall obtain the gift of the Holy Spirit which is called discernment of spirits: if, that is, we obtain those gifts which are proper to ourselves, and bestow on our neighbor those given to us for the advancement of others."[3] A more immediate application is to the virtues of compassion and justice, which must flourish together in religious superiors, so they do not break the bruised reed or quench the smoking flax. The spirit of discretion, he says, enables us to do the right thing at the right moment; it teaches us how to be zealous for divine justice and to offer pardon at one and the same time.[4]

On the other hand, Bernard makes the point that even the most experienced observer of interior stirrings and thoughts will not be able to discern, to separate out one from the other, the evil that already exists in the heart, and that which has been sown there (*malum innatum et malum seminatum*). Indeed, who can understand sins? Nor does it make much difference to know the source of the evil in us, as long as we acknowledge that it is there. The point is to watch and pray lest we consent to it, no matter whence it comes.[5] Nonetheless, in the sermon that the English author examines, Bernard distinguishes the various spirits, or rather their speech—and mainly of the three wicked spirits, the devil, the world, and the flesh. His last few sentences are devoted to the one whose word is truth: "You must listen constantly to what the Lord speaks in you, for he speaks peace."[6]

In this sermon to his community, the abbot Bernard takes his text from Galatians (5:25): "If we live by the Spirit, let us also walk by the Spirit." He offers the image of the money-changer testing the coins, separating the true from the counterfeit, the precious metal from the base. Flesh must be converted to spirit; it must become its servant, in fact like the centurion's (Mt 8:9); and thus we shall be saved through our children, good works, as we become like the fruitful vine under the eaves of our house (Section 1).

With the above prologue, Bernard proceeds by way of 1 John (4:1) to distinguish first the human spirit from God's Spirit, which speaks in man, and from the good angel who likewise speaks in man, especially the prophets, and from the bad angels who make their inroads into the human heart (Section 2). With Colossians (2:18) and 1 Corinthians (2:12) for texts, he then distinguishes the spirits of the flesh and of the world, who are "the satellites of that malicious prince of darkness, the Spirit of wickedness." These three speak of self-indulgence, of worldly vanities and of bitter things, so that we know them by what they say. We are to answer the flesh and the world as the Lord answered Peter, who was tempting him to the standards of world and flesh (Mk 8:33): "Get behind me Satan, for you do not savor (*sapis*) the things of God." Bernard adds, with typical word-play, "rather your wisdom (*sapientia*) is God's enemy." Any thought that is less than friendly or discreet, or gives occasion for indignation, is straight from the devil (Section 3).

We are not only tempted, Bernard goes on, but sometimes we fall, and so grievously that our own spirit takes over from all three evil spirits, "giving birth itself to voluptuous, vain or bitter thoughts." From this point of view (and Bernard repeats this elsewhere) the source of the various speeches is of secondary importance. "If he is an enemy, resist him stoutly; if he is your own spirit, take him on, groan at yourself because you have fallen into such misery and servitude" (Section 4). Good thoughts, he continues, when they come into the mind, indicate that the Spirit of God is speaking, either directly or indirectly, by his angel in whom God likewise speaks (Section 5). Section 6 teaches how to deal with temptations—not to listen to our blood, to recollect that worldly thoughts are none other than those wicked children of Babylon in Psalm 136, who are to be dashed against the rocks—and offers the various motives for resisting bad thoughts and cultivating good ones. We are to turn constantly to the Lord God and say with the young Samuel: "Speak, Lord, for your servant is listening" (3 Kgs 3:9). St. Bernard is equally aware that Satan has been able from the beginning to simulate the voice of God (Gn 3), and that this is particularly true of those who come to the grace of devotion. They must fear the noonday devil, for even Satan transforms himself into an angel of light (2 Cor 11:14). "He who prepares all his spiritual exercises with abundance of delight, might destroy the body through inordinate exertions. . . . Let him then be illumined by the light of discretion which is the mother of virtues and the consummation of perfection."[7]

The Translation

The English translator, omitting Bernard's prologue, follows his source substantially and faithfully in the distinction and description of the spirits of world, flesh, and wickedness; and this corresponds to a little over half the original sermon.[8] After this, the use of the Latin is minimal and also coincidental. The English author is concerned to develop three subjects. First, temptations at the hands of the three bad spirits, which as Bernard points out have to do with self-indulgence, vainglory, and that peculiarly English vice, "grouching." (In the *Cloud*, this last is contrasted with chaste and perfect love; a smiling and a "grouching" countenance are contraries, while the young disciple can be "grouching against counsel"—be ill-disposed to his spiritual director).[9] Such temptations, especially of the third kind, militate strongly against contemplation and its peace. This theme (4–6) is central both in its position in the sermon and to the author's substance. It has no equivalent in Bernard's Latin; and if it has a source other than the author's own accumulated reading on contemplation and the discretion that is a necessary condition for it, this may be found in Augustine's commentary on Psalm 64 (as the annotations indicate). It may be significant that after his summary statement of all that he teaches in the *Cloud* and elsewhere—"the vision of the high peace of the Godhead which is the highest and best part of contemplation that may be had in this life"—he proceeds, as does Walter Hilton, to draw the distinction between true and false light. The latter says: "Now beware of the midday fiend, who counterfeits light as though it were come out of Jerusalem, but it does not."[10] The former goes on in the next section (7) to explain how Satan sometimes assumes the mantle of true light. For this the translator uses the first paragraph of Bernard's sermon 24 *De diversis*, preached, the saint himself tells us, the day after the one on discernment, on the Lord's speech and its many-sided fruitfulness.[11] In our author's scheme, the citation and its short interpretation are merely introductory to another subject dear to his heart, which he develops at length in *Assessment of Inward Stirrings:* that singular "devout observances," like fasting and wearing cloth, are normally diabolic suggestions, because they invariably lead to dissensions and scandal. (Here the translator uses Bernard's short Section 4, but with the object of reinforcing the teaching on avoiding the devil's darts, which "kill love and simple souls under the pretext of holiness and charity.")

The English author's next subject is the importance, for this discernment of temptations and their sources, of the interior witness, one's conscience, and the exterior witness, the spiritual director. Bernard in another place has said, quoting the Roman poet Juvenal, that this discernment is so rare a bird that it is necessary to supply for it with obedience.[12] The translator is more circumspect. The direction here concerns, not inward thoughts and stirrings in general, but those that afflict, for example, the *ex professo* contemplative, when, by accident or design, he fails to follow the advice given earlier here, and at length in the *Cloud*, of "treading down" any new thought concerning anything or anyone, and particularly any sin. It is grace, wisdom, and experience that enable the conscience to identify the inward speaker. Confession is to be according to the law of the Church and the advice and judgment of confessor or counsel; the author does not say clearly whether the two are identical. This confession is itself our assurance that the temptations that follow it, "no matter how frequent, evil or numerous they may be," are the suggestion of flesh, or world, or devil. They are not thoughts of your own spirit, and the tendency to accept them as such is itself a lack of discretion and a dangerous illusion, one that easily leads to scruples and to despair. After a good and truthful confession, then, new thoughts or feelings toward sin have already been rejected and thus can only be fleshly, worldly, or devilish in origin.

In his penultimate section (13), the English author returns once more to his source, to make the point that there are certain thoughts and feelings belonging to the order of salvation that indicate that "it is the spirit of God speaking, either by himself or by one or other of his angels." It would seem from the list of thoughts—chastity, temperance, contempt of the world, voluntary poverty—that our author is again thinking of the *ex professo* contemplative life, even though there is no other evidence leading us to suppose that he, like Bernard, is exhorting a monastic community. He does, however, bring his reflections on discernment to a happy conclusion. Though he has been concerned almost entirely with evil thoughts and stirrings, he looks forward to a totally different state of mind and heart; the soul, who through its assimilation to God by contemplation is now enabled to have the stirrings of thoughts of peace and charity and fulness of heart, "wherever it will and with constant awareness."[13]

Discernment of Spirits would appear to have been written, like the *Cloud* itself and all the other treatises, to help the apprentice contemplative to become more proficient. The central sections (4–6) are clearly pivotal to the structure of the piece, and are analogous to those chapters in Hilton's *Scale of Perfection*, introduced by the allegory of the pilgrimage to Jerusalem, that concern the "reform in feeling" of the *ex professo* contemplative. To achieve his purpose, the *Cloud* author makes use of Bernard's homily in distinguishing and identifying the temptations and impulses of the evil spirits of the flesh, the world, and wickedness. Once it is established that the last spirit to be dealt with, because the hardest to overcome and the most inimical to the contemplative life, is the wicked Spirit himself, the author describes how the apprentice proceeds: by making his confession, as in the *Cloud*, and by consulting and following the advice of his spiritual director. Detailed advice is minimal—as indeed it is in

THE DISCERNMENT OF SPIRITS

Bernard's sermon; but the translator does not overlook the main difficulty in the way of contemplative progress. As the soul sets itself to listen to the voice of God's Spirit, under whatever form it can be heard, as the antidote to the voices that tempt us to sins of the flesh—gluttony, intemperance, lechery, and soft living; of the world—the ephemeral honors, empty pride, and vain joys; and finally of the spirit of malice—wrath and wickedness that rob us of the "best thing of all" (and here we are reminded of the *Cloud* author's frequent reference to Luke 10:10, "Mary has chosen the best part"), "charity which is God," it is to be reminded of Satan's ability to masquerade as a good angel, and to tempt and deceive under the color of holiness. Here we have the inevitable digression of the *Cloud* author: his belief that the singular observances of religious life—vigils, fasts, and corporal penances—are normally temptations to Pharisaism, to do everything so as to be seen by men (Mt 23:14). The freedom of grace, which is essential to a flourishing contemplative life, is acquisitive of self-knowledge, and this operates by means of conscience informed by experience and by spiritual counsel. As is usual in the contemplative milieu, any new beginning in the interior life has confession as its starting point. It is doubly demanded in the search for progress through discernment, since purification is best acquired sacramentally. Only one difficulty remains, and it is one that has no mention in the Latin sermon of St. Bernard. As the author indicated elsewhere, every form of despair, whether sloth or sorrow, is highly inimical to contemplation, and indicates the devil's frontal attacks on those who practice it. Yet nothing induces the state so quickly and dangerously as does that lack of discernment in attributing to one's own spirit every evil thought that assails the human consciousness. This would be not simply to tempt oneself to sin, but to take on the office of the devil. A frequent contrary thought of the *Cloud* author is that great penitents have become God's special saints in this life. It is true that temptation and consent to it does make us fragile, but the power of sacramental confession is greater. Grace always abounds, and we become "spiritual by purity of life and devotion." The translation ends with a prayer for this grace.

It has been alleged that "it is [more] difficult to adduce proof that *Of Discerning of Spirits* should be included in a canon of this author's works," because, "though it resembles them in its use of language, its choice of ornament and its sentence construction, it is little more than a paraphrase of St. Bernard's *De diversis*, sermon 23, and is entirely different in theme from the other treatises." On the contrary, it must be affirmed that the English treatise never moves beyond the set themes of the author's other works and it uses its source sparingly and with great ingenuity. In fact, it illustrates better than the *Study of Wisdom* itself the straight relationship that exists, in the Victorine tradition followed by the *Cloud* author, between Joseph and Benjamin, discretion and contemplation.

The Discernment of Spirits[1]

1. Because there are different kinds of spirits, it is necessary for us to know how to distinguish them; especially as we are taught by the Apostle St. John not to give credence to all spirits.[2] For it might seem to those who have but little education in spiritual things especially,[3] that every thought that resounds in the human heart[4] must be the utterance of no other spirit except man's own.[5] And this is not so: as both the faith and the witness of Holy Scripture clearly show.[6] "For I shall hear," says the Prophet David, "not what I myself speak, but whatever my Lord God speaks in me."[7] And another prophet says that an angel spoke in him.[8] And besides this, we are taught in the Psalm that wicked spirits send evil thoughts into men.[9] Furthermore, the Apostle Paul clearly shows that there is a spirit of the flesh that is not good, where he says that some men are all puffed up with the spirit of their flesh.[10] And he also plainly declares that there is also the spirit of the world, when he rejoices in God,[11] not only for himself but also for his disciples that they had received, not the spirit of the world, but that which is sent of God: that is, the Holy Spirit.[12]

2. Now these two spirits, of the flesh and of the world, are, as it were, servants or men-at-arms[13] of that accursed spirit, the foul fiend of hell; so that the spirit of wickedness is the lord of the spirit of the flesh and also of the spirit of the world.[14] Whichever of these three spirits speaks with our own spirit, we must not believe any of them, because they never speak without the intention of bringing about the loss of both body and soul.[15] And which one it is that speaks to our

108

spirit, the speech of that spirit shall make fully plain.[16] For the spirit of the flesh always speaks of things soft and comfortable to the body;[17] the spirit of the world, of vanities and the inordinate desire of honors;[18] and the spirit of the fiend, of cruel and bitter things.[19] So whenever any thought of food, drink, of sleep and of fine apparel and of all other things belonging to the flesh which make our hearts burn, as they say, with a longing desire for all such things, we may be very sure that it is the spirit of the flesh speaking.[20] We must therefore drive him away as best we can by the help of grace; for he is our adversary.[21] And whenever any thought of the empty joys of this world beats upon our hearts, firing us with a desire to be considered attractive and to be approved of, to be reckoned as of noble birth and extremely intelligent, to be counted as wise and worthy, or else to hold high rank and have special standing in this life,[22] and all other such thoughts that would make a man appear important and worthy of esteem, not only in other people's eyes but also in his own: have no doubt that it is the spirit of the world that utters them all.[23] He is a far more dangerous enemy than is the spirit of the flesh and he must be driven off with much greater urgency.[24]

3.   Now it often happens that these two servants and men-at-arms of the dread fiend, the spirit and prince of wrath and wickedness,[25] are put down and firmly trodden underfoot by grace and the soul's spiritual strategy.[26] On the other hand, they may be skillfully withdrawn by the cunning tactics of their malicious master,[27] the foul fiend of hell, when he takes it into his head to rise up himself with great malice and wrath, running around like a savage lion[28] to attack our souls in their weakness and helplessness.[30] This is what happens whenever the thought of our heart stirs us, not to the lusts of the flesh, nor to the fruitless joys of this world, but to murmuring, to complaining and airing our grievances, to bitterness of soul, to pining and to impatience, to wrath, to melancholy, to ill-will, to hatred, to envy, and to all such misfortune.[31] This spirit makes us take it badly if anything is said or done to us less amicably and less thoughtfully than we would wish. It arouses in us all kinds of evil suspicion. If any sign or look is given, any word or deed that could in any way be made an occasion of malice or heaviness of heart, this spirit persuades us to take it that way.[32]

4.   All these thoughts, and any like them that would rob us of peace and restfulness of heart, we must resist as we would the fiend of hell himself. And we must flee from them as we would from the losing

of our soul.[33] There is no doubt that the other thoughts, that come from the spirit of the flesh and the spirit of the world, labor and toil toward the loss of our soul with all their might. But his work in this regard is the most perilous. For he can bring it about by himself, whereas without him they are powerless.[34] No matter how purified a soul may be from the lust of the flesh and the empty joys of this world, as long as it is defiled with this spirit of malice, wrath, and wickedness, it is in the condition of damnation,[35] notwithstanding all its purity. And no matter how defiled a soul may be with the lust of the flesh and the empty joys of this world, as long as by the help of grace it remains at peace and in restfulness of heart with regard to its fellow-Christians—though this is very hard to achieve when the thoughts of the other two are habitual—it is further from the condition of damnation, in spite of all the impurities of the flesh and the world, mentioned above.

5.   The lustful thoughts of our sinful flesh are bad, because they rob the soul of its liking for devotion.[36] The empty joys of the world are worse, because they rob us of the true joy that we should have in the contemplation of heavenly things, which are ministered and taught to us by the angels of heaven.[37] For those who have an inordinate desire to be honored, admired, and served by men here on earth deserve to forgo the honor, admiration, and service of angels in the spiritual contemplation of heaven and heavenly things all their lifetime:[38] that contemplation which is better and more worthy in itself than the delight and consolation of devotion. But the worst spirit of them all I call this spirit of malice, of wrath, and of wickedness, because of this bitterness.[39] And why? Surely because it robs us of the best thing of all: that is, charity, which is God.[40] For whoever lacks peace and restfulness of heart lacks also the living presence and the lovely vision of the high peace of heaven, the good and gracious God, his own dear self.[41]

6.   This is the witness of David in the Psalm, where he says that God's homestead is established in peace, and his dwelling-place in Sion.[42] Sion is as much as to say "the vision of peace."[43] The soul's vision is its thought. And truly, in the soul that is most occupied with thoughts of peace, God has made his dwelling-place.[44] So he says himself through the mouth of the Prophet when he says: "Upon whom shall my spirit rest, but on the meek and the restful?"[45] And therefore he who would have God dwelling in him constantly, and live in love and in the vision of the high peace of the Godhead, which

is the highest and best part of contemplation that may be had in this life,[46] such a man must be vigilant night and day to put down the spirit of the flesh and the spirit of the world whenever they come. But he must be most vigilant in putting down the spirit of malice, of wrath, and of wickedness, for he is the most unclean and the worst of all.[47]

7. Hence it is very necessary and helpful to know his cunning tricks, and not to be ignorant of his crafty deceits.[48] For that wicked accursed wretch will sometimes change his likeness into that of an angel of light,[49] in order that, under the color of virtue, he may do more mischief.[50] However, if we pay careful attention, what he does is to sow nothing but the seed of bitterness and discord, though at its first appearance it seems ever so holy and good.[51] He persuades very many to embrace a special type of holiness above the common law and custom of their state of life.[52] The signs of it are fasting, wearing hair-cloth, and many other devout observances and forms of behavior, and openly reproving the faults of other men when they have no authority for it.[53] He leads them on to things like this and many other such, and always under the pretext of devotion and charity; not because he takes any delight in works of devotion or of charity, but because he loves dissension and scandal, which is generally the outcome of these unseemly singularities.[54] For wherever, in any pious association,[55] there are one or two who go in for these forms of exterior observances, as far as the foolish are concerned, they are a stumbling-block to all the rest; but, as the wise see it, they are a stumbling-block to themselves.[56] Yet since there are more fools than wise men, because these people have the fools' approval, they imagine themselves to be wise in their outlandish doings. Whereas if the matter were judged wisely, they and all their supporters would be recognized as fools: darts shot by the devil to kill true and simple souls, under pretext of holiness and charity. In this way the fiend can introduce many sly tricks. But he who refuses to consent, and truly humbles himself by recourse to prayer and direction, shall, by the help of grace, keep clear of all these wiles.[57]

8. But sad to say, and even more to experience, sometimes our own spirit is so overcome by all these three spirits—of the flesh, the world, and the devil—and brought into subjection and so bound in bondage, servitude, and slavery to them all, that it is most distressing to realize it. To its great bedevilment and despoilment, the soul, of its own power, now performs in itself the task of each one of them.[58]

This happens through the inveterate habit and custom of giving way to them when they come; until at last the soul becomes so fleshly, so worldly and so malicious, so wicked and evilly disposed, that of its own full accord, and without the promptings of any other spirit, it engenders and brings to birth in itself not merely lustful thoughts of the flesh and thoughts of the world's vanities, but, worst of all, bitter and wicked thoughts, such as backbiting, rash judgment, and evil suspicion of others.[59]

If this is the case with our own spirit, then I am sure that it cannot easily be discovered when it is our own spirit speaking, or when it is hearing any one of the other three spirits speaking in it, as was said above.[60] But what difference does it make when all that is said is one and the same thing? What good is it to know the person who speaks, when it is sure and certain that every word spoken is evil and perilous? If it is your enemy, do not give him your consent, but humble yourself by recourse to prayer and to direction, so that you can strongly resist your enemy.[61] If it is your own spirit, upbraid him bitterly, and mourn and sorrow that you ever fell so deep into this wretched state, this bondage and slavery to the devil.[62] Confess your habitual consenting, and your past sins;[63] and so you may come by the help of grace to recover your freedom.[64]

9. By the freedom of grace you may come to know with wisdom and to discern truly by experience when it is your own spirit speaking these evil things or when it is other, evil spirits speaking them in you.[65] Hence this knowledge can be a most efficacious means and help in resisting them. For oftentimes unknowing is the cause of grave error; while knowing is the cause of great truth.[66] You can attain to this kind of knowledge in the following way. If, when these evil thoughts come you are in doubt or perplexity whether they are the thoughts of your own spirit or of one or other of your enemies, examine them diligently according to the witness of your conscience and the spiritual direction you have received;[67] if, that is, you have made your confession and amends, according to the Church's law and the judgment of your confessor, of every consent you have given to the particular sins that your thought brings to mind. And if you have not been shriven, then make your confession as truly as you can by the help of grace and your spiritual counsel.[68] Then you can be certain that the thoughts that come to your mind after your confession, tempting you again to the same sins, are the suggestions of spirits other than your own—of one or other of the three mentioned before.[69] Nor are you to blame for them, no matter how frequent,

evil, or numerous they may be—when they first come to mind, that is—unless there is carelessness in resisting them.[70] And if you withstand them vigorously, you can merit release from the purgatory you have deserved for the sins committed in the past, whatever they may be,[71] as well as many graces in this life, and great reward in the bliss of heaven.[72]

10.   When these evil thoughts come and tempt you to any sin, and you have consented to them, before you are sorry for that consenting and have decided to go to confession, it is no danger to you in accepting them as your own, and to confess them as thoughts of your own spirit. But there is great peril in accepting as your own all those other thoughts which you have judged by true discernment (as we have said before) to be the suggestions of spirits other than yourself.[73] For in this way you could easily lead your conscience astray, reckoning something as sinful which is no sin. This would be a very serious error, and lead you into extreme danger. For if it were true that every evil thought and temptation to sin were the work and suggestion of none other spirit than man's own, then it would follow that man's own spirit was a devil, which is clearly false and damnable lunacy.[74] For while it is true that through weakness and sinful habits a soul can fall into such a wretched state that in its enslavement to sin it takes over the work of the devil, and tempts itself increasingly to sin, without any suggestion being made to it by any other spirit, as we said before; yet even so, it is not a devil by nature. Yet it does take on the function of the devil and can be called devilish: in that it tempts itself to sin, which is the work of the devil.[75] Yet in spite of all this enslavement to sin and this likeness to the devil in its working, by the grace of contrition, confession, and amendment the soul may recover its freedom and enter again on the way of salvation.[76] Yes, and a soul that was once ripe for damnation in living a most wicked life can become one of God's special saints in this life.[77]

11.   Hence, if it is most perilous for a soul in a state of sin not to accuse his conscience and to make amends, it is equally perilous, and perhaps we ought to say even more so, for a man to accuse his own conscience of every evil thought and temptation to sin that may come into his mind.[80] For by such scrupulous self-accusations he might easily acquire an erroneous conscience, and be led into a despair that lasts all his lifetime.[81] And the cause is ignorance about discernment of spirits; while the knowledge of it can be acquired by practical experience, by anyone who is quick to examine himself as soon as his

soul has been properly cleansed in confession, as has been said before.[82]

12.   Immediately after confession a soul is like a clean page. It is ready to receive whatever anyone wishes to write on it. God and his angels on the one side, the devil and his angels on the other:[83] Both are eager to write upon the soul when it is made clean by confession.[84] But it remains within the free choice of the soul to accept what impression it prefers.[85] This acceptance on the soul's part is its consent. A new thought or feeling toward any sin which you have previously rejected in your confession—what other source of it is there except one of the three spirits, who are your enemies mentioned before, attempting to write on your soul the same sin once again? Such a thought is not from yourself, because there is no such thing written on your soul. It has all been washed off in your confession, and your soul is left clean and unadorned, with nothing on it but a fragile and free consenting;[86] tending rather toward the evil in it habitually practiced in the past,[87] but more suited for the good than the evil because of its cleanness and the power of sacramental confession.[88] Of itself, then, it has nothing whereby it may conceive or stir itself to good or evil. Hence it follows that whatever thought comes to it at this time, whether good or evil, is not of itself.[89] The consent to the good or the evil, whichever it be—that is always the work of the soul; and it deserves punishment or joy in proportion to the rightfulness or wrongfulness of this consent.

13.   If the soul's consent is to the evil, then with the burden of sin it takes on the function of that particular spirit which first offered the temptation to the sin. And if the consent is to the good, then, through grace, it takes on the function of the particular spirit which caused the movement toward that good.[90] For whenever any salutary thought comes into our mind—of chastity, temperance, contempt of the world, voluntary poverty, patience, meekness, and charity, without doubt it is the spirit of God speaking, either himself or by one or other of his angels: that is, either his angels of this life—those who are true teachers—or his blessed angels, who assuredly move and inspire us to good.[91]

14.   Just as we have said of the other three spirits—that the soul who is habitually accustomed over a long period to giving its consent to them can become so carnal, so worldly, and so malicious that it takes upon itself the office of them all; in the same way, the soul who

is similarly accustomed with regard to goodness can become so spiritual by purity of life and devotion in spirit against the spirit of the flesh, so heavenly minded against the spirit of the world,[92] and so like to God by peace and charity and restfulness of heart against the spirit of malice, wrath, and wickedness, that it now discharges the office of thinking all these good thoughts, whenever it will and with constant awareness, as perfectly as the frailty of this life will permit.

So it can be seen that every thought that knocks upon our heart, whether good or evil, is not always the utterance of our own spirit, but the consent to the thought, whatsoever it be, is always our own.

May Jesus grant us his grace to consent to the good and to stand firm against the evil. Amen.

Notes

Introduction

1. A short piece entitled "How a man shall know which is the speech of the flesh in his heart, and which is of the world, and which is of the fiend, and also which is of God Almighty, our Lord Jesus Christ." It is known in three MSS of the mid-fifteenth century: Trinity College, Cambridge B 14, 19; Downside College, 26542; and Yale University Library, 223.

2. *Sermones in Cantica* 49, 5: P.L. 183, 1018.

3. *Sermones de diversis* 88, 1–3: P.L. 183, 766–67.

4. *In tempore resurrectionis: ad abbates* II, 6: P.L. 183, 285.

5. *Sermones in Cantica* 32, 6: P.L. 183, 948.

6. *Sermones de diversis* 23; *De discretione spirituum:* P.L. 183, 600–03. The other ME translation, to which we have referred above, insists that it is not a question of identifying the various spirits but their speech. In the first paragraph, he translates: "Know you well that this stirring and this thought is of the speech of the flesh." Cf. C. Kirchberger, *The Coasts of the Country,* pp. 75–77.

7. *In circumcisione Domini, sermo* III: P.L. 183, 42.

8. Nos. 1–3 of the translation (the numbers are inserted for easy reference) correspond to the original's 2–3 in Migne, cols. 600–03.

9. General meanings of the many ME forms of "grudge," "bear a grudge," "grudging," are: discontent, resentment, vexation, and the words piled up in this tract—wrath, malice, murmuring, bitterness, impatience, melancholy, ill-will, hatred, envy, "and all such sorrow."

10. Cf. *infra,* n. 43.

11. Scale II, 26: Underhill, p. 330. The sins that come from the false light, says Hilton, are disobedience, indignation and backbiting, and other such sins: tokens by which the false light can be distinguished from the true.

116

THE DISCERNMENT OF SPIRITS

12. *In circumcisione Domini, sermo* 3, 11: *At vero, quia omnino rara ista avis est in terra* (Juvenal *Sat.* VI), *huius discretionis locum in vobis suppleat virtus obedientiae*. P.L. 183, 142.

13. P.H., p. lxxxi.

The Discernment of Spirits

1. Discernment—ME: Discrescyon. Discernment did not displace the word discretion in English theological language until the late sixteenth century, though the verb was in use at the turn of the fifteenth.

2. *Quia spirituum diversa sunt genera, necesse est nobis eorum discretio: praesertim cum ab apostolo didicerimus non omni spiritui esse credendum.* The ME is a literal translation of the lead sentence from St. Bernard's sermon, entitled variously *De discretione spirituum*—"On discretion of spirits," and *De septem spiritibus*—the seven spirits (of God, of the good angel and the bad angel, of man himself, of the devil and his two satellites, the world and the flesh) and not an allusion to the "seven more wicked spirits" traditionally referred to in the Gospel (Mt 12:45). Our author identifies Bernard's apostle: the first letter of John, 4:1–6.

3. ME: that ben bot litil in kunnyng and namely of goostly thinges; Latin: *minus eruditis et qui parum exercitatos habet sensus.* There is a reference here to a classical text of the Vulgate on discernment—Heb 5:14: the senses of the mature are trained to distinguish between good and evil. Our author seems to have missed the allusion. He does not attempt to translate *exercitatos sensus.*

4. ME: that sounith in mans herte—a neat addition of the translator, to indicate that thoughts are the utterances of the human spirit heard in the heart, with an allusion to Mt 15:18–20: it is the evil thoughts coming from a man's heart that defile.

5. Cf 1 Cor 2:11—"For what man knoweth the things of a man, but the Spirit of a man that is in him?"

6. Latin: *certa fidei veritas probat et divinarum testimonia scripturarum*—"the certain truth of faith and the witness of the divine scriptures prove." There is contamination in the copying of the translation.

7. Both texts add to the Scripture of Ps 84:9, which simply reads "I shall hear what the Lord God will speak in me."

8. "And the angel who spoke in me said to me"—Zach 1:9.

9. Evil thoughts. The reference is to the Vulgate Ps 77:49: "He sent upon them [the Israelites] . . . his indignation and wrath and immersions . . . by evil angels" (*Deus misit in eos . . . indignationem, et iram et tribulationem, immissiones per angelos malos*). Bernard's text reads *in psalmo didicimus fieri immissiones per angelos malos* (We learn in the psalm that immissions happened through evil angels). This is the only use of the noun *immissiones* in the Latin Vulgate. The Douai translates "trouble." The wicked angels are God's avenging messengers. In all probability, the translator is following the

117

teaching of St. Thomas, that "wicked angels assail man in two ways: firstly, by tempting them to sin . . . sometimes they are sent (*immittuntur*) by God . . . their assault (*impugnatio*) is a punishment to man" (*Summa Theologica* I, 114, 1 ad 1).

10. "Let no one seduce you, willing in humility and the religion of angels, walking in the things he hath not seen, in vain puffed up by the sense of his flesh"—*frustra inflatus sensu carnis suae*. Neither Bernard nor his translator is concerned with textual difficulties; the phrase is excised from its context.

11. Latin *ubi gloriatur in Domino:* cf 1 Cor 1:30–31. The Apostle's reference is to Jer 9:23–24: "Let not the wise man glory in his wisdom, and let not the strong man glory in his strength, and let not the rich man glory in his riches. But let him that glorieth glory in this, that he understandeth and knoweth me, for I am the Lord." The translator ignores the primary sense of *gloriatur*.

12. 1 Cor 2:12: "Now we have received not the Spirit of this world, but the Spirit that is of God: that we may know the things that are given us from God"—*ut sciamus quae a Deo denator sunt nobis*. Bernard cites, his translator paraphrases.

13. ME: seriauntes; Latin: *satellites*. In ME, the term is an early form of "sergeant," denoting a military rank below that of knight. The common meaning of *satelles* is an attendant on a distinguished person. It does not occur in the Latin Vulgate. The translator introduces the military flavor by giving us two words "servauntes or seriauntes of that cursid spirite."

14. "Lord" translates Bernard's *spiritus nequitiae* and *principis tenebrarum*—the Gospel titles: cf Lk 22:53 and Jn 14:30. The translator is more anxious to distinguish the spirit of wickedness from the spirit of this world.

15. The translator here expands his text, perhaps with an allusion to Lk 12:4–5.

16. In the *Cloud* it is stated that the angelic messenger usually resembles his message. Cf. *ed. cit.*, ch. 55, p. 227.

17. The reference is to the parable in Lk 12:19–20, where those who require the soul are the evil spirits. Cf 1 Cor 6:10. The *molles*, the self-indulgent, will never possess the kingdom. So the pampered in the palaces of kings are contrasted with the asceticism of the Baptist, Mt 11:8.

18. The tradition of the Fathers on the violence and savagery of Satan against mankind is summarized in St. Thomas's treatment of "the power of Christ's passion" (cf. *Summa Theologica III*, 46, 3).

19. Bernard here refers the spirit of the world to Satan—"we must repel him as the adversary, saying: Go behind me, Satan" (cf. Mk 9:33). Our author wishes to retain the clear distinction between the three spirits, so he omits this allusion.

20. Cf. Eccl 2:10: "And whatsoever my eyes desire, I refused them not. And I withheld not my heart from enjoying every pleasure and delighting itself."

21. ME: "by grace." This is the translator's addition.

22. "firing us with a desire . . . " The Latin speaks first of "ambition, pride and arrogance."

23. Another addition of the translator.

24. Traditionally, pride and vainglory are taken to be much more aggressive and subtle than gluttony, lechery, and avarice, and particularly for the solitary. Cf. Cassian, *Coll.* 5, 10; the *Cloud:* "The pleasure and vainglory which comes from men's flatterings" (*ed. cit.*, ch. 8, p. 136).

25. ME: stifly put doun and troden doune under fote. The language and context of the *Cloud* is almost identical with that of the translator's addition here: "any new thought . . . concerning any other sin . . . bravely step above it with a fervent impulse of love and tread it down under your feet" (*ed. cit.*, ch. 31, p. 180). Ch. 4 ME: be born doun and stifly troden doun under fote (cf. P.H. 22/20).

26. ME: goostly sleight. No Latin equivalent. The term is used several times in the *Cloud* and in the author's other writings.

27. The translator, in an addition to his text, stresses the subtlety of the devil's activity, as he does in the *Cloud*, e.g., (*ed. cit.*) ch. 52, pp. 150–51.

28. "Your adversary the devil, like a roaring lion, goeth about seeking whom he may devour" (1 Pt 5:8).

29. St. Paul lists these assaults of the spirit of the world as "works of the flesh": sc. "enmities, contentions, emulations, wraths, quarrels, dissensions, envies" (Gal 5:20). The whole passage is an addition to the original.

30. These two sentences are not in the Latin. They form an acute psychological observation from a very sensitive spiritual director.

31. The next three paragraphs, which are the substance of the translator's own contribution and concern discretion for contemplative souls "purified from the empty joys of this world," have no equivalent in the Latin.

32. The extremely popular *De Arca Noe morali* of Hugh of St. Victor begins from an examination of "the instability and restlessness of the human heart" (*de humani cordis instabilitate et inquietudine*) (P.L. 176, 618).

33. Cf. 1 Tm 6:9: "For they that will become rich fall into temptation and into the snare of the devil and into many unprofitable and hurtful desires which drown men into destruction and perdition."

34. ME: losable. The first recorded use of this word in O.E.D. is 1611. It clearly translates *periculosum*. Bernard says that it is of no value to know which spirit (world or flesh or devil) speaks, while what is said is equally dangerous (*periculosum*).

35. The original is more interested to distinguish man's spirit from the evil spirit than to distinguish the three evil spirits—of devil, world, and flesh. There is no equivalent in the English for the following: "If it is the enemy, resist the enemy manfully; if it is your own spirit, argue with him, bitterly complain that he has landed you in this miserable plight."

36. In the "Letter on Prayer," the English author quotes with approval St. Thomas's definition of devotion—"the readiness of man's will to do what belongs to the service of God" (cf. *infra*).

37. If carnal thoughts rob us of our desire of devotion, worldly thoughts

rob us of devotion itself. Bernard says elsewhere that devotion fills the soul with joy, sweetness and gentleness (*sermo in Circumcisione*, P.L. 183, 140–41). Hugh of St. Victor tells us that devotion enflames the spirit and guides the soul to pure prayer in the ardor of charity (*De modo orandi*, 2, P.L. 176, 980). Richard in fact identifies devotion with contemplation. Ecstasy "comes to pass through exaltation of devotion" (cf. Kirchberger, *Beniamin Maior*, pp. 189ff.).

38. A medieval Dionysian reference to angelic hierarchical activity that is repeated by the author in "Private Direction" (cf. *infra*). The immediate source is perhaps Hugh of St. Victor's commentary *Expositie in Hierarchia Coelesti S. Dionysii* IX (P.L. 175, 1087ff.). The angels as the lowest order in the nine heavenly choirs communicate to us the divine illumination (1089 D). They minister to us, "reduce for us the fulness of his illumination" (1094 A).

39. Cf. Mt 6:5. Hugh of St. Victor says that there are those who out of self-love love themselves more than God and seek their own glory, and are thus deprived of the divine knowledge (ibid., 1092, A–C). There is no contemplation in the strict sense except by the ministration of angels; but man is still free to accept or reject God's gifts (1092–3).

40. This distinction between contemplation and devotion is made neither by St. Bernard nor the Victorines, Hugh or Richard; for devotion is the perfection of prayer. Richard underlines the intellectual role of devotion: it discerns and judges all things (*De eruditione hominis interioris*, P.L. 196, 1259 B). The English author is clearly referring to the dark contemplation that is the work of the *Cloud*.

41. Cf. "Inward Stirrings" on choosing and loving the best, which is God, where the Dionysian antithesis is elaborated.

42. Examples of this typical English style and vocabulary—lively . . . lovely, good and gracious, own dear self—are frequent in "Private Direction": cf., e.g., *infra*.

43. Vulgate Ps 75:3: *Et factus est in pace locus eius, et habitatio eius in Sion.* The *locus classicus* for the traditional rendering of Jerusalem/Sion as "vision of peace" is Augustine on Ps 64:2. *Te decet hymnus, Deus, in Sion:* "Jerusalem is interpreted vision of peace . . . the fatherland is Sion. Jerusalem and Sion are the same. As Jerusalem is interpreted vision of peace, so Sion is sight (*speculatio*): that is, vision or contemplation. . . . It is God himself who founded the city" (P.L. 36:774).

44. "Jerusalem is as much as to say a sight of peace and betokeneth contemplation in perfect love of God. For contemplation is nought else but a sight of God, which is very peace" (Hilton, *Scale II*, 21; Underhill, p. 305). Our author's source is rather Augustine. There is a distinction between *contemplatio* and *speculatio*, which is love translated "thought." Cf. Introduction, *supra*.

45. An earlier version of the Isaiah (66:2—Vulgate) reads: "Upon whom shall I turn my gaze, except on the humble and restful" (*nisi humilem et quietum*). St. Jerome notes that this is the Septuagint reading, as opposed to the

THE DISCERNMENT OF SPIRITS

Latin *nisi ad pauperculum et contritum spiritum*. In any case, the author has conflated this with another text of Isaiah—11:2: "And the Spirit of the Lord shall rest upon him: the spirit of wisdom and understanding." However, the last image of Isaiah remains uppermost: "Rejoice with Jerusalem, and be glad with her, all you that love her: rejoice for joy with her . . . be filled from the breasts of her consolation . . . behold I will bring upon her as it were a river of peace, and as an overflowing torrent the glory of the Gentiles" (66:10–12).

46. A summary of the *Cloud's* teaching on the "third" life, of dark contemplation, the best, "which is begun in this life and shall last without end" (*ed. cit.* ch. 8, p. 137). Cf. also "Private Direction"—"This simple and delightful exercise, which is in fact the high wisdom of the Godhead descending through grace into man's soul, knitting it and uniting it to himself" (*infra*).

47. St. Bernard takes the thoughts and temptations of the three spirits together: "Let us consider how to put down the suggestions of those malicious (*malignorum*) spirits from the sight of our heart," and likens them to the Babylonian children of Ps 136:9, who are to be dashed against the rock. The English author grades the thoughts, but omits the unpleasant image.

48. Bernard begins his next sermon with a recapitulation of "yesterday's on the discernment of spirits" (P.L. 186, 603). The author here inserts two paragraphs based on it.

49. Bernard's short comment on 2 Cor 11:14 is followed exactly in the English: "From time to time that wicked and malignant Spirit transforms himself into an angel of light, that he might do more harm under the color of virtue."

50. The doctrine finds its origin, in the West, in Cassion: "The devil . . . tries to achieve our downfall by the attractive nature of vices or by secret ambush seeking to present evil under the color of the good with all his cunning and transferring himself before our eyes into an angel of light" (*Coll.* 1, 19).

51. "There commeth the wicked one, and catcheth away that which was sown in the heart . . . and he that receiveth the word with joy is he that received the seed upon stony ground . . . and when there ariseth tribulation he is presently scandalized . . . his enemy came and oversowed cockle among the wheat . . . the enemy that sowed them is the devil" (Mt 13:3–41).

52. The association of holiness, and more particularly diabolical trickery, with penitential and ascetical practices is an important theme in the *Cloud* (cf. *ed. cit.*, chs. 45–46; 52–53), and the preoccupation of "Inward Stirrings" (*infra*). For Bernard, however, exterior penance—and only fasting is cited—is simply an example of a singularity that occasions scandal.

53. Cf. the *Cloud*, *ed. cit.*, ch. 30 (p. 178)—"Who should judge and reprehend other mens' faults."

54. Latin: *singularia*. Like the English "singular", the noun is indifferent. The English author qualifies it with the epithet "unseemly."

121

55. ME: devoute congregacioun. In "Inward Stirrings," the author, in condemning these same singularities, makes an exception for those "performed by religious or those upon whom they are enjoined by way of penance" (cf. *infra*). The "devout congregation" is thus not a religious order as such, though it could quite easily refer to a local religious community. As the *Cloud* insists, one of the common temptations among "young disciples in God's school" is "disordered and unseemly behavior"—*ed. cit.*, chs. 51–53, pp. 218ff.

56. St. Bernard speaks of the divine wisdom enabling man to seek the chaste and the peaceful (Jas 3:17); the translator underlines human folly to which the true and simple are prone: the deceptions which are the darts of the most wicked one (Eph 6:11, 16).

57. "God resisteth the proud, but to the humble he giveth grace . . . your adversary the devil goeth about seeking whom he may devour" (1 Pt 5:5–10).

58. The translator returns to Bernard's *Sermo* 23. The same notion occurs in *The Ladder:* "As in fleshly works a man is overwhelmed that he loses all the guidance of his reason, and becomes wholly fleshly . . . " (p. 89).

59. ME: bacbiting and deming and ivel surpecian of other—an elaboration on the Latin text, which merely says "the soul itself brings to birth voluptuous, vain or bitter thoughts."

60. "the other three," i.e., the spirit of the flesh, of the world, and of wickedness.

61. Again the translator alludes to the key text from 1 Pt 5: "You young men be subject to the elders"—the spiritual fathers "all show humility to each other" (v. 5), and resist the adversary (v. 8).

62. "And ought not this daughter of Abraham, whom Satan hath bound, be loosed from this bondage?" (Lk 13:16).

63. ME: Schrive thee: It is the constant teaching of the *Cloud* author that if direction—the *sine qua non* of discernment, particularly in the contemplative life—is to be profitable, it must be preceded by sacramental confession.

64. "For sin seduced me. . . . Unhappy that I am, who shall deliver me from the body of this death? The grace of God . . . " (Rom 7:11, 24–25).

65. So Richard of St. Victor: "Let the discernment of these spirits be known by means of which the devout soul may judge and assess all things" (*Explicatio in Cantica Canticorum*, ch. XVII P.L. 196, 457). The grace of which the English author speaks here is not properly the grace of discernment. Cf. Introduction, *supra*.

66. Exactly the same phrase occurs in the "Letter on Prayer," where the context is also discernment—cf. *infra*.

67. To use a later terminology, there are those who possess the infused grace of discernment—the gift to which Paul refers: "To another is given by the Spirit . . . discerning of spirits" (1 Cor 12:10). Western spiritual writers generally follow Gregory the Great in restricting the numbers of those so endowed to "holy men who discern by an inward sense (*intimo sapore*) visions and locutions from illusions" (*Dialogues* IV, 48; cf. Introduction, *su-*

pra.). Great importance is attached to acquiring through prayer and study the art of discernment for one's own spiritual proofs, as here and, in the case of spiritual directors, for that of others.

68. This passage makes it clear that the translator, while distinguishing between the role of the spiritual director and the confessor, sees the two roles as one; this is especially true of interior temptations and the thoughts of the heart.

69. He gives the reason for this below, with his image of the "clene paper leef" (*infra*).

70. "No one can keep absolutely clear of venial sin in this mortal life. However, carelessness in venial sin should always be avoided by all true disciples of perfection" (*Cloud, ed. cit.*, ch. 11, p. 144).

71. The thoughts and impulses that are temptations to sin, says the *Cloud* author, we are to work earnestly to destroy; the inference is that such work is meritorious, as here.

72. The English author echoes what he writes in "Inward Stirrings" on the text "Blessed is the man who bears temptation patiently for when he has been proved, he shall receive the crown of life" (Jas 1:12; cf. *infra*).

73. The author enunciates the fundamental principle for recognizing and rejecting what are commonly called scruples—to reckon something as sinful that is no sin. Ignatius Loyola makes the point that here we have, not scruples in the strict sense, but an erroneous judgment (*Exx* 346).

74. Here we have the underlying distinction between a coarse and a delicate conscience. This principle is equally important for discernment, and the example is simple and clear.

75. The tempter is one of the principal names of the devil throughout the Western tradition, and the entire Christian life, for many of the Fathers, is seen as a battle against him. Augustine calls him "the prince of all sin" (*Ennarratio in Ps.* 58, 5).

76. "Whoever commits sin is the slave of sin" (Jn 8:34); ". . . you were the slaves of sin . . . but now being made free from sin, and slaves to God, you have your fruit unto sanctification, and the end, life everlasting" (Rom 6:20–23).

77. Cf. the identical passage in the *Cloud, ed. cit.*, ch. 29: ". . . some that are now wicked sinners will take their rightful place in his sight with the saints" (pp. 177–78).

78. The contemplative for whom this little disquisition is written will be well on his guard against any form of lax moral behavior. He is much more likely to err in the other direction. Ignatius Loyola quotes Gregory the Great: "It belongs to the good souls to acknowledge a fault where there is no fault at all" (*Exx* 348).

79. The last part of the treatise, which shows no dependence on St. Bernard, is the English author's teaching on the formation of conscience, derived from some source such as the Cistercian *Tractatus de interiori domo seu de conscientia aedificanda* (P.L. 184, 507ff.; cf. Introduction, *supra.*).

80. Cf. Eccl 38:19: "For of sadness comes death, and it overwhelmeth the

strength, and the sorrow of the heart." . . . Despair, particularly among religious, was a common malady.

81. "For our glory is thus," says St. Paul, "the testimony of our conscience, that in simplicity of heart and sincerity of God, and not in carnal wisdom but in the grace of God, we have lived in this world" (1 Cor 1:13).

82. Doubtless the author has in mind considerations such as those of the English writer of the *Ancrene Riwle*, who instructs his audiences at great length on a true or proper confession: It must be accusatory, bitter, integral, unadorned, frequent, speedy, humble, made with shame, fear, and hope, prudent, truthful, made willingly and unasked, with a purpose of amendment, with diligent preparation (Salu, *Ancrene Riwle*, pp. 133–53).

83. The author seems hardly concerned to distinguish between God's action on the soul and that of the angels; nor does he mention guardian angels here. The angels' role as spiritual guide never ceases to be stressed, teaching souls the knowledge of divine things (Origen, *In Num*, 14).

84. "I will plant my law deep within them; I will write it on their hearts. . . . I will forgive their iniquity and will remember their sin no more" (Jer 31:33–34).

85. Cf. the *Ancrene Riwle:* "Confession washes from us all our impurities, for thus it is written, 'All things are washed by confession. . . . Confession shall make man just as he was before he sinned, as clean and as fair and as rich in all the good that belongs to the soul' " (Salu, p. 134).

86. Among the traditional reasons God allows us to be tempted is "that we may recognize our own frailty, our great lack of strength" (Salu, *Ancrene Riwle*, p. 103).

87. Bad habit is offered as a powerful reason for frequent and speedy confession. The *Ancrene Riwle* cites Augustine: "With what difficulty does he rise upon whom there presses the weight of sinful habit" (Salu, p. 145).

88. "Confession has many powers . . . it confounds the devil, cuts off his head, and puts his army to rout. Confession washes us of all our impurities, gives back to us all that we had lost, and makes us children of God" (Salu, *Ancrene Riwle*, p. 133).

89. Cf. the capital text in Hebrews (5:14)—"the perfect: who customably have their sense exercised to the discerning of good and evil."

90. ME: wilful pouert: sc. the evangelical counsel and the profession a religious makes of it.

91. This sentence is lifted from Bernard's sermon, though the list of salutary virtues in *De discretione spirituum* reads differently. Bernard has: "of chastising the body, humbling the heart, preserving the virtue of patience, showing charity to the brethren or acquiring conserving and increasing the rest of the virtues" (P.L. 186, 602 B).

92. "Let us therefore, as many as are perfect, be thus minded, there are many whose mind is on earthly things. But our dwelling . . . is in heaven . . . we look for the Savior, our Lord Jesus Christ. He will reform these lowly bodies of ours, making them into the image of his glorified body" (Phil 3:14–21).

The Assessment of Inward Stirrings

Translator's Introduction

One of the perennial questions asked about the *Assessment of Inward Stirrings* (or Impulses) that has never been answered to anyone's satisfaction is whether the epistolary form is genuine or conventional. Of the seven works left us by the author—and this includes the great *Cloud of Unknowing* itself—we can speak only of the specifically literary nature of three: *The Mystical Theology*, the *Pursuit of Wisdom*, and the *Discernment of Spirits*. Each one can lay claim to the title of translation, though in every case it must be said that nomenclature is deceiving rather than revealing. The version of the famous *Mystical Theology* of the fictitious Denis the Areopagite is a paraphrase of a paraphrase (or two paraphrases) with the translator's own additions and idiosyncratic variants on another man's interpretations, in which none of the several hands, if they know, believe it important that the work was originally written not in Latin but in Greek.[1] The treatise drawn from one of the sermons *De Diversis* in the *Discernment of Spirits* by Bernard of Clairvaux retains a certain closeness to its original, and is sparing with its additions.[2] The third rendering, from Richard of St. Victor's *Benjamin Minor*, which has for subtitle in the Latin *De Praeparatione Animi ad Contemplationem*, ("The preparation of the Soul for Contemplation") and which the English translator entitles *A Treatise of the Pursuit of Wisdom, called Benjamin*, is a reasonably faithful précis of its original, but the translator is in no way concerned to treat the Latin according to the proportions given it by the author, whether by way of brevity or prolixity.[3]

The letters are in another category altogether. Even the *Cloud* itself

127

begins on a highly intimate note, and thus, apart from its prologue which stresses at great length that it is addressed to all and sundry,[4] as long as the reader is able to understand it,[5] will take the trouble to read it with attention from beginning to end,[6] has some ability to read works on contemplation and a real possibility of practicing prayer proper to the solitary life;[7] and finally is ready, according to the tradition concerning the perusal of treatises on the spiritual life, to give the author the benefit of the doubt in every case. *Private Direction* defines prayer as reverent affection,[8] and the *Cloud* itself, "that privy love put." It is also in the *Cloud* that we are told that the *Mystical Theology* will help to elucidate certain difficulties that may present themselves in the former work;[9] nor would we be captious in concluding that the author of the *Cloud* and of the *Pursuit of Wisdom* are one and the same.[10] The same can reasonably be added of *Discernment of Spirits*, though this is a question of entirely internal evidence.[11]

In the case of the *Letter of Private Direction*, the *explicit* of an important manuscript—Douce 262—informs us that the author and the addressee are the same as those of the *Cloud*.[12] The relationship between the *Letter on Prayer* and the *Pursuit of Wisdom* has been shown to be very close, while there are over twenty analogues in *Inward Stirrings* with the *Cloud* itself and three or four with *Private Direction*.[13] None of this, however, says any more than a unity of authorship, and really has nothing to offer concerning an addressee. The question still remains whether the disciple was a conventional imaginary "novice" of a contemplative community or someone beginning a spiritual relationship with the *Cloud* author. The latter seems more likely.[14] However, if this is so, the literary quality of this letter, as of the rest of the *Cloud* corpus, is extraordinary. The grammatical and syntactical care of its composition, as well as its easy use of the *colores* of the rhetoric of the author's time,[15] lifts it into the category of those English authors who did employ the letter form not only to develop their material but consciously to declare the excellence of the language.[16]

The Relationship between the Author and Addressee

If we accept, as most students of the *Cloud* corpus do, that the author was addressing a real disciple, whose status in the religious life, as far as the *Cloud* and *Private Direction* are concerned, is fixed,[17] and whose age is twenty-four at the time the *Cloud* was addressed to him,[18] then the first question with which we are concerned is what of the man or men to whom *Prayer* and *Inward Stirrings* are offered. Both have the same form of address: "Goostly freend in God"; and the same *envoi*, "in the name of Jesu. Amen." Both plunge *in medias res*, apart from the brief invocatory blessing in *Inward Stirrings*, "that same grace and ioye that I wil to myself I wil to thee at Godes wile."[19] In *Inward Stirrings*, however, the author makes much of the fact that his acquaintance with his correspondent is recent and of a limited kind: "Your interior dispositions and the sort of schooling you have had for the practices you mention in your letter are not yet as fully known to me as it would be expedient for them to be in order that I might give you solid advice on this matter."[20] It would appear more than reasonable to argue that *Prayer* was addressed to the same man as the *Cloud* itself and *Private Direction;*[21] but not, however, *Inward Stirrings*. The author says in the former letter that he is determined to become the spiritual counselor of the addressee.[22] There appears to be no such desire in *Inward Stirrings;* in fact, the author voices his suspicions that his correspondent is not as adept as he might be in discerning on the evidence of his own dispositions.[23] On the other hand, there are indications enough that the addressee is known to the author as a contemplative of no mean standing. He writes to one who is in the way of perfection, and ripe for dark contemplation of him "who cannot be found by any work of your soul, but only by the love of your heart . . . he can be loved and chosen by the true and loving desire of your heart. Choose him then."[24]

The Contemplative Penitent

Julian of Norwich has much to say about a class of contemplatives who are known as penitents. She is shown a procession of them, headed by David, St. Peter, St. Thomas of India, and St. Mary Magdalen,[25] who figures so largely in the *Cloud.*[26] So the author uses the celebrated image of the "sely schip" to designate "any sinner that came to the perfect knowing of himself,"[27] "the poor soul" which comes at last to dry land and a safe harbor.[28] He takes it for granted, as well, that his correspondent is well versed, like himself—and unlike the addressee of the *Cloud*—in the Latin of the Vulgate;[29] and it is also accepted that he is trained in medieval exegesis; for the author with his *Beatus Vir* text offers him the anagogical and tropological meanings, as well as the allegorical.[30] The composite meaning, applied to the addressee, that of "a sinful man [the penitent, who] has been proved by various trials in rising and falling, the one by grace, the other by frailty, he shall never in this life receive from God the spirit of wisdom, which is the clear knowing of himself and his inward dispositions; nor full discernment in teaching and directing other souls; nor the third gift which is the perfection of virtue in the love of God and his neighbor."[31]

An educated addressee

Quid credas, allegoria	(the allegorical sense: what you must believe)
moralis, quid agas	(the moral sense: how you are to behave)
Quo tendas, anagogia	(the anagogical sense: where you should be going)

The author gently insinuates that the addressee, when he finally receives wisdom, discernment, and the perfection of virtue in God's love, will be able to direct himself to the perfect love of God, which is the highest or anagogical meaning of Scripture. Not only does the word point whither it is that the sinner makes his pilgrimage; it is also the crown of life here as well, that perfect patience and meekness which enables us to continue to wait on the Lord's will.[32]

The moral or tropological sense of Scripture shows us how one is to behave in the contemplative life, and this in fact is the burden of the rest of the letter. At the back of the reflection on discernment is the *ne plus sapere quam oportet* ("not to be more wise than it behoveth to be wise") of St. Paul, as we shall see later on.[33]

St. Bernard, for one, is very emphatic in his teaching about direction. He who presumes to direct himself, he says, for example, has a fool for a director.[34] The contemplative spirituals will insist that the director—one who has long experience in the solitary life—[35] be both wise and holy. There is no such thing as nondirective direction, though, as Bernard will remark, there are so few competent directors that the vast majority of contemplatives need perfect obedience.[36] Here, the author speaks of the dirigée submitting himself night and day to God and a good spiritual director, throwing himself away,[37] and martyring himself,[38] rather than following his own will with regard to these impulses. "Thoroughly test your stirrings and their origins," says the author.[39] Ultimately, then, he returns to the capital text from the first Johannine letter: "Dearly beloved, believe not every spirit, but test the spirits to see if they be of God; because many false prophets are gone out into the world."[40]

The Doctrine of Discernment

In the Christian tradition, the choices that face a man in the context of the divine will always seem to involve a certain darkness and obscurity, often imposed by an authority that one has difficulty in "reading," in which the reasons for the directives or demands are unclear. Hence the question of faith is always in the context: "For I knewe never yit no synner that myght come to the parfite knowing of himself and of his inward disposicioun, bot if he were lernid of it before in the scole of God by experience."[41] It seems that we have to take it for granted that the one who chooses sees something of mysterious value in the object of his choice: "For nowadays they who keep strict silence, unusual fasts, and who dwell in solitude are often considered to be very holy."[42] So, in the simpler approach of the Old Testament, we hear the voice of God, of Satan, of God's adversary, as in the stories of Eden, of the Flood, of Babel, and of the Golden Calf. Man often seems plunged into darkness: the darkness of God who enters on the scene without letting himself be seen; of Satan who dissimulates and suggests rather than affirms, proposes rather than imposes, proffers dreams and not the reality. Man, too, is a mystery unto himself, incapable of looking into his own heart and finding the truth, of accepting the responsibility for and the consequences of his own actions, as so often he listens to two voices. To choose seriously first demands discernment.

In the light of the Gospel and particularly Pauline teaching, the author first describes through his curial image of the wise king well able to govern his people because he can govern "himself and all his thoughts and movements in body and soul with strength, wisdom and prudence,"[43] the principles of discretion: knowledge of self, ability to direct others, and "the perfection of virtue in the love of God and his neighbor," with the simple crown and its *fleur-de-lis* as the preacher's *exemplum*.[44] As in the *Cloud*, he shows a fondness for the show-pieces of medieval life. There it was the boar-hunt and the bear-baiting;[45] here it is the antics of the monkey on the chain in the marketplace that can imitate whatever it sees its keeper doing.

Indifference, he teaches, has to do with means, not ends; and it is in the context of midday, when, as Richard of St. Victor notes, the light is stronger and the heat more intense, that the noonday devil turns himself into an angel of light.[46] So the solution of the author is to seek the mean between what can turn out to be true or false. This mean is God. As the author has already suggested when trying to forget faults and defects during the course of contemplative effort:

"Try to look over their shoulders, as it were, as though you were looking for something else: that something else is God . . . a longing desire for God, to experience him and see him as far as it may be possible here below. The desire is charity."[47]

Discernment and Charity

The paragraphs that follow, describing this discernment that leads us "to this loving choice of God" and moves *via* the *Cloud* author's trademark, the target, the bull's-eye, and the arrow, represent some of the most sincere and affective "love-talk" between God and the contemplative spirit contained in our language. This may be because our modern English has fashioned for us intelligible words that can express the feelings of affective contemplation: words whose first meanings can reach through to our loving passivity and its response:

> Soche a louely chesing of God, thus wisely lesing and seking him onto with the clene wille of a trewe herte betwix alle soche to, levyng hem bothe whan thei come and profen hem to be the poynt and the pricke of oure goostly beholding, is the worthiest trasing and sekyng of God that may be getyn or lerned in this liif. . . . For if God be thi love and thi menyng, the cheef and the pointe of thin herte, it suffiseth to thee in this liif, thof al thou se never more of him with thee iye of thi reson alle thi liif tyme. Soche a blinde schote with the scharp darte of lon-gyng love may never faile of the prik, the whiche is God.[48]

The author then moves smoothly into the medieval exegesis of the verse of the Canticle—*The Book of Love*, as he calls it, "where he spek-ith to a langwisching soul and a loving, seiing thus. . . . 'Thou hast wounded myn hert, my sistre, my lemman and my spouse.' "[49]

The Victorines, Hugh and Richard, will agree here and say that "there is more loving than understanding, and love enters where knowledge waits without." Bernard interprets the text from the Canticle as do the Victorines.[50] It is, of course, Thomas of St. Victor in his Commentaries on the Canticle who draws out the text to the same length as does the *Cloud* author, but it would not be possible here to say who it is the letter writer is following, Bernard, Richard, or *Vercellensis*, since all are at one in their interpretations.[51]

Discernment and the Contemplative Life

The author then links his response to the matter of discernment to the question of the vocation to the contemplative life. The emphasis here, with the triple quotation from St. Paul and the citation in the Vulgate Latin, makes it almost certain that he is referring to vocation in the *ex professo* sense: a professed member (or novice) of a religious community—which in the context means Benedictine, Cistercian, or Carthusian. In no sense would he refer to Mendicants as "verrey contemplatyfe."[52] In view of the fact that one of the matters about which the addressee is asking help in his discernment concerns "comoun etyng . . . and comoun wonyng in companye,"[53] this would seem to leave only the eremitical state where the anchorite is under the supervision of the local bishop.[54] In the *Cloud*, the two sisters are types of three kinds of religious life, whereas here Martha is simply introduced to identify Mary as "Martha cister." The addressee's call "is to be verrey contemplatyfe, ensaumplid by Mary." And he is admonished to do as Mary did. "Set the poynte of thin herte upon o thing . . . the whiche is God." The rest of the paragraph is constructed of balanced phrases,[55] and other rhetorical *colores* abound, including the brilliant Latin equivalent of the triplet:

Maria, inquit Optimus	(Mary, said the Best)
Optimam partem elegit	(has chosen the best part)
Que non auferetur ab ea	(which shall not be taken from her),[56]

where not only do we have three *cola* of eight syllables each, but five other figures: *adnominatio, chiasmus, compar, gradatio,* and *traductio.*[57] Small wonder that we have second thoughts about this being an ordinary run-of-the-mill letter of direction.[58]

Finally, as the notes to the text indicate, besides Aristotle and Aquinas, there are three analogs here with Cassian, Bede, Augustine, and Gregory the Great, as well as to writers nearer to the author's time and subject—Bernard, Hugh, and Richard. Here again, the *Cloud* author betrays both in the substance and context of a treatise that certainly contains *multum in parvo*, the sureness of touch and occasionally the brilliance that mark him as one of the preeminent writers of his century.

The Assessment of Inward Stirrings

My Spiritual friend in God: the same grace and joy that I wish for myself, I wish for you, according to God's will.[1]

You ask my advice about silence and about talking,[2] about following a normal diet and fasting above the ordinary,[3] about living with others and the solitary life.[4] You say that you are greatly exercised over what you should do. For, you say, your progress is hindered by talking and eating as other folk do and with ordinary life in the company of others.[4] And on the other hand, you are afraid to keep a strict silence, unusual fasts, and to live in solitude,[5] lest you be thought to be holier than you are, and because of many other dangers.[6] For nowadays they who keep strict silence, unusual fasts, and who dwell in solitude are often considered to be very holy, and fall into many perils.

It is true, of course, that these are very holy if grace alone is the cause[7] of that silence, unusual fasting, and solitary living,[8] whilst nature merely endures and gives a simple consent.[9] If the case is otherwise, there is nothing but peril on all sides. For it is very dangerous to overtax nature by any such exercise of devotion,[10] whether this involves silence or talking, following an ordinary diet, or singular fasting, living with others or in solitude—I mean going beyond what is normal and natural in any of these things—unless the soul is led by grace.[11] I am speaking of practices which are indifferent in themselves;[12] that is to say, sometimes good and sometimes evil, now for you now against you, now helping now hindering.[13] It could happen

134

that, if you followed your inward stirring toward keeping a strict silence, extraordinary fasting, or to solitude, often you might be keeping silence when it was time to speak, oftentimes to be fasting when it was time to eat, oftentimes [to be alone when] it was time to be in company. Or again, if you indulged yourself in speaking when you felt like it, or to normal eating habits or to living with companions, then, perhaps, you would sometimes be talking when it was time to be quiet, eating when it was time to be fasting, in company when it was time to be on your own. And so you could easily fall into error, to the great harm not only of your own soul but also of others.[14]

It is to avoid such errors that you ask me, as I gather from your letter, two things. First, what do I think of you and your inward stirrings; and second, what is my advice in this case, and about all such stirrings whenever they happen.[15]

As to the first, I answer and say that I am very fearful of offering my untutored opinion, such as it is, in matters such as these; and for two reasons.[16] One is this. I do not dare to lean hard upon my opinion and affirm it as certainly true. The other is this. Your interior dispositions and the sort of schooling you have had for the practices you mention in your letter are not yet as fully known to me as it would be expedient for them to be in order that I might give you solid advice on this matter.[17] As it is said by the Apostle, *Nemo novit quae sunt hominis nisi spiritus hominis qui in ipso est*—"No-one knows what are the hidden dispositions of a man except the spirit of that man which is within himself".[18]

Furthermore, perhaps you do not yet know your own inward dispositions as fully as you might, later on, when God lets you experience them by the occasion of frequent fallings and risings.[19] For I never knew any sinner that came to the perfect knowing of himself and of his inward dispositions, unless he were first apprised of it in God's school by the experience of many temptations and of many fallings and risings.[20] For just as the little ship must ride high waves, storms, and heavy seas as well as gentle winds, calm seas, and fair weather before she comes to land and harbor; even so, among the variety of temptations and tribulations which come upon a soul in the ups and downs of this life—like the ship in the storms and high waves of the sea—as well as the grace and goodness of the holy Spirit and his manifold visitations, sweet consolations, and spiritual comfort—like the ship in gentle winds and fair weather—the poor soul comes at last to dry land and a safe harbor: that is, to the clear and true knowing of himself and of all his inward dispositions.[21]

Through this knowing he rests quietly in himself, like the sovereign king in his realm, governing himself and all his thoughts and movements in body and soul with strength, wisdom, and prudence.[22]

It is of such a man that the wise man says: *Beatus vir qui suffert tentationem, quoniam cum probatus fuerit, accipiet coronam vitae Deus repromisit diligentibus se*—"He is a happy man who bears temptation patiently, for when he has been proved, he shall receive the crown of life, which God has promised to all who love him."[23] The crown of life may be interpreted in two ways. First, spiritual wisdom, true discernment, and perfection of virtue—these three fastened together may be called the crown of life, which may be achieved by grace here in this life.[24] Or, on the other hand, the crown of life may represent the endless joy which every faithful soul shall have hereafter in the happiness of heaven. But certainly no man can receive either crown unless he has been well tried beforehand in the enduring of hardship and temptation, as the text says: *Quoniam cum probatus fuerit, accipiet coronam vitae;* that is: "Once he shall have been proved, then shall he receive the crown of life."[25] This, as I said before, I believe to mean that unless a sinful man has been proved by various trials in rising and falling, the one by grace, the other by frailty, he shall never in this life receive from God the spirit of wisdom, which is the clear knowing of himself and his inward dispositions;[26] nor full discernment in teaching and directing other souls;[27] nor the third gift, which is the perfection of virtue in the love of God and his neighbor.[28]

All these three, wisdom, discernment, and perfection of virtue, make a whole, and can be called the crown of life. In a crown there are three elements:[29] Gold is the first, precious stones are the second, and turrets of the fleur-de-lis which stand up from the circlet make the third.[30] The gold represents wisdom, the precious stones discernment, and the turrets of the fleur-de-lis represent the perfection of virtue.[31] The gold encircles the head,[32] and by wisdom we order all our spiritual activities. Precious stones give light in seeing people: and by discernment we teach and direct our brethren.[33] The turrets of the fleur-de-lis are two branches on either side to the right and to the left, and a third straight up above the head: and by perfection of virtue, which is charity, we have two side branches of love, spreading out on the right to our friends, on the left to our enemies; and the third rises up to God himself, above man's understanding, which is the head of the soul.[34] This is the crown of life, which we can receive in this life by grace.

And therefore keep yourself humble in your struggle,[35] and endure your trials with meekness until you have been proved. For once

proved you shall receive either the one crown here or the other hereafter, or both the one here and the other hereafter.[36] For whoever
receives the one here is most certain to receive the other hereafter.[37]
There are many truly proven here by grace, and yet they never attain
to that which may be won in this life.[38] But if with patience and
meekness they continue to wait upon the Lord's will, they will receive it hereafter in great abundance in the bliss of heaven. Does it
seem to you that the crown that may be won here is beautiful? Well,
no matter how meekly you may live by grace, in comparison with
the heavenly, the other, it is like a single gold piece against a world
of gold.[39] I say all this to give you comfort and assurance of strength
in the spiritual contest which you have undertaken, trusting in our
Lord.

I say all this to let you see how far you still are from knowing truly
your own interior dispositions; and second to give you warning not
to surrender to nor to follow too quickly, in inexperience, the unusual movements of your heart, for fear of illusion.[40] I say all this to
explain to you what my opinion is of you and your stirrings, as you
have asked me. For I feel that you are overinclined and too eagerly
disposed toward these sudden impulses for extraordinary practices,
and very swift to seize upon them when they come. And that is very
dangerous.

I do not say that this inclination and overeagerness of yours, or of
any other person who is disposed as you are, even though it is dangerous, is evil in itself.[41] No, I would not say that; and God forbid
that you should take it so. Rather I say that it is very good in itself,
and is a very great power for very great perfection; indeed, for the
greatest perfection possible in this life. What I mean is that a soul
with this disposition must earnestly, night and day, submit itself to
God and to a good spiritual director, and bear up strongly and martyr itself, by casting away its own intelligence and its own will in all
these sudden and extraordinary stirrings, and say sharply to itself
that it will not follow these stirrings, no matter how desirable, lofty,
and holy they appear to be, unless it have the approval and consent
of spiritual teachers—I mean those who have had long experience in
the solitary life. Such a soul, by spiritual perseverance in this meekness, may deserve, through grace and the experience of this spiritual
combat with itself,[42] to win that crown of life mentioned above.

But if this kind of disposition is a great power for good in the soul
which humbles itself in the way I describe, it can be equally dangerous to another soul—one which determines to follow on the in-
stant, without any advice or direction, the stirrings of its impetuous

heart, according to its own opinion and desire. And therefore, for God's love, treat this power and disposition I speak of, if it is in you, with caution; and submit yourself constantly to prayer and direction. Break down your own opinion and desire in all these sudden and extraordinary stirrings; do not follow them too easily, until you know whence they come, and whether they are right for you or not.

You also ask my advice and counsel about the stirrings themselves. I must say that I am suspicious of them, in case they are conceived apishly. It is a common saying that the ape does as he sees others doing.[43] Please forgive me if my suspicions are ill-founded; but the love that I have for your soul moves me to voice them, through the example I learnt of a spiritual brother of yours and mine who was recently in your district. He too was moved with the same impulses to very strict silence, extraordinary fasts, and the solitary life; but apishly, as he admitted after a long talk with me, and after he had made trial of himself and his stirrings. For, he said, he had seen a person in your district—one who, as is well known, always keeps strict silence and extraordinary fasts and lives entirely alone. And certainly I have every reason to suppose that this man's stirrings are genuine, coming only from the grace which he has experienced within himself, and not from without, from what he has seen or heard of any other man's silence. If that were the cause, such impulses should, according to my simple understanding, be called apish.

Take care, then, and thoroughly test your stirrings and their origins. For whether you are being moved from within by grace or apishly from without, God knows; I do not. Yet I can tell you this, to help you avoid this sort of peril: take care that you do not behave apishly; that is to say, make sure that your stirrings to silence or to speech, to fasting or eating, to living alone or in company, come from within, out of abundance of love and spiritual devotion, and not from without, by the windows of your bodily senses—your ears and eyes. For Jeremiah says very plainly: "Death comes in by such windows"—*Mors intrat per fenestras.*[44] Short as it is, this is a sufficient answer to your first question, where you ask me what I think of you and the stirrings which you mention in your letter.

As to your second request, for my advice about these particular stirrings and similar ones when they come: I beseech almighty Jesus, under his title of Angel of Great Counsel[45], to be, of his mercy, your counselor and strengthener in all your trouble and need, and to teach me with his wisdom that I may to some extent justify by my teaching, simple as it is, the trust of your heart, that you have in me above

138

many another, simple ignorant wretch that I am, unworthy to teach you or anyone else, for littleness of grace and lack of understanding.[46] But still, however great my ignorance, I shall say something in answer to your request, as far as my simple understanding permits, trusting in God that his grace will be the teacher and leader, when common sense and theological learning are wanting.

You are well aware yourself that neither silence nor speaking, extraordinary fasting nor ordinary diet, solitary living nor company— none of these in themselves nor all of them are the true end of our desire.[47] But they are to some men, though not to all, true means which help to the end, as long as they are used lawfully and with discernment; otherwise they are more a hindrance than a help.[48] Hence I do not intend to counsel you here simply to speak or to be silent, simply to fast or to eat, simply to live in company or alone. And why? Because perfection does not lie in any of these.[49] But I can give you some general advice which you may follow with regard to these and all other similar stirrings, wherever you find two contraries[50] such as are silence and speaking, fasting and eating, living alone and in company, the common dress of christian religious,[51] and the special habits which distinguish different brotherhoods, and all other such contraries whatever they are; for in themselves they are simply human, natural activities. For it is according to nature and to the law of the exterior man, now to speak and now to be silent, now to eat and now to fast, now to be in company and now alone, now to wear ordinary dress and now a special habit—whenever you wish and when you see that any of these are expedient and helpful to you for the increase of the heavenly grace working inwardly in your soul; unless you or anyone else should be so stupid or so blinded (which God forbid!) by the distressing temptations of the noonday devil as to bind yourselves by any crooked vow to any such singularity, as it were under color of a holiness which feigns such a holy thraldom.[52] This would be the full and final destruction of the freedom of Christ, which is the spiritual garb of the highest holiness possible in this life or the next, as St. Paul witnesses when he says: *Ubi spiritus Domini, ibi libertas*—"Where the Spirit of God is, there is freedom".[53]

When then you see that all these things can be both good and evil in their use, I beg you to leave them both alone; that is the easiest thing to do if you wish to be humble. And leave off this detailed introspection and searching of your mind to find out which is better. Rather do this. Set them both aside, one here and one there, and choose for yourself something which is hidden between them. When you once have this third thing, it will permit you to take up and to leave aside either of the other two in freedom of spirit, at your own good pleasure, without incurring any fault.[54]

And now you ask what this third thing is. I shall tell you what I understand it to be. It is God. For him you must be silent, if you are to be silent; for him you must speak, if you are to speak; for him you must fast, if you are to fast; for him you must eat, if you are to eat; for him you must be solitary if you are to be solitary; for him you must be in company if you are to be in company; and so for all the rest, whatever they be. For silence is not God, nor is speaking God; fasting is not God, nor is eating God; being alone is not God, nor is company God, nor yet any one of every such pair of contraries. He is hid between them; and he cannot be found by any work of your soul, but only by the love of your heart. He cannot be known by reason. He cannot be thought, grasped, or searched out by the understanding. But he can be loved and chosen by the true and loving desire of your heart.[55] Choose him then, and you are silent in speaking and speaking in silence; fasting in eating and eating in fasting; and so with all the rest.

This loving choice of God, which is attentively to gather him up and seek him out with the true will of a clean heart from between all such contraries—so that when they come and offer themselves as the target, the bull's-eye of our spiritual gaze,[56] we leave them aside; this is the best searching and seeking for God that one may have or learn in this life—I speak of those who would be contemplatives.[57] And this is true even if the person who makes this search sees nothing that can be conceived with the spiritual eye of reason. For if God is your love and your intent, the choice and the ground of your heart, this is enough for you in this life; even though you never see more of him with the eye of reason all your life long.[58] Such a blind shot with the sharp arrow of a love that longs can never miss the bull's-eye, which is God.[59] He himself says in the Book of Love, where he is speaking to a soul languishing with love: *Vulnerasti cor meum, soror mea, amica mea, sponsa mea, vulnerasti cor meum in uno oculorum tuorum*—"You have wounded my heart, my sister, my beloved, my bride; you have wounded my heart in one of your eyes."[60] There are two eyes of the soul, reason and love.[61] By reason we may search out how mighty, how wise, and how good God is in his creatures, but not in himself.[62] But whenever reason falls short, then it is love's pleasure to look alive and to learn to occupy itself.[63] For by love we can find him, experience him, and reach him, as he is in himself. It is a high and wonderful love, when our Lord says of the loving soul: "You have wounded my heart with one of your eyes"; that is, with the love that is blind to many things and sees only the one thing that it seeks. And thus it finds and experiences, hits and pierces the target and the bull's-eye at which it aims, much sooner than it would if its sight were distracted by looking at many things,[64] as it is when reason ransacks and seeks among all these various things such as silence and speaking, extraordinary fasting and normal diet, living alone and in company, in order to find out which is better.

I pray you, then, to leave this kind of activity and conduct yourself as though you did not know that there were any such means—for reaching God, that is. And truly no more are there, if you would be a genuine contemplative and achieve your purpose quickly.[65] And so I pray you and everyone like you, as the Apostle does when he says: *Videte vocationem vestram, et in ea vocatione qua vocati estis, state*—"Consider your calling, and stand firmly in the state to which you have been called,"[66] and abide in it in the name of Jesus. Your calling is to be a true contemplative, after the pattern of Mary, Martha's sister. Do then as Mary did; set the fine point of your heart on one thing.[67] *Porro unum est necessarium*—"For one thing is necessary," and this is God. Him you would have; him you would seek; him you desire to love. Him you wish to experience; him you would live by; and not by silence nor by speaking, by extraordinary fasting nor a normal diet, by solitary living nor living in company. For sometimes silence is good, and at that same time, speaking would be better; and again, sometimes speaking is good, but at that same time silence would be better. And so with all the rest, fasting, eating, solitary living, and living in company; for sometimes the one is good, but the other is better. Neither of them is ever the best.[68] And therefore leave the good with all that is good and the better with all that is better; for both will decay and have an end. And choose the best, with Mary for your mirror; it will never perish. *Maria, inquit, optimus, optimam elegit, quae non auferetur ab ea*[69]—the best is almighty Jesus, and he said that Mary, the type of all contemplatives, had chosen the best, which would never be taken from her. And therefore I pray you, leave the good and the better, and choose with Mary the best.[70]

Let be, then, all such things as these—silence and speaking, fasting and eating, solitary living and company and the rest, and take no heed of them. You do not know what they mean, and, I pray you, do not desire to know.[71] And if you must at any time think or speak of them, then think and say that they are such high and noble means to perfection—this knowing when to speak and when to be silent, when to fast and when to eat, when to be alone and when to be in company, that it would be folly and wicked presumption in such a weak wretch as yourself to meddle with matters of so great perfection.[72] Because to speak and to be silent, to eat and to fast, and to be alone and to be in company whenever we will—all this we can do by our natural powers; but to know how to do them, this we cannot except by grace.

And without doubt, such grace is never obtained by way of the strict silence, extraordinary fasting, or the solitary living of which you speak, if these are suggested from without, by hearing and seeing such singular behavior in another person. If this grace is ever to be won, it must be taught from within, of God,[73] when you have yearned longingly after him for many a day with all the love of your heart, and by emptying out from your inward beholding every sight of anything beneath him;[74] and this even though some of those things that I bid you empty out should seem in the sight of some to be very worthy means whereby to come to God.[75] Let men say what they like; you must do as I tell you, and let experience be your witness. For to him who wishes to achieve his spiritual purpose, the actual awareness of the good God alone suffices as the means along with a reverent stirring of lasting love. He needs no other. Have, then, no means for coming to God except God himself,[76] and if you keep intact your stirring of love and do not dissipate your inward beholding,[77] you may experience it in your heart by grace.

And then your heart's experience will know well how to tell you when to speak and when to be silent. It will guide you with discernment in all your living without error, and teach you in mystical manner how you are to begin and leave off in all your natural doings with a great and perfect discernment.[78] And if, by grace, you can make a habit of this loving awareness and exercise yourself in it constantly, then, if you need to speak, follow a normal diet, or dwell in company, or do anything else that belongs to the good and common custom of human nature and Christian men, it will first gently move you to speak or to do the ordinary natural thing, whatever it is.[79] And if you fail to do it, this awareness will wound you as sorely and painfully as if your heart were pierced, and let you have no peace until you do it.[80] And in the same way, if you happen to be speaking or doing anything else that belongs to normal human activity, and it is necessary and profitable to you to be still and set yourself to the contrary, such as fasting in place of eating, living alone instead of in company, and all other such works of singular holiness, this loving awareness will move you to do these.

Thus, by experience of this blind stirring of love for God, the contemplative will arrive at the grace of discernment, in the matter of speaking and being silent, eating and fasting, living in company and alone, and so on; and that much sooner than by the peculiarities of which you speak, whether the motivation is from within, by the stirrings of man's own reason and will, or outwardly by the example of other men's activity, whatever it be. Because such ascetical practices,[81] when occasioned by natural stirrings and not by those of grace, are most painful, and at the same time profitless, unless they are performed by religious or by those upon whom they are enjoined by way of penance;[82] in which case there is profit because of obedience[83] and not because of the austerity of the external practices, which are painful to all who experience them. But to desire lovingly and with eager longing to have God brings great and surpassing ease, true spiritual peace, and an earnest of everlasting rest.

And therefore speak when you like and leave off when you like; eat when you like and fast when you like; be in company when you like and by yourself when you like—as long as God and his grace are your directors. Let them fast who so wish, and live solitary, and keep silence. But you, have God as your guide, who leads no one astray. Silence and speaking, fasting and eating, living solitary and in company—all these can beguile us. And if you hear of any man who speaks or is silent, of any who eat or fast who live in company or by themselves, then think and say, if you will, that they know how to act as they ought, unless the contrary is clearly proven. But take care not to do as they do; I mean apishly, just because they do so. For either you are unable to do so, or perhaps their dispositions are not yours. And therefore avoid acting according to other men's dispositions; but act according to your own, insofar as you can discover what they are. And until such time as you can discover what they are, act according to the advice of those who know their own dispositions; but not according to their dispositions. Only such men should give counsel in these cases, and no one else. This should be answer enough to all your letter.

May the grace of God be with you always, in the name of Jesus. Amen.

Notes

Introduction

1. Though the *Cloud* author knew Sarracenus's Latin translation, and presumably its prologue, in which John speaks of a search in Greece for Dionysian MSS (*Si forte per illum vestrum monachum qui in Greciam profectus esse dicitur ipsam et alios libros . . . obtinueritis*) and tells us that *mistica* is a translation of *mio*, it still remains possible that the English translator was unaware that Sarracenus was speaking of a Greek text. Cf. Théry, *Thomas Gallus*, p. 8.

2. Cf. *supra*.

3. For example, the Victorine's disquisition on the aversion from sin and the sense of shame occupies fourteen columns in the Migne edition. The English author deals with the same material in six short paragraphs. Cf. *supra*.

4. *"To you, whoever you are, who may have this book in your possession"* (*The Cloud*, ed. cit., p. 101).

5. "He will be one who is doing all that he can . . . to fit himself for the contemplative life" (ibid., p. 102).

6. " . . . take time to read it . . . right through" (ibid.).

7. " . . . those whose state belongs to the active life . . . are enabled by an abundance of grace to share in the work of contemplation at the highest level; not of course continually . . . but every now and then" (ibid., p. 103).

8. "This . . . is that reverent affeccion . . . the cloude of unknowyng . . . the Arke of the Testament. This is Denis devinite, his wisdom and his drewry, his lighty derknes and his unknowyn cunnyngs" ("Private Direction," *infra*).

9. " . . . whoever cares to examine the works of Denis, will find that his

144

words clearly corroborate all that I have said or am going to say" (The *Cloud*, *ed. cit.*, p. 256).

10. Most clearly, perhaps, in the *Cloud*'s disquisition on the principal and secondary powers of the soul, chs. 63–66. Cf. *supra*.

11. In *Discretion*, the image of treading down underfoot is used, verbally and conceptually. Cf. *supra*.

12. "Here followeth the Epistle of Private Counsel, the which dependeth upon the Cloud and of the self Cloud's making." Cf. McCann's edition, p. 101. For a description of this MS and its importance, cf. *infra*, Appendix.

13. Cf. *infra*, nn. 5, 8, 24, 28, 34, 39, 43, 47, 49, 50, 55, 57, 58, 64, 65, 67, 68, 74, 77, 78, 79, 80.

14. The cautious way in which the author couches his doctrine on discernment and applies it to the addressee adds a note of veracity to the letter, as does the greeting: "Goostly freend in God, that same grace and ioie that I will to myself I wil to thee at Godes wile."

15. Cf. P.H. "Denis's Hidden Theology," *infra*, pp. xlvii–lvi.

16. We have noted the quality of the descriptive writing and the free use of the rhetorician's *colores*.

17. Cf. the description of the four states of the Christian life—ordinary, special, singular, and perfect, in ch. 1 of the *Cloud*, *ed. cit.*, pp. 115–17.

18. Cf. the *Cloud*, *ed. cit.*, ch. 4, pp. 124–25.

19. *Infra*.

20. *Infra*.

21. "For this same werk, if it be verrely conceyvid, is that reverent affeccion . . . that I speke of in thi lityl pistle of preier" (*Private Direction*, P.H. p. 154).

22. "I make no secret, as you see, of the fact that I want to be your spiritual father" ("Private Direction," *infra*).

23. "I say all this to let you see how far you still are from knowing truly your own interior dispositions; and secondly to give you warning not to surrender to nor to follow too quickly the unusual movements of your heart" (*supra*).

24. *Supra*.

25. " . . . and then there came truly to my mind David, Peter and Paul, Thomas of India and Mary Magdalen, how they are known, with their sins, to their honour in the Church" (*Showings*, ch. 17, p. 154).

26. Cf. the *Cloud*, *ed. cit.*, chs. 16–23.

27. *Infra*, nn. 19–20.

28. Ibid., nn. 21–22.

29. In the *Cloud* itself, the author never cites from the Latin Vulgate, and this is also true of the *Pursuit of Wisdom*, *Hidden Theology*, and *Discernment of Spirits*. Of the remaining three treatises, it may be argued that they were written later than the rest, when the opposition to the Lollard translations was intensifying, particularly in ecclesiastical circles. Cf. the *Cloud*, *ed. cit.*, p. 11, where another opinion is advanced.

THE ASSESSMENT OF INWARD STIRRINGS

30. On the medieval exegesis, cf. also the *Cloud, ed. cit.*, pp. 67–68.

31. *Infra.*

32. The *Cloud, ed. cit.*, pp. 148, 150.

33. Cf. Rom 12:3.

34. *Qui se sibi magistrum, constituit stulto se discipulum subdit. Epistolae* 87, 7; P.L. 182, 215.

35. The author repeats elsewhere, particularly in "Private Direction," that fitness for the contemplative exercise always depends on Scripture, the spiritual director, and the individual's conscience; and further, that the director himself be practiced in dark contemplation. Cf. "Private Direction."

36. Cf. Sermo III In Circumcisione Domini, 11; P.L. 183, 142.

37. "For soche a soule, thus loveliche naughtyng itself, and thus heely allyng his God" ("Private Direction"). The scriptural allusion is clearly Phil 2:7: ". . . he emptied himself." Julian of Norwich uses the same word and image. There seems no doubt that the word entered the language through spiritual writing. The O.E.D.'s first example of the verb *nought* is Hilton, the Latin verb being *adnihilare.* Cf. *Book of Showings*, Short text, ch. 5, p. 216.

38. The reference is to the martyrdom of the schoolboys Justus and Pastor at Alcalà. Their feast is commemorated in the Roman Martyrology for 6 August. We read in "Private Direction"—ME: thei kasten here instrumentes . . . children here tables in the scole, and ronnen . . . to the martirdom. The literal translation of the Martyrology reads: "At Alcalà in Spain, the feast of the holy martyrs Justus and Pastor who, whilst they were still children learning their letters, threw down their tablets in school and ran to their martyrdom."

39. ME: prove wel thi sterrynges and whens thei come.

40. I Jn 4:1.

41. Cf. *infra.*

42. ME: For oft-tymes now thees dayes, thei ben demid for most holy and fallen into many periles, that most aren in silence, in singulere fastyng and in only dwellyng.

43. ME: mightly, wisely and goodly governing himself and all his thoughtes and sterynges, both in body and in soule. The triple adverb would naturally be read by a contemporary as trinitarian, might (for the Father), wisdom (for the Son), goodness (for the Holy Spirit). In fact, the image is strikingly like the description given by Julian of Norwich of the Indwelling, where she writes: "In the midst of that city sits our Lord Jesus . . . most awesome king. . . . He sits erect there in the soul, in peace and rest, and he rules and guards heaven and earth, and everything that is. The humanity and the divinity sit at rest . . . and the soul is wholly occupied by the blessed divinity, sovereign power, sovereign wisdom and sovereign goodness" (*Showings*, ch. 68, p. 313).

44. Note that the first meaning of *ensaumple*, the noun, is derived from the Latin *exemplum*, the preacher's or orator's "citing of something done or said in the past, along with the definite naming of the doer or author" (Ca-

plan, *Cicero*, p. 383). But by the end of the fourteenth century, the term had already been extended. Cf. O.E.D. s.v.

45. Cf. *Cloud, ed. cit.*, ch. 32, p. 181.

46. Cf. 2 Cor 11:14.

47. Cf. *Cloud, ed. cit.*, ch. 32, p. 181; *infra*.

48. *Infra*.

49. Sg 4:9.

50. *Infra*.

51. Vercellensis comments on *in uno oculorum tuorum:* "that is, in your reason" (*in intelligentia tua*). J. Barbet, *Thomas Gallus: Commentaire du Cantique des Cantiques* (Paris: Vrin, 1967), p. 182.

52. *Infra*.

53. *Infra*.

54. Cf. R.M. Clay, *Hermits and Anchorites of England* (London, 1914).

55. For the importance of the *cola* used by the *Cloud* author, see General Introduction, *supra*.

56. Kk.vi.26 omits *optimus;* Harley 2373, Pepwell's printed version of 1521, and Ff,vi.31 write *in quid*—a failure on the part of all these scribes to understand the "triolet."

57. For the rhetorical *colores* of the author, cf. General Introduction, *supra*.

58. An outstanding example of the literary consciousness of the author is the following sentence: "Bot louely and listely to wilne have God is grete and passing ese, trewe goostly pees and erles of the eendles rest."

The Assessment of Inward Stirrings

1. ME: Goostly frend in God—exactly the same greeting as at the beginning of the *Cloud, ed. cit.*, ch. 1, p. 115. The titles in the various MSS offer the following composite: "Here biginnith a (followeth also a veray necessary) pistle of discrecioun of (in) stirrings (of the soul)."

2. The Abbot Moses in Cassian's Conferences speaks of "inmoderate and inopportune fasts, of excessive Vigils and inordinate conversations" (Coll *I*, *XX: S.C.* 42, p. 103).

3. "He [the devil] persuades us to engage in business and pious visits which under colour of charity draw us out of the spiritual cloisters of the monastery and the privacy of peace and friendship" (ibid.). It is suggested that the recipient of "Stirrings" is not a religious, which seems likely. But we cannot argue, in view of statements such as the above, from the fact that it is open to him to be a solitary and to live in community as well. Cf. Introduction.

4. Cassian teaches that progress from the cenobitic life to the perfection of the eremitical is achieved by the love and practice of the virtues, of solitude especially, of every kind of hardship and frugality (Inst. *V*, 36: *S.C.* 109, pp. 247–48).

THE ASSESSMENT OF INWARD STIRRINGS

5. In the *Cloud*, as well, the author stresses the traditional teaching that lack of moderation in spiritual exercises is illusionary, and that "from such illusions as these come great mischief, great hypocrisy, great heresy and great error" (*ed. cit.*, Ch. 43, pp. 206–07).

6. The scriptural source here is the hypocrisy of the Pharisees and other "religious" Jews, so fiercely condemned by Jesus in the Gospels as pursuing external practices of devotion "so as to be seen by men" (Mt 23:5ff.). Richard of St. Victor notes that the fraud of the hypocrites serves their ambition to be held in honor. "Ambition is nothing else than the affectation of eminence, when a person is anxious to be considered by all a man of great prudence and holiness" (*De eruditione hominis interioris* XIII: P.L. 196, 1360).

7. ME: the kinde bot suffring and only consentyng. In "Private Direction," the same distinction between suffering and consenting is used in the interpretation of the text (Jn 15:5) "Without me you can do nothing." God is the principal partner in a contemplative's doing—"asking of them nothing else but their yielding and their consent" (*infra*).

8. The *Cloud* author will have nothing to do with "holy indiscretions"; they damage the health and "often pull you down from the height of this [contemplative] exercise"; cf. ch. 41, p. 199. Hilton concurs, though less forcefully and directly: "meekness and charity . . . shall rule and measure thee full how thou shalt eat and drink and succour all thy bodily need" (*Scale I*, ch. 77: Underhill, p. 189).

9. The common and classical doctrine is well expressed by St. Bernard: "For those who come to the grace of devotion, there appears to be one peril. Those who perform all their exercises with great delight must be on their guard in following their affections lest their physical strength be destroyed by such over-exertion. The result can be most detrimental to spiritual exercises: one becomes preoccupied with care of the body through the ill-health which follows. So we need to be illumined by the light of discretion, lest we are stricken down whilst we are running" (*Sermo in Circumcisione* 3, 11: P.L. 183, 142).

10. The author defines *indifferent;* which is as well, because O.E.D. cannot produce an example of the word with this meaning before 1538.

11. The reference to indifference, as well as the verbal reminiscence, makes the allusion to Eccl probable: ch. 3.

12. Richard of St. Victor postulates five elements in discretion: judgment (*dijudicatio*), deliberation (*deliberatio*), ordering (*dispositio*), appropriateness (*dispensatio*), and moderation (*moderatio*). Here the first four elements are being exercised. *Adnotationes mysticae in Psalmos* CXLIII: P.L. 196, 381.

13. The Abbot Moses tells a cautionary tale of two of the brethren who "possessed by a spirit of imprudence and lack of discretion" decided that, when they were about to cross the desert of the Thebaid, they would not take any food with them, but would rely on God to provide for them. After wandering through the desert, already perishing of hunger, they meet tribesmen whom one brother thinks have been sent by God to feed them.

148

The other refuses to accept food at the hands of mere man. They both perish. Cf. Cassian Coll II, 7: *S.C.* 42, pp. 117–18.

14. St. Bernard insists that the gift of discretion is primarily a *gratia gratis datae*, a charism given us for the benefit of others. Cf. *Sermo 88 de diversis* P.L. 183, 706.

15. This letter, like *Prayer*, is stated to have been written at the specific request of the addressee, who at this point is both a novice, very likely a priest—cf. Introduction—and not yet well known to the author. The suggestion that here we have a stylistic fiction or a *captatio benevolentiae* would seem otiose.

16. Bernard quotes Juvenal in support of this view—"the virtue of discretion is a rare bird on earth (*rara avis in terra*)" (*Sermo in Circumcisione* 3, 11: P.L. 183, 142). He further says that "he who has no other master than himself makes himself the disciple of a fool" (*Ep.* 87, 7: P.L. 182, 215).

17. It is through the manifestation of self that the disciple makes to the director that this sort of knowledge is acquired. So the Abbot Moses says that it is impossible to be deceived in this matter, as long as a person refuses to rely on his own judgment or to hide the thoughts that come to birth in his heart, but presents them for mature scrutiny by the elders (Cassian, Coll 2, 10: *S.C.* 42, p. 120).

18. 1 Cor 2:11. The disciple knows his Latin Vulgate, as do the addressees of "Prayer" and "Private Direction." Cf. Introduction, *supra*.

19. Prv 24:16: "The just man will fall seven times and will rise."

20. It is a cardinal principle of Victorine spiritual doctrine that the soul arrives at perfect knowledge through the virtue of discretion. Hugh: *De meditando*, P.L. 176, 996; Richard: *Benjamin Minor*, 76.

21. "We are all in the ship," says Augustine; "some are the crew, others the passengers; all are in danger in the tempest, all are safe when in harbor" (*Enarr. in PS. CVI*, 12: P.L. 37, 14, 25). Hugh of Tobieto, in his *Claustrum Animae*, begins from St. Paul's ship in Acts (28), wrecked on the island of Malta: "Allegorically, the sea is the world, the ship is this present life, the shipwreck represents its dangers, the coming into port the renunciation of this world, and the harbour is the true life" (P.L. 176, 1018). For the commonplace nature of the allegory, see Owst, *Literature and Pulpit in Mediaeval England*, pp. 67ff. Not many, however, match the quality of the descriptive writing here.

22. Julian of Norwich is shown "my soul in the midst of my heart . . . large as it were an endless world . . . a blessed kingdom . . . He sits in the soul established in peace and rest. And he rules and governs heaven and earth and all that is. The manhood with the Godhead . . ." (ch. 68). Richard of St. Victor writes of "the heart which is tossed on the sea of its desires, subject to the storms of worldly cares, which has not yet reached that blessed land, that certain tranquillity of heart, when the spirit is wholly gathered within itself" (*Benjamin Minor* 38).

23. Jas 1:12. The same text is cited in the *Benjamin Minor*, ch. 26, of abstinence and patience, but is omitted in the translation.

24. The *Cloud* author uses the phrase "crown of life" in his proemium: cf. pp. 115 and 236, note 379. Cf. Eccl 1:22: "The fear of the Lord is a crown of wisdom, filling up peace and the fruit of salvation."

25. Richard of St. Victor says that the crown given to the Lamb in the Apocalypse "signifies the prize of eternal blessedness, which shall have no end." It also signifies the human condition, according to which Christ receives all things through grace (*In Apocalypsim VII*, 4: P.L. 196, 761–62.

26. According to Bernard, knowledge of self consists in the self-consciousness of the disfigured divine image (*De diversis* 12, 2; P.L. 183, 571); so that we first know what we have done, second what we have deserved, third what we have lost (*De diversis* 40, 3: P.L. 183, 648).

27. St. Thomas teaches that the charism of discretion enables us to discover by what spirit a person is moved to act or to speak, for example, by the spirit of charity or the spirit of envy (*Comm. in 1 Cor 12*, lect. 2).

28. The author expounds the nature of perfect charity in the *Cloud*, and adds that all the other virtues are subtly and perfectly contained in "this little blind impulse of love as it beats upon this dark cloud of unknowing" (*ed. cit.*, ch. 24, p. 169).

29. Bede, in his Commentary on the Epistle of James (P.L. 93, 13) links the "crown of life" with Apoc 2:10: "Be faithful until death, and I will give thee the crown of life." He glosses: "The crown of life will be given to those who in the love of God are proved to be truly faithful, that is, perfect and blameless, deficient in nothing."

30. Hodgson opines that "the whole symbolism of the passage may have been borrowed from some "wench writer", on the supposition that the crown described is that of France (or of Scotland) in the time of Charles V. But she quotes W. Jones, *Crowns and Coronations*, p. 471, to the effect that in the time of Edward III the fleur-de-lis on the English crown had three turrets (*Demise*, 138/65).

31. This appears to be the author's own allegory. For Richard of St. Victor, gold and precious stones represent sacred eloquence—as in the name of John Chrysostom and John Chrysologus. Gold is also human nature purified in Christ.

32. Encircles—ME: environneth. Cf. the description of wisdom, "the worker of all things" (Wis 7:21ff.): "For in her is the spirit of understanding: holy, one, manifold, subtle, eloquent, active, undefiled, sure, sweet, loving that which is good."

33. If the other gifts grow in us through the grace of the Holy Spirit—wisdom and knowledge, that is—we should take care to share them with the brethren. And thus we shall obtain that gift of the Holy Spirit which is called discernment of spirits (*discretio spirituum*) (St. Bernard, *De diversis* 88, 2: P.L. 183, 706–07).

34. In the *Cloud*, the author speaks of "the second, the lower branch of charity," which is directed to all men, kinsman or stranger, friend or foe (*ed. cit.*, ch. 24, pp. 169–70). By implication, the first branch is the love of God for himself above all creatures.

35. Cassian, speaking of the spiritual combat, says that Israel was humbled under the attacks of his enemies, so that he might never feel the absence of the Lord's protection (Col IV, 6: *S.C.* 42, p. 172).

36. Sc. wisdom, discernment, and the perfection of virtue here, and the joys of heaven hereafter.

37. Julian of Norwich says that those who deliberately choose God in this life for love are to be "as sure, in hope, of the bliss of heaven whilst we are here, as we shall be, in surety, when we are there" (*Revelations*, ch. 65).

38. Discretion, as the author of "The Pursuit of Wisdom" teaches, is the last step, the crowning virtue in the soul's preparation for the contemplative life and vocation (cf. *supra*). As he indicates in "Private Direction" and elsewhere, not every soul is called to it, since it is supreme among the gratuitous gifts of God. Cf. Introduction, *supra*.

39. This is the only place in his writings where the author explicitly compares the beatific vision with the act of contemplation. He says in the *Cloud* that "the contemplative life [which] is begun in this life and shall last without end" (*ed. cit.*, ch. 8, p. 138).

40. The Abbot Moses tells the story of the monk Hero, who kept so vigorous a fast, and was so jealous of his solitude, that he refused to eat with his brethren even on Easter day. But in his presumption he was deceived by the angel of Satan disguised as an angel of light, who persuaded him that he could throw himself unharmed down a well. But he killed himself instead (Coll II, 5: *S.C.* 42, pp. 116–17).

41. "The virtue of discretion languishes without the fervour of charity, and intense fervour falls headlong unless tempered by discretion" (St. Bernard, *Sermones in Cantica* XXIII, 7: P.L. 180, 888).

42. To Cassian: "True discretion is acquired only at the price of true humility; and its first proof is when all one's impulses as well as one's actions are left to the scrutiny of the elders, so that no one puts any trust in his own judgment, but accepts theirs in all things and receives as good or bad whatever is recognized as such by their agreement" (Coll II, 10: *S.C.* 42, p. 120).

43. Solitary life—ME: singular lenyng. The most perfect state of life to which the Christian may be called—the eremitical, after he has made proof of the "special," the cenobitical. It is in this form of living that the disciple may "win through to the crown of life that lasts forever" (*Cloud, ed. cit.*, ch. I, proemium, p. 115).

44. Jer 9:21. A traditional metaphor. Cf. the *Cloud, ed. cit.*, ch. 2, p. 119 and note. Hilton, commenting on the same text writes: "These windows are our five wits, by the which sin cometh into the soul . . . as by the eye to see curious and fair things, by the ear for to hear wondrous and new tidings, and so of the other wits" (*Scale I*, 78).

45. The old Latin variant from the Christmas verse in Is 9:6 (Vulgate): "For unto us a child is born, unto us a son is given, and the government shall be upon his shoulder: and his name shall be called Wonderful Counsellor, the Mighty God, the Everlasting Father, the Prince of Peace."

46. Cf. the *captatio benevolentiae* in similar terms in the *Cloud, ed. cit.*, ch.

73, p. 261: "I am a wretch, unworthy to teach any creature . . . speaking childishly and foolishly."

47. That is, the desire of the *ex professo* contemplative. In the *Cloud* (*ed. cit.*, ch. 75, p. 265), the author cites Gregory the Great on the subject of contemplative desire; and Gregory in turn is citing the Song of Songs (3:1): "I sought him whom my soul loves" (*Homiliarum in Evangelia II*, 25, 2: P.L. 76, 1190).

48. So Hilton: "What work or what stirring it be that may help thy desire, strength it and nourish it, and make thy thought . . . more whole and more burning to the love of God, whether it be praying or thinking, stillness or speaking, reciting or hearing or communing, going or sitting; keep it for the time and work therein . . . and keep discretion in thy working, after counsel . . . " (*Scale II*, ch. 23; Underhill, p. 317).

49. "The substance of all perfection," says the author in the *Cloud*, "is the good will directed to God, and a kind of satisfaction and gladness that you experience in your will concerning all that he does" (*ed. cit.*, ch. 49, p. 215). The author, as he will make clear here, is speaking of the perfection of unitive love (cf. ch. 21, p. 163), which is identical with the *culmen contemplationis:* that oneness of love and union of wills "where a marriage is made between God and the soul" (cf. "Letter on Prayer," *supra*).

50. ME: comoun clothing of Cristen mens religion and singulere abites of dinerse and deuisid brotherhedes. The view of P.H. that "the vehemence of this passage . . . strongly suggests that the writer was not himself bound in any 'holy thraldom' but that he was a free lance" is doubtful on several counts: first it is the "common clothing of Christen men's religion," i.e., the cowl and scapular etc., common to all members of the various monastic Institutes (as well as to the friars) that is the religious habit of professed monks (ad frieurs) including the eremitical Carthusians; secondly, it is precisely the "free-lance" who is castigating—as St. Bruno cautioned his monks against the *gyrovagi* (*Cloud*, *ed. cit.*, Introduction, p. 52); thirdly, the diverse and distinct brotherhoods may well be Lollards or Wycliffites. There was at least at hand the example of the heretical groups of *Fraticelli*, who splintered off from the Friars Minor (cf. *Fraticelles*, Dsp 5, 1167–78). Cf. Introduction, *supra*.

51. We read in the *Book of Margery Kempe* that she was ordered by Our Lord to wear a white habit indicating her vow of chastity, her husband being still alive (Butler-Bowdon, ch. 15, pp. 58ff.).

52. ME: midday deuel. Cf. Ps 90:6 (Vulgate): "Thou shalt not be afraid of the terror of the night, of the arrow that flieth in the day, of the thing that walk about in the dark, of invasion, or of the noonday devil." Richard of St. Victor comments: "Who is ignorant of the fact that at the hour of noon the light is stronger and the heat more intense? So the fiends come upon us as it were with great light and heat; with their wickedness and fraud hidden under the colour of holiness, they scheme and plot to bind us. Light belongs to discretion, heat to devotion. . . . It often happens that we are so infa-

tuated by his fraudulent temptation that our mind grows stupid" (*Annotationes mysticae in Psalmos* 90: P.L. 196, 395).

53. 2 Cor 3:17. Cf. St. Bernard, *De gratia et libero arbitrio V* 15: "Only contemplatives can enjoy perfect liberty in this life; and this only minimally and very rarely" (P.L. 182, 1009).

54. Is 45:15: "verily thou art a hidden God, the God of Israel, the Savior."

55. Cf. Aquinas, *Summa Theol.* 2–2ae, 180, 1: "The contemplative life belongs to the knowing power (*intellectus*), as far as the essence of the act is concerned; but insofar as what moves the knowing power to carry out the operation, this belongs to the loving power (*voluntas*), which moves all the other powers, including the knowing power, to their acts." Cf. the *Cloud*, *ed. cit.*, ch. 4, p. 122–23.

56. Dt 26:17: "Thou hast chosen the Lord this day to be thy God, and to walk in his ways . . . and to keep all his commandments. And the Lord hath chosen thee this day to be his special people . . . that thou mayst be a holy people of the Lord."

57. ME: Soche a lovely chasing of God, this wisely lesing and seking him out. P.H. wants "lesing" to mean either "to release" or even more unlikely, "to gean." But the allusion is clearly to the Canticle of Canticles 3:1. "I sought him whom my soul loveth; I sought him and I found him not." St. Bernard says that there are three reasons why those who seek God are frustrated in their search: They seek at an inopportune time, or in the wrong way, or in the wrong place (*aut non sicut oportet, aut non ubi oportet*) (*Sermones in Cantica* 77, 3–11: P.L. 183, 1145–30).

All the phrases in this sentence are integral to the author's equipment as a director of contemplatives who has adopted the Dionysian method: *Cloud*, *ed. cit.*, ch. 20, "our loving Lord"; "you experience in your will a simple reaching out to God," ch. 3, p. 121; "the target, the bull's eye of your spiritual gaze," "Private Direction," *infra*; "tracing," ibid.

58. ME: the loue and the mening, the cheef and the pointe of thin herte. The author attempts many times, in all his extant writings, to find satisfactory equivalents for the *apex animae/affectus/intellectus*, the "place" in the human psyche where the transforming union is effected—the sovereign point of the spirit.

59. ME: Soche a blinde schote with the scharp darte of longing loue may never faile of the prik. Cf. *Cloud*, *ed. cit.*, ch. 6, p. 131.

60. Sg 4:9. "The soul has two eyes. One by which it understands, the other by which it investigates. And of these two, the right eye is love, which wounds by its penetrating search" (St. Bernard, *Tractatus de caritate* 3, 16: P.L. 184, 592).

61. "*Vulnerasti cor meum . . . in uno oculo.*" There are two sights or eyes: one by which we contemplate the things that are above, and the other, transitory and earthly things. "The Savior comes to open the eye whose object is heavenly things . . . the contemplation and desire of our salvation. You

have wounded my heart, o soul, whom I chose as spouse when I joined you to me in the oneness of love and will" (Richard of St. Victor, *Explicatio in Cantica*, ch. 27: P.L. 196, 484).

62. "The first degree is wounding love. . . . Do you not feel sometimes as though you were pierced through the heart when the fiery arrow of this love penetrates the inmost spirit, and pierces his affections. . . . This first degree affects the thought . . . restricts thinking. . . . It fastens the mind indissolubly by preventing it from passing over to other concerns. . . . So God is loved by judgment and deliberation, by desire and affection" (Richard of St. Victor, *De IV Gradibus violentae caritatis*, P.L. 196, 1207ff.).

63. "This is the eye which is never closed . . . which is never covered over, in which darkness plays no part . . . the eye which no earthly affection can turn aside. A simple and prudent eye which no harmful curiosity can deter from looking incessantly on him upon whom the angels long to gaze; the vehement love, which as St. Augustine says cannot see the one it loves, for love is the eye, and to love is to see" (Richard of St. Victor, *De gradibus caritatis*, ch. III: P.L. 196, 1203).

64. ME: ransakith and sekith. The *Cloud*, chs. 6–11, is concerned to deal with this activity of the reason as the main hindrance to dark contemplation.

65. " . . . in this exercise man must use no intermediaries, nor can they come to it through intermediaries. All good means depend on it, but it depends on none of them; nor can any one of them lead you to it" (*Cloud, ed. cit.*, ch. 34, p. 186).

66. There is a pastiche of two and possibly three Pauline texts here, indicating that the author is citing from memory, and implying that the addressee has a good working knowledge of the Vulgate Latin: 1 Cor 1:26: *Videte enim vocationem vestram, fratres;* 1 Cor 7:20: *Unus quisque in qua vocatione vocatius est, in ea permaneat* (Let every man abide in the same calling in which he was called); Eph 4:1: *Obsecro vos . . . ut digne ambuletis vocatione qua vocatiestis* (I beseech you that you walk worthy of the vocation in which you are called).

67. The author's longest digression in the *Cloud* (*ed. cit.*, chs. 16–23, pp. 153–69) concerns the figure of "Mary, who stands for all sinners that are called to the contemplative life, indeed for all contemplatives" (ch. 17) and for "the contemplative life" (ch. 21). We may well ask why the author here makes no reference to his protracted treatment of the story of Martha and Mary in the *Cloud*. Cf. Introduction, *supra*.

68. In the *Cloud*, the Gospel text of Lk 10:42 "Mary has chosen the *best*" is to elucidate the three parts of the "two lives," the lower, the middle, and the higher. The external practices normally associated with the *ex professo* contemplative life, silence, fasting, and solitude, are here, as the author says, indifferently the good and/or the better. In the *Cloud*, too, the one thing necessary is "that God may be loved and praised for himself, above all other business, bodily or spiritual, that man can do" (*ed. cit.*, ch. 20, p. 162). Here it is God, or almighty Jesus.

Augustine, the first in the West to interpret the Lucan text *unum est ne-*

cessarium as indicating the *otium* and *negotium* of the contemplative and active lives, says that the *unum* is "that supernal one, where the Father, Son and Holy Spirit are one" (*Sermo* CIII, 3, 4: P.L. 38, 614).

69. The words *inquit optimus* (says the best man-person) have caused havoc among the MSS copyists, one of whom omits *optimus*, another writes *in qui* for *inquit*, while others again have *in quid*. The author expects his addressee, however, to have enough Latin (and to know his Vulgate well enough) to appreciate the ingenious rhetorical figures: adnominatio, chiasmus, compar, gradatio, and traductio: *Maria, inquit Optimus/Optimam partem elegit/quae non auferetur ab ea.* Cf. Introduction, *supra.* Ps 101:26–28.

70. St. Bernard says that the order of charity in the household of Martha and Mary consisted in a threefold distribution: to Martha was assigned the administration, to Mary the contemplation, and to Lazarus the penitence. The perfect soul would combine all three functions, but ordinarily speaking they have to be shared among individuals. This said, "Rejoice and give thanks, Mary, for you have chosen the best part. Blessed are the eyes which see what you see and . . . receive the veins of the divine whisper in silence" (*Sermo III in Assumptione B. Mariae Virginis* 4, 7: P.L. 183, 423, 425).

71. The classic anti-intellectual statement, reversing the opening of Aristotle's *Metaphysics:* "It is man's nature to desire to know."

72. "Lord, my heart is not proud, nor are my eyes lifted up, neither have I conversed about great matters, nor in marvels above me . . . " (Ps 130).

73. Heb 8:10–11 (Jer 31:33–34): "I will be their God and they shall be my people. And they shall not teach every man his neighbor and every man his brother, saying, 'Know the Lord,' for all shall know me from the least to the greatest of them." Cf. Jn 6:45; Is 54:13.

74. Emptying out entirely—ME: utterly voiding. The author doubtless has in mind that the contemplative movement matches the divine self-emptying. Cf. Phil 2:7: "Anything beneath him." Though the author greatly prefers the image of "trending down" to emptying out, especially in the *Cloud* itself, this specific reference to the distinctions "above, beneath, within" treated at length in chs. 62 and 67 presents us with the same contemplative process.

75. If the author ever defines concisely the act of contemplation it is this phrase, "a reverent stirring of lasting love." In the *Cloud* (*ed. cit.*, ch. 50, p. 217) we have: "this reverent and humble stirring of love and union of wills." It is in "Private Direction," of course, that the "passive" aspect of the contemplation is stressed: "This simple and delightful exercise, which is in fact the high wisdom of the Godhead descending through grace into man's soul, knitting it and uniting it to himself in spiritual wisdom and discernment" (*infra*).

76. Julian of Norwich is less dogmatic on the question of means: "It pleases him that we seek him and worship him by means: but understanding and knowing that he is the goodness of them all. For the highest prayer is to the goodness of God which comes down to us . . . it is the very grace for which the soul seeks and ever shall" (*Revelations*, ch. 6).

77. ME: and scaterst not this goostly beholding therfro. In the *Cloud*, the author offers us a graphic description of this scattering process—the dissipation of concentration (*ed. cit.*, ch. 7, p. 132).

78. ME: mistely. Perhaps the best rendering would be "anagogically," since "mystically" has ceased to have any precise sense. The "work" of the *Cloud* is certainly to lead us where we wish to go—to God, in love and in union of wills. Cf. *Cloud, ed. cit.*, Introduction, pp. 68–69.

79. The author here briefly repeats instructions that he gives at length in the *Cloud:* "never cease . . . but constantly beat upon this cloud of unknowing with a sharp dart of longing love" (*ed. cit.*, ch. 16); "no matter how much you fast or keep watch . . . and cause your body all the pain you could think of, it would be of no avail" (ibid.); "your silence is peaceful, your speech edifying, your prayer secret, your pride proper, your behavior modest, your laughter very soft" ("Private Direction," *infra*).

80. "Work at this exercise without ceasing and without moderation, and you will know where to begin and where to end all your other activities with great discretion" (*Cloud, ed. cit.*, ch. 42, p. 200).

81. ME: streynid doinges.

82. The author is here speaking of the penances given to penitents in the confessional as a measure of their desire to atone for their sins.

83. The author accepts that in religious communities penitential practices are legitimately imposed. But he will not assign to them any merit of themselves.

A Letter on Prayer

Translator's Introduction

It must have been particularly galling for the *Cloud* author to face yet another barrage of criticism[1] and, indeed, quite vehement accusations of heretical tendencies,[2] after the publication of the *Letter on Prayer*.[3] Its first paragraphs are a simple expression of the *ex professo* contemplative who at last comes to realize that all his fears are quite simply a masking of the great fear of death,[4] and a veiled allusion to the truth that the Christian has always found it difficult to accept the implications of a realized eschatology.[5] Hope, however, seems to have been a special function of the spirituality of the English fourteenth century,[6] and the *Cloud* author sees the virtue as a fruit of as well as a means toward the dark contemplation, which even in this simple little letter represents the sum total of all that he has to say.

Here again he insists that the contemplative prayer that he is advocating is sacramentally rooted in the penitence of ecclesial reconciliation,[7] and though, surprisingly, the Eucharist is never on a single occasion mentioned in this context, or—at least directly—in any other in the entire corpus of his writings, his thoroughly Thomistic teaching on grace,[8] as well as the descriptions of a Carthusian solitary like Richard Methley of the exercise of the *Cloud*'s method,[9] assures one that the celebration of the Eucharist is certain to be the essential element in the liturgical structure of the contemplative life of eremitical solitude.

The third aspect of the preparation for contemplation here described, and one that flows spontaneously from the prayer of hope, is gratitude: "It may not be bot that thou schalt fele a grete stering of love unto him that is so good and merciful unto thee, as the steppes of thi staf hope pleinly schewith unto thee in the time of thi preier, if thou do it deweliche as I have tolde thee bifore."[10]

For the Dionysians, Mount Sinai is naturally the symbol of the climb to perfection,[11] and equally appropriate that one of the more distinguished of them, Bonaventure, should have entitled a spiritual treatise of his *Itinerarium mentis in Deum*. However, it is Augustine in the West who seems to be the first to equate the ascent of the "very high and steep mountain" with "charity, the end of all fulfilment."[12]

"Alle amendement standen in two, in levyng of ivel and doing of good." Guigo the Angelic makes prayer, which he defines as the petition to avoid evil and to do good, the third of the four-runged ladder[13] "by whiche men might well climb to heaven," since it is an image of the contemplative process. The first two are reading and Scripture-reflection, which with this third, prayer, constitute the chief occupation, for the *Cloud* author, of the contemplative apprentice.[14] Reflection or meditation is proper to the proficients,[15] and the activity will lead them, "insofar as they are such, here below," to true prayer.[16] In the *Cloud*, we are not given any definition or description of the prayer of petition, which is traditionally an essential element in the process.[17] It is here that we find it, in the context of sacramental confession, and as the amalgam of fear and hope; for the *Cloud* author, it constitutes the beginnings of the contemplative climb that leads up the high mount of perfection, to reverent affection.[18] What is more, in describing meditation in the *Cloud*, the author speaks of it as increasing devotion. The effect, then, of this beginning and proficient exercise that combines fear and hope, is that one's will is readied to do what belongs to the service of God, and to do it, moreover, swiftly and gladly.[19] These spiritual and academic definitions apart, "devotion" is clearly a key word for the work of the *Cloud*, and describes its fruits. Guigues du Pont, for example, tells us that anagogical union "means that the devout mind enjoys God's company and takes its joyous repose in him. We must realize that the way of this upward contemplation consists in the filial affection of blessed devotion. There is no other road to it."[20]

The author may be said to be obsessed by the danger of indiscreet ascetical practices for *ex professo* contemplatives, and he takes every means, direct and indirect, to warn his penitents that the clear signs of false devotion are, in general, indicative of the unprofitable nature of such practices in the context of the contemplative pilgrimage. As we have seen, silence, fasting, and physical solitude are taken as typical in *Inward Stirrings*,[21] and what is more, the attitudes and dispositions to these practices of the "verrey contemplative" are, as it were, a touchstone of his sincerity. In fact, the author's ability to handle them is a demonstration of the Pauline adage "Freedom is where the Spirit of God is."[22] Here, in *Prayer*, there are named "fasting, waking and scharp weryng": "fasting" being common to the two denunciations, and the wearing of a hair shirt something new. Here again, the reasons for damning the practices with faint praise are different: that in comparison with the prayer-exercises as means of obtaining their object, they have nothing to offer. "This [sc. reverent affection] is onliche it by itself, withouten ani other maner of doing, as is fasting, waking, scharp weryng and alle theese other, the whiche onliche bi itself pleseth to Almighty God and deservith to have mede of him. And it were impossible any soul to have mede of God withouten this."[23] In *Inward Stirrings* a special point is made, perhaps surprisingly in the ascetical context, about the wearing of something akin to a religious habit, such as Margery Kempe adopted and refused to put off at the instance of a bishop.[24] The author lists it with "spekyng, fastyng and etyng, onlines and companye, comoun clothing of Cristen mens religion and singulere abites of diverse and devisid brotherhedes."[25] All these practices have their worth only insofar as they are genuine means to reverent affection.

To describe the next step in the contemplative ascent, the author elaborates the image of gardening, the fruit and the tree, a commonplace in contemporary spiritual writing for contemplatives. In the Middle English version of Mechtild of Hackeborn's *Book of Special Grace*, we read that "to this maiden's seeming our Lord delved in the earth in the likeness of a gardener."[26] It is, however, Julian of Norwich in her parable of the Lord and the Servant who elucidates the image with a detail similar to the *Cloud* author here. It is worth quoting her extensively:

> There is a treasure in the earth which the Lord loved. . . . I was answered in my understanding: It is a good which is delicious and pleasing to the Lord. . . . The servant was to be a gardener, digging and ditching and sweating and turning the soil over and over. . . . He was to persevere in his work, and make sweet streams to run, and fine and plenteous fruit to grow, which he was to bring before the Lord and serve him with to his liking. And he was never to come back again until he had made all this food ready, as he knew was pleasing to the Lord; and then he was to take this food and drink, and carry it most reverently before the Lord.[27]

In our annotations, we have listed the various aspects of this complex biblical image as the patristic and medieval writers continued to interpret it from generation to generation, with a multitude of borrowings and developed interpretations.[28] The *Cloud* author's main concern, however, is how the contemplative prayer that he is describing is to develop. He has moved his penitent from fear to hope, and from fear and hope to the beginnings of the obscure contemplative love. This is, first, the fruit of anagogical devotion, never to be confused with the ascetical devotional practices that may or may not be authentic means to reverent affection. Now through the image of the unripe and ripe fruit, he turns to the quality of contemplative love that reverent affection enshrines, and discusses how this is to be purified so that it becomes "fit for the king."

"Chaste love" is a term that is current among all the Dionysians of the author's acquaintance, and a chapter of the *Cloud* itself is devoted to it.[29] There, the focus is first on the distinction between sensible or spiritual sweetnesses and consolations, and "this meek stirring of love in your will." The danger is that one could be loving God for the sake of the sweetness, in which case "your love is not yet chaste or perfect."

These consolations "depend entirely on the disposition and the ordinance of God, who looks to the different advantages and needs of his creatures." The author also speaks of God's being perfectly loved for himself, when the contemplative apprentice takes no account of pain or joy.[30] Thomas Gallus, in his comment on the verse in the Song of Songs, "the voice of the turtle-dove is heard . . . ," says that the affection of the dove for its little ones signifies that the *sponsa* embraces the spouse most chastely, and pours out to him her most chaste prayers (*castissimas orationes*).[31] "This most chaste love is so powerful that it excites God to ecstatic love;" and Gallus cites Proverbs 8,17, of Wisdom: "I love them who love me." Again the love of the spouse for the bride is the most chaste love which guards the spiritual heart (*amor iste castissimus mentem circumcingit*).[32]

In the handbook of medieval rhetoric *Cicero ad C. Herrenium de ratione dicendi*, much is made in the rhetorician's art of the *argumentatio perfectissima*. The *Cloud* author is well versed in the use of this figure, and we are given an excellent example of it in this disquisition on the most chaste love that begins to touch the perfection of reverent affection:

1. *And thus it is that I mene when I say "lovyng hym with chast love for himself and not for his goodes."* (This is the *first part* of the argumentation, the *proposition*, which sets out what is to be proved.)
2. *Not as if I seide, thogh al I wel seide, mochel for his goodes, bot withoute*

comparison more for himself. (This is the *second part*, the *reason*, which repeats the proposition in different words.)

3. *For if I schal more heilich speking in declaring of my mening of the perfeccioun and of the mede of this reverent affeccioun,* (The *third part*, confirming and reiterating the reason, *confirmationis ratio.*)

4. *I say that a soul touched in affeccioun bi the sensible presence of God, as he is in hymself, and in a parfite soule illumind in the reson by the clere heme of everlastyng light the whiche is God, for to se and for to fele the lovelines of God in himself, hath for that tyme and for that moment lost alle the mynde of any goode deed or of any kindnes that ever God did to him in this lif.* (Here is the *fourth part,* the embellishment or *ornatio,* the illustration of the argument.)

5. *So that cause for to love God fore, feleth he none or seeth he none in that tyme, other than his God.* (This is the *fifth part,* the conclusion, *complexio,* which finally states what had to be proved.)[33]

Now the author begins to illustrate in terms he uses elsewhere the *culmen contemplationis,* which he has been expressing simply as reverent affection: "Beholding to the pointe and the prik of perfeccioun . . . chast love is to love God for himself and not for his goodes." The meaning of the parable—chaste versus unchaste love—is drawn out in the scriptural manner. The author shows that he can discourse on the very same point of the perfection of contemplative love, even using the same imagery, but without making us feel that he is repeating himself. For instance, early on in the *Cloud,* he has the addressee speak of the multitude of stirrings emerging from heart and will in one hour as dissipated because of the concupiscence caused by the fall.[34] Here he says: "a soule . . . that offreth the frute ripe and departeth it fro the tre, may unnoumerable tymes in one oure be raisid into God sodenly withouten mene."[35]

The description of the union that is the fruit of the contemplative effort so often described by the author is perhaps most succinctly expressed in the paragraph that begins with the citation from first Corinthians, "He who is joined to God is one spirit [with him]," continues with the image of marital union, and ends with the words from the Song of Songs: "My beloved to me and I to him." Thomas Gallus, in his Third Commentary on the Canticle, interprets thus the phrase *Dilectus meus mihi et ego illi:*

"My beloved to me and I to him." It would seem that some word of love must have been inserted, for example, "is fastened" (*adhaeret*), "cemented with glue" (*conglutinatur*), or "is joined" (*iungitur*) or something similar as in I Cor 6:17, "He who is fastened to God"; Jer 13:11, "I have

163

glued to me (*conglutinavi mibi*)"; *Divine Names*, 1, 6, "we are joined to them." But he does not insert any of these, because he has not discovered any word worthy of expressing so sublime a coupling (*copulae*). The union is above mind (*super intellectum fit coniuncto*) and thus is ineffable. Or, perhaps, the lover is become his love, and is the "bond of perfection" (Col 3:14).[36]

We can see how the pastiche of citations, as given in these annotations, is gathered together in the Commentary of *Vercellensis*. The phraseology used to express the "spiritual marriage" by Hilton in Book II of the *Scale* and the author here is so exactly repetitious that one must have simply copied from the other. This makes no matter to the *Cloud* author. It could have happened either way in view of the constant theme of Gallus, as he studies and studies again the union of which the Song of Songs constantly speaks to him. Our author here refers to the fact that the union cannot be broken. *Vercellensis*, commenting on the phrase "on the day of his espousals,"[37] writes: "that is, in the union of the joining that unites (*unitione unitivae coniunctionis*) which is of the essence of these espousals, still separable here, but preceding and preparing for these heavenly nuptials (*patriae nuptias*), the final union which is for ever inseparable, 'on the day of the hearts gladness.' "[38]

It is from the Canticle, too, that we would expect a moral or anagogical reflection on "the odour of sweetness." "There is a super-intellectual sense of smell (*olfactum mentis superintellectualis*)," says Gallus, "which is different from any spiritual sweetness to be sensed when mind and heart are operative. This is often signified in Leviticus and other books of both Old and New Testaments as 'a most sweet odour.' " Genesis 27:27: "Behold the sweet smell of my son"; Ecclesiastes 24:21: "My odor is as the purest balm"; Ecclesiastes 50:8: "As the sweet-smelling frankincense in the time of summer, in hearts, that is, which are full of light and eagerness."[39] The image of the hard shell and bitter rind is found in the *Ladder of Four Rungs* (*Scala Claustralium*): "Reading is outside in the bark; meditation is inside in the sweet kernel."[40]

At the end of the *Cloud*, the author draws out, from Richard of St. Victor's *Benjamin Major*, three different kinds of contemplation,[41] and takes it that the way of working described in the *Cloud* may not fit the bodily or spiritual disposition of the addressee, in which case "take another safely and without reproach, as long as it is with good spiritual counsel."[42] Here, the director considers that the method of contemplative prayer he has described in the letter is the right one for his penitent, and that he himself is being inspired by God to teach him. He even sets forth the *argumentatio perfectissima* to prove his point. "Here is the reason why I counsel you thus," he begins; "and, secondly, the reason is. . . . " To confirm the reason, he stresses that hope and fear do indeed correspond to the two substances in the human composite. He then embellishes his argument by pointing out what the real fear of death and the certain hope of forgiveness will assure. "And therefore . . . ," he concludes.[43] Yet, even though he is convinced that he has set out the right method for this penitent, he is still experienced enough to leave him free to judge for himself and to take the appropriate advice. The proof will be in the frequent making of the contemplative exercise. "Sett thee scharply to the profe; and fle all letting and occacyons of letting, in the name of our Lorde Jesu. Amen."[44]

A Letter on Prayer

My spiritual friend in God:

   With regard to your question about how you shall keep your heart during the time of your prayer, I answer as best I can, out of my frailty. It will be very profitable to you, I believe, at the very beginning of your prayer, whatever it is to be, long or short, to tell your heart very plainly, without any pretense, that you are going to die at the end of your prayer; and, unless you get on with it seriously, even before you come to the end of your prayer.[1] And realize that what I am telling you is no mere whimsy, and understand why. For there is no man in this life who would dare take it upon himself to say the contrary: that is to say, that you shall live longer than your prayer lasts. So it is salutary to think like this; and I advise you to act on it. For if you do, you will see that the consideration of your sinfulness in general, and of the shortness of the time left for amendment in particular, will bring into your heart a truly effective fear.[2] And you shall feel the effect of it hidden deep in your heart, unless—and God forbid!—you happen to deceive and beguile your false, carnal, blind heart with lies and false, deceitful promises of a longer life. For though in fact it may be true that you will live longer, it is still a lying falsehood for you to think so beforehand and to promise your heart accordingly. For the truth of it is only in God. In yourself, there is only a blind waiting on his will, without any surety with regard to duration. For the reality is as short as the twinkling of an eye, or less.[3]

   Therefore, if you would pray wisely, as the prophet bids when he

166

says in the Psalm *Psallite sapienter*, see to it that you obtain at the beginning this truly effective fear.[4] For, as the same prophet says in another Psalm: *Initium sapientiae est timor Domini*; that is, "The beginning of wisdom is fear of our Lord God."[5]

However, since there is no solid foundation in fear alone, in case you sink into an unbearable heaviness[6] you must fasten to the first consideration this second one: Keep it firmly in mind that if, by the grace of God, you can pronounce distinctly the words of your prayer and come to the end of it—or even if you die before you come to the end, as long as you do all that lies in your power—then your prayer will be received by God in full satisfaction of all your carelessness from the beginning of your life until the present moment.[7] I am taking it for granted that you will have made the proper amendment guided by your intelligence and your conscience, according to the ordinary law of the Church, in confession.[8]

This short prayer of yours, little as it is, will then be accepted from you by God, for your final salvation, even if you were to die in that moment; and if you live longer, for a great increase of perfection.[9] This is the goodness of God, who, as the Prophet says, never forsakes those who truly trust in him with the desire of amendment.[10]

Since amendment consists in two things, in avoiding evil and in doing good,[11] there are no readier means of achieving these two than spiritual exercise in the two reflections mentioned above. For what rids the spirit of sinful inclination more quickly than a right understanding of the fear of death? And what moves the spirit more fervently to do good than a sure hope in the mercy and the goodness of God, which is brought in by means of this second consideration? For when the spiritual feeling born of this second reflection is properly related to that of the first, it will be for you a sure staff of hope[12] to support you in all your good deeds. With this staff you may safely climb the high mountain of perfection, that is to say, the perfect love of God;[13] even though its beginning is imperfect, as you shall hear later on.[14] For through the general understanding that you have of the mercy and goodness of God, along with this special awareness that you feel of his mercy and goodness; that is, his acceptance of this little and short service for such long negligence; and as full satisfaction, so to say, for so much carelessness—as we mentioned above—it is impossible that you should not feel a great stirring of love[15] for him who is so good and merciful toward you. The steps you take with your staff of hope will clearly show you this during your prayer, if you carry it out in the way I have explained to you before.

The spiritual experience which is the effect of this exercise consists in the reverent affection a man has toward God during the time of his prayer, achieved by this fear in the very substance of the exercise, and by this upsurge of love which consists in the spiritual steps made with this staff, hope, which I mentioned before.[16] For reverence is nothing else but the mingling of fear and love, along with the staff of certain hope.[17] The effect of this exercise may be called devotion. For devotion, as St. Thomas the Doctor says, is nothing else but the readiness of man's will to do what belongs to the service of God.[18] Let each man take the measure of this in himself; for he that serves God in this way knows by experience how prompt is his will for it. I believe that St. Bernard takes the same view of this exercise when he says that everything should be done swiftly and gladly.[19] And see why: swiftly out of fear, and gladly because of hope and loving trust in his mercy.[20]

And what is more,[21] I would sooner have the reward of the man who has persevered in this work, though he never did any bodily penance in his life except that which is enjoined by Holy Church, than the reward of all those who, from the beginning of the world to the present day, have concentrated on doing penance, but without the experience of this kind of exercise.[22] I am not saying that simple reflection on these two considerations is so profitable, but that they are very special means, on man's part, for obtaining that reverent affection; this, I say, is what is so profitable.[23] This is the only exercise, independently of any others, such as fasting, keeping vigil, wearing hair-cloth, and the rest, which is, of itself, pleasing to Almighty God and deserves to have his reward.[24] It would be impossible for a soul to have God's reward without this reverent affection. And the reward shall be in proportion to it. For he who has much of it shall have a great reward, and he who has less of it, shall have less.

All these other things, like fasting, keeping vigil, wearing hair-cloth, and so on, are profitable only insofar as they are helpful in obtaining this reverent affection. Without it they are nothing; while reverent affection is sometimes completely sufficient in itself without these other things. And it is often obtained and possessed in its full splendor by very many without any of these other things.[25] I say all this because I would have you know how to give proper weight and commendation to everything according to its worth: more to the more worthy and less to the less. For ignorance here is often the cause of much error. It often leads men to give greater weight and commendation to bodily exercises of penance, like fasting, keeping vigil, wearing hair-cloth, and the rest, than they do to spiritual exercises in the virtues or to this reverent affection I have been talking about. And therefore I shall say a little more than I have yet said about the merit and worth of this reverent affection, in the hope that through my exposition you may be better instructed in this exercise than you are at present.[26]

The nature of the aforesaid exercise in this reverent affection, when it is introduced by these two reflections on fear and hope, may well be compared with a tree that is laden with fruit.[27] Fear is that part of the tree within the earth, that is, the root; and hope is that part of the tree which is above the earth, that is, the trunk and the boughs. Inasmuch as the hope is sure and stable, it resembles the trunk; inasmuch as it draws men to works of love, it resembles the boughs. But this reverent affection is always the fruit. As long as the fruit is hanging on the tree, it shares in some way the unripe savor of the tree. But some time after it has been plucked from the tree, and is fully ripe, then it loses all taste of the tree.[28] Before, it was fit only for the servants; now it is fit for the king.

It is at this time that this reverent affection is as profitable as I said. So set yourself to gather this fruit from the tree, and to offer it, as it is, to the high King of Heaven.[29] And then you shall be called God's own child, loving him with a pure love, for himself, and not for his gifts.[30] What I mean is this. The innumerable good gifts which Almighty God has given to every soul in this life are wholly sufficient reasons, and more, for every soul to love him with all its mind, all its understanding, and all its will.[31] Yet if it were possible (which, of course, it is not) for a soul to be as powerful, worthy, and intelligent as all the saints and angels in heaven taken together, and not to have received its worthiness from God nor to have been shown any kindness by God in this life; if such a soul saw the loveliness of God in himself and the abundance of it, it would be ravished above its powers to love God until its heart burst: so lovable and so attractive, so good and so glorious is he in himself. Oh, what a wonderful thing, and how high a thing to speak of, is the love of God, and beyond the comprehension of man;[32] in such wise that no man can speak of it so as to give the right understanding of the least degree of it, except by impossible examples.

This is what I mean when I say "loving him with a pure love for himself and not for his gifts." It is not the same as saying—though this would be well said—"loving him much for his gifts, but infinitely more for himself."[33] If I may use more elevated language to clarify what I mean by the perfection and the profit of this reverent affection, I say that a soul whose affection is energized by the felt

169

presence of God as he is in himself and as he dwells in a perfect soul, whose reason is illumined by the clear beam of the everlasting light which is God, so as to see and to experience the loveliness of God as he is in himself; such a soul has, during that time and moment, lost all consciousness of any good deed or any kindness that God ever did for it in this life.[34] And so during this time the soul neither sees nor appreciates any other reason for loving God except God himself.[35]

So though it may be said, when we speak of ordinary perfection, that the great goodness and the great kindness that God has shown us in this life are noble and worthy reasons for loving God, yet the perfect lover of God, who directs his gaze to the bull's-eye in the target of perfection[36] (and it is toward this that I intend to direct you by writing in these terms), for fear of missing his perfection—that is to say, its supreme point[37]—now seeks no other reason for loving God except God himself. This is what I mean when I say that pure love is to love God for himself and not for his gifts.

And therefore, in the language of my parable,[38] set yourself to pluck the fruit from the tree and to offer it alone to the King of Heaven, so that your love will be chaste. For as long as you offer him the fruit while it is still unripe and hanging on the tree, you may well be compared to a woman who is not chaste, because she loves a man more for his gifts than for himself.[39] See then why I make this comparison. I believe that it is your fear of death and of the shortness of time, together with hope of forgiveness for all your carelessness, that makes you as reverent as you are in God's service. If this is how it is, then your fruit has the unripe savor of the tree. And though it pleases God up to a point, it does not please him perfectly; and this is the reason why your love is not chaste. Chaste love is when you ask God neither to be freed from pain nor to have increase in reward, nor for the sweetness of his love in this life—unless it be, at any given time, that you desire the sweetness for the restoring of your spiritual strength, so that it does not fail you along the way;[40] it is when you ask God for nothing but himself.[41] And you do not care nor take account of whether you are in pain or bliss, as long as you have him whom you love. This is chaste love. This is perfect love. And therefore set yourself to pluck the fruit from the tree: that is to say, pluck your reverent affection from the thoughts of fear and of hope which come before, so that you can offer it, in itself, to God, ripe and chaste, having as its source nothing that is beneath him nor mingled with him (though it were the best of all these), but him alone, by himself.[42]

Then is it as rewarding as I say it is. For it is plainly known without any doubt to all those who are experienced in the science of God's knowledge and God's love that whenever a man's affection is stirred toward God without a cause, that is, without any specific thought acting as messenger to occasion the stirring, then it deserves everlasting life.[43] And because a soul that is so disposed (that is, one who plucks the fruit from the tree and offers it ripe) can be lifted up to God, suddenly and without cause, innumerable times in one hour,[44] it merits, more than I can say, to be brought up into joy through the grace of God who is the chief worker. So prepare yourself to offer the fruit when it is ripe and has been plucked from the tree.

At the same time, the fruit which is offered on the tree as constantly as man's frailty will permit, merits salvation. But fruit ripe and plucked from the tree, suddenly offered to God without any cause, that is perfection.[45] And by this you can see that the tree is good, even though I bid you pluck the fruit from it for your greater perfection. So I am planting it in your garden,[46] for I would have you gather its fruit and preserve it for your Lord; and also because I would have you know what sort of exercise it is that knits man's soul to God and makes it one with him in love and union of wills.[47]

According to those words of St. Paul, *Qui adhaeret Deo, unus spiritus est cum illo*, that is, "he who draws near to God," by the sort of reverent affection mentioned above, "is one spirit with God,"[48] although God and he are two, and distinct according to nature, nevertheless they are so knitted together in grace that they are but one spirit: and all this in oneness of love and union of wills. In this oneness the marriage is made between God and the soul that shall never be broken except by mortal sin,[49] even though the ardor and fervor of this work cease for a time. In the spiritual awareness of this oneness a loving soul can say, or sing, if it will, the holy word that is written in the *Book of Songs* in the Bible: *Dilectus meus mihi et ego illi*, that is, "My beloved unto me and I to him;" understanding thus: "It shall be fastened with the spiritual glue of grace" on God's part, and "with loving consent in gladness of spirit" on your part.[50]

Climb up this tree, then, as I said at the beginning, and when you come to the fruit—that is, to the reverent affection which will always be in you as long as you think steadfastly on those first two considerations and refuse, as I said, to deceive yourself with lies—you must take good care of the work that is done in your soul at that time, and set yourself, as best you can through grace, to humble yourself under the highness of your God.[51] Then you will be able to make the exercise at other times, directly, without having to climb to it by other considerations.[52] In truth it is this exercise which, as I said, is so rewarding. And the longer this fruit has been gathered from the tree, that is to say, separated from any thought, and the oftener the exercise is done suddenly, eagerly, lovingly, and without any means, the sweeter it smells and the better it pleases the King of Heaven.[53] And whenever you experience sweetness and consolation in this exercise, it is because he breaks open the fruit and gives you a part of your own present.[54]

And when, in the first beginning, you feel this exercise to be so hard, heart-constricting, and without consolation, this means that the greenness of the fruit still hanging on the tree, or else just plucked, puts your teeth on edge.[55] Nevertheless it is profitable for you; for there is no way of eating the sweet kernel without first cracking the hard shell and biting on the bitter rind. However, if your teeth are weak, that is to say, your spiritual strength, then my counsel is that you have recourse to stratagems, for "skill is better than brute strength."

There is another reason why I am planting this tree in your garden for you to climb. For although God can do whatever he will, yet, as I understand it, it is impossible for any man to attain to the perfection of this exercise without these two means, or others like them, coming before. And yet it belongs to the perfection of this exercise to be sudden and without any means. And therefore I counsel you to make these considerations your own; not yours by right, for to think that would be sinful, but yours as a gracious gift of God sent by me as his messenger, unworthy though I am.[56] For you must understand full well that every thought that moves you to good, whether it comes from within by your angel messenger or from without by a human messenger, is simply an instrument of grace, given, sent and chosen by God himself to work within your soul.[57]

Here is the reason why I counsel you to use these two considerations rather than any others. Man is a composite of two substances, corporeal and spiritual; so that it is necessary to have two separate means whereby to come to perfection, especially as both these substances will be joined immortally in the resurrection at the last day.[58] Hence both substances must be brought to perfection in this life by a common concord with it; which consists, for the corporeal substance, in fear; and for the spiritual, in hope. And this, it seems to me, is very right and proper. For as there is nothing that will detach the body from all liking of earthly things so soon as will a real fear of death, so there is nothing that will lift up the affection of a sinful soul to the love of God so soon or so fervently as will the certain hope of forgiveness of all its carelessness. And therefore I have directed you to climb by these two considerations.[59] However, if your good angel (or any man either) teaches you in your spiritual understanding another two means which appear to be more according to your disposition than these two, you can safely and without blame take them and leave these. But still in my opinion, and until I have more understanding, I believe that these will be very helpful to you and not unsuitable to your disposition, insofar as I have experience of it.[60]

If, then, you think they are doing you good, thank God heartily. And for God's love, pray for me. Please do so, for I am a wretch, and you do not know in what case I am. No more now; but God's blessing and mine to you.[61] Read this often; do not forget it; set yourself this exercise diligently, and avoid all hindrance and occasion of hindrance. In the name of Jesus. Amen.

Notes

Introduction

1. The "Letter of Private Direction" was certainly written after this "Letter on Prayer," since the author refers to it there: "For this same werk, if it be verrely concevyd, is that reverent affeccioun and the frute departyd fro the tre that I speke of in thi lityl pistle of preier". There are two long passages in "Private Direction" that indicate the severity of the attack on the author.

2. In the *Cloud, ed. cit.*, ch. 18, the author shows a very sensitive awareness of such criticism; cf. pp. 158–59.

3. The "Letter on Prayer" was certainly written after the *Cloud*, and therefore after the translation of the *Mystical Theology*. It is difficult to say where it stands vis-à-vis *Pursuit of Wisdom* and the two pieces on discretion.

4. The point is made strongly, for instance, in ch. 4 of the *Cloud*, pp. 123–25.

5. Once the Christian community realized that the *eschaton* might well not happen tomorrow, the pagan philosophy of *carpe diem*, which Christianity had rejected, always remained both a threat and a promise.

6. Cf. Julian of Norwich: *Showings, passim.*

7. He refers to sacramental confession as integral to the work of the *Cloud* five or six times. Cf. *Cloud, ed. cit.*, pp. 152, 176, 189, 219, 264.

8. Cf. *Cloud, ed. cit.*, pp. 29–42 and *passim;* and David Knowles, "The Excellence of the Cloud," in *Downside Review* lii: (Jan. 1934).

9. Methley records one of his mystical experiences as taking place while celebrating mass; and in one of his works, *Refectorium Salutis* (ch. vii), he insists that the desire for contemplation to the detriment of liturgical celebration is a diabolic temptation.

10. *Infra.*

11. Cf. Denis's *Mystical Theology*, ch. 1, *supra*.
12. Cf. *infra*.
13. Cf. E. Colledge and J. Walsh, *The Ladder of Monks*.
14. Cf. The *Cloud, ed. cit.*, ch. 35, pp. 187–88.
15. The Lesson, the meditation, and the petition are linked together for the beginners and the proficients; ibid. and n. 246.
16. Cf. *infra* and the *Cloud, ed. cit.*, pp. 116–17.
17. Cf. ch. 35.
18. *Infra*.
19. The author, in ch. 70, expresses his reluctance to cite other authors in support of his views. Here we have a rare exception, and it is significant that they should be Bernard of Clairvaux and Thomas of Aquin.
20. The *Cloud, ed. cit.*, p. 174, n. 198.
21. Cf. *supra*.
22. 2 Cor 3:17.
23. *Infra*.
24. W. Butler-Bowden, *The Book of Margery Kempe* (London: Jonathan Cape, 1936).
25. Inward Stirrings, *supra*.
26. Julian of Norwich, *Showings* (crit. ed.), p. 530, n. 190.
27. Ibid. (ed. Classics of Western Spirituality), ch. 51, pp. 273–74.
28. *Infra*, nn. 26–29.
29. The *Cloud, ed. cit.*, ch. 50, pp. 216–17.
30. Ibid., ch. 24, p. 169.
31. Barbet, *Thomas Gallus*, p. 31. All authentic prayer is chaste, but the positive, *oratio casta*, petitions (for oneself or for others) for material goods; the comparative *castior*, for spiritual goods; the superlative *castissima*, for God Himself.
32. Ibid., p. 92.
33. *Infra*.
34. Cf. The *Cloud, ed. cit.*, ch. 4, p. 122.
35. *Infra*.
36. Barbet, *Thomas Gallus*, p. 164.
37. Sg 3:11.
38. Barbet, *Thomas Gallus*, p. 175.
39. Ibid., pp. 138–39.
40. *Ed. cit.*
41. The *Cloud, ed. cit.*, ch. 73, pp. 260–61.
42. Ibid., ch. 74, p. 262.
43. *Infra*.
44. Ibid.

A Letter on Prayer

1. ME: reule thin hert . . . make it ful knowen to thin hert. Cassian, who stands at the head of monastic teaching in the West, inherits from Origen that the heart is the principle of our knowledge of God and divine things, the seat of wisdom and understanding, the descriptive word for the spirit of man. Cf. K. Rahner, "Coeur de Jésus chez Origène," *RAM*, 1934, p. 171. "Private Direction" likewise begins with reflection on prayer (*infra*) and the *Cloud* itself introduces the question of prayer and the shortness of time at the head of the treatise. Cf. *ed. cit.*, ch. 2, pp. 117ff.

2. Gregory the Great says that as long as the day of our death is unknown to us, we can believe that it is always nigh, and hence be more fervent in our love for God and neighbor (*Homil in Ezech II*, 5, 7: P.L. 76, 988). The liturgy for the souls of the faithful departed and the practice of multiple masses for the dead explains the importance of death in the life and prayer of the medieval Church. John of the Cross sums up the tradition for the contemplative in his *Spiritual Canticle:* "The soul, taking account of her obligations, knowing that God has created her for himself alone, for which she owes him all the rest of the love of her will . . . and that a great part of her life has vanished. . . . In order to remedy so much evil and harm, especially as she sees God to be far distant and hidden . . . she is touched with fear and inward grief of heart at so great perdition and peril, and renounces all things, ceases from all business, and delays not a day nor an hour" (E. Allison Peers, *Complete Works of John of The Cross, II*, pp. 186–87).

3. "Our Lord has wished our last hour to be unknown to us, so that we might always keep it in view; for as long as we are unable to foresee it, we shall always be in a state of readiness for it" (Gregory, *Homil in Evang* I, XIII, 6: P.L. 76, 1126). 1 Cor 15:52: "In a moment, in the twinkling of an eye at the last trumpet. For the trumpet shall sound, and the dead shall rise again incorruptible, and we shall be changed."

4. Ps 46:7 (Vulgate): "Sing praises to our God, sing praises to our King. For God is king of all the earth: sing wisely." This contemplative prayer is to be offered to "the high King of heaven." "He shall think on the greatness of his trespass, and, on the other hand, on the power of the judge. From such consideration comes fear" (Benjamin, ch. 1, *supra*).

5. Ps 110:10. The *glossa ordinaria:* "Fear of the judgment is the gateway to conversion."

6. The author seems to be recalling the apostles' reaction to Jesus' agony in Gethsemane. Cf. Mt 26:37–39, 43. In the *Cloud* he addresses the contemplative who is beginning his prayer: "A weary and wretched heart indeed, and one fast asleep in sloth . . . " (*ed. cit.*, ch. 2).

7. The prayer exercise of the *Cloud* destroys all sin and acquires the virtues (cf. *ed. cit.*, ch. 12, p. 146).

8. This is the characteristic teaching of the *Cloud* author, who stresses the importance of auricular confession in his every work. Cf. Introduction, *su-*

pra. In the *Cloud* itself, he directs that the prayer exercise must not be begun until the exercitant has been to confession (*ed. cit.*, ch. 28, p. 176).

9. The author follows Gallus in teaching, here as elsewhere, that ultimate salvation and the summit of human perfection are one and the same. It is ecstatic union—*unicio super memtem*—that constitutes the highest perfection of the heart and spirit.

10. This idea is commonplace in the Psalms and other hortatory OT literature. The scribe of a Harley MS glosses Psalm 36 (v. 28 and 40); PH offers 33:23 (cf. 50/I). Most apposite would appear to be Ps 9:11 "and let them trust in thee who know thy name; for thou has not forsaken them that seek thee, O Lord." However, no Psalm versicle reproduces the four ideas of the author: "the goodness of God . . . never forsakes . . . truly trust . . . desire of amendment." The sentence is made up of four balanced cola.

11. Guigo *II*, in the *Ladder of Monks* describes the prayer of the contemplative process as "the heart's devout turning to God to drive away evil and obtain what is good" (p. 82). The *Cloud* uses the same definition, "God" as appropriate in the context. But neither here nor elsewhere does our author link amendment with the *oratio* of the contemplative.

12. Two Vulgate uses of staff (*baculus*) are highly relevant to this image of hope: *Tob* 10:4: " . . . the light of our eyes, the staff of our old age, the comfort of our life, the hope of our posterity"; and Ps 22:4: "For though I should walk in the midst of the shadow of death, I will fear no evils, for thou art with me; thy rod and thy staff they have comforted me."

13. A very high and steep mountain, writes Augustine, and the end of all fulfilment: the fulfilment of the law, which is charity—*Christus Deus, Deus Charitas.* Cf. *In Epistolam Joannis ad Parthos* X, v., 4: P.L. 35, 2057.

14. Cf. *infra*, where he develops the Augustinian doctrine of hope and chaste love. In the *Cloud*, he simply writes of perfect charity: "the love of God for himself above all creatures" (*ed. cit.*, ch. 24, p. 169).

15. In the *Cloud* it is rather a little impulse—"this litil blynde love put, when it is betyng upon this darke cloude of unknowyng" (ibid.). However, both terms are synonymous for the *extensio*, the Dionysian contemplative effort, in response to the God who presents himself to the human spirit: here in his mercy and goodness and willingness to receive a little, short service as satisfaction for carelessness and long negligence.

16. "Pursuit of Wisdom" lists seven affections—fear, sorrow (for sin), hope, love, joy, hatred, and shame (cf. *supra*). Here, fear, love, and hope together constitute what the author calls reverence or reverent affection, and it turns out to be one description of the contemplative effort, which the *Cloud* calls "work" or "the work of this book." Thomas Gallus gives us a by no means exhaustive list of synonyms, linked with *mens*, "mind," the spiritual faculty that embraces reason, will, imagination, and sensuality. Cf. chs. 63–67, pp. 243ff.

17. Julian of Norwich, in a memorable chapter, speaks of "reverent drede"—reverential fear. She belongs to the same tradition as the *Cloud* au-

thor here, of which Augustine is the head, in his commentary on 1 Jn 4:18: "Fear is not in love, because perfect love casts out fear" (in *Epistolam Joannis* IX, iv, 5: P.L. 35, 2049). Julian writes that only reverent dread fully pleases God, "and the more it is had, the less it is felt, because of the sweetness of love. Love and dread are brethren . . . and thus we shall, in love, be homely and near to God, and in dread, gentle and courteous to God" (*Revelations*, ch. 74).

18. The *Cloud* author will later declare against quoting authorities in support of his views (*ed. cit.*, ch. 70, p. 256). Here he is clearly basing himself firmly on Augustine. Aquinas is merely additional corroboration. Cf. *Summa Theol.* 2–2ae, 82, 1: "Devotion is manifestly nothing else than a certain will promptly to hand oneself over to the things that belong to God's service (*voluntas quaedam prompte tradendi se ad ea quae pertinent ad Dei famulatum*)".

19. St. Bernard defines devotion as "exultation which arises from the hope of pardon" (*Serm. in Cant.* XVIII, 3: P.L. 183, 161). Elsewhere, in his commentary on Is 6:1–2, he speaks of the two wings of the seraphim as knowledge and devotion (*agnitio et devotio*).

20. Presumably the author's gloss on Bernard.

21. "And what is more . . . this, I say, is what is so profitable." These sentences do not occur in the late Bodleian, Oxford University MS 576—early sixteenth century; nor in Pepwell's printed edition of 1521. Certainly, the introduction of the matter of bodily penance is very abrupt here: no previous reference either to the need for it or to its advantage has been made.

22. The only bodily penance enjoined by the Church at this period was fasting and abstinence. Mention is made in "Inward Stirrings" of silence, fasting, solitude, and other regular practices in religious orders, "or those upon whom they are enjoined by way of penance" (cf. *infra*).

23. ME: I say not that the nakid thinking of thees two thoughtes is so medeful. In the *Cloud* (*ed. cit.*, ch. 4, p. 122), the author reflects that before the fall, all the "stirrings" of the soul were directed to God—impulses or thoughts of pure love. The "two thoughts" in question here are, however, fear (of eternal punishment) and "hope and loving trust in his mercy," which would have had no place in a person's life had man not sinned, or before the fall. Hence the thoughts in themselves are means and not ends.

24. In "Discernment of Spirits," "the signs of a special type of holiness" are "fasting, wearing [hair-cloth], and many other devout observances and forms of behavior and openly reproving the faults of other men" (*infra*); in "Inward Stirrings," it is said that men "who keep strict silence, unusual fasts, and who dwell in solitude are often considered very holy" (*infra*); while in the *Cloud*, discretion is counseled in eating and drinking, in the length of time given to prayer or reading and conversation (*ed. cit.*, ch. 41, p. 199).

25. Synonymous with reverent affection is the term in the *Cloud* that the author borrows from Richard of St. Victor's *Benjamin Major* (IV, 22–23), "the grace of contemplation, prefigured by the Ark of the Testament in the

Old Law." Moses, as opposed to Aaron and Besebeel, had to labor long and hard for it. Cf. chs. 71 and 73, pp. 258 and 260.

26. "Private Direction" and "Stirrings" were also written at the request of the author's penitent(s). In the former, as he expatiates on the spiritual exercise that is the "work" of the *Cloud*, the author singles out for specific mention, among several other titles, "that reverent affeccion and the frute departed fro the tre that I spake of in thi lityl pistle of preier" (*infra*).

27. This paragraph is an apt summary of the spiritual exegesis of the Bible in the Church of the West during the Middle Ages. Apple trees, fig trees, vines, and pomegranates all belong to the allegorical texture of the Song of Songs (cf. 2:3, 2:5; 5,1,7,8, 8,5—apples and apple trees; 2:13, 2:15; 6:10; 7:8—figs and vines: 4:3, 4:13; 6:6; 7:2—pomegranates). For St. Bernard, the living wood of the tree of the vine is the wisdom of contemplation, and we are to save one another with its fruits, which are the fruits of the Spirit listed by Paul in Gal 5:22. These fruits of the Lord are our spiritual progress. *Serm in Cant* (5:1) 63: P.L. 183, 1081–82.

28. Gilbert of Hoyland, who set himself to complete St. Bernard's Sermons on the Canticle of Canticles, comments as follows on the verse "Let my beloved come into this garden and eat the fruit of his apple trees" (5:1): "Happy the soul which is worthy of your [sc. Christ's] invitation to eat the ripe fruit which has nothing bitter about it" (*Serm. in Cant* 40, 1: P.L. 184, 207–08).

29. We have here the common pastiche of biblical images to represent the "digging and delving" of what Thomas Gallus calls antecedent contemplation—for the highest work of redemption in which we are called to co-operate in Christ. So we have the vine of which the Father is the husbandman (Ps 79:9–16) and the son the heir (Mt 21:33–42). This is given eucharistic significance in the allegory of the vine and branches (Jn 15:1–7), and in the Apocalypse we have allusion to Gn 3 and Ez 47:12, when the tree of life yields its fruit in the midst of the new city (Apoc 22:1–3).

30. This is a regular theme with the author. Cf. *Cloud, ed. cit.*, ch. 50, where his point is illuminative consolations, "sensible and spiritual," as with Walter Hilton, *Scale II*, ch. 11. In "Stirrings," it is the active aspect of contemplative love—"the blind shot with the sharp arrow of a love that longs" (*infra*). In "Private Direction," "the love is chaste and perfect," when one has arrived at mortification's ultimate goal—utter self-despoilment (*infra*). The source is Augustine: "Let us love God with a pure and chaste heart. The heart is not chaste if it cares for God for the sake of the reward" (*Enarr. in Psalm* 55, 17: P.L. 36, 658).

31. ME: with alle his mynde, with alle his witte and with all his wylle. Richard of St. Victor says that across the four degrees of violent love God is loved wholly with the heart, the soul, and the mind. The second degree is binding love: We are bound to God by his gifts, his blessings of nature grace and glory—creation, redemption, eternal glory. Cf. Clare Kirchberger, ed. *Selected writings*, pp. 222, 214.

32. Richard says something similar in speaking of the third kind of ec-

179

stasy in his *Benjamin Major*, 14: "The human soul . . . passes beyond itself in ecstasy of mind, and leaving itself altogether, it is immersed in divine things by contemplation and devotion. . . . The abundance of delights is the cause of the ascent; for by the infusion of divine sweetness, the devout soul does not understand what she feels in her inmost heart, inasmuch as the greatness of her exultation and joy . . . ravishes her above herself."

33. "God is loved gratis; one asks for no other gift. Whoever seeks another gift from God, makes what he desires to have a more precious gift than God himself. God's gift is himself" (Augustine, *Enarr. in Psalm* 72, 32: P.L. 36, 923).

34. The paragraph is another example of the author's deft handling of his sources: here the long description by Richard of St. Victor of what he designates the second kind of ecstasy in his *Benjamin Major* (V), where the key text is 2 Cor 3:18—"by looking on the glory of the Lord we are transformed from glory to glory into the image of his likeness, as by the Spirit of the Lord." Cf. Kirchberger, pp. 195–202. This paragraph constitutes an *argumentatio perfectissima* with its five steps: the proposition, the reason, the confirmation of the reason, the illustration, and the conclusion.

35. "If you long for him when you consider his kindnesses towards you, and your heart is restless in your desire for him, do not seek from him anything outside himself; he himself is enough for you" (*Enarr. in Psalm* 55, 17: P.L. 36, 658).

36. The same image of the bowman and the target is used in the *Cloud*, *ed. cit.*, ch. V p. 129.

37. ME: in the pointe of perfeccioun. The perfection of the exercise described in the *Cloud* "is to strive by grace to reach a point to which you cannot come by nature: that is to say, to be made one with God in spirit and in love and in oneness of wills" (*ed. cit.*, ch. 67, p. 249).

38. ME: ensaumple. The O.E.D. says that the modern archaistic use of the word is taken from its N.T. usage: the principal one being the Lord's washing of the feet: "I have given you an example"—*exemplum dedi vobis.* In 1 Pt 2:29 we have "Christ suffered for us, leaving you an example," and in Jd (v. 7) "Sodom and Gomorrah were made an example." In Ez (Vulgate 14:8), "example" and "proverb" are synonymous. As a rhetorical figure, *exemplum* is defined as the citing of something said or done in the past, along with the definite naming of the doer or author (Caplan, *Cicero*, p. 383).

39. "If you praise God that he might give you something, you do not love him for nothing. You would be ashamed if your wife loved you for your riches; and perhaps if poverty befell you, she would be thinking of adultery" (*Enarr. in Psalm* 53, 10: P.L. 36, 626).

40. The same concession is made in the *Cloud*, *ed. cit.* ch. 50, p. 217.

41. Julian of Nowich emphasizes the same Augustinian doctrine in her beautiful prayer: "God of your goodness, give me yourself, for you are enough for me, and I can ask nothing that is less that would be full worship of you" (*Revelations*, ch. 5). And cf. the legend of the aged St. Thomas Aqui-

nas, who heard the Lord ask: "You have spoken well of me, Thomas; what reward would you have?" He answered: "Nothing but yourself, Lord."

42. Augustine, reflecting on "the perfect love which casts out fear" (1 Jn 4:18), quotes Eccl (1:28) "If a man be without fear, he cannot be justified," and the Psalm (18:10) "Fear of the Lord is chaste, and remains forever." Fear, he says, is the remedy, charity health. In *Epistolam Joannis ad Parthos* X, 4, 5: P.L. 35, 2049.

43. The exercise of "the stirring of love unto God" is first described in detail in chs. 3 and 4 of the *Cloud:* It is the work that pleases God most; angels and saints take joy in it; the fiends try to destroy it; it eases the pains of purgatory; it purifies and makes virtuous the exercitant; it enables him to comprehend the infinite God; it gives some taste here of the sweetness of everlasting life; it assures the full taste of the happiness of heaven; it is a sudden impulse, coming without warning. Cf. *ed. cit.*, pp. 119–26.

44. Cf. the *Cloud, ed. cit.*, ch. 4, pp. 121–22, and footnotes.

45. The author frequently contrasts salvation and perfection; in fact, the distinction for him coincides with that between Martha and Mary, and the active and contemplative lives, as he divides and subdivides in the *Cloud*— e.g., ch. 20, p. 162. However, he does postulate more forms of contemplative prayer than his own dark contemplation. Cf. *ed. cit.*, ch. 74, p. 262.

46. The same metaphor is used in the contemplative classic the *Scalae Claustralium.* "It is fitting," says the twelfth-century Carthusian author, "that I should offer these first results of our work together . . . so that you may gather the first fruits of the tree which . . . you set in its place among the ordered rows" (cf *The Ladder of Monks*, p. 83).

47. ME: that knitteth mans soule to God and that makith it one with him in loue and acordaunce of wile. In the *Cloud* we have to be knit to God "in spirite and in oneheed of wile." (*ed. cit.*, ch. 8, H 32/15).

48. The author offers scriptural Latin in *Prayer, Stirrings*, and *Private Direction*, but not in the *Cloud* and the other three pieces attributed to him. Cf. Introduction. "Draw near" is a rendering of the Vulgate *adhaeret* (1 Cor 6:17). It is more accurately translated at the end of the paragraph—"fastened." The Vulgate text does not read *cum illo* (with him, sc. God). It is supplied by the author, indicating a citation from memory.

49. ME: And in this oonheed is the mariage maad bitwix God and the soule, the whiche schal never be broken. Hilton (*Scale I*, 8) has: in this onyng is this mariage made betwix God and the soule, whilks schal never be broken (MS Cambridge AL Add.6686, p. 283). The theme of the spiritual marriage and the *aulmen contemplationis* is traditional in Western spirituality; for "the book most read and most frequently commented on in the monastic cloister was the Canticle of Canticles." Cf. Introduction, *supra;* LeClercq, *The Love of Learning*, p. 106.

50. ME: the goostly glewe of grace. Richard of St. Victor speaks of the *glutinum amoris* in *De Gradibus Caritatis:* "The glue of love is so tenacious that it may be said not so much to join as to unite" (P.L. 196, 1204). The ref-

erence to the Song of Songs is 2:16. The *glossa ordinaria* on the verse of the Song reads: "*My beloved* will give his grace and dispense his fruits *to me* and to none other; *and I to him*, I will be fastened (*conglutinabor*) to him and to none other in entire obedience and devotion" (P.L. 113, 1142). This is clearly a likely source for our author's interpretation.

51. 1 Pt 5:5: "God resists the proud, but gives grace to the humble. Be humbled therefore under the mighty hand of God, that he may exalt you in the time of his visitation."

52. "There are some who are so refined by grace and in spirit, and so familiar with God in this grace of contemplation that they may have the perfection of it wherever they will" (*Cloud, ed. cit.*, ch. 71, p. 258).

53. The ascent of the soul is common both to the metaphors of the tree (cf. reverent affection) and of the mount of perfection, and the attitudes and dispositions of contemplative movement are traditional—sudden, eager, joyfully, longingly. Cf., e.g., the *Cloud, ed. cit.*, ch. 6, p. 131. The "sweet smell" recalls the Pauline "we are the good odor of Christ" (2 Cor 2:15); "Thy name is as oil poured out" of the Song (1:2); and of the anointing of Christ's feet with the precious ointment, whose scent filled the whole room (Jn 12:3).

54. Guigo II, the Carthusian, extends this metaphor in his Meditation on holy communion: "Unless this dry bread be first moistened by the saliva of wisdom coming down from the Father of light, you will labor in vain, for what you have gathered up by thinking does not penetrate your understanding" (*The Ladder of Monks*, p. 133).

55. Jer 31:29; Ez 18:2: "The fathers have eaten sour grapes, and the teeth of the children are set on edge."

56. "Sometimes we make progress in this grace [of contemplation] by other men's teaching. . . . I am fashioning and making plain on your behalf the nature of this spiritual ark [of contemplation]" (*Cloud, ed. cit.*, ch. 73, p. 261).

57. St. Bernard: "The Lord sometimes fills our souls with splendors by himself, and sometimes his visitation is carried out by angels; at other times he instructs us by human beings, and then again he consoles and teaches us by means of the Scriptures" (*In Psalmum Qui habitat* XI, I: P.L. 183, 225).

58. This is the common teaching of the schools, following the Sentences of Peter Lombard (Lib. IV, dist. 43–44).

59. Again the author uses the rhetorical device—the *argumentatio perfectissima*:

Here is the reason . . . any others: the propositions
Man is a composite . . . last day: the reasons
Hence both substances . . . in hope: the confirmation of the reasons
And thus, it seems . . . carelessness: the embellishments
And therefore . . . two considerations: the conclusion.

60. Similarly at the end of the *Cloud*, though he expresses his preference with all due emphasis, he still leaves the addressee free: " . . . you can leave it and take another . . . " (*ed. cit.*, ch. 74, p. 262).

61. No other treatise carries a blessing, except the *Cloud* itself.

A Letter of Private Direction

Translator's Introduction

A most important aspect of the *Cloud* corpus that has never been given sufficient attention by its students is the doctrinal cohesiveness internal and external alike, of its various treatises, and with this the traditional nature of the spirituality it teaches. This coherent body of doctrine is what Dom Cuthbert Butler, in his account of the teaching of Sts. Augustine, Gregory the Great, and Bernard of Clairvaux on contemplation and the contemplative life, has called "Western Mysticism." But over and again in recent years there has been frequently expressed an uneasiness and even a studied reluctance to allow the author of the *Cloud* to take what I believe to be his rightful and indeed his prominent place in this tradition, and it is one that, in the English context at least, has also had a deep formative influence in language and literature.

For example, a distinguished spiritual theologian, an acknowledged authority on the mysticism of the East as well as of the West and a serious student of the *Cloud* for many years, has written recently of his unhappiness[1] with the author's reflections on the prayer of Mary the Magdalene, favorite among dark contemplatives: how she "was contemplating with all the love of her heart the supreme and sovereign wisdom of our Lord's Godhead clothed in the dark words of his manhood," and paying scant attention to his human voice and words.[2] The point is not that the *Cloud* author is here advocating the Neoplatonic flight from the body, or manifesting a fear of the senses, as William Johnston alleges. He is speaking rather of the Christian mystical phenomenon of ecstasy to which Paul refers in describing his own spiritual experience,[3] which has been granted to a comparatively small number of solitaries, and belongs to the prayer-process proper to the "higher part of the contemplative life,"[4] to which only very few are destined here below.[5]

There are doubtless those who will say that he has only himself to thank for the fact that so many in recent times have equiparated his essential teaching with the brand of Neoplatonic metaphysic adopted by the Pseudo-Dionysius with its philosophical dryness and eccentric language, since the author insists that Denis's words "clearly corroborate all that I have said or am going to say."[6] The point is (and again I must insist) that our author believes that the Dionysian sayings involve the whole Gospel-teaching of St. Paul, in addition to what is not written in the Apostle's letters but was confided to St. Denis of France, that he in turn might pass it on to the Christian initiates and contemplatives such as Timothy. Not only this, but the prayer proper to the higher part of the contemplative life is what "our ancient Fathers before us have written and taught on that which is the fruit and flower of Holy Scripture."[7]

Another conceivably important point that has hardly been thought worth considering is a possible relationship between the contemplative process taught by the *Cloud* author throughout his works and the current of spirituality that was given the name *Devotio Moderna*. This originated in the Low Countries in the last part of the fourteenth century. It is accepted that the idea of devotion here conceived meant the service of God as understood by Christians in general, and more probably by traditional monastic theology and language. It is worth recalling that our author in his *Letter on Prayer* cites with approval the definition of St. Thomas Aquinas and of St. Bernard of Clairvaux: "The readiness of man's will to do what belongs to God's service," and "Everything should be done swiftly and gladly."[8]

There has been, however, in this century, during the great revival of theological and historical interest in Western spirituality and the newly found conviction of its crucial moment in the modern Church, an over-precious concern with "schools" of spirituality, and an equal anxiety to set up distinctive lines of demarcation between them. The first in order of importance in the Western tradition has been "action" and "contemplation," with the typological pairs Leah and Rachel, Martha and Mary. None of the great masters and practitioners of the contemplative life, however, from Simon Stylites to Charles de Foucauld, have been able to conceive of the one without the other. It is generally accepted that the purest form of the contemplative life in the West is the eremitical vocation of the Carthusian, and it is the author of their twelfth-century *Consuetudines*, the venerable Guigo, the fifth prior of the Grande Chartreuse, who writes so emphatically of their apostolate of spiritual and pastoral writing and copying. "As many books as we write," he says, "so many heralds of the truth we make for ourselves . . . and thus we may hope that God will reward us for all those who are saved from their errors or make progress in the Catholic truth by means of our books, or are pierced to the heart for their sins and vices, or are fired with longing for their heavenly home."[9]

"Being pierced to the heart and fired with longing" are the two strands of compunction, so dear to the heart of the great St. Gregory, a monk turned pope by force of circumstances and mourning thereafter his lost contemplative solitude.[10] Joseph de Guibert has demonstrated the part played by compunction in apostolic preaching from Peter's first sermon on the morning of Pentecost: "Now when they heard this they were pierced to the heart, and said to Peter and the rest of the apostles: Brethren, what shall we do?"[11] The words reflect a profound and complex experience of remorse, fear, and astonishment, but also of confidence.[12] Peter, and all those committed to the apostolic life after him, have preached the same message and exercised the same priesthood, whether this is immediately ministerial or belonging to the people of God as a whole: "Repent and be baptized everyone of you in the name of Jesus Christ for the forgiveness of your sins, and you shall receive the gift of the Holy Spirit."[13]

The manual of the *Devotio Moderna* is acknowledged to be *The Imitation of Christ*, written in some form or other between 1360 and 1380, and thus in all probability exactly contemporaneous with the *Cloud* at one term and *Private Direction* at the other. Perhaps one of its most celebrated sentences occurs in its very first chapter: "I would much rather feel compunction than know its definition."[14] The aphorism highlights another alleged difference in spiritualities across the centuries, the anti-intellectualism so often considered typical of the *Devotio Moderna* and other spiritual movements, including fourteenth-century English spirituality.[15] It is, however, a question of preference and of opting for what is considered to be more essential, and indeed more in accord with the psychology of Christian contemplation, which has its organized beginnings in Augustine of Hippo, and tells a consistent story until the treatises of St. John of the Cross, and of all who take up contemplative theory from his *Ascent of Mount Carmel*, *Dark Night*, and *Living Flame of Love*.

187

Augustine, who in no sense can be considered an anti-intellectualist, is also second to none in his affective language as he writes his autobiographical *Confessions*, as we shall see. Doctrinally and scripturally, he makes his position clear at the very beginning of his commentary on John's Gospel, when he says that the Prologue—"In the beginning was the Word, and the Word was with God, and the Word was God"—cannot tell the mystery of God as it is. Each one can only catch what he can, even when God's mercy is with him. John, though inspired, does not reveal the divine mysteries as they are, but only as a man can grasp them.[16]

When the author in *Private Direction* tries to describe both the actual experience of knowing God by unknowing, and the negative, affective way leading to it, he is doing no more than translating into late medieval language the description given by Augustine a thousand years before, of what would seem to be his own experience:

If one could silence the clamorous appetites of the flesh, and hush one's perceptions of earth, the waters and air; if one could silence the vault of heaven; and could one's very soul be silent to itself, and by ceasing to think of itself, mount above the awareness of self; if one could silence all dreams and images which the mind can imagine; if one could hush all tongues, and signs and symbols that pass: for all these say to any who listen, "we did not make ourselves, but he made us that abides for ever"; if after speaking thus, they were then to be silenced after drawing the mind's attention to him who made them, and he were now to speak alone not through them but by himself, so that we might hear his Word, not through human tongue, nor through the voice of an angel, not through a voice speaking out of a cloud, nor through any false appearance, but that we might hear instead without these things, himself in his very Being—himself whose presence we love in those things; that we might hear him now with our spirit as we reached out with our swift impulse of thought to that Eternal Wisdom which dwells unmoved beyond all things; if this movement continued on, and all other visions were to pass away as totally unequal; and this one vision were to ravish the beholder, immerse him and draw him into these inner joys, so that life might be for ever like that fleeting moment of awareness which we have longed for; would not this be "Enter into the joy of your Lord?"[17]

The *Imitation of Christ*, surprisingly to many who can scarcely conceive of the author engaging in the Dionysian exercise of anagogical contemplation, expresses this same yearning and longing: "Oh, when shall it be given to me, at the full, to be still and to see how sweet the Lord is? When shall I gather myself at the full, so that, for your love, I no longer feel myself, but only you, above all feeling and all human modes, and in a way that is hardly known to everyone?"[18]

It is Gerard Groote who is accepted as the real founder and initiator of the *Devotio Moderna*. Born into a wealthy bourgeois family in Deventer in Flanders in 1340, he studied in the Faculty of Arts in the University of Paris and became the recipient of rich benefices without becoming a cleric; he was converted from a frivolous life in 1370. Significantly he entered the Charterhouse of Munnikhuizen near Arnhem, and this served him as a novitiate and an introduction to the eremitical life and spirituality. The authors he studied and who influenced him—Cassian, Gregory, Jerome, Suso—drew him into the mainstream of monastic theology. He was then ordained deacon in order that he might exercise the ministry of traveling preacher, but he frequently lost the favor of the ecclesiastical authorities because of his violent denunciations of the vices of the clergy, and was eventually forbidden to preach. He died in 1384.[19]

Groote's teaching on contemplation was presented as much more simple than that of the Rhineland mystics, though he and Ruysbroeck were friends and he translated some of the former's works. For him the reality of contemplation was declared to be the perfection of love: *contemplatio seu perfectio charitatis*.[20] Unlike the *Cloud* author, he does not describe the contemplative process. He does, however, press home the need for the contemplative—"and not everyone is bound to be contemplative or reach out after the absolute perfection of charity"[21]—to strip himself totally in spiritual poverty and exercise himself in the effective practice of the virtues. He is also at one with the doctrine of *Private Direction* in his insistence that one enters into the divinity by means of contemplating Christ in his humanity—which is the *imitatio humanitatis Christi*.[22] Whatever is of prime importance in the various kinds of spirituality that came to flower in the second half of the fourteenth century across the face of Western Europe is here, whether it is labeled Carthusian, Cistercian, Dionysian, Franciscan piety, or "Modern Devotion." Groote looked not only to the Greeks Climacus and Chrysostom, but to Bernard, David of Augsbourg, and Bonaventure's *De Triplici Via*. For all of them, there is no other way to the summit of unitive contemplation than the affective meditation on the suffering humanity of Christ: "That is," writes Thomas of St. Victor, "in the careful consideration of the blessed, beautiful and wounded Christ. For among all the mind's exercises for the ascent of the spiritual intelligence, this is the most efficacious. Indeed, the more ardent we are in his most sweet love, through the devout and blessed imaginative gazing on him, the higher shall we ascend in the apprehension of the things of the God-head."²³ The universality of the spiritual teaching is inevitable. In the person of Christ, in the manner of his living on earth, the divine exemplars and virtues are seen in their most holy effects. The true test of the soul's advance in virtue, of her growth in the divine like-ness, is her imitation of the Christ who loved us first and left us an example.²⁴ As our author insists, "He who does not enter by this door, is . . . a nocturnal thief and a daylight prowler."²⁵

The Structure and Doctrine of Private Direction

Though *Private Direction* in many ways has the appearance of a meta-physical (Neoplatonic) and theological (apophatic) treatise on the un-derpinning of anagogical contemplation, it is in fact what the author declares it to be: a detailed account of how this individual spiritual "son" of the author should habitually practice the "inward occupa-tion," the prayer proper to the eremitical contemplative life. What has been described at length and embellished with a multitude of digressions in the *Cloud* itself, where the author deals with every-thing that occurs to him from his reading, reflection—his *lectio divina* in the fullest sense,²⁶ and in particular his own long and varied ex-perience as a director of *ex professo* contemplatives, he now brings to bear for the benefit of the addressee of this letter. The author wishes to restrict himself to the needs and profit of this individual, "the tar-get and the bull's-eye of his intention." Not that he will not digress; his style and manner of thought makes this inevitable.²⁷ He will, however, take special pains to separate his digressions from the main thread of his narrative, and freely acknowledge them. In his rather rambling exegesis of "Without me you can do nothing," he concludes by saying, "Here indeed are many words and only a little meaning in them. . . . Now that this has been said, let it stand, even though it has little to do with our subject."²⁸ In the main, he strictly adheres to the promises made in his prologue.

In the *Cloud*, the "higher part of the active life and the lower part of the contemplative life" are shown to be the virtuous life. The au-thor defines virtue after Richard of St. Victor and St. Augustine: the ordered and controlled affection that has God himself for its single object.²⁹ However, Richard speaks at length of the virtues whose practice prepares the soul for contemplation, in his *Benjamin Minor*; and the *Cloud* author provides his English contemplatives with an appropriate paraphrase of Richard's work in the vernacular, which he calls "a treatise on the pursuit of wisdom," by which he means contemplative wisdom;[30] and Thomas of St. Victor called it *Sapientia Christianorum*. In the *Cloud*, the author, in treating of the most important of contemplative virtues—humility and charity—introduces the distinction between imperfect and perfect virtues: the former being a preparation for dark contemplation, and the latter its true effects:

> During this time [of abundance of the grace] which increases its desire as often and for as long as God deigns to grant it, a soul living in this mortal flesh may lose and forget all awareness and experience of its own being, so that it takes no account of its holiness or its wretchedness. . . . During this time it is made perfectly humble.[31]

Here then is the remote preparation for anagogical contemplation, and the author in *Private Direction* begins by describing its proximate preparation—the entering into—this prayer. Unlike Hugo de Balma,[32] who not only recommends a place, time, and even a posture (*in aliquo loco occultissimo*—a very secret or private place; *maxime in secreto noctis silentio*—in the deep silence of the night; *faciem suam dirigendo in coelum*—with face upturned toward heaven), or Richard Methley,[33] who recommends one's own choir-stall in the nave of the cruciform Carthusian Church, outside the time of community liturgy, our author simply refers to solitude "when you come away by yourself."[34]

When, however, he first describes the nature of the exercise proper to the prayer of dark contemplation in the *Cloud* itself, he first says, "Look up now, feeble creature. . . . Press on with speed, I pray you. Look ahead now and never mind what is behind."[35] No words or any word can be appropriate to express this humble impulse of love by which one lifts up one's heart to God,[36] this "simple extension of your will, reaching out to God."[37] This is the sole activity of the mind that is proper to the exercise. The author calls it the "nakid entent," and it signifies the substance of the contemplative effort. The traditional word in the spiritual vocabulary of the West is *extension*, inherited from the Vulgate translation of the Pauline phrase in Philippians: . . . *quae quidem retro obliviscens, ad ea vero quae sunt priora extendens meipsum, ad destinatum persequor ad bravium supernae vocationis Dei in Christo Jesu: "forgetting the things behind me, and reaching out to what lies ahead*, I press on toward the goal which is the prize of God's heavenly call in Christ Jesus."[38] Further than this, Augustine will not hesitate to use the same word "to extend" in terms of ecstasy and assimilation: "insofar as the human spirit can reach out toward that which is eternal (*mens, quantumcumque extenderit se in id quod eternum est*), in that far, it becomes conformed to the image of God."[39]

"Let faith be your foundation."[40] Thomas Gallus assures us that it is faith in the Incarnate Word that is all-important here. It is a living and growing faith whose term is the superintellectual union with God that the Dionysians called deification: "It is only if you believe that you will come to understand."[41] Hugo de Balma points out in the consideration at the end of his *Mystical Theology:* "Whether the soul by means of its affect can be united with God (*moveri in Deum*) simply through ardor or desire, without any preceding or concomitant activity of the intellect" (*sine aliqua cogitatione intellectus praevia, vel concomitante*).

> This unitive wisdom is the wisdom of Christians alone. Hence it presumes the knowledge of faith and charity as its foundation. No mortal man, no matter how great his love of wisdom no matter how much of a savant he may be, could ever, by transcending the faculties of the human spirit, apprehend this wisdom, which dwells in the supreme point of the loving power, by the exercise of his understanding. It entirely belongs to the children—and to them alone—as they look forward to the consolations of the one Eternal Father, who in the depths of his paternal affection and merciful love unlocks his hidden treasure for them. That is why it is called mystical, that is to say closed or hidden, because it is known only to the few.[42]

In the *Cloud* chapters on the prayer belonging to the process of reading, thinking, and praying, as applied to dark contemplation, the author, following Aquinas,[43] first distinguishes between the Divine Office and personal prayer: "I am speaking of their personal prayers, and not of those ordained by Holy Church." In the *Cloud*, the spontaneity of these dark prayers is emphasized,[44] while the form of words is pronounced unimportant; they could be liturgical or nonliturgical.[45] Their qualities are first their total spiritual nature: *totus sine voce erit, et totus unietur ineffabili*, "when the ascent is complete, there will be no words at all, and all will be made one with the Ineffable," where there is no further regard for word or concept, as we read in Denis's *Mystical Theology*.[46] Then there is the total immediacy—"sudden awarenesses," "hidden intuitions"—according to the celebrated example of the cry of one "suddenly seized with fear of fire or death." There is also the entire disregard of the length of the prayer, with the allusion to the Lord's own teaching.[47] All this is repeated in highly summary fashion here in *Private Direction*, whereas the *Cloud* extends it over three chapters,[48] an indication of the fact that the disciple is now familiar with the exercise and is aware of its purposes.

Familiarity with the *Cloud* as a whole is also taken for granted in the paragraphs following, which are in their turn a development of the author's metaphysical instruction, allied to his medieval exegesis of various scriptural passages.[49] Toward the end of the *Cloud*, the author offers a special disquisition on the powers of the soul as they apply to the anagogical ascent to union with God; and as here, in *Private Direction*, he cites the Pauline epigram, "He who cleaves to God is one spirit with him." Earlier in his book, after distinguishing the various states of soul that are proper to the three states of life, "the lower part of the active life" in which "a man is outside himself and beneath himself," "the higher part of the active life and the lower part of the contemplative life," in which he "is within himself and on a par within himself," and finally "the higher part of the contemplative life," in which he "is above himself and under his God," in Chapter 67 he explains his theological teaching on God and the soul, and how it gives substance to the spiritual reflections on the beginning of this contemplative prayer:

> For he is God by nature from the beginning; and there was a time when you were nothing in substance, and even afterwards when you were by his power and love made something, then deliberately by sin you made yourself worse than nothing. It is only by his mercy and without any merit of yours that you are made a god in grace, united with him in spirit without any division between you, both here and in the happiness of heaven without end. So though you are one with him in grace, you are yet far, far beneath him in nature.[50]

Ecce ipsi idioti rapiunt caelum, ubi nos sapientes in inferno mergimur— "See how the illiterates take heaven by violence, whilst we, the wise of this world, are sunk into hell." Saintly scholars, from Augustine to Pasteur—who wrote of the high holiness of his washerwoman— have been at one in considering secular knowledge as worthless in comparison with the *Sapientia Christianorum*, the unitive knowledge of God. We can take it for granted that the *Cloud* author is not here feeling himself under suspicion of the numerous heresies condemned earlier in the thirteenth century, whether of the Beguardi, the *Fraticelli*, or Meister Eckhart, let alone the Lollards.[51] It is much more likely that he is thinking of those who have little or no acquaintance with anagogical contemplation, and are genuinely concerned that the uneducated, such as Margery Kempe shows herself to be, should not be deceived by some form of Illuminism.[52] It may be, too, that he is referring to learned priests of his own community who are themselves genuinely concerned about the spiritual well-being of their novices and younger brethren, as well as their *conversi.*[53] Thomas Gallus tells us in the preface to his *Explanation of the Angelic Hierarchy* of the Pseudo-Denis that he is writing for those devout who are less than erudite in profane letters, for it is to these that the piety of God (*divina pietas*) opens up the heart of the Scriptures that the efforts of human reason cannot reach.[54] Thomas has his own version of the Augustinian adage that would have a special appeal for the *Cloud* author, with his strong personal devotion to the Holy Name:[55] *Nos miseri innumeras scripturas et innumera percurrimus volumina, cum in uno nomine Jesu totius religionis forma et totius sanctitatis norma scribatur* (We turn over innumerable pages and peruse countless volumes in our wretchedness, when all the time the entire nature of religion and the principles of all holiness are found inscribed in the single name of Jesus).[56]

However, the specific *locus* of this controversy between our author and the "theologians" is easy enough to spot. It is the traditional battleground of the schoolmen and the monks, which has been marked out now for several centuries: the struggle between monastic theology and the "new learning" of the universities. The *Cloud* author could easily have figured among the "grett clerks in scole," as his very confident grasp of the developed teaching of the Scholastic theology on grace amply demonstrates;[57] and he still retains his deep respect for "Seint Thomas the doctour."[58] The Carthusian Priory is now his university—as it is of his disciple. A friend of St. Bernard, the abbot of the Premonstratensian Monastery of Good Hope in central France, writes that in the monastery cloister there is little place for vanity. The only pursuit is holiness; and there it is that the good monk gives himself over to the hymns of the Divine Office, to sacred reading, tears, and prayer. He says that his correspondent considers no knowledge worth mentioning that has not been hammered out in the workshop of the secular universities, but the truer knowledge is the instruction in the Law given by God himself; we are to listen, as does the Psalmist, to what the Lord God says within us. It is an honor to have been educated from childhood in the school of religious life.[59] "There are some," writes Peter Comestor, "who pray more than they read; these are the ones who inhabit the cloister.

There are others who spend all their time reading, and pray but seldom. These are the schoolmen."[60]

One holy contemporary of the *Cloud* author, a certain John Whiterig († 1371) and known as the Monk of Farne, until recently anonymous, who after several years as a member of the Benedictine community in Durham and the novice-master there around A.D. 1350, became a solitary on the Isle of Farne, off the Northumbrian coast, in 1363. He had studied in the University of Oxford in his youth, and in his *Meditations* he writes trenchantly of the learning of the schools:

> The reason why the Psalmist confesses that he understands the things of God. He does not say, "because I have attended the schools, because I have learnt from learned men," but "because I have sought out your commandments." . . . Let the sons of the bond-woman listen to this, those who seek the wisdom of the earth, the sons of Belial puffed up with learning, who tend to despise the simple and ignorant because they are not powerful in letters. . . . Let the humble listen and be glad that there is a knowledge of holy Scripture learnt from the Holy Spirit which often the layman knows and the theologian does not, the fisherman, not the lawyer, which the old woman has learnt, but not the doctor in the schools.[61]

In section II, the author insists again, as he has done in the *Cloud* itself as well as in the *Letter on Prayer*, that sacramental confession is essential as a general preparation for understanding the anagogical exercise that is to be the main feature of the disciple's interior life. In the *Cloud*, answering the question when the contemplative work should be begun, he writes: "not er thei haue clensid theire concience of alle their special dedis of sinne done bifore, after the comoun ordinaunce of Holi Chirche." In *Prayer*, he promises that if the disciple should die before he has finished the contemplative exercise, God will receive it as satisfaction for all his lifelong sins, "standing that thou hast before tyme, after thi connyng and thi concience, lawfulich amendid thee after the comoun ordinaunce of Holy Chirche in confession." Here he varies the formula somewhat, but retains many of the same words and certainly the same sentiments: "so that thou haue before-tymes, as I suppose thou hast, ben lawefuly amendid of alle thi sinnes in special and in general after the trewe counseil of Holi Chirche."[62] Not that he expects the contemplative to go to confession each time he sets himself to perform the exercise: This was probably a practical impossibility, in view of the fact that the work must be done perseveringly[63] (Richard Methley performed it four times daily[64]). But the implication still is that the disciple will go to confession with great frequency.[65]

The later Dionysians, and particularly the Carthusians in the wake of the Victorine Vercellensis, cannot conceive of the dark contemplative exercise outside the threefold scheme based on Denis's angelic triad: Angels, Archangels, and Principalities, representing the purgative; Powers, Virtues, and Dominations, the illuminative; Thrones, Cherubim, and Seraphim, the unitive.[66] The anagogical contemplative ascent always involves the purgative and the illuminative, but these elements of contemplation are to be understood in the context of unitive love. It will follow that they will be subordinated to the purified and graced affection and in no sense will they operate under the guidance, much less the domination, of the knowing power of the mind. We may recall that the *Cloud* author begins his investigation into the nature of the exercise under the direction of Thomas Gallus:

> Now all rational creatures, angels and men alike, have in them, each individually, one chief working power which is called a knowing power, and another chief working power, called a loving power; and of these two powers, God, who is the maker of them, is always incomprehensible to the first, the knowing power. But to the second, which is the loving power, he is entirely comprehensible in each one individually; in so much that one loving soul of itself because of love, would be able to comprehend him who is entirely sufficient, and much more so, without limit, to fill all the souls of men and angels that could ever exist. This is the everlastingly wonderful miracle of love, which shall never have an end.[67]

The contemplative effort is precisely this loving power that cooperates with the sacramental graces in Confession—*gratia sanctificans et gratia sanans*—to the extent that it destroys the root and ground of sin (concupiscence, as the Scholastic theologians call it) insofar as this is possible here below. It is also acquisitive of those cardinal virtues on which all the others turn: prudence, justice, fortitude, and temperance; and the result is that all a man's affections are ordered and controlled and directed Godward.[68]

For our author then, as for Gallus and de Balma, the purgative element is always incorporated in the anagogical exercise. Gallus accepts the Dionysian principle that the purpose of the purification is illumination, but he passes beyond Denis when he insists that purification is more powerfully effected by longing love. Here the contemplative effort is the spirit's constant striving actively to purify itself, in cooperation with the contemplative graces, which do in fact cleanse by illumination. "The effort itself separates the soul from its contraries; and once separated, it is purified from its own proper darkness and restored to the pristine purity and innocence." De Balma gives us a real summary when he says: "The purgative way purifies by means of sorrow, frequent contrition and tears. But purification through the ascent of ardent love is much more efficacious."[69]

Implicit in *Private Direction*'s teaching here is that the penitent's individual sins have already been specifically forgiven in his confession. There remain two other reasons why he should leave them alone, particularly during the exercise of dark contemplation. The first is, as the author has stressed at length in the *Cloud*, that there is the constant danger that to give them attention is to expose oneself to further temptation. Instead, the contemplative is to bring the affections to bear on the *via negativa*, the *sécheresse métaphysique* of Denis. He must avoid thinking *what* he is made up of—those various filths that pursue and attach themselves to the nature of wretched man by reason of his coarseness and ignorance—and simply think *that* he is.[70] In any case, the intellect is unable to achieve anything by any speculation upon or probing into any of the qualities that belong to its own being or to God's. The image the author uses to describe this blind movement is the rather bizarre one of plastering himself under the Divine Being. Possibly he has in mind the story of the prophet Eliseus, who stretched himself on top of the child of the Shunamitess, with "mouth on his mouth, eyes to his eyes, hands on his hands," and so gave warmth and the breath of life to the boy.[71] The *Cloud* author has already spoken of the God of the contemplative as one who "fits himself exactly to our souls by adapting his Godhead to them," so that "our souls are fitted exactly to him by the worthiness of our creation after his image and likeness."[72] Still, he hastens to change the image at once for one drawn from a vivid and very familiar Gospel scene—the woman healed of her issue of blood. Augustine had said, in a celebrated comment on this text: *Visne tu tangere Christum?* "Do you wish to touch Christ?" *Intellige Christum, ubi est, in sinu Dei Patris.* "Think Christ, where he is, next to the Father's heart."

Another Carthusian work our author was most likely to have studied was the *Liber de quadripertito exercitio cellae* ("The fourfold exercise of the cell")[73] by Adam the Scot, who was first a Premonstratensian abbot in his native Berwickshire, of the Abbey of Dryburgh near

Melrose. He then joined the Charterhouse of Our Lady of Witham in Somerset, whence his friend and patron Hugh, the first English Carthusian saint, was taken to become Bishop of Lincoln in 1186.[74] In the twenty-ninth chapter of Adam's book, "Of that kind of meditation we should practice in the inmost recesses of our hearts when we labor to think on God, and what it is permissible and becoming to feel about him," he writes:

> Speaking of God, we cannot say what he is, because we cannot understand this. Certainly whatever he is, is either himself, or it is the creature whom he has created. But the creature is so far away from God's essence that one can only speak of what the creature is not; whilst God is wholly alone.[75]

He then cites a passage from the *Heavenly Hierarchy* of Denis: "For he is above all knowledge and life, and no light can identify him, and every act of reason and understanding fails to approach him." The conclusion is that "in your cell you are to love God unceasingly with all your heart, you are to pray to God with all devotion, you are to long to come to God in the midst of your heart [*medullitus*]. And in this love, this prayer, this longing, what do you understand God to be? A beginning without beginning, an end without end; above everything but not lifted up, below everything but not underneath; within and without, but not enclosed nor excluded; always and everywhere himself, but neither in time nor in space."[76]

In the *Cloud*, we have a moral theological disquisition on distinctions between perfection and imperfection, venial and serious sin. This is certainly "the probing of the rational faculties," as the author lists the capital sins for the disciple. Doubtless, by the time the *Letter of Private Direction* is written, the disciple has studied some moral theology for himself.[77] However, while the introduction of theological learning into some aspects of meditation will be useful and profitable, it has no part to play in this exercise, as our author insists in everything that he teaches: "Him I covet, him I seek and nothing but him."[78] As Hugo de Balma says of the whole matter of this book, against all the divines and their theological speculations, that it is not through the consideration of creatures nor investigation by means of our natural talents that we shall come to the immediate knowledge of the Creator, but by the burning aspirations of unitive love.[79]

In the section that follows (III), the author introduces us to his theological method, which is proper to the monastic cloister and has little relationship with or regard for the Scholastic system, even though, in our author's day, it had almost entirely replaced monastic learning. The latter's end has always been contemplation, and its starting point the spiritual exegesis. Here, for example, the author pays not the slightest attention to the literal meaning of his text. Solomon is speaking to the spiritual intelligence of the reader, and the author considers himself fully competent to speak in Solomon's person: "The text that Solomon spake to his son bodely, as if he had seyde to thin understondyng, as I schal sey in his persone unto thee goostly." It is not simply that there are two meanings of Scripture here, the literal and the anagogical; rather, the literal is a pejorative sense, unspiritual or devoid of any real significance.[80] This is the way in which "our Fathers before us" thought and expressed themselves. Their written theology was largely contained in their commentaries on Holy Scripture, and there was a certain way of approaching it and treating it. "In the exposition of sacred and mystical words we must proceed with simplicity and caution," says St. Bernard. "We are to adopt the ways and manners of Scripture, so that the wisdom hidden in the mystery will express itself in our words. When it portrays God for us, Scripture suggests him in terms of the range of our own experience. His unknown and invisible attributes, so precious to us, become accessible to our human minds—those vessels made of such worthless material—by comparisons with realities known to us through our senses."[81]

It is more than likely that the author is following the later medieval tradition, which has its beginnings in Origen and St. Gregory the Great as much as in John Scotus Erigena's expositions of the Pseudo-Denys, when he seizes upon these verses of the book of Proverbs to elucidate for his disciple the anagogical ascent. As we have noticed elsewhere,[82] the Cistercian Garnier de Rochefort, abbot of Clairvaux in 1192, has a sermon on John the Baptist, in the course of which he analyzes the progressive anagogical exercise that links this spiritual exegesis with the heights of contemplation:

> The human spirit, by its sacred inquisition of the divine words, contemplates in its upward ascent the heavenly secrets. It rises to the summit of perfection assisted by two kinds of vision which were infused into the minds of the theologians and prophets through the grace of divine revelation. The first kind of vision is called in the Greek "theophanies," which means "divine manifestations." The other is called anagogical, in which the ascent and transport of the mind is naked and simple and without any concealment, and strives to contemplate that most sacred of heavenly objects.
>   In this second kind of vision the human spirit trembles and quivers,

wrapped in the darkness of its unknowing; nor can it escape to that clarity and light of truth unless it be guided. It is as it were blind, needing to be led by the hand, and goes where it cannot see. It also begins to be melted by this vision and visitation of the Beloved. It cannot think what it ought, or might want of God, nor can it speak of what it thinks, no matter how much it tries to speculate on the heavenly kingdom which is in total obscurity.[83]

The monastery, as Le Clercq notices, was for the theologians a school of charity for the service of God.[84] Any speculative contemplation in the course of the anagogical exercise was a deviation, a wanting in respect for the Divine. The philosophers, said William of St. Thierry, were metaphorically unkempt and unwashed.[85] The last scriptural citation in this letter is the Pauline dictum *Scientia inflat*, "Learning puffs up with pride."[86]

The monk of Farne tells us that in a crisis of despair in his solitude, Christ appeared to him and consoled him, and said "merrily and with mild countenance, Love and thou shalt be saved."[87] He too alludes to the Pauline *Scientia inflat:* "The psalmist did not say, I went to school, or, I was taught by the learned, but, I have sought your commandments. There is a knowledge which is called love or charity, because, according to Gregory the Great, love itself is knowledge of him in whom it is directed, because in proportion as we love, to that extent we know."[88] Since the time of St. Ambrose, who had said, "God has not chosen to make the salvation of his people depend on philosophical subtleties" and "we do not put our faith in the philosophers," the monks would tend to suspect "the busying of yourself in speculative searching and ransacking with your rational faculties any of the qualities belonging to your being and to God's being as well."[89] From the time of Cassian, as well, the monks in the West had collected, preserved, and experimented with what had been the common doctrine of the Eastern tradition about hesychasm (contemplative leisure) and had given it expression in language drawn from the Psalms and the Wisdom literature and adapted it to the usages of monastic theology in the High Middle Ages of the Western Church.[90] The great St. Basil speaks for them all when he says: "The soul will be saved through love; so that it seeks no other wisdom, knows no other loyalty than to accept and to recognize that form of life which will lead it most surely to the most supreme love."[91] It is not surprising then that the Carthusian founder, St. Bruno, should write to Raoul le Verd, first assistant to the Archbishop of Rheims and provost of the Cathedral Chapter, who wished

to be excused from following what Bruno and even he himself believed to be an authentic eremitical vocation, that he was preferring
the needs of his archbishop to the divine love. "What is more con-
genitally appropriate and serviceable for human nature than to love
the Good? So the devout soul who has a true feeling for the incomparable beauty and splendor of this Good will be set on fire with its
heavenly love and say: My soul is thirsting for the strong and living
God. When shall I come and appear before the face of the living
God?"[92] Hugo de Balma, in counting his blessings at the beginning
of the *Viae Sion Lugent*, will reckon his Carthusian vocation as the one
that Christ himself chose, the divine and wordless eloquence of living for the world's salvation that excels all human teaching.[93]

At the same time, this attack (IV) on the intellectual subtlety of
the schools is itself conducted by our author with a rhetorical brilliance and a doctrinal and hermeneutical assuredness that refuses to
counter the *scientia quae inflat* with *rusticitas*—the illiterate simplicity
of the village yokel.[94] Bernard had said that the Lord's spouse should
never be a simpleton.[95] Our author's theological thesis, which the
Scholastic professors would have approved, is established by the testimony of Scripture, by the teaching and actions of Christ in the
Gospel, and also by rational argumentation. But one of the principles
that he has in mind constantly is that once we allow the contemplative process to be drawn into a discursive complexity, the mind becomes agitated and dissipated. As he had already written in the
Cloud, "Before you are even aware of it, your concentration is gone,
scattered about you know not where." And Jean Le Clercq tells us
in his consideration of holy simplicity:

> Questions, objections, argumentations rapidly lead into an inextricable
> forest; like a deer one makes one's way through it laboriously. To offset
> these undesirable effects, the mind must be brought back to a single
> occupation and preoccupation. A single search and a single quest must
> be substituted for all these questions. To seek God, not to discuss him,
> to avoid the inner turmoil of over-subtle investigations and disputa-
> tions, the manifold arguments, to flee from the outer noise of contro-
> versies and to eliminate futile problems: such is the role of simplicity.

Here the author first links dark contemplation with the liturgical
action, in the Eucharistic Canon of the Mass: *Memento, Domine, fa-
mulorum famularumque tuarum . . . quorum tibi fides cognita est et nota
devotio . . . qui tibi offerunt hoc sacrificium laudis pro se suisque omnibus,
pro redemptione animarum suarum, pro spe salutis et incolumitatis suae, ti-*

bique reddunt vota sua aeterno Deo vivo et vero.[96] Three times in these paragraphs he returns to the same concepts and words. First, he says, "offer up the substance of your being, which is the first of your fruits, in continual praise to God both for yourself and for all others, as charity demands"; then, of Christ in his Passion, he adds, "when he offered himself in the truest sacrifice, the whole of himself in general and not his manhood in particular, not for any particular man living, but generally and commonly for all"; and finally, "similarly, the man who makes a true and perfect sacrifice of himself, with a common intention for all, does all that in him lies to fasten all men to God as effectively as he himself is."

The Church had taught explicitly, on the authority of Augustine, for close on a thousand years, that through the sin of Adam, all had lost their natural powers of innocence,[97] and at the Council of Orange (A.D. 529), for example, it was decreed that "the nature which was lost through Adam was restored by Christ, who had said that he had come to seek out and to save whatever was lost;"[98] and that the chalice of human salvation, which was mixed from the weakness of our human nature and the divine power, contains something that is of profit to all. Further, the Bull of Clement V, contemporary with the author (A.D. 1341) had declared that humankind, children of the loving Father, had been endowed with the treasure of Christ's Passion and death—an infinite treasure "which made men sharers in the friendship of God."[99] It is this teaching the author synopsizes here.

For the monks, the end of theology is to search the mysteries of the divine love; this is its effect as well as its purpose. This is eminently true of the Eucharistic mystery, and we see an example of it here. The author's "ready reason" follows on his examination of the scriptural text from Romans: "By one man sin entered into this world, and by sin, death; and so death came upon all men . . . if by the offense of one, many died, much more the grace of God, and the gift, by the grace of one man, Jesus Christ, has abounded unto many. For if by one man's offense death reigned through one; much more they who receive abundance of grace, and of the gift, and of justice, shall reign unto life through one, Jesus Christ."[100] It is not so much the way in which the Eucharistic mystery is accomplished, but what it accomplishes: the loving union with the Lord in the here and the hereafter, where the abundance of the earthly fastening, which literally keeps body and soul together, fails, and the soul moves from the lower part of the contemplative life to the higher, from salvation to the greatest perfection. Yet, as Augustine observes in his *De quan-*

titate animae, the soul nourishes itself as does the body; it draws it together and keeps it together, not allowing it to flow and melt away; it distributes nourishment proportionately to each member.

Our author, as we note in his text, takes exactly the same list of Divine Names or attributes as does Hugo de Balma in his discourse on the purgative way in the *De Triplici Via.*[101] For Hugo the names provide spiritual sustenance as he prays his prayers of purification; the *Cloud* author uses them simply to indicate that the *isness* of God, which is equally the first of the fruits flowing from our creation, contains them all. The emphasis, though it is still on the abandonment of all speculation, remains affective rather than metaphysical. He is speaking of an affection "filled with the fulness of love and with powerful faith in God, your foundation and your purity of heart." So the contemplative effort is always at the heart of faith, never going beyond it; it remains always an act of faith. And in his spiritual exegesis of the last verse of his text from Proverbs, "and your wine presses shall run over, full of wine," he will say that by this wine "is truly and mystically understood spiritual wisdom in true contemplation and high savor of the Godhead." As St. Bernard had said, the teaching of the Spirit does not sharpen the curiosity; it enkindles the fire of love.[102] "If the incomprehensible can be grasped at all, it is holiness which will comprehend it. If you are a saint you will already have understood. If you are not, become one and you will learn through your own experience."[103]

At the beginning of V, the English author offers what appears to be the most succinct and simplest description of what the ultimate moment of this work of dark contemplation is: that which affects the actual experience of knowing God by unknowing, rather than the steps in the negative affective process leading to it. "The high wisdom of the Godhead descending through grace into a man's soul, knitting it and uniting it to himself in spiritual wisdom and discernment." The unitive experience is Trinitarian: it is the Wisdom, the Second Person, flowing forth from the Divine Power in the Godhead personified in the Spirit to whom is primarily attributed the divine creative work—every creative act, every emanation revealed as caused in virtue of the ineffable Heavenly Perfection as revealed to man: God's almighty Word leaping down from heaven from his lofty throne,[104] "Intelligent, Holy One, Manifold, Subtle, Eloquent, Mobile, Undefiled, Sure, Sweet, Loving what is good, Quick, Keen, Irresistible, Beneficent, All-Powerful, All-Watchful, Gentle, Kind, Steadfast, Assured, Unanxious, Penetrating . . . the breath of God's

Power, pure Emanation of the Glory of the Almighty . . . the Reflection of the Eternal Light, the Spotless Mirror of God's working and the Image of his Goodness."[105]

"Knitting it and onying it unto hymself in goostly sleight and prudence of spirit." Peter Damian, in what seems to us an overelaborated piece of spiritual exegesis of Solomon's dedication of the temple he had built to the Lord,[106] speaks of the heavenly temple dedicated under the eternal lordship of the true Solomon, no longer adorned with the splendor of sparkling gems but with the radiance of spiritual virtues.[107] This is exactly the kind of biblical interpretation our author takes for granted. The literal interpretation of the Scriptures has its analogy with the lower part of the active life; but once we begin to contemplate in the lower part of the contemplative life, our eyes are on the allegorical; and in the higher part that begins here and is consummated in heaven, the Scripture is dominated by the anagogical sense. Thomas Aquinas explains it to us, using the example of God's word in Genesis, "Let there be light:"

> When I say, *fiat lux*, I am speaking about the literal sense, of corporeal light. But once the phrase is understood of Christ's being born in the Church, *fiat lux* is being used in the allegorical sense. And once *fiat lux* means the light by which our intelligence is enlightened and our affection inflamed by Christ, we are speaking in the moral sense. Finally, if *fiat lux* means that we are carried by Christ to glory, we have the anagogical sense.[108]

When the English author says here, "By gold and silver is understood morally all other knowing, natural and spiritual," he is speaking of the divine things proper to the lower part of the contemplative life and its spiritual exercises: "consisting in good spiritual meditations and earnest consideration of a man's own wretched state . . . and of the wonderful gifts, kindness and works of God."[109]

"The frute of this worching is highe goostly wisdom, sodenly and frely riftid of the spirit inly in itself and unformid, ful fer fro fantasie, impossible to be streinde or to falle under the worching of naturele witte." So runs the author's exegesis of *Primi et purissimi sunt fructus eius*—"first and purest ben the frutes of it." It is in fact St. Bernard who first appropriated the word and the image, for which the translator of the first English Psalter, half a century before the *Cloud* was written, coined the term "rift."[110] *Eructavit cor meum verbum bonum; dico ego opera mea regi:* "My heart has belched forth a good word; I will tell my story to the King." The psalm has no other parallel in the Old Testament (it is both an epithalamion—a bridal song—and messianic as well) except the Canticle of Canticles; and Bernard entitles his sixty-seventh *Sermo in Cantica* "The wonderful affection of the bride's love, which is uttered forth (*eructat*) out of love for Christ her spouse."[111] The author is at one with Bernard in the firm belief that the soul's capacity to understand the anagogical sense of the Scriptures—their *medulla*—is strictly the equivalent of the closeness of union—*Dilectus meus mihi et ego illi:* "my beloved to me and I to him."

Bernard is followed by a whole host of cloistered contemplatives— particularly his own Cistercian Spirituals, William of St. Thierry, Guerric of Igny, Gilbert of Hoiland, Aelred of Rielvaux[112]—in pressing into service the digestive system to explain to his brethren the affective contemplative process:

> He [Bernard] sees his monastic audience as rows of hungry mouths [which in all probability they were] eagerly agape to receive the good bread which he, the *fidelis coquus*, will serve them smoking hot from the ovens of his meditation . . . or he encourages them to chew on the honeycomb of the letter, or extract the sweetness of the Spirit, or it may be from the marrow of the bone or the nut from its shell. The word of God is to be ground up by these ruminants, to be relished and savoured, digested and assimilated. Then at last comes the *ructus*, which are his Sermons [on the Canticle].[113]

The food, says Bernard, is delicious to the taste, it is solid as nutriment, and it is also good as medicine. The resultant regurgitation is from the heart's abundance—*ex abundantia cordis os loquitur*. It is the affection that speaks, not the intellect. This vehement love cannot be constrained—*se intra se cohibere non valet*. It is when it is replete with the Spirit that it is belched forth. *Eructavit cor meum verbum, eodem quippe(sponsa)repleta Spiritu.*[114]

The gathering together of various descriptions of the *culmen contemplationis*—the author uses the rhetorical figure *expolitio*, "the striking effect"[115]—includes one that has become celebrated in fourteenth-century English mystical literature.[116] Walter Hilton says: "The knitting and fastening of Jesus to a man's soul is by a good will and a great desire for him alone, to have him and to see him in his spiritual bliss." But for Julian of Norwich, the good will or godly will is that which the Holy Spirit, the Spirit of Life, constantly pours into the higher part of the soul by the way of love. St. Bernard's contemporary, the Abbot William of St. Thierry, says that this good will toward God is love (*amor*), and another love (*dilectio*) is a clinging or uniting to him, and a third love (*charitas*) is delight in him. "Yet the oneing of the Spirit with God in a man who lifts up his heart towards God is the perfection of his will, when he not only wills God's will, not only is he drawn to God, but in that drawing he is so made perfect that he can will nothing but that which God wills."[117]

The author can even offer us a spontaneous anagogical interpretation of the phrase "beauty to your cheeks," *gratia faucibus tuis*.[118] "If a man were practiced in this exercise," he writes in the *Cloud*, using the same phrase "semely governaunce," "it would give him true decorum both of body and soul, and would make him truly attractive to all men or women who looked upon him."[119] Anagogical contemplation is universally corrective and protective. Conversely, if one allows oneself to be mistaken in distinguishing between speculative and anagogical contemplation, and particularly if one should succumb to the temptation of prizing the first over the second, the consequences are hazardous indeed. The last part of this section is given over to describing the ways in which the eremitical contemplative can be exposed to the attacks of the devil—but to no avail as long as he is faithful to the anagogical exercise. From the time of Athanasius and his life of Antony the Hermit, much attention, and of course credence, was given to Cassian's collection of diabolical stories concerning the stalwarts of the eremitical life in the Thebaid desert. The *Cloud* author is no exception to the general naiveté of his age in his easy acceptance of the science of necromancy.[120] Before the end of the fifteenth century Richard Methley, Carthusian of Mount Grace in Yorkshire, would write in his *Experimentum Veritatis:* "The evil angel (*angelus malus*) has appeared to me under a variety of bodily guises. He has taken on the form of practically every kind of man, woman and beast." François Vandenbroucke coined the phrase *fièvre satanique* for the malaise that affected Christendom for nearly four centuries from c. 1300.[121] However, the *Cloud* author is far more restrained than, say, Bl. Henry Suso, who offers us in his *Horologium Sapientiae* a lurid description of hell and of the activities of the demons there. "You shall not fear any peril, nor any deceit of the devil," is the author's anagogical exegesis of his text here.[122] The devil is confused and blinded by his own ignorance and perplexity when confronted by the exercise of dark contemplation. In any case, as the Lord promised to Julian of Norwich in a locution full of consolation: "He did not say: You shall not be troubled, you shall not be in travail, you shall not be distressed; but he said, You shall not be overcome."[123] Julian tells us that she felt the extraordinary heat of the devil's presence, and that there was a fearsome stench.[124] Our author, too, promises that "you shall certainly see and feel or else smell, taste or hear some strange thing devised by the devil to affect some of your five outward senses." The author in the main is surprisingly free of the irrational fear attaching to diabolic superstition. He is well aware that it is all "treachery and guile of your enemies, the devil and his minions." "Our Lord and his love" overcome the devil. "The power of evil is powerlessness. All the devil can do is just trickery and mirage. . . . By his death Jesus brought the devil to nothing."[125]

Julian of Norwich tells us in her very first revelation that God the Trinity—power, wisdom and goodness—is the Maker, the Lover, and the Keeper. Our author's initial reflection on the spiritual meaning of his text here (VI), which describes the final and full renunciation of the self in the negative ascent to union, serves as introduction to one of the outstanding scriptural pastiches in all his writings.[126] His intent is to emphasize with full force the Trinitarian nature of the contemplative exercise, in which this darkness is the unfathomable mystery of three Persons in one God. So we move from a basic statement in the third chapter of Ephesians to the publican in Luke's Gospel with his head bowed in the presence of the God of unfathomable mercy; the teaching of the same Luke and 1 Peter on the meaning and need of humility in the exercise, in which in our nothingness we are called to engage the God who is all. The point of departure is again Eucharistic: The soul is to turn from itself entirely in order to be "so louely led and fed in the loue of our Lorde." The goal is to be "ful knowing and felying" of the Trinitarian splendor: "his almightyheed, his unwetyn wisdom and his glorious goodnes."

In *Inward Stirrings*, our author was concerned to lead his contemplative disciple to the right perspective with regard to ascetical practices. Apart from the genuine search for holiness by those external means, which are hard enough wisely to use or to leave alone, there is always the danger inherent in slavishly imitating those who have gained a reputation for holiness because of their extreme asceticism. The safest and surest procedure is to go to God by unknowing, by choosing him who lies between fasting and eating, watching and sleeping, and so on.[127] It is clear that what the author wishes to teach, without discouraging his disciple, is the ultimate form of abnegation involved in the negative contemplative ascent, which he now begins to elucidate in detail. This, in fact, is not some form of apophatic metaphysic inherited from the Pseudo-Denis's Neoplatonic mentors, Plotinus or Proclus. Rather it is the author's own reflection on the mortification taught by Paul through the Christological hymn he sings in Philip "to dispose oneself to receive the grace from the Lord, and listen to what he says: 'If anyone will come after me. . . . ' "

St. Bernard, in his little treatise *On Loving God*, speaks of the third degree—to love God not for one's own sake, but for himself, and says that one stays there for a long time. He wonders whether the fourth degree is ever truly achieved in this life—namely, to love oneself simply for God's sake. He feels that it is impossible, because it involves being forgetful of oneself in some extraordinary way. The person falls away from self, as it were, and penetrates wholly into God, and by clinging to him, is destined to become one spirit with him.[146] Our author, at least, takes it for granted that this fourth grade is the object of the contemplative exercise. He is one with Bernard also in seeing the second and third degrees of love as the situation "in which the soul finds itself forced to turn to God and frequent his company. This it does by consideration, reading, prayer and obedience, until God gradually and experientially becomes known to him." Here the transition to the third degree takes place, in which he tastes how sweet the Lord is.[147] This is what Guiges du Pont was to call the first kind of contemplating.[148]

The abandonment that is taught in the first chapter of Denis's *Mystical Theology* is given an affective context by all the late medieval Dionysians, but never with such unction as by the *Cloud* author here. As we have seen, the *locus classicus* for the Neoplatonic ascent to God is Moses' ascent to Mount Sinai, where the passage in Exodus (19:16) is pressed into service. The Pseudo-Denis, addressing Timothy, supposedly the disciple of Paul, whom he calls his fellow-priest, explains to him the manner of the ascent: all sensible and intellectual operations as well as their objects, in fact anything existing at all either outside or inside human faculties, are to be trodden firmly underfoot (*forti contritione . . . derelinque*).[149] The author uses the image first of "fancy, false imagination, subtle opinion . . . and proud and elaborate speculations [which] must always be pushed down and heavily trodden underfoot";[150] and then, with Richard of St. Victor, who appears to have coined the term, he says: "You must put beneath you a cloud of forgetting between you and all the creatures that have ever been made."[151] Here, however, the author offers an entirely new explanation for his direction to the disciple "to forget everything but the being of yourself." The cloud of forgetting turns out to be a device of the same nature as the one he suggests in the *Cloud*, of hiding the desire of one's heart from God,[152] while the negative metaphysic of the Platonic search for God takes on a new and affective dimension: It becomes the reaching out for the spiritual feeling of the being of God who is ultimately, but still darkly, conceived as our own being. The affective knowledge of God and the self becomes ever more contrarious. Our purpose and desire is to arrive at the high awareness of himself, and to match his all-comprehending purity of spirit; and "this is a love-making that none can know save the one that has experience of it" (this is the werk of loue that none may knowe bot he that felith it). It is the person of the Lord—"whoso would love me let him forsake himself."

In the *Cloud*, as in his version of *Denis's Hidden Theology*,[153] the author has translated *forti contritione*, which previously simply meant "forcefully treading down" under the cloud of forgetting all sensible and intellectual operations and all their objects in ridding the mind of all rational activity in the process of dark contemplation. It now becomes "a special grace which God gives out of his absolute bounty, and along with it a corresponding capacity on your part for receiving the grace."

This capacity is nothing else but a strong and profound spiritual sorrow (a stronge and a deep goostly sorow).[154] The author here has joined the stream of Western tradition with regard to the spiritual grace of the gift of tears, first gathered early in the ninth century at the Carolingian Abbey of St. Mihiel by the abbot, the celebrated Latinist Smaragdus.[155] Le Clercq says that there are "tears, born of the compunction of love and the Divine sweetness and by the desire to enjoy eternally, accompanied by sighs which are not signs of sadness, but of love-longing; and a whole literature on tears developed in the monastic ambience."[156] So here the advice is: You must sorrow in earnest and long with all your heart for the feeling of God. It is a sentiment the Lord himself manifests in many Gospel-doings: the mother grieving over the people of Jerusalem like the hen with her chicks, the dead son of Naim waiting to be raised from the dead to assuage the tears of his widowed mother; for Lazarus, the beloved friend, and his own dear friends, Peter and Magdalen, who are the types in the tradition for the sorrowful whom the Lord will comfort.[157] The author's comparison between the sorrowing of Jesus and his friends and contemplative sorrowing is carried to its term: "Ye, Jhesu help thee thanne, for than thou hast nede. For all the woo that may be, withoutyn that is now a poynte to that." The weeping "till my heart should break," is to have and to long for the feeling of God.

We have seen how the author makes known his devotion to the Holy Name of the Incarnate Word, in his final addition to the first instruction on contemplation, which he shares with his most favored mentor, Richard of St. Victor.[158] The heart of the contemplative exercise, with which he begins the *Cloud*, may be called the love of Jesus—"Love Jesus and everything is yours."[159] Here in Section IX we have one of the most powerful names attributed in the Gospel to Jesus, the Good Shepherd; one of the most descriptive and loved identifications of God spoken through the great prophets, Isaiah, and especially Ezekiel—"It is the Lord who speaks!" The functions of his Father, in the traditional attribution of caring, protecting, soothing, healing, and especially feeding, now fall to the Son, who has received the power from the Father's hands.[160] The observation is repeated: the *culmen contemplationis*—the coming of the Spirit upon the contemplative—in this exercise, is to be lovely, led and fed by this God, who is now proclaimed the door to the sheepfold.[161] The tradition is consistent, from Augustine until now: Christ is the one gateway to faith; the Christ born of the Virgin, who has suffered, is risen.

The meditations (a fuller term is "contemplative reflections") on the Gospel mysteries of Christ are, as we have seen, the prayer proper to those who pertain to the lower branch of the contemplative life and the higher branch of the active. Of the latter the author has little to say; he is concerned to instruct solitaries, and in particular, his fellow-Carthusian and neophyte. In the *Cloud*, borrowing from the Carthusian prior Guigo II,[162] he has indicated the contemplative refinement that is brought to the meditation of the solitary: "sudden awareness and obscure feelings of their own wretchedness, or of God's goodness."[163] It is by way of the Incarnate Word, the Way to the truth and the Life, that we go to the Father: and "no one comes to the Father except by me."[164] For the solitary, Jesus became man in order that this union might happen—and happen here in this life; and it is thus that the author offers us the anagogical meaning of his text from John 10. Jesus is both door and door-keeper of the house of the interior life. There is no way into it except by him—by contemplating his Passion and mourning for the wickedness that caused it, with pity and compassion for the mystical Christ. We are to "lift up our hearts" at the Eucharistic sacrifice, to contemplate the love and goodness of Jesus' Godhead, as he stoops to humble himself. And thus we enter the door to contemplate this love and goodness.

It seems certain that in the author's time the main description of the solitary life—and certainly for him, as for Richard Methley, monk of the Charterhouse of Mount Grace, the Carthusians were the last English hermits,[165]—was the assumption that the high reaches of contemplation were not only available to them all without exception, but were their due under grace. It would seem that the ascetical life of the community, because of prevailing heretical views, was in abeyance. We know, for example that James Grenehalgh of the Shene Charterhouse had opinions that inclined him to the Brethren of the Free Spirit—a condemned heretical sect—and that for some reason he had to leave his own charterhouse, and died in the one at Hull.[166] So he concludes the section with the observation that the young contemplative can so easily think that all his activity is good, and is inclined to follow his own violent desire without submitting himself to direction.

After this short digression, the author continues his instruction, which he has based on the spiritual exegesis of "I am the door." The contemplative is to stand there without advancing further until the purifying graces have done their work, and the Holy Spirit beckons and draws him further in, by giving him a growing desire to draw near to God. Such solitary monks are those who are called even in this life to move from the state the author simply calls salvation, into perfection. The distinction is shorthand for those he has already made: in general, between the active and contemplative lives, but more refinedly between the lower and higher parts of these two lives.[167] He is not thinking here of active works of mercy, but simply the prayer and devotion proper to the two different states. He has already written in the *Cloud* that one coming to the higher part of the active life must leave for a time the lower part in the outward corporal works and devote himself to meditation.[168]

The author here introduces another digression on a point already mentioned in the *Cloud*—not to judge another's prayer experience in the light of one's own. He assumes the role of the theologian, instructing his disciples with the aid of further spiritual exegesis. Here in Section X, it is the text *Sine me nihil potestis facere* (Without me you can do nothing), another Johannine text (Jn 15:5), that introduces a point he wishes to make on operative and cooperative grace, a subject that is a constant concern of his in the *Cloud*.[169] Here, however, the author is more practical, simple, and direct. He gives us an example of how the bishop, whose rank is the highest in the active life, is assisted by grace, and the principles according to which "with God's consent and grace," the human faculties are brought into cooperation. He reaches his conclusion with the simple observation that in the work of contemplation our God asks nothing more of us but to receive him and give him our consent, to our great perfection "and goostly onyng of oure soule unto hym in parfite charite."

The section to which we now address ourselves (XI) is one of the greatest pieces of rhetorical prose in the whole of Middle English literature. The author begins with a rhetorician's question, taking up the position of the disciple and supposing him to expect an answer that will assure him that this call he feels to dark contemplation in his daily exercises is truly from God, to the more special work of grace so often described in all the author's works.

Typically, the tokens or signs by which authenticity can be affirmed have to do with holy desires. The *Cloud* concludes with a celebrated quote from Gregory the Great, and one from Augustine for good measure:

> Because it is not what you are nor what you have been that God looks at with his merciful eyes, but what you desire to be. And St. Gregory is witness that "all holy desires grow by delay; and if they diminish by delay then they were never holy desires." And he who experiences less and less joy in the new experiences and sudden presentations of his own desires, though they all must be called natural desires for the good, nevertheless they were never holy desires. Of this holy desire St. Augustine speaks, when he says that "the whole of life of good Christians is nothing else but holy desires."[170]

The holy desires of Gregory stand over against his struggle with constant physical illness. Le Clercq has written that Gregory's illness was one of the great events of the history of spirituality,[171] his striving within his *inquietudo*, agitation, lack of tranquility and peace, and with the dark side of compunction, *formido*, positive fears to offset the *compunctio amoris, contemplationis*. Gregory is the doctor of desire, and he stresses the humility, the ardor, even the impatience of this desire for God that drives the contemplative to long for death itself. Equally, such desire confers a certain possession of God, which gives the longing its dynamism and increase.[172] Our author has thoroughly imbibed this teaching on desire with that of Augustine,[173] and uses it to answer the first question: Is there interior evidence that the disciple is indeed called to the exercise of dark contemplation?

Naturally enough he is much more voluble, vivacious even, when he deals with his second point, the manifestation of exterior signs that one is called to the exercise. In one long sentence, he asks question after question—are you full of joy without knowing why? Is everything a consolation and nothing can upset you? Would you run a thousand miles to speak to someone who feels as you do, and when you get there, find that you have nothing to say? Do you feel full of unction and fire, while what you have to say seems foolish and irrational? Is your silence peaceful, your speech edifying, your prayer secret, your pride proper, your laughter very soft? The words are those of a man in love himself, one convinced that he is indeed called to lift himself to God in this kind of contemplation, one long practiced in it, and well able to read the desires and dispositions of others who are called to it.

There remains one problem with which the author feels he must deal. It is a well-known fact of the interior life, and one that John of the Cross, in some senses master of them all, is to devote much time and explanation to. You have given up your customary spiritual exercises of the past—your "meditations," which so often brought you sensible sweetness, feelings of pains, when he exhorts his addressees to tune their minds and attitudes to those of the Word Incarnate, as he sets himself to love his Father to the end. "Let that mind be in you, those feelings fill your heart and soul, which Jesus himself understood and experienced when he gazed upon his Father and accepted to be humble and obedient unto death, even the death of the Cross." Here is the truth of the mortification of the Incarnate Son of the eternal Father on the way to the supreme manifestation of the divine power, wisdom, and goodness: the resurrection of Christ. "It was for this reason that God has exalted him and has given him a name that is above every name . . . Jesus Christ is Lord in the glory of God the Father."[128] Christ it is who teaches us by his own experience—"the things he suffered"—to be "truly humbled in the . . . royal reduction of the self to nothing in true humility and the high exaltation of God, its All, in perfect charity . . . deeply immersed in God's love, fully and finally forsaking itself."[129] It is then that God's love sustains it, keeps it, and defends it with his power, wisdom, and goodness.

In the *Cloud* itself, the author had taught that the first and continuous requisite for the practice of dark contemplation is this perfection of humility; and he is there at pains to distinguish carefully from the perfect, the imperfect humility that is the consciousness of one's wretchedness and weakness, the experience of one's sinfulness. This was not Christ's, and the contemplative must put it behind him, precisely as "God deigns to grant it, that a soul living in this mortal flesh may suddenly lose and forget all awareness and experience of its holiness and wretchedness."[130] The author's source is here Richard of St. Victor and his distinction between voluntary humility, where by the use of one's reason one can see one's own weakness and sinfulness, and devout humility, which the perfect soul possesses by grace.[131] So, in replying to the detractors of his contemplative method, who seem to have centered their objections on this ultimate mortification, the loss of one's identity, he marshals Bernard as well as Richard, but without naming them or going further. Doubtless he has in mind the former's fourth degree of love, where the lover, "made drunk on the richness of God's indwelling, in some marvellous way forgets himself and ceases to belong to himself. He passes entirely into God, and becomes one spirit with him."[132] Doubtless the author has in mind the psychological fear that the consideration of this full and final forsaking of oneself might engender in those who have experience only of the imperfect aspect of humility—those who as yet are no more than half-humbled. He also wishes to make yet again the point that it is the prayer proper to the lower part of the contemplative life—also the higher part of the active—that leads to the acquisition of imperfect humility. Its perfection is so far removed from the imperfect that it is won only when the soul passes over from death to life by way of crucifixion, in imitation of the journey of Christ done to death but now risen. The image used by the author— of Rachel, Jacob's wife, dying in the act of giving birth to the little Benjamin—is a commonplace of Western spirituality; our author, of course, has already translated and paraphrased Richard's *Benjamin Minor*, which is where the soul should begin in preparing itself to pass over into unitive contemplation. Yet this is not his only similitude. He has already written in the *Cloud* that "as long as we are aware that we are moved and called by grace to be contemplatives, there is then another cause for being humbled. This is as far above the first . . . as the life of Christ is above that of any other man in this life."[133] Thomas Gallus, in his *Explanation of the Heavenly Hierarchy* of Dionysius, reminds us that the mysteries of Christ Incarnate form a kind of ladder by which we ascend to the heights of dark contemplation, while it is contemplative humility that brought the wisdom of God to earth.[134]

Perfect humility, in the form of these extremes of mortification, remains a constant in the tradition of Western spirituality. St. Ignatius of Loyola speaks of three kinds or modes of humility, of which the third is the most perfect: "when, in order the better to imitate Christ our Lord and to become actually more like him . . . I desire to be accounted as worthless and a fool for Christ, who was first held to be such, rather than wise and prudent in this world."[135] Much earlier in the tradition, with Irenaeus and Origen, this "noble naughting of the self" was designated *martyrium conscientiae*. It was the perfect substitute for martyrdom unto blood, once the violent Roman persecutions began to recede in the Church. The divine endowment of those who went to martyrdom with Christ, such as Pastor and Justus, the schoolboys of Alcalà de Henares, in the persecution on the Iberian peninsula during the reign of the Emperor Dacian, still illustrates the immediacy and gratuitousness of the grace of dark contemplation.

After this excursus on perfect humility and mortification, with its trenchant criticism of those theologians who continue to speak and write against contemplative solitaries,[136] the author offers his concluding exegesis of the verse *Si dormiens, non timebis* (If you sleep, you shall not fear). The traditional contemplative exegesis of the text of the Canticle of Canticles, "I sleep, but my heart wakes" (*Ego dormio, sed cor meum vigilat*) is the definition of rapture.[137] Indeed, the author appears to begin to refer to this when he writes: "In sleep the use of the natural faculties is suspended." However, this final paragraph is a summary of his teaching on the cloud of forgetting, in the wake of his mentors, Gregory the Great, Thomas Gallus, Guigues du Pont, and Hugo de Balma: all rational investigation, natural knowledge, and intellectual acumen must be suppressed in this exercise.[138]

One of St. Bernard's sermons on the Circumcision, of which our author seems to be aware in his translation from another sermon of the saint, *Discernment of Spirits*,[139] shows the Cistercian in satirical mood. Quoting Juvenal, he says that the monk who has the power of discretion is a *rara avis*, so that normally "the virtue of obedience will have to supply for discernment."[140] Though the point is well taken, it can only apply to what is said about the contemplative exercise and its practice, and hardly about the contemplative's general life-style. It remains that the author takes for granted three prerequisites for beginning and persevering in the exercise of dark contemplation. The first is the constant perusal of God's Word—the *lectio divina*, the sacred reading that itself embraces antecedent contemplation (as Gallus calls it); and in the *Cloud*, the author summarizes the classic teaching on reading, meditation, and prayer as he had found it in Guigo's *Ladder of Four Rungs*, as an essential part of the contemplative neophyte's instruction.[141] The second is sacramental confession, as we have noticed above. Finally, there is competent spiritual direction, which our author, along with all the great masters of monastic theology and practice since the time of the great Cassian and of Benedict himself, can never emphasize enough. Here in Section VII, our author is concerned not simply with the matter of the direction and the quality of the director's teaching, but with the former's personality; and, most important of all, with the relationship between director and disciple.

To submit oneself to a spiritual father is integral to the humility that, with charity, is the prime virtue energizing the exercise. It firmly negates intellectual pride and independence, which maintain that we are clever enough to draw out the spiritual meaning of the Word of God—as does Guigo II for instance, in reflecting on the mystery of Christ's encounter with the Samaritan woman—and cull from it our own lessons. More than that, there is the constant danger of taking it for granted that, by the exercise of our reason, we persuade ourselves that such spiritual reflection must be superior to the apparently mindless exercise of dark contemplation. The author accepts that his disciple has a point, and agrees to argue in the former's terms. The disputation is carried out on the author's behalf with the help of his favorite mentors, St. Bernard and Richard of St. Victor.[142] He finally routs the disciple by recalling the many references to contemplative virtues in his letter to him on prayer, in the *Cloud* itself, in Richard's *Benjamin Major*, and in his translation of the Dionysian *Hidden Theology*. This exercise, he concludes, is "Denis deuinite, his wisdom and his drewry, his lighty derknes and his unknowyn kunnynges"—the mystical theology of Denys, his wisdom and treasure, his luminous darkness and his secret knowledge. "It is this that brings you to silence, in your thoughts as well as in your words. It makes your prayers short indeed; and in it you are taught to forsake and to despise the world."

Finally, it is worth noticing that, as in the *Cloud* itself, the author is content to mention the breadth of his experience as a director of *ex professo* contemplatives, to express his confidence that he is himself called to the same vocation; and that by the vocabulary he uses to designate his role as spiritual father to the disciple—"Lo, here maist thou see that I couete souereinte of thee"—along with his citation of St. Bernard,[143] he has no doubt of his own ability to direct, and this in spite of his *captatio benevolentiae*:

I trowe loue sterith me therto more than any abilnes that I fele in myself in any height of kunnyng or yit of worching or degree of my leuyng. God amende that is amys, for he wote fully, and I bot in party.[144]

All this goes to indicate that the two are brothers, perhaps not in the same local community, but certainly of the same order. It is one more indication among many that they are fellow-Carthusians, and that a developed spiritual affectivity is part of their stock-in-trade.

The section that follows (VIII) is a Gospel reinforcement of the author's teaching on contemplative mortification. The solitary is reminded at length that it can only be in the footsteps of the Incarnate Word that he can reach the perfection of the Godhead. In virtue of the hypostatic union, Jesus is destined by nature to manifest his Sonship by bearing the cross and making light of the shame in virtue of the joy that was set before him by the Father. It is to be the same for the contemplative: "as if he spoke thus in present circumstances to your understanding. If any man will come in humility, not with me, but after me, up to the bliss of heaven and the summit of perfection, 'let him bear his cross and follow me.' "

Here the author embarks on a short discursus concerning the grace of contemplation. He is doubtless led into this digression by his reflection on the union of love—of the child for the parent—between the Eternal Son and himself in nature, and love in grace in us, his rational creatures. The way in which we make progress in the grace of contemplation—so he has already told us in the *Cloud*—[145] is three-fold: by grace alone, by our spiritual skill supported by grace, and sometimes in this grace, by others' teaching. He is developing here what he has said earlier about his own role as a spiritual father in this work of guiding contemplative apprentices. St. Irenaeus had said long ago that to be spiritual father meant to participate in the Divine Fatherhood, and that such a one's first task was to pray for his spiritual child's advancement, always having regard to the Father's most holy will—which is, as the author says, fervor, and burning desires; and you no longer enjoy these consolations. Rather—and the author uses again the stock simile—"now arte thou in the goostly see, to my licnes, schipping over fro bodelines unto goostlines."[174] The author is at his most encouraging here (some might say, today, at his most directive), as he offers the traditional reasons, beginning with the spiritual exegesis of the Canticle of Canticles, how it is and why that God the lover hides himself.[175]

The final point the author wishes to make, that the contemplative must be indifferent to sensible consolations because they are merely the tokens and not the reality of the Divine Presence, again is a *locus classicus* for the direction of contemplatives, as indeed is the affective language he employs. "He wishes to test the quality of your patience. . . . He never withdraws his grace from his chosen ones. . . . Do not be dismayed. . . . He will come, I promise you, as soon as it is his will, to free you . . . far more wonderfully than he ever did before . . . more marvelously and joyfully." He also makes brief allusions to other traditional instructions of the masters—on chaste love and perfect love, on rapture—of which he has already written in the *Cloud*,[176] and on the limitations of the experience while "here on earth." Typically, he ends his instruction here with a short metaphysical excursus. The seeing and feeling experience of the contemplative, his sight and feeling of himself contemplating, his sight and experience of God, and the *totum esse* of God—all these are one, in the union of nature and grace.

The author, in his general view of anagogical contemplation, is firmly traditional. Contemplation is in no sense the term of discursive intellectual activity; it is an act of faith and hope and love. Where the Pseudo-Dionysius is outside the Christian milieu, it is that he pays scant attention to the eschatological nature of the Christian's unitive life and prayer. If the possession of God here below is dark and obscure, it is certainly because it is not possession in the light, the superabundance of light, as Denis writes in his fifth Letter to Dorotheus. It is also because it is possession in holy desire; the reality is in heaven, and the possession will be increased as the desire increases. So his final text is the Lord's word to his disciples at the supper: "It is to your advantage that I go" (Jn 16:2). In the physical absence of the Incarnate Word, we receive the gift, in contemplation, of grasping with the understanding of faith that unity of God which is at once immense and unchanging. The contemplative effort, Anselm had written, must be worthy of eternity, at least by our desires. "It is by the quality of our holy desires that we search for the Christ, to be united to him, and to love him."[177]

The concluding paragraphs reveal that the disciple is still a novice in the practice of dark contemplation, since he seems to expect him, with another rhetorician's question, to be exposed to the mortification of which he has spoken so fluently. The note on which this author ends is not all that encouraging, even though he hopes that it will be, and one wonders what has happened, textually perhaps, to the conclusion. We have grown used to affectionate and paternal blessings since the author wrote so warmly in the *Cloud,* "Farewell, spiritual friend, in God's blessing and mine. And I beseech almighty God that true peace, sane counsel and spiritual comfort in God with abundance of all grace, always be with all those who on earth love God."[178] The *Pursuit of Wisdom* has an *envoi* addressed to "what so thou be that couetest to come to contemplation"; *Prayer* imparts a blessing, as does *Inward Stirrings* and *Discernment of Spirits.*[179] Maybe the letter was never sent, or had a covering letter. At least, a late-seventeenth-century manuscript does have a formal colophon.[180]

A Letter of Private Direction

Prologue

My spiritual friend in God,

It is to you personally that I now address myself about the interior exercise[2] for which I believe you to be ready, and not to all those who may read or listen to what is written here.[3] For if I were to write for all, I would have to write what suited them all in general. But since at this time I am writing to you individually, I shall say nothing except what I believe to be most profitable and suited to your own disposition. If anyone else is of similar disposition to yourself and finds this letter as profitable, so much the better; I shall be well content. All the same, at this moment it is your own interior disposition, as far as I understand it, and that alone, which is the target and bull's-eye of my intention.[4] It is to you, then, as representing all those in like disposition, that I say what follows.[5]

I

When you come away by yourself,[6] do not be thinking ahead of time what you are to do next; forsake good thoughts as well as evil thoughts. And do not pray with words unless you feel really inclined to do so.[7] And then, if you feel you should say anything, do not reckon how long or how short the prayer should be.[8] Pay no heed to what it is or what it means, whether petition, psalm, hymn, or antiphon, or any other form of prayer, with a particular or general intention, whether mental or interior, expressed merely in your mind, or vocal, by pronouncing the words.[9] Take care that nothing remains for your mind's activity but the simple extension of your will, reaching out to God,[10] not dressed up in any particular thought concerning God as he is in himself, or as revealed in any of his works; simply that he is as he is. Let him be just so, I pray you; do not make anything else of him. Do not seek to penetrate any deeper into him by subtle reasoning; let faith be your foundation.[11]

This simple extension, freely established and grounded in true faith, must be nothing else, as regards your thinking and your feeling, except a simple thought and blind feeling of your own existence;[12] as if you were to speak to God inwardly, with this for your meaning: "What I am, Lord, I offer to you, without looking to any quality of your being, but only that you are what you are and nothing else."[13] This humble darkness is to be the reflection of yourself and your entire mind. Think no further on yourself than I bid you do on your God, so as to be one with him in spirit, and this without dividing or dissipating your awareness.[14]

For he is your being and you are what you are in him, not only by cause and by being: but he is also in you both as your cause and your being.[15] So in this exercise think on God as you do on yourself, and on yourself as you do on God: that he is as he is and you are as you are; so that your thinking might not be dissipated or divided, but kept one in him who is all things; saving this difference between you and him, that he is your being, and you are not his.[16] For though it is true that all things are in him by cause and by being, and that he is in all things as their cause and their being, yet he alone in himself is his own cause and his own being. For as nothing can subsist without him, so he cannot subsist without himself; he is being both to himself and to all things.[17] And in that alone he is separated from all things, because he is the being both of himself and all things; and in this he is one in all things and all are one in him, because all things have their being in him and he is the being of all.[18] Thus your thought and your feeling shall be made one with him in grace, without any separation,[19] while all intellectual inquiry into the subtle qualities of your unseen being or of his are banished far away.[20] See to it that your thought is single and undefiled; that you yourself, unencumbered, just as you are, may be touched by grace and secretly fed in your feeling with him alone, be just as he is; remembering that this union shall be blind and incomplete, as it can only be here in this life, so that your longing desire may always be active.[21]

A LETTER OF PRIVATE DIRECTION

Look up, then, with joy and say to your Lord, either aloud or in your heart: "What I am, Lord, I offer to you; for you are what I am." And think single-mindedly, plainly, and vigorously that you are as you are, without racking your brains at all. To think in this way requires little expertise, even of the most illiterate man or woman alive, with the minimum of natural intelligence; or so it seems to me. And that is why I am quietly amused, but also ruefully amazed sometimes, when I hear some folk say—and I am not speaking of illiterate men and women but of very learned theologians—that what I write to you and to others is so difficult and so profound, so subtle and so unfamiliar, that it can scarcely be understood by the subtlest theologian or most intelligent man or woman alive: This is what they say. To such as these I must answer and say that here is great reason for sorrow and for severe though merciful scorn and condemnation on the part of God and those who love him. For nowadays not only a few people but practically everyone, except perhaps for one or two of God's specially chosen somewhere or other, is so blinded by the subtleties of knowledge, acquired by learning or possessed by natural intelligence, that they can come no nearer in truth of spirit to the understanding of this easy exercise, through which the soul of the most ignorant man or woman alive is truly made one with God in loving meekness and perfect charity, than a little child still learning its A.B.C. can come to the knowledge of the greatest theologian in the schools; or not even as near as that, because of this blindness and curiosity. Because of it they mistakenly call such simple teaching intellectual subtlety; whereas, if we look at it properly, we find it to be a simple and easy lesson given by an illiterate. For I would consider him too illiterate and uncultured by far who could not think and be conscious of himself—that he is. Not what he is, but that he is. For clearly it is an attribute of the most ignorant cow or the most irrational animal—if it could be said, as it cannot, that one were more ignorant or more irrational than another—to be aware of its own individual being.[22] Much more then is it an attribute of man, who alone above all the other animals is endowed with reason, to think and to be conscious of his own individual being.

II

So come down to the lowest point of your understanding which some maintain by experience to be the highest,[23] and think in the most ignorant way, which some maintain to be the wisest, not what

221

your own self is, but *that* it is. Because to think what you are according to all your distinctive qualities requires great learning and intellectual ability, and very skillful investigation into your natural faculties. You have been doing this now for some time, with the help of grace,[24] so that you now have some knowledge—as much, I suppose, as is good for you at the moment—of what you are; that you are a man, by nature, and by sin, a foul, stinking wretch. You know well how it is; and sometimes perhaps it seems to you that you know too well the various filths that pursue and attach to wretched man. Fie on them! Leave them alone, I pray you.[25] Do not stir them up any further, for fear of the stench. But you can think *that* you are, by reason of your own ignorance and coarseness, without any great fund of theological knowledge or natural intelligence.

I pray you then to do no more in this matter than to think without subtlety that you are as you are, no matter how foul or wretched you may be; as long as you have been absolved, as I suppose you have, of all your sins, particular and general, in the proper way, according to the true teaching of Holy Church.[26] Otherwise, neither you nor anyone else shall make so bold as to take up this exercise, at least with my consent. But if you feel that you have done all that in you lies, then you may apply yourself to this exercise. And even though you still feel yourself to be so vile and so wretched, and so hampered by your own self that you scarcely know what is best to do with yourself, you must do this, just as I tell you.[27] Take the good, gracious God, just as he is, without qualification, and bind him, as you would a poultice, to your sick self, just as you are.[28] Or, to put it another way, take your sick self as you are, and strive to touch by desire the good, gracious God as he is. For the touching of him is endless health, as witness the woman in the Gospel: *Si tetigero vel fimbriam vestimenti eius, salva ero*—"If I touch but the hem of his clothing, I shall be safe."[29] You shall be healed of your sickness much more by this high heavenly touch of his own being, of his own dear self. Step up then strongly and taste this wonderful medicine.[30] Lift up your sick self, as you are, to the gracious God, as he is, without any speculation or special probing into any of the qualities that belong to your own being or to God's, whether they are clean or unclean, of grace or of nature, divine or human. You have no business now except to make sure that your dark contemplation of the substance of your being be lifted up in gladness and loving desire to be joined and made one in grace and in spirit with the precious being of God just as he is in himself, and nothing more.[31]

And if your wayward and inquisitive rational faculties can find no nourishment for themselves in this kind of exercise, and therefore grumble all the time[32] and bid you abandon the exercise and achieve something worthwhile in their own probing fashion, for it seems to them that what you are doing is worthless simply because they have no knowledge of it, it would please me all the more: It is a sign that this activity is worth more than their own. And why should it not please me all the more, particularly since there is nothing I can do, nothing that can be achieved by the probing of rational faculties, outwardly or inwardly,[33] that could bring me so close to God and so far from the world as would this simple, almost imperceptible experience, this offering up of the substance of my being? Hence, though your rational faculties can find no nourishment for themselves in this exercise, and for that reason would like to take you away from it, make sure that you do not leave off for their sakes. You are to be their master and refuse to go back to feed them, no matter how vexed they are. You go back to feed them, your rational faculties, when you permit them to be occupied in various speculative reflections on the qualities of your being.

And though these meditations are very good and profitable, yet in comparison with this dark experience and offering up of your being, they are a cause of dissipation and scattering from the perfection of unity which ought properly to exist between God and your soul. So keep on as before, in the first point of your spirit, which is your being;[34] and do not go back for anything at all, no matter how good or holy the thing seems to be that your rational faculties would lead you to.

III

Follow the direction of Solomon when he said to his son: *Honora Dominum de tua substantia et de primis frugum tuarum da pauperibus; et implebuntur horrea tua saturitate et vino torcularia redundabunt*—"Honour the Lord with your substance, and with the first of your fruits feed the poor; then your barns will be filled to bursting; and your cellars abound with wine."[35] This is the literal sense of the words which Solomon spoke to his son;[36] but it is as if he had said to your understanding, in the spiritual sense, what I say to you now on his behalf:

My spiritual friend in God, see to it that you leave behind all the speculative reflections of your natural faculties and give complete worship to God with your substance, offering your own self simply and entirely to him, all that you are and just as you are, but in general and without qualifications—that is, without regard to what you are in particular: so that your contemplation is not distracted nor your affection contaminated in any way which would make you less one with God in purity of spirit.[37] "And with the first of your fruits feed the poor": that is, with the first of your spiritual or bodily qualities which have grown up with you since first you were created until this day.

All the gifts of nature and of grace which God ever gave you, these I call your fruits. With these you are bound to nourish and feed, both bodily and spiritually in this life, all who are your brothers and sisters by nature and by grace, as you are your own proper self.[38] The first of these gifts I call the first of your fruits. The first gift in every creature is simply the being of that creature.[39] For though it be true that the qualities of your being are so firmly fastened to the being itself that they are inseparable from it, yet since they are so dependent upon it, your being itself may rightly be called, as it is, the first of your gifts. And so it is your being, alone, that is the first of your fruits. For if you draw out the mind's weapon of speculative contemplation to penetrate any one of the refined qualities and worthy characteristics that belong to man's being, which is the noblest of all created things,[40] you will always find that the ultimate target and bull's-eye of your contemplation,[41] whatever its primary object, is the substance of your being. It is as though you said within yourself, in every act of contemplation, as you bestir yourself by means of this contemplation to the love and praise of your Lord God, who gave you not only existence, but a nobility of existence to which the qualities you contemplate are witness:[42] "I am and I see and experience that I am; and not only that I am, but that I am this, and this, and this, and this," reckoning up in your contemplation all the specific qualities of your being. And then—and this is more than all that has gone before—you wrap them all up together and say: "What I am and the way I am, in nature and in grace alike, I have received it all from you, Lord; and you are what it is. I offer it all to you, chiefly for your praise and also for the help of my fellow Christians and myself." And so you may see that the ultimate target of your contemplation essentially consists in the single vision, the dark experience of your own being. And so it is your being alone which is the first of your fruits.[43]

IV

But even though it be the first of every one of your fruits, and although all the other fruits depend from it, it is not profitable for you now in your present state, to wrap up or clothe your contemplation of it in one or all of its subtle qualities, which I call your fruits and which your mind has worked on in the past. Now it is enough for you to give complete worship to God with your substance: to offer up the substance of your being, which is the first of your fruits, in continual sacrifice of praise to God both for yourself and for all others,[44] as charity demands, without qualification or particular contemplation of anything that belongs or may belong to your own being or that of any other; even though you may wish by such contemplation to help the needs, further the well-being, or increase the progress in perfection of yourself or any other. Pay no attention to such contemplation. It will not be helpful in your case, believe me. This dark, unfocused contemplation is much more profitable for the needs, the well-being, and the progress in purity of spirit of yourself and all others than is any specific object of a man's contemplation, no matter how holy it appears to be.

The truth of this is shown by the testimony of Scripture, by the example of Christ, and by ready reason. For all men were lost in Adam because he fell from this unitive affection; and all men who bear witness to their desire of salvation with good works according to their vocation are saved, and shall be, by the power of Christ's Passion alone, when he offered himself in the truest sacrifice, the whole of himself in general and not his manhood in particular, not for any particular man living but generally and commonly for all. Similarly, the man who makes a true and perfect sacrifice of himself, with a common intention for all, does all that in him lies to fasten all men to God as effectively as he himself is.[45] And no man can do greater charity than thus to sacrifice himself for his brothers and sisters in grace and in nature.[46] For as the soul is more noble than the body, so the fastening of the soul to God, who is its life, by the heavenly food of charity, is better than the fastening of the body to the soul, which is its life, by any earthly food in this life.[47] This second fastening is good in itself; but without the first it is never well done. The first fastening along with the second is better; but the first fastening in itself is best of all. For the second never merits salvation; but the first, in the point where the abundance of the earthly fastening fails, not only merits salvation, but leads to the greatest perfection.[48]

Hence there is no need, in order to increase your perfection, to go back and feed your faculties by contemplating the qualities of your being; that by such contemplation you might feed and fill your affection with sweet and loving feelings about God and spiritual things, and your reason with the spiritual wisdom of holy meditations in seeking after the knowing of God. For if you will earnestly exercise yourself in the first point of your spirit, without slackening, as best you can with the help of grace, offering up to God that simple awareness of the substance of your being which I call the first of your fruits, you may be sure that the other, the secondary purpose of Solomon's teaching, shall be truly fulfilled as he promises, without your busying yourself in speculative searching and ransacking with your rational faculties any of the qualities belonging to your own being and to God's being as well.

For you are to know very well that in this exercise you must have no more regard for the qualities of God's being than for those of your own being. For there is no name, nor awareness nor sight, which is in as much or more accord with the eternal, which is God, as that which may be possessed, seen, and experienced in the dark and loving contemplation of this word *is*.[49] For if you say Good or Fair, Lord or Sweet, Merciful or Righteous, Wise or All-knowing, Mighty or Almighty, Knowledge or Wisdom, Power or Strength, Love or Charity, or whatever else you say about God,[50] it is all hidden and stored up in this little word *is*. For with God, simply to be is to be all these. And if you were to add to these words good, fair and so on, a hundred thousand other words as sweet as they are, still you would not get away from this word *is*. And if you were to name them all, you would not add to it. And if you were to name none of them at all, you would take nothing from it.[51] So be as blind in the loving contemplation of the being of your God as you are in the simple contemplation of the being of yourself, without any speculative searching in your faculties after any quality proper to his being or to your own. But with all speculation abandoned and left far behind,[52] give worship to God with your substance—all that you are, just as you are, to the whole of him who is as he is. For he alone, in himself and without any thing else, is his own blessed being and yours.[53]

And so through this union, in a way that is wonderful, you shall worship God with God himself. For what you are you have of him and he is what it is. And although you had a beginning in your substantial creation, which at one time was nothing, yet your being has always been in him without any beginning, and always shall be without any ending, just as he is himself.[54] And so I often cry out, and

always with one cry: "Give worship to your God with your substance and give the same well-being with the first of your fruits to
all who are men; and then your barns shall be filled to overflowing."
That is, then your spiritual affection shall be filled with the fulness
of love and with powerful faith in God, your foundation and your
purity of heart.[55] "And your wine-presses shall run over, full of
wine."[56] That is, your interior, spiritual faculties, which you are accustomed to force and press together with various speculative meditations and rational investigations into the spiritual knowing of God
and yourself, in contemplation of his qualities and your own, shall
then run over, full of wine. By this wine, in Holy Scripture, is truly
and mystically understood spiritual wisdom in true contemplation
and high savor of the Godhead.[57] And all this shall happen suddenly,
delightfully, and through grace, without effort or labor of your own,
but only by the service of angels through the power of this dark exercise of love.[58] For all the angelic spirits of knowledge render special
service to it,[59] like the serving maid of her lady.[60]

V

It is in great praise of this simple and delightful work, which is in
fact the high wisdom of the Godhead descending through grace into
man's soul, knitting it and uniting it to himself in spiritual wisdom
and discernment,[61] that Solomon cries out and says:

> Beatus homo qui invenit sapientiam et qui affluit prudentia. Melior est ac-
> quisitio eius negotiatione auri et argenti. Primi et purissimi fructus eius. Cus-
> todi, fili mi, legem atque consilium: et erit vita animae tuae et gratia faucibus
> tuis. Tunc ambulabis fiducialiter in via tua, et pes tuus non impinget. Si dor-
> mieris, non timebis; quiesces et suavis erit somnus tuus. Ne paveas repentino
> terrore, et irruentes tibi potentias impiorum, quia Dominus erit in latere tuo
> et custodiet pedem tuum ne capiaris.[62]

All of this means, for your understanding:

> He is blessed who can find this unitive wisdom and be filled in his spir-
> itual exercises with this loving simplicity and spiritual discernment,
> offering up his own obscure awareness of his own being and leaving
> far behind all the subtleties of knowledge both natural and acquired.
> To achieve this spiritual wisdom and this simple exercise is better than
> winning gold or silver. By gold and silver is understood morally all
> other knowing, natural and spiritual,[63] which is obtained by the spec-

227

ulative investigation and operation of our natural faculties on what is beneath us, within us, or on a par with us,[64] in the contemplation of any of the qualities proper to the being of God or of any created thing.[65]

And he adds the reason why it is better, when he says: for *primi et purissimi fructus eius*—that is, "for the fruits of it are the first and purest." And no wonder. For the fruit of this exercise is high spiritual wisdom, which is suddenly and without constraint belched forth by the spirit inwardly, within itself.[66] It is without definition, the antithesis of illusion; it cannot be controlled by or become subject to the working of the natural faculties. For the natural understanding, no matter how keen or sanctified it may be, is to be called, in comparison to this, mere foolishness formed and devised in illusion; as far removed from the real truth[67] seen in the light of the spiritual sun as is the dark light of the moon, shining through the mist of a midwinter's night, from the brightness of the sunlight at the height of a mid-summer's day.[68]

"My son," he says, "keep this law and this counsel"; in which all the commandments and the counsels, as well of the Old Testament as of the New, are truly and perfectly fulfilled: without considering specially any particular one in itself.[69] For no other reason is this kind of exercise called a law except that it contains wholly within it all the branches and the fruits of the law.[70] For if we look at it rightly, the ground and the strength of this exercise shall be seen to be nothing else but the glorious gift of love, in which, as the apostle teaches, all the law is fulfilled.[71] *Plenitudo legis est dilectio*—"The fullness of the law is love."[72] This loving law and counsel of life, as long as you keep it, shall be, as Solomon says, "the life of your soul" interiorly, in your tender love of God; "and beauty in your cheeks" outwardly, in the truest teaching and seemliest behavior toward your fellow Christians in your outward manner of life.[73] "On these two," the one within and the other without, "depend the whole of the law and the Prophets," as Christ teaches. *In his enim duobus tota lex pendet et prophetae; scilicet, dilectio Dei et proximi.*[74]

And therefore, when you are thus made perfect in your exercise, inwardly and outwardly, you may go forward in hope, with grace as your support and guide for your spiritual journey,[75] lifting up the substance of your being, in love and in darkness, to the blessed being of your God: They are one in grace though separate in nature. "And the foot of your love shall not stumble." That is to say, once you have experience of your spiritual exercise with inward perseverance, you shall not be so easily hindered or pulled down by the searching questions of the mind's speculation, as you are now, in your beginnings. Or else he may mean: "Then the foot of your love shall not stumble" nor trip on any kind of illusion occasioned by the mind's speculative searching; because in this exercise, as was said before, all the speculative inquiry of any of your natural faculties is abandoned and wholly forgotten for fear of any illusion or deception that may occur in this life,[76] which in this exercise would contaminate the simple awareness of the substance of your being and draw you away from the perfection of this exercise.

For if any kind of idea of any particular thing, other than the simple substance of your being, which is your God and your goal, should come into your mind, immediately you are off course and pulled back to subtle and enquiring speculation, which dissipates and separates both yourself and your mind from yourself and God. So keep yourself recollected and undistracted as far as you can by grace and the strategy of spiritual endurance.[77] For in this dark contemplation of the substance of your being, in which, as I have told you, you are one with God, you must do all that you have to do: eat and drink, sleep and awaken, walk and sit, speak and be silent, lie down and get up, stand and kneel, run and ride, labor and rest. Every day you must offer it up to God as the most precious offering you can make. It must take the first place in all your activity, whether what you are doing be styled active or contemplative. For as Solomon says in this passage, "if you sleep" in this dark contemplation, away from all the agitation and temptation of the dread fiend, the false world, and the frail flesh,[78] "you shall not fear any peril" nor any deceit of the devil; because he is utterly confused and blinded by a painful ignorance and a frenzied perplexity about what you are doing in this exercise.[79] Do not worry about that; for "you shall rest pleasantly" in this loving union of God and your soul. "And your sleep shall be very sweet," for it shall be a spiritual nourishment and inward strength, to your body as well as to your soul. For as Solomon immediately goes on to say, *Universae carni sanitas est*—"It is health to all the flesh's frailty and sickness." And this is well said. For since all sickness and corruption attacked the flesh when the soul fell away from the practice of this exercise, so all health shall return to the flesh when the soul rises again to this same exercise, by the grace of Jesus who is the chief worker of it.[80] And you must hope to obtain this health only through the mercy of Jesus and your loving consent.[81] And, therefore, I pray you, as does Solomon in this passage, to persevere steadfastly in this exercise, constantly lifting up to him your loving consent with the eagerness of love. *Et ne paveas repentino terrore, et irruentes tibi potentias impiorum*—"And do not be dismayed by any disquieting fear," though the fiend should come, as indeed he will, "bringing sudden panic,"[82] banging and beating on the walls of your house, as you sit within, or should incite one of his powerful limbs "to rush in upon you" suddenly, as they do, without any warning.[83] You must take it as certain that it shall be so, whoever you are who prepare yourself to carry out these exercises properly. You shall certainly see and feel or else smell, taste, or hear some strange thing devised by the devil to affect some of your five outward senses.[84] It is all done to pull you down from the heights of this precious exercise. And therefore keep a good watch on your heart in the time of this torment, and lean eagerly and confidently on the love of our Lord.[85]

Quia Dominus erit in latere tuo, et custodiet pedem tuum ne capiaris—that is, "for our Lord shall be at your side," ready and near to help you, "and he shall watch your step," that is, the climbing up of your love by which you ascend to God; "so that you shall not be caught" by the trickery or guile of your enemies, the devil and his minions, the world and the flesh.[86] Yes, my friend, it is thus that our Lord and our Love, with his power, wisdom, and goodness shall sustain, keep, and defend all those who because of the loving confidence that they feel in him are willing entirely to abandon care for themselves.[87]

VI

But where shall such a soul be found, one that is so securely rooted in and founded on the faith, so utterly humbled in the annihilation of itself, so lovingly led and fed in the love of our Lord; one that has full knowledge and experience of his almighty power, his hidden wisdom, and his glorious goodness, how he is one in all and all are in him: so much so that unless a loving soul entirely surrenders to him all that is from him, by him, and in him, it is never truly humbled in the complete reduction of self?[88] It is only by this royal reduction of itself to nothing in true humility and the high exaltation of God, its all, in perfect charity, that the soul deserves to have God. When it is deeply immersed in God's love, fully and finally forsaking itself as nothing or less than nothing—if there could be such a thing as less than nothing—then God's love sustains it, keeps and defends it with his power, wisdom, and goodness from all adversity, without any industry or effort, consideration, or reflection on the soul's part.[89]

Cease from your all too human objections, you half-humbled souls, and do not say, in your wearying excursions into logic, that such a humble and utter forsaking of self-consciousness, whenever a man is aware of being touched by grace, is to tempt God: simply because you feel that you dare not do so yourselves.[90] No, be content with your own part—the active life, which is enough for the saving of your souls; and leave others alone, the contemplative souls who dare do so. Do not muse over or marvel at their words and deeds, even though it seems to you that they go beyond the normal limits and balance of your reason.[91]

Oh, for shame! How much longer are you going to read and to listen and still refuse to give credit or credence to it? I mean all that our ancient Fathers before us have written and taught, that which is the flower and the fruit of all Holy Scripture.[92] It would seem either that you are blind and cannot see with the eye of faith what you read or hear read, or else you are moved by some secret kind of envy, so that you cannot believe that so great a good can happen to your brethren, since you do not have it yourselves. It is well for you to be on your guard, for your enemy is subtle; his purpose is to make you give more credence to your own intellectual powers than to the truthful teachings of the old Fathers or the working of grace and the will of our Lord.

How often have you read and heard, and from so many holy, wise, and truthful writers that as soon as Benjamin was born, his mother Rachel died? Benjamin stands for contemplation, Rachel for reason.[93] As soon as a soul is touched by true contemplation, as it is in this royal reduction of itself to nothing and this high extolling of God as all, it is certain and true that all a man's reason dies in that moment.[94] Seeing that you read this so often, not just in one or two writers but in very many who are really holy and of real account, why do you not believe it?[95] And if you believe it, how dare you ransack and search with your reason the words and deeds of Benjamin? Benjamin stands for all those who are ravished above the mind's powers by ecstasy of love, as the Prophet says: *Ibi Beniamyn adolescentulus in mentis excessu*[96]—that is to say: "Here is Benjamin, a young child, in ecsasy of mind." Take heed then that you do not imitate those wretched women who literally slay their children as soon as they are born.[97] It is good to take care, lest you aim the point of your presumptuous spear with all the strength you possess at the power, the wisdom, and the will of our Lord, thinking in your blindness and lack of experience that you are best advancing his cause when, in fact, you are aiming to bring him down.

For in the first beginnings of Holy Church, in the times of persecution, many different kinds of people were so wonderfully and without warning affected by a sudden infusion of grace, that straightway and without any previous spiritual preparation craftsmen threw down their tools and children ran to martyrdom with holy men.[98] So why should not men believe that now in a time of peace God may, can, will, and indeed does affect different people in the same sudden way with the grace of contemplation? And I believe that it is his will to do this with the fulness of grace in chosen souls. For it is his will to be known at the last for what he is, to the wonder of all the world.[99] Such a soul, then, that, for love, reduces itself to nothing and makes its God everything, shall be preserved in the fulness of grace from being overthrown by its spiritual and earthly enemies, by the goodness of God alone and without any industry or effort on its own part.[100] For the divine logic demands that he should keep truly safe all those who, making his love their business, cease to worry about themselves and have no desire to do so. And it is no wonder that they are marvellously well looked after, because they are so truly humble in their strong and daring deeds of love.[101]

If there is anyone that does not dare the same and speaks against it, either the devil is in his heart,[102] robbing him of the loving confidence he should have in his God, and the goodwill he should have toward his fellow-Christians, or else he is not yet as perfectly humble as he needs to be—I mean if he intends to lead a life of a true contemplative. So do not be afraid to humble yourself in this way before your Lord, or to sleep in the dark contemplation of God as he is, away from all the noise of this wicked world, the false fiend, and your frail flesh. "For our Lord shall be ready to help you, and to watch your steps that you may not be ensnared."

This exercise is rightly compared to sleep. For just as in sleep the use of the natural faculties is suspended in order that the body may obtain complete rest, for the nourishing and strengthening of its natural powers; even so in this supernatural sleep the extravagant questioning of the untamed spiritual faculties, their imaginative speculations, are thoroughly tamed and got rid of, in order that the simple soul may sleep and rest softly in the loving contemplation of God as he is, for the nourishing and strengthening of its supernatural powers. Tame, then, your senses, and offer up this dark awareness of the substance of your being. And take constant care, as I keep on saying, that it is the substance of your being unadorned with any quality. For if you dress it up in any quality, such as the nobility of your being or any other special characteristic belonging to man's being as against the being of any other creature, then straightaway you are giving sustenance to your natural faculties, by which they have occasion and strength to draw you down to many things, so that you become distracted in some way or other. I beg of you to watch out for this pitfall.[103]

VII

But perhaps at this point, influenced by the clever and searching scrutiny of your rational faculties—for they have no knowledge at all of this exercise—you are beginning to wonder about its method and hold it in suspicion. This is not surprising; because up to now you have been too clever by half[104] to know anything about this sort of thing. Perhaps you are even asking yourself whether this exercise is pleasing to God or not; or, if indeed it is pleasing to him, how it can be as pleasing as I say it is. My answer here is that your question springs from intellectual curiosity; and this will effectively prevent your consenting to practice this exercise, until such time as this curiosity is assuaged by some good logical argument.[105] So I will not stand in your way, but up to a point I will imitate you and flatter your intellectual pride; so that later on you may become like me, accepting my direction, and refusing to set bounds to your humility. For, and St. Bernard is my witness, "Perfect humility knows no bounds."[106] You set bounds to your humility when you refuse to accept the direction of your spiritual master unless your reason sees that this is the thing to do. I make no secret, as you see, of the fact that I want to be your spiritual father; indeed I do, and intend to be so.[107] I believe that love is my motive rather than the awareness in myself of any great ability either in the theory or the practice, or a high degree of spiritual perfection.[108] May God put right what is wrong, for he knows the whole, and I only a fraction. But now, since I must give some satisfaction to your intellectual pride in my praise of this exercise, I tell you truly that if a soul which is occupied in it had a form of speech and a vocabulary to describe its experience, all the theologians in Christendom would be amazed at its wisdom.[109] Yes, indeed; and in comparison to this wisdom, all their profound theological learning would appear plain foolishness.[110] No wonder, then, if I cannot describe the excellence of this exercise in my crude and earthly speech. God forbid that it should be contaminated by

233

the distortion which earthly language would give it. No, this must not and surely will not happen, and God forbid that I should want it so. For all that is said of it does not define it, but is said about it. So now, since we cannot define it, let us speak about it—to the confusion of all intellectual pride, and yours in particular, which is the sole cause or at least the occasion of this present letter.[111]

My first question is: What is the perfection of man's soul, and what are the qualities which characterize this perfection? I shall answer for you, and say: The perfection of man's soul is nothing but the union made in perfect charity between God and itself.[112] This perfection is of itself so noble and pure, so far above human understanding, that in itself it cannot be known or perceived. But we may take it that the perfection is substantially and vigorously present wherever the qualities that characterize it are truly seen and perceived. So now, if we are to demonstrate that this spiritual exercise excels all others, we must know the qualities of that perfection.

The characteristics of perfection, which every perfect soul must possess, are the virtues.[113] Now if you will examine carefully in yourself both this exercise and the quality and state of each virtue separately, you will find that all the virtues in their clarity and perfection are presupposed in this exercise, as long as there is no deviation or perversion of the intention. I shall not examine any particular virtue here; there is no need for it. You will find them discussed in several places in my other writings.[114] For this same work, properly understood, is the reverent affection, the fruit plucked from the tree,[115] of which I wrote in my short letter to you on prayer. It is also the Cloud of Unknowing;[116] it is the hidden love offered in purity of spirit;[117] it is the ark of the Testament.[118] It is the mystical theology of Denys,[119] his wisdom and his treasure,[120] his luminous darkness and his secret knowledge.[121] It is this that brings you to silence, in your thoughts as well as in your words.[122] It makes your prayer very short. And in it you are taught to forsake and to despise the world.

VIII

And what is more, in this exercise you are taught to forsake and to despise your own self, according to the teaching of Christ in the Gospel, when he says: *Si quis vult venire post me, abneget semetipsum: tollat crucem suam et sequatur me*[123]—"If any man will come after me, let him forsake himself, let him bear his cross and follow me." It is as if he spoke thus in present circumstances to your understanding: "If any

234

man will come in humility, not with me but after me, up to the bliss of heaven and the summit of perfection."[124] For Christ went before,[125] by nature, and we follow after, by grace. His nature is nobler than grace,[126] and grace is nobler than our nature.[127] Here he gives us clearly to understand that we cannot by any means follow him to the summit of perfection, which is the proper object of this exercise, unless we are driven and led by grace.[128] This is the truth. And you, and all others like you who may read this letter or hear it read, must take full account of it; for though I bid you so simply and so boldly to apply yourself to this exercise, yet my true feelings in this, beyond error or doubt, are that almighty God with his grace must always be the one who prompts and carries out the exercise whether he uses instruments or not.[129] You, and anyone else like you, merely give your consent to the exercise and accept its working in you,[130] even though during the exercise your consent and acceptance must be actively disposed and proportionate to it in purity of spirit, and fittingly offered to your sovereign Lord.[131] Your spirit's inward sight can give you the proof of this.

And since it is true that God in his goodness affects different souls by the touch of his goodness in different ways, some by the use of instruments, and others without them, does anyone dare to say that God does not affect you and others like you who may read this writing or hear it read, by using me, unworthy as I am, as his sole instrument, always having regard to his most holy will, for it is his pleasure to act in the way it pleases him?[132] This, I believe, will be the way of it. The exercise itself will prove it, once you have practical experience of it.[133] And therefore I beg you to dispose yourself to receive this grace from your Lord and listen to what he says: "If any man will come after me," in the sense expounded above, "let him forsake himself." How, I pray you, can a man abandon himself and the world more completely, despise himself and the world more positively, than by disdaining even to think of the qualities of his own and the world's being?

You must take it as certain that, although I direct you to forget everything but the feeling of the being of yourself, yet it is my wish, and it was my intention from the beginning, that you should forget the feeling of the being of yourself in exchange for the feeling of the being of God.[134] That is why I proved to you at the beginning that God is your being. But because it seemed to me that you were not yet capable of being lifted up suddenly to the spiritual feeling of the being of God because of your lack of experience in your own spiritual feeling of yourself, in order to help you to climb up to it gradually I directed you to gnaw on the dark and obscure feeling of your own being unadorned until such time as you might be made ready, by spiritual perseverance in this hidden exercise, to arrive at the high awareness of God. For your purpose and desire in this exercise must always be to feel God. For though at the beginning, because of your coarseness and lack of spiritual experience, I bade you to wrap up and clothe the feeling of your God in the feeling of your own self; later on, when through perseverance you are become wiser in purity of spirit, you must strip, despoil, and utterly divest yourself of every kind of feeling of yourself, so that you can be clothed in the grace-giving feeling of God's own self.[135]

And this is the way in which the perfect lover behaves, wholly and entirely to despoil himself of himself to have the thing he loves, and refusing to allow himself to be clothed in anything except the thing he loves; and this is not merely for a time, but to be wrapped in it forever, in the full and final forgetfulness of self.[136] This is a love-making that none can know save him that has experience of it.[137] This is what our Lord is teaching when he says: "If any man love me, let him forsake himself," as though he said: "Let him despoil himself of himself if he truly wishes to be clothed in me, who am the rich garment of everlasting love that shall never have an end."[138]

And therefore whenever you consider your spiritual exercise and see and feel that it is yourself and not God whom you are feeling, then you must sorrow in earnest and long with all your heart for the feeling of God.[139] It must be your constant and ceaseless desire to be rid of this woeful knowing and miserable feeling of your blind being; you must yearn to escape from yourself as you would from something poisonous. Then it is that you forsake yourself and despise yourself most bitterly, as your Lord commands you.[140] And then when you long so desperately, not to cease to be, for that would be madness and contempt of God,[141] but to be rid of the knowledge and the feeling of your being, which must always happen before God's love can be felt as perfectly as it may here on earth; then indeed you see and feel that you can in no way attain your purpose, because no matter how occupied you are, a naked feeling of your blind being will always accompany and follow you in all your actions.[142] There may however be a rare and brief occasion when God permits you to experience him in the fulness of love.[143]

So this naked feeling of your blind being will always press in above you, between you and your God, just as at the beginning the qualities of your being will press in between you and yourself. Then it is that the burden of yourself will seem so heavy and so painful. Yes, indeed, may Jesus help you then, for then you have need of him.[144] For all the sorrow that exists, apart from that, is nothing in comparison. It is then that you are yourself a cross to yourself. This is the authentic exercise and the way to our Lord, as he says himself: "Let him carry his cross": first, the painful heaviness of self, and then "follow me" into joy or the mount of perfection,[145] tasting the sweetness of my love, the godlike experience of myself. Here indeed you can see that you need this sorrowing desire to be rid of the feeling of yourself, and painfully to bear the burden of yourself as a cross, before you can be joined to God in this spiritual feeling of himself, which is perfect charity. So you can both see and feel to some extent why this exercise is nobler than any other in proportion as you are touched and spiritually sealed with this grace.[146]

How then, I ask you, could you come to make this exercise by the use of your rational faculties? Indeed, never; not even by good means, as are your well-devised imaginative, speculative meditations: not even if these concern your sinful life, the passion of Christ, the joys of our Lady or of all the saints and angels in heaven, or any quality or refinement or condition pertaining to your own or God's being.[147] Certainly, I would rather have that dark unencumbered feeling of myself which I described above.[148] It is a feeling not of my activity, but of myself. Many men identify themselves with their activity, but there is a distinction; I myself that do is one thing, my deeds that are done are another. It is the same with God; he is one thing in himself, his works are another. I would rather weep till my heart should break because I lack this feeling of God and of the painful heaviness of the self, and thus inflame my desire to have and to long for that feeling of God, rather than enjoy all the well-devised imaginative and speculative meditations that men can tell of or find written in books, no matter how holy or worthwhile they appear to the subtle regard of your speculative mind.[149]

IX

At the same time these meditations are the truest way that the sinner may have in his new beginnings for the spiritual feeling of himself and of God. I would even say that human understanding cannot conceive of the possibility—granted that God can do whatever he will—of a sinner coming to rest in the spiritual feeling of himself and of God, unless he first saw and felt by imagination and meditation the earthly activity of himself and of God, mourning over what is sorrowful and rejoicing over what is joyful.[150] Whoever does not come along this way does not really come at all. He must therefore stand outside; there he stands when he thinks that he is well and truly inside. For many think that they are inside the spiritual door when they are still standing outside; and they shall continue so until they seek the door in meekness. There are some who find the door almost immediately and enter in before others; and this is clearly due to the doorkeeper and not to what they pay or deserve.

The interior life is a wonderful house,[151] for the Lord himself is not only the doorkeeper but also the door.[152] He is the doorkeeper by his Godhead, and the door by his manhood. He says this himself in the Gospel: *Ego sum ostium. Per me si quis introierit, salvabitur; et sive egredietur sive ingredietur, pascua inveniet. Qui vero non intrat per ostium sed ascendit aliunde, ipse fur est et latro.*[153]

If we interpret according to our context, it is as if he said to your understanding:

> I who am almighty by my Godhead can lawfully, as doorkeeper, let in whom I will and by what way that I will. But because I want there to be one clear way for all, one open entry to all that wish to come in, and in order that none can plead ignorance of the way in, I have clothed myself in the nature common to all men, and have made myself so open that by my manhood I am the door; whoever enters by me shall be safe.[154]

They enter by the door who contemplate the Passion of Christ and mourn for their wickedness which is the cause of that Passion, bitterly reproving themselves in that they have deserved to suffer and have not suffered, and have pity and compassion for our good Lord who suffered so cruelly and deserved none of it.[155] Then they lift up their hearts to contemplate the love and the goodness of his Godhead, in which he stoops so low as to humble himself in our manhood doomed to death. All these enter by the door and they shall be safe. And whether they go in and contemplate the love and goodness of his Godhead, or stay outside and behold the suffering of his manhood, they shall find spiritual nourishment for devotion in plenty, enough and more than enough for the health and safety of their souls;[156] even though, in his life, they never penetrate further.

But whoever does not enter by this door, but seeks to climb in to perfection by some other way, by speculation, extravagant to the point of illusion, of the unruly reason, ignoring the common straightforward way described above and the sound advice of our spiritual fathers; such a one, whoever he is, is not only a nocturnal thief but a daylight prowler.[157] He is a nocturnal thief, because he goes abroad in the darkness of sin, presumptuously trusting to his own intellectual powers and his own will rather than to sound advice or the common straightforward way described above. He is a daylight prowler because in the disguise of one who lives the contemplative life he steals the outward signs and words of contemplation without possessing its fruits.[158] And because he sometimes experiences in himself the traces of a longing in his intellectual subtlety to come near to God, dazzled by the appearance of this, he thinks that all his activity is good; when, in fact, there is nothing more dangerous than for a young man to follow his own violent desire without submitting himself to direction. This is specially true when his desire is focused on the ascent to higher things—things not only above himself but above the common straightforward way of Christians described above; which, after the teaching of Christ, may be called the door of devotion: the surest entrance to contemplation that there may be in this life.

X

But now we must develop the subject matter of this letter insofar as it concerns you particularly and all those who are disposed as you are. If Christ's manhood is the door to contemplation for people like you, when a man has once gained the threshold, shall he continue to stand there, or just outside, hesitating to penetrate further in? Let me answer for you. I say that it is good for a man to continue to stand there until, in the judgment of his directors and his own conscience, the heavy rust of his coarse earthiness is scrubbed away;[159] and, most important of all, until he is summoned to advance further in by the quiet teaching of the Spirit of God. This teaching is the readiest and surest witness that we can have in this life that the soul is called and drawn further in, by grace, to a more special working of grace. A man can have proof that he has received the touch of this grace if he experiences, as he constantly perseveres in his exercise, a gentle but growing desire to draw as near as possible to God in this life; and this by way of that special spiritual awareness which he has heard men speak of, or has seen described in books. But if he is unaware of being affected by a growing desire to draw near to God, when he hears spiritual exercises discussed or reads about them, or particularly when he prefers his own daily exercises, then he must continue to

stand still at the door, as one who is called to salvation, but not yet
to perfection.

And here is a warning to all those who read this letter or hear it
read, whoever you may be; particularly when you come to this point
where I make a distinction between those called to salvation and
those called to perfection.[160] Whether you feel that your own vocation is to salvation or to perfection, take care that you refrain from
judging or criticizing the activity of God and of man alike—apart
from your own;[161] I mean deciding whom he attracts and calls to perfection and whom he does not; or discussing the length of time—why
he calls one sooner than another.[162] If you are determined not to err,
take care that you do not judge; just listen for once, and understand.
If you are called, then give praise to God and pray that you do not
fail. And if you are not yet called, pray humbly to God that he might
call you when such is his will. But do not try to teach him what he
should do. Let him alone. He is powerful, wise, and willing enough
to do the best for you and for all who love him. Be at peace in your
vocation, whichever one it is. You have no call to complain, since
both are precious.[163] The first is good, and is always necessary.[164]
The second is better, and may they take it who can; or rather, to
speak more correctly, may they take it who are taken by grace and
called to it by our Lord. We may strain stumblingly after our good
in our proud independence; but certainly without him what we do
is nothing, as he himself says: *Sine me nihil potestis facere*[165]—that is,
to your understanding: "Unless I initiate the movement and remain
the chief mover, while you merely consent to it and accept it, you
can do nothing that is perfectly pleasing to me."[166] And so it must
be with the exercise described in this letter.

I have written all this to confound the false presumption of those
who, relying on their speculative theology or their natural acumen,
always want to see themselves as the chief workers, and God as
merely consenting to and accepting their work; when of course, in
matters contemplative, the opposite is the truth. For in these matters
alone must all the reasonings of speculative theology and natural acumen be left behind, so that God is the principal. At the same time,
in the lawful occupations of the active life, a man's theological learning and his natural intelligence must be working partners with God,
once his consent to the work is established by these three witnesses,
Holy Scripture, direction, and the bounds set by a man's nature,
state of life, age, and temperament. So much so that a man should
not follow the inclination of his spirit—I mean, of course, in matters
pertaining to the active life—no matter how attractive or holy it

seems to be, unless it comes within the compass of his theological or natural knowledge: and this no matter how strongly the inclination is supported by any one or all three of the witnesses mentioned above. And indeed it is very reasonable to expect that a man should amount to more than his works. This is why the law of Holy Church ordains that before a man is admitted to the office of bishop, which is the highest rank of the active life, it must be shown through examination that the duties of the pastoral care are within his compass.[167] Hence, in the active life, a man's theological learning and his natural acumen, must, with God's consent and his grace, and given the approval of these three witnesses, be employed to the full in all that he does; and rightly so, since all things belonging to the active life are inferior and subject to human wisdom.[168] But in matters contemplative the highest wisdom that man can possess in the natural order is utterly submerged, that God may play the leading part whilst man merely consents and follows the lead.[169]

It is thus that I interpret these words of the Gospel, *Sine me nihil potestis facere*—"without me you can do nothing":[170] in one sense for those living the active life, in another for contemplatives. He must be with the actives either by sufferance or by consent or by both, in whatever is to be done, whether what is done is lawful and pleasing to him or not. He must be with contemplatives as the chief worker, asking of them nothing else but to receive him and to consent to what he does.[171] The general interpretation is this: In all that we do, lawful or unlawful, active or contemplative, we can do nothing without him. When we sin, he is with us both by sufferance and not by consent, which at the last shall be our damnation, unless we humbly repent. In our works that are active and lawful, he is with us both by sufferance and consent: to our discredit if we fall back, and for our great reward if we advance.[172] In our contemplative works he is with us as the first mover and chief worker while we merely receive him and give him our consent, to our great perfection and the spiritual joining of our soul to him in perfect charity. And since all men alive can be divided into three kinds, sinners, actives, and contemplatives, these words of our Lord can be applied to the whole generally: "Without me"—I am with sinners by sufferance and not by consent, with actives both by sufferance and consent, or, in the way which is more perfect, with contemplatives, as first mover and chief worker—"you can do nothing."[173]

Here indeed are many words and only a little meaning in them. But I have said them all to let you see on what matters you should use your rational faculties and on what you should not; and the way in which God is with you in one work and in a different way in another. Perhaps you will now be able to avoid certain mistakes which you might have made if I had not said all this. Now it has been said, let it stand, even though it has little to do with our subject. We must now get on with that.

XII

You could ask me a question like this:[174] Could you please tell me by what sign or signs I might know most quickly and without error whether this growing desire which I experience in my daily exercises, and this attraction which comes upon me when I hear of this contemplation or read about it, is a true vocation from God to a more special work of grace,[175] the one you describe in this letter? Or is this desire and attraction simply for the nourishing and strengthening of my spirit, to stay where I am and to continue to work in the realm of ordinary graces—those which you call the door and the common entrance of all Christians?

I answer as well as my feebleness permits. You realize that I have set before you in this letter two kinds of evidence by which you can put it to the test whether you have a truly spiritual call from God to this exercise: One is interior, the other exterior. I do not think, in this case, that either of the two is sufficient without the other. But where you find them both together and in agreement, then your evidence is complete and strong enough.[176]

The first of these two, the interior one, is this growing desire which you experience in your daily exercises. And you can learn this much more about it: Although the desire is in itself a blind work of the soul—the soul's desire is analogous to the body's sense of touch or of movement; you know yourself that using the hands and feet are acts of the body which have not sight, yet however blind the working of this desire may be, it is always associated with and followed by a kind of spiritual sight, which is partly the cause and the means of the desire's growth.[177] You must earnestly examine the nature of your daily exercise. If it is the consciousness of your own sinfulness, the Passion of Christ, or any other that belongs to the common entrance of Christians mentioned above; and if, in addition, this spiritual sight, associated with and following on your blind desires, comes from these devotional contemplations, this is to me undoubtedly a sign that this growing desire is the nourishing and strengthening of your spirit, to enable it to stand patiently and to continue to work with ordinary graces; and not that you are being called or drawn by God to more special graces.[178]

And now the second, the exterior evidence; this is the attraction you feel whenever you hear this exercise spoken of, or read about it. I call it exterior evidence, for it comes from outside through the windows of your bodily senses,[179] through your ears or your eyes during your reading time. Concerning this evidence, if it happens that this attraction which you feel when you hear or read about this exercise does not last or continue with you longer, but only while you are actually reading or listening, but stops then or soon after; if, that is, you do not wake up and go to sleep in it or with it, and especially if it does not accompany you in your daily exercise, coming and forcing itself, so to say, between you and your prayer, stirring up and bringing forth your desire;[180] if it is not like this, then, in my judgment, this attraction which you feel when you hear or read of this exercise is simply the natural gladness which every Christian soul has when he hears or reads about the truth, particularly the truth which goes to the heart of and clearly expounds the qualities which characterize the perfection of man's soul, and more particularly the perfection of God.[181] It is not the spiritual touch of grace, nor the call of God to a more special work of grace than that which is the door and common entrance of all Christians.

But if it happens that this attraction that you feel in reading or hearing about this matter is of itself so overwhelming that it goes to bed with you, gets up with you in the morning, accompanies you all day in all that you do, separates you from your normal daily exercise by inserting itself between your prayers and you; if it is associated with and follows your desire to the extent that it seems to be just the one desire,[182] or you scarcely know what it is that alters your outlook and brings a cheerful smile to your lips;[183] if, while it lasts, everything is a consolation and nothing can upset you; if you would run a thousand miles to have speech with someone whom you know has truly felt as you do; and if, when you get there, you have nothing to say, no matter who speaks to you, since you do not wish to speak except about that one thing; if your words are few but full of unction and fire;[184] if one brief word of yours holds a world of wisdom but seems mere foolishness to those who have not passed beyond reason;[185] if your silence is peaceful, your speech edifying, your prayer secret, your pride proper, your behavior modest, your laughter very soft;[186] if your delight is like that of a child at play;[187] if you love to be alone and sit apart, because you feel that others would hinder you, unless they did what you are doing; if you do not wish to read or listen to reading unless it be about this one thing; then indeed your two kinds of evidence, the interior and the exterior, will be in agreement, forming a whole.[188]

But what if both kinds of evidence and all the indications in their favor which I have just enumerated, after you have once possessed some or all of them, should disappear for a time, and you are left as though you were sterile, deprived not only of your new fervor but also unfitted for your customary spiritual exercises of the past? It seems in fact that you have fallen between two stools: You now have neither, but are deprived of both.[189] You are not to be too despondent about this; rather you must endure it humbly, and wait patiently on the Lord's will. For, as I see it, you are now on the spiritual ocean, being shipped across from the active state to the contemplative.[190]

It can happen that great storms and temptations will arise during a time like this, and you will be at a loss where to run for help. As far as you can see, everything has gone—ordinary graces as well as the more special. But you must not be too disturbed, though it seems that you have every reason to be. Rather trust lovingly in our Lord, as much as you can at the time, however feebly; for he is not far off. He will turn his face to you, perhaps very soon, and affect you again with a touch of that same grace more ardently than you ever experienced before.[191] And then it will seem to you that you are completely restored, well in every respect; but only while it lasts. For suddenly, almost before you know it, it will be gone again,[192] and you are left flat in your boat, tossed about and floundering now hither, now thither, not knowing where you are nor where you are going. But do not be dismayed; he shall come, I promise you, as soon as it is his will, to relieve you and mightily to free you from all your trouble, far more wonderfully than he ever did before. Yes, indeed; whenever he goes away, he will come again soon. And each time he will come more marvellously and joyfully than he did before, as long as you have that patient endurance. For his purpose in all this is to make you as close-fitting to his will, spiritually as a soft leather glove is to the bodily hand.[193]

And inasmuch as he is sometimes absent and sometimes present, he wishes by this coming and going to test you secretly and to form you for his own work.[194] He wishes to test the quality of your patience by this withdrawal of your fervor. It is this that you take to be his absence, though it is not so. You must understand that though God sometimes withdraws sensible sweetness, feelings of fervor and burning desire, at the same time he never withdraws his grace from his chosen ones.[195] And certainly, I cannot believe that his special grace could ever be withdrawn from his chosen ones who have once been endowed with it, except by mortal sin. But all this sensible sweetness, feelings of fervor and burning desire which in themselves are not grace but tokens of grace, these are often withdrawn to test our patience, and for our spiritual profit in many other ways as well, beyond our reckoning. For grace is in itself so high, so pure, and so spiritual that it cannot be perceived by our senses; its tokens can be, but not the grace itself. Thus our Lord will sometimes withdraw your feelings of fervor both to strengthen and to purify your patience, and not for this reason alone, but for many others which I do not mention here. But let us return to our subject.

By the quality, frequency, and growing intensity of these sensible consolations mentioned above—which you take to be his presence, though it is in fact not so—he wishes to nourish and strengthen your spirit to live and persevere in his love and service. And thus, by your patience in the absence of these sensible consolations—the tokens of grace—by that vital nourishing and loving strengthening of your spirit when they are present, it is his will to make you, alike in consolation and desolation, eagerly inclined and sweetly fitted to perfection and spiritual union with his will: for this union is the perfection of charity.[196] When this happens, you will be as glad and pleased to forgo these sensible consolations, if such be his will, as you would be to possess them and experience them without interruption all your life long. When you are in this state, your love is both chaste and perfect:[197] Now it is that you see your God and your love of him, both together; and you also experience him directly, as he is in himself, in the highest point of your spirit, by being made spiritually one with his love.[198] This experience is, however, a blind one; it cannot be otherwise here on earth. You are utterly despoiled of yourself and your nakedness is clothed in him, as he is. You are unclothed: that is, you are not wrapped in any of the sensible consolations which may be experienced in this life, no matter how sweet or holy they may be. He can be perceived and felt, truly and perfectly as he is in himself, only in purity of spirit—which is very different from any imaginative picture or false notion such as may come to us in this life.[199]

This sight and this feeling of God as he is in himself cannot be separated, in the mind of the person who sees and feels like this, from the being of God himself, any more than God himself can be separated from his own being: for God's self and his existence are one, both in substance and in nature.[200] For just as God cannot be separated from his existence because of natural union, so the soul who sees and feels in the way described cannot be separated from what he sees and feels, because of union in grace.[201]

XIII

See then how by these tokens you can to some extent experience and up to a point make trial of the condition and the noble nature of your calling,[202] and how you are being led by grace, interiorly by means of your spiritual exercise and exteriorly by reading or hearing about this subject. And then, from the time when you or anyone else like you in spirit have had true experience of all these signs or of some of them—for there are very few who are so specially affected and sealed with this grace from the start that they are enabled, immediately or almost immediately, to make trial of them all by genuine experience; but even though a man may not experience them all at the start, it is enough to experience one or two; when therefore you feel that you have true experience of one or two, and this is supported by the true witness of Scripture, your director, and your conscience—then it will be profitable for you to cease for a time from speculative meditations and imaginative considerations about the qualities of your being and God's, and the activity of yourself and of God. Your faculties have been nourished on these meditations, and you have been led by them from a worldly life and a purely earthly existence to that state of grace in which you now dwell. It is time for you to learn to be occupied spiritually, in the awareness of yourself and God, whom you learned to understand so well in the past from your activity, by thought and imagination.

Christ in his earthly life gave us an example of this. For if it were true that there could be no higher perfection in this life than in contemplating and loving his manhood, I do not believe that he would have ascended into heaven while this world lasted: nor would he have withdrawn his bodily presence from his special lovers on earth.[203] But because there is a higher perfection to which man can attain in this life, namely, a true spiritual awareness, in love, of his Godhead, he therefore said to his disciples, who were loath to lose his bodily presence, in rather the same way as you are to lose your speculative meditations and the subtleties of intellectual investigation, that it was to their profit for him to leave them bodily. *Expedit vobis ut ego vadam*—"It is to your profit that I leave you bodily." The doctor comments on this text: "Unless the physical form of his manhood be withdrawn from our bodily sight, the love of his Godhead cannot be fixed in our spiritual sight."[204] And so I say to you that it is sometimes profitable to abandon the speculative investigations of your intellect and learn to taste a little of the love of God, in your spiritual feeling.[205]

XIV

You are to come to this feeling by the way that I tell you and by the help of the grace that anticipates your needs. This way is that you always, without ceasing, turn toward the naked awareness of yourself, ever offering your being to God as the most precious sacrifice you can make. But take care, as I have often said, that it is naked, unless you wish to be deceived. And if it is naked, it will be most painful to you to stay with it for any length of time at first. And the reason is, as I said before, that your natural faculties find in it no nourishment for themselves. But that is no drawback: Indeed I like it better that way. Let your faculties abstain for a while from the natural pleasure they take in their knowing. For though, as has been well said, a man naturally desires to know,[206] it is also true that he cannot experience God by spiritual taste except through grace, no matter how much knowledge he has, natural or acquired.[207] And therefore I ask you, seek rather experience than knowledge. For knowledge often leads us astray through pride, but humble loving awareness cannot beguile us: *Scientia inflat, caritas aedificat.*[208] In knowing there is labor, in experience rest.

And now you may well say: "What is this rest that you speak of? For it seems to me that it is no rest at all, but hard work and painful. For when I set myself to do as you say, I find nothing but pain and strife on every side. For on one side my faculties would have me turn away but I do not want to: and on the other side I want to feel God and be deprived of the awareness of myself, and I cannot. So there is strife and pain on every side. A strange rest this, that you speak of, or so it seems to me." My answer is this: It is because you are not used to this exercise that it is painful to you. If you were only practiced in it and knew by experience how much profit there is in it, you would not willingly abandon it in exchange for all the earthly joy and rest this world could give. And yet it is a great affliction and very hard work. But I still call it rest: for the soul is in no doubt as to what it must do, and also the soul is made sure—I mean during the time of this exercise—that it cannot go far wrong.[209]

Notes

Introduction

1. William Johnston, *Christian Mysticism Today* (London: Collins, 1984), p. 91.

2. The *Cloud*, *ed. cit.*, ch. 17, pp. 156–57, and n. 143.

3. 2 Cor 12:1–4.

4. The *Cloud*, nn. 141 and 142.

5. Both the *Cloud* and *Private Direction*, we must continue to insist, are intended only for solitaries—hermits or Carthusians, and those who "are enabled by an abundance of grace to share in the work of contemplation at the highest level" (The *Cloud*, *ed. cit.*, p. 103). Cf. *supra*, Prologue.

6. The *Cloud*, *ed. cit.*, ch. 70, p. 256.

7. *Supra*, VI, and nn. 93–96.

8. *Supra*, but cf. nn. 18 and 19. The service of God, however, in "Modern Devotion" is that conceived and practiced in Flanders by the newly founded Brothers and Sisters of the Common Life, and the Canons Regular of Windesheim, themselves *ex professo* contemplatives. Cf. *s.v. Devotio Moderna* D.Sp. III.

9. Cf. *infra*, Appendix. n. 14.

10. For the paramount importance of compunction in the classical spirituality of the West, cf. the chapter "St. Gregory, doctor of desire," in Le Clercq, *The Love of Learning*, pp. 36–44.

11. Acts 2:37.

12. Joseph De Guibert, *"La componction du coeur," RAM* 15 (1934): 225–40.

13. Acts 2:38. Cf. J. Walsh, "Apostolic Spirituality," *Supplement to the Way* 28 (1976): 9–19.

14. *Opto magis sentire compunctionem quam scire eius definitionem.*

248

15. Cf. François Vandenbroucke, "La spiritualité du Moyen Age," in *Histoire de la Spiritualité Chrétienne*, tome II, deuxième partie, p. 512.

16. Cf. *In Joannis Evangelium*, tract. 1,1: P.L. 34, 1379.

17. Augustine, *Confessions* IX, 25.

18. *Imitation of Christ*, Bk. 3, ch. 21, 3.

19. Cf. Vandenbroucke, *La Spiritualité du Moyen Age*, pp. 512–16.

20. Cf. W. Mulder, *Gerardi Magni Epistolae* (Anvers, 1933), Ep. 45.

21. Ibid.

22. *Ingrediendo ad divinitatem per contemplationem* (ibid., Ep. 9).

23. From the first Commentary of Vercellensis on the Canticle of Canticles, in Bernhardus Pez, *Thesaurus Anecdotorum Novissimus II* (Augsburg, 1721), 551.

24. Cf. J. Walsh, "Thomas Gallus et l'effort contemplatif," *Revue d'Histoire de la spiritualité (RAM)* 51 (1975): 1–2, p. 41.

25. Cf. *infra*, X.

26. He has described this, with particular reference to eremitical contemplatives, in chs. 35–39 of the *Cloud*.

27. We have noted that twenty-five out of the seventy-five chapters of the *Cloud* are digressions, at least *prima facie*. Cf. Prologue, p. 102, n. 8.

28. Cf. *infra*, XI.

29. The *Cloud*, *ed. cit.*, ch. 12, p. 147 and n. 115. Augustine says that "virtue is no other than to have what should be loved . . . and this is God." Cf. Epistle 145, 13: P.L. 33, 671.

30. Cf. *supra*.

31. Cf. the *Cloud*, *ed. cit.*, ch. 13, pp. 148–49.

32. De Balma, cap. I, Particula II, *De Modo Purgativa*, p. 5. Hugo also offers an example of a preparatory prayer: "Lord Jesus Christ, I am the most wicked sinner, wretched and unhappy, worse than the worst criminal. I cannot count the ways in which I have offended you . . . " The posture of "head upturned" is reminiscent of the representation of figures, depicted in catacomb wall paintings and early mosaics, standing with arms outstretched. Cf. Ex 17:11–12.

33. "Methley advises his Carthusian brethren to retire to their accustomed place of prayer, concentrate their whole attention on God, hide from every creature, close their eyes and begin with a simple affective preparatory prayer" (The *Cloud*, *ed. cit.*, pp. 17–18).

34. The three authors have a common source: Mt 6:6, " . . . pray to your Father in secret."

35. The *Cloud*, *ed. cit.*, ch. 2, pp. 117–18. Cf. Phil 3:13.

36. Ibid., ch. 3, p. 119.

37. Cf. *infra* I.

38. My italics: where the situation expresses not only the extension, but also the "forgetting" (cf. the *Cloud*, *ed. cit.*, ch. 5, p. 128), the ascent and the goal. As William of St. Thierry says in his *Golden Letter* to the Carthusians of Mont-Dieu: "The perfect forgetting of those things that are left behind, and the perfect reaching out to those things that lie ahead."

A LETTER OF PRIVATE DIRECTION

39. *De Trinitate* XII, ch. 7.

40. ME: That byleue be thi grounde. The prime importance of faith in the dark contemplative effort assures us against P.H. that this reading is correct. See her note, 135/24.

41. The old translation of Is 7:9: *nisi credideritis, non intelligetis.* The Vulgate has *nisi credideritis, non permanebitis*—If you will not believe, you shall not continue.

42. *Sapientia ista dicitur solum Christianorum; unde fidei cognitionem supponit et caritatis fundamentum. Unde nullus mortalis, quantumcumque sit philosophus vel sciens, hanc sapientiam, quae est in supremo affectu, mentis humanae facultatem transcendens, nec potuit nec poterit apprehendere rationum investigatione vel intelligentiae exercitio; sed solis filiis a solo Patris aeterno consolationem exspectantibus, paterno etiam affectu misericorditer reseratur et ideo mystica, id est, clausa vel occulta dicitur, quia a paucis cognita (Quaestio unica,* p. 49).

43. *Summa Theol.* 2, 2ae, 83, 12.

44. The *Cloud, ed. cit.,* ch. 37, p. 191. We have remarked there that the distinction and the manner of making it establish both the author and the disciple as members of an *ex professo* contemplative order, bound to the celebration of the Divine Office in community.

45. Here he indicates that the ejaculation may be a snatch of a psalm, a liturgical hymn, or an antiphon.

46. Cf. *supra,* "Denis's Hidden Theology," III.

47. Mt 6:7–13.

48. The *Cloud, ed. cit.,* chs. 37–39, pp. 191–96.

49. *Infra.*

50. The *Cloud, ed. cit.,* ch. 67, p. 250.

51. There is no indication, here or elsewhere in his writings, of any real concern to protect himself from the charges of heresy.

52. Margery, of course, was accused on many occasions of Lollardy. See her *Book, passim.*

53. Dom David Knowles has suggested that the disciple of the *Cloud* author was a Carthusian lay brother.

54. R2, r2.

55. Cf. the end of Benjamin, *supra,* and the *Cloud,* ch. 4, p. 125.

56. From his treatise *Oleum effusum nomen tuum* (Your name is as oil poured out).

57. Cf. the *Cloud, ed. cit.,* Introduction, pp. 26–42.

58. *Letter on Prayer, supra.*

59. Philip of Harvengt (†1182), *Epistolae* V: P.L. 203, 58.

60. *Sermo* IX; P.L. 198, 1747. Cited in Le Clercq, *The Love of Learning,* p. 244.

61. Cf. H. Farmer, "The Monk of Farne," in *Pre-Reformation English Spirituality,* ed. J. Walsh (London: Burns and Oates, 1963), p. 145ff.

62. Cf. *infra;* "Prayer," *supra* the *Cloud, ed. cit.,* ch. 28, p. 176, and ch. 15, p. 152.

63. The *Cloud, ed. cit.,* ch. 29, p. 177.

64. Ibid., Introduction, pp. 17–18.

65. The practice of auricular confession of devotion, with its traditional emphasis on sacramental grace as a principal means to Christian and religious perfection as well as to the purity of heart and intention desirable for those who celebrate mass or receive communion daily, was linked in terms of frequency to the reception of the Holy Sacrament. The ancient rule of St. Columban recommends its practice in the cloister several times a day. Cf. D.T.C. s.v. *Confession*, vol. 3, 884.

66. These are the hierarchies of the created mind—spiritual and corporal. Cf. J. Walsh, "Thomas Gallus et l'effort contemplatif," *Revue d'histoire* (*RAM*), pp. 24ff.

67. Cf. the *Cloud, ed. cit.*, ch. 4, p. 123 and n. 43, where the parallel passage from Gallus is cited.

68. Cf. the *Cloud, ed. cit.*, ch. 12, pp. 146–47.

69. Ibid., n. 112.

70. The author here uses the devotional language of the time, such as we find in a work like Walter Hilton's *Goad of Love*, a translation of a thirteenth-century Franciscan spiritual treatise. A typical passage reads: "My heart is full of venom, full blown with pride and poisoned with malice and bitterness of the fiend, and with fleshly lust . . . all full of wicked thoughts as a stinking carrion" (cf. C. Kirchberger, ed., *The Goad of Love* [London: Faber and Faber, 1952], p. 111).

71. Cf. 4 Kgs 4:32–36.

72. Cf. the *Cloud, ed. cit.*, ch. 4, p. 122.

73. *The fourfold exercise of the cell* (P.L. 153, 785ff.) was long attributed to Guigo II, author of the *Scala Claustralium*.

74. Cf. H. Pawsey, "Adam of Dryburgh," in *Pre-Reformation English Spirituality*, ed. J. Walsh (London: Burns and Oates, 1963), pp. 81–92.

75. P.L. 153, 855–56.

76. Ibid., 857–58.

77. Cf. *supra* II, "This hast thou done now many a day with help of grace."

78. The *Cloud, ed. cit.*, ch. 7, p. 131.

79. *De Mystica Theologia*, c. III, Particula 2, p. 27.

80. Cf. *infra*.

81. *Sermons on the Canticle*, 74, 2: P.L. 183, 1139. Cf. *The Love of Learning*, p. 246.

82. Cf. *supra*.

83. *Sermo 23:* P.L. 205, 730.

84. Le Clercq, *The Love of Learning*, p. 251.

85. *The second disputation against Abelard*, P.L. 180, 321.

86. *Infra*.

87. Cf. Walsh, *Pre-Reformation English Spirituality*, pp. 149–50.

88. Cf. Le Clercq, *The Love of Learning*, ch. 9, n. 99, p. 397.

89. *Infra*.

90. Cf. Walsh, *The Ladder of Monks*, p. 23.

91. Ibid., p. 24.

92. Saint Bruno, "Lettre à Raoul le Verd," in *Lettres des premiers Chartreux*, S.C. 88, p. 78.

93. *Mystica Theologia*, Cap. 1, Particula II, p. 6.

94. The *Cloud*, *ed. cit.*, ch. 7, p. 132.

95. Le Clercq, *The Love of Learning*, pp. 253–54.

96. A translation might run: "Remember, Lord, your servants, men and women, and all those here present with us; you know their faith and their devotion to you. For them we offer you this sacrifice of praise, or they offer it to you on their own behalf and for one and all, to obtain redemption for their souls, the salvation they hope for and freedom from all harm; it is to you, the eternal, living and true God, that they offer their vows." This is now the commemoration for the living in the first Eucharistic Prayer.

97. Denzinger and Schönmetzer, *Enchiridion Symbolorum*, 237 and 239.

98. Ibid., 391, 624.

99. *Unigenitus Dei Filius*, January 1343. Cf. Denzinger and Schönmetzer, *Enchiridion Symbolorum*, 1025. The Bull cites 1 Cor 1:30, "You are in Christ Jesus; for us God has made him, wisdom and justice, holiness and redemption." Cf. *infra*, n. 45.

100. Rom 5:12–21 (Vulgate).

101. *Infra*, n. 50.

102. *On the Canticle*, 8, 5–6: P.L. 183, 842.

103. *De Consideratione* V, 30.

104. Cf. Wis 18:15.

105. Wis 7:22–29.

106. Cf. 3 Kgs 8.

107. Cf. H. De Lubac, *Exégèse Médiévale* I, tome 2, p. 632.

108. *Commentary on Galatians* V, lect. 7. Cited by de Lubac, *loc. cit.* p. 644.

109. The *Cloud*, *ed. cit.*, ch. 8, pp. 137–38, and nn. 87–88.

110. Cf. O.E.D. s.v. "rift." The first reference for this figurative meaning is to the *Early English Psalter* xliv, 1.

111. Sermo LXVII: *De mirabili affectu dilectionis sponsae quem eructat propter amorem Christi sponsi* (P.L. 183, 1102–08).

112. Dumontier, *S. Bernard et la Bible*, p. 89.

113. W. Yeomans, "St. Bernard of Clairvaux," in *Spirituality through the Centuries*, p. 112. Guigo II, in *The Ladder*, uses the same analogy of the contemplative process: Reading puts food into the mouth, meditation ruminates on it, prayer extracts its flavor, and contemplation tastes its sweetness (*ed. cit.*, p. 28).

114. Sermo LXVII, 1–4: P.L. 183, 1102–04.

115. Cf. *infra*, n. 66.

116. The *Cloud*, *ed. cit.*, ch. 49, pp. 214–15.

117. The Golden Epistle to the Brethren of the Charterhouse of Mont-Dieu: P.L. 184, 348. For this love, which is the godly will according to Julian of Norwich, see her *Revelations*, ch. 37.

118. Cf. *supra*, n. 73.

119. The *Cloud*, *ed. cit.*, ch. 54, p. 224.

120. Ibid., ch. 55, pp. 227–29. The author is quite serious when he says, "I have learnt from students of necromancy, who make it their study to win the help of wicked spirits, and from others to whom the devil has appeared in bodily likeness."

121. "Démon en Occident," D.Sp. III 225ff.

122. Ibid., 226. Vandenbroucke comments: "One perceives here a very lively imagination, and it may well be asked how much of this is true vision, how much pure literary fiction."

123. Julian of Norwich, *Showings*, ch. 68.

124. Ibid., ch. 67.

125. J. Lefèvre, "Angel or Monster?" in *Satan*, ed. B. de Jésus-Marie, *Etudes Carmelitaines* (Paris, 1946).

126. Cf. *infra*, nn. 88–89.

127. Cf. *supra*.

128. Phil 2:4–11.

129. Heb 5:7–10.

130. The *Cloud*, *ed. cit.*, ch. 13, pp. 148–49.

131. Richard of St. Victor, *Expositio in Cantica*, xiv.

132. Bernard of Clairvaux, *De Diligendo Deo*, xv, 40.

133. The *Cloud*, *ed. cit.*, ch. 15, p. 152.

134. In his Third Commentary on the Canticle—*humilitas deposuit sapientiam Dei in terram*.

135. *Exercises*, 167.

136. Cf. *infra*, nn. 101–02.

137. The *Cloud*, *ed. cit.*, ch. 71, p. 237.

138. Ibid., chs. 7 and 8, *passim*.

139. Cf. *supra*.

140. *In Circumcisione Domini* 3:11. Cf. *supra*.

141. The *Cloud*, *ed. cit.*, chs. 35–39, pp. 187–96.

142. *Infra*, nn. 112–13.

143. ME: Parfite meeknes settith no merkes. Cf. *infra*.

144. *Infra*, p. 100.

145. The *Cloud*, *ed. cit.*, ch. 73, pp. 260–61.

146. XV, 40. Cf. *infra*, n. 134. *Quasi enim miro quodam modo oblitus sui, et a se penitus velut deficiens, totus perget in Deum, et deinceps adhaerens ei, unus cum eo spiritus erit.*

147. Ibid.

148. Cf. The *Cloud*, *ed. cit.*, Introduction, pp. 23–26.

149. Cf. *supra*, *Hidden Theology*.

150. The *Cloud*, *ed. cit.*, ch. 4, pp. 126–27.

151. Ibid., p. 128, and n. 60.

152. Ibid., p. 210.

153. The *Cloud*, *ed. cit.*, ch. 44, p. 203; *Hidden Theology*, *supra*.

154. Ibid.

155. He gathered the patristic and scriptural references as far as Gregory the Great, in his *Diadema Monachorum*, ch. 94. Cf. Jean Le Clercq, *L'amour des lettres et le désir de Dieu* (Paris, 1957), pp. 48–49, 60–61.

156. Ibid., p. 61.

157. Mt 23:36; Lk 7:11–17, 24, 62; Jn 11:35–36, 12:1–8, 20, 1–2, 11–17.

158. "Pursuit of Wisdom," *supra*.

159. The *Cloud*, ed. *cit.*, ch. 4, p. 125.

160. This is the burden of John's Gospel: Jesus' mission is to do what he sees the Father doing. The prime example is his teaching on the Eucharist in ch. 6.

161. Cf. Jn 10:1–17. *Infra*, n. 154.

162. Cf. *The Ladder*.

163. Cf. the *Cloud*, ed. *cit.*, ch. 36, p. 190.

164. Jn 6:37–44.

165. Cf. the *Cloud*, ed. *cit.*, Introduction, pp. 14–19.

166. Cf. Sargent, "Medieval Spiritual Writings."

167. Cf. the *Cloud*, ed. *cit.*, ch. 8; *infra*, nn. 101–02.

168. Ibid., The *Cloud*, ed. *cit.*, p. 138.

169. Cf. the *Cloud*, ed. *cit.*, Introduction, pp. 29ff.

170. The *Cloud*, ed. *cit.*, ch. 75, pp. 265–66.

171. Le Clercq, *L'Amour des lettres*, p. 33.

172. Ibid., pp. 35–37.

173. Cf. *infra*, n. 177.

174. Cf. "Inward Stirrings, *supra*.

175. Guigo II, in *The Ladder*, is perhaps nearest to the author, being the simplest and most graphic, and we recall that there was an abundance of Middle English translations available to him. Cf. *infra*, nn. 191–95.

176. V. Cf. the *Cloud*, ed. *cit.*, chs. 71 and 73.

177. Cited in Le Clercq, *L'amour des lettres*, pp. 68–69.

178. The *Cloud*, ed. *cit.*, ch. 75, p. 266.

179. Cf. *supra*.

180. Cf. *infra*, n. 209.

A Letter of Private Direction

1. Nine MSS out of seventeen listed by Phyllis Hodgson (pp. ix–xxvii) contain this *Letter of Private Direction*. It is entitled severally *The Book* (once), *A Tretyse* or *Treatyse* (three times), an *Epistle* or *Pistle* or *Pystell* or *Pystelle* or *Pystle*, of *Prive Counselling* or *Privey Counseile* or *Private Counsell* or *Pryvate Cowncell* or *Priveye Conseyle* or *Privat Councelle* or *Pryvate Counsell* or *Pryve Conseille* or *Pryvate Cownsell*. The MSS range from early fifteenth century to mid-sixteenth. The inconsistencies in spelling may indicate how frequently the work was copied, as well as the fluidity of Tudor English.

A LETTER OF PRIVATE DIRECTION

2. "Interior exercise"—ME: inward occupation: the contemplative "work" of the *Cloud*. In MSS Douce 262, we have the following special introduction: "The Epistle of Private Counsel follows, which depends on the *Cloud* and is written by the same author as the *Cloud*, and it is very profitable for contemplative men who desire to come to divine love."

3. ". . . may read or listen to . . . "—ME: scholen here. "Listening is a kind of reading," says Guigo II the Carthusian, "and that is why we are accustomed to say that we have read not only those books which we have read to ourselves or aloud to others, but also those which our teachers have read to us" (*Ladder*, pp. 93–94, xiii; cf. also *Cloud, ed. cit.*, ch. 75, p. 261).

4. "The target and bull's-eye of my attention"—ME: the poynte and the prik of my beholding. Cf. *Cloud, ed. cit.*, ch. 5, p. 129; "Inward Stirrings," *supra*.

5. As several of the MSS witness, though *Private Direction* is cast in the form of a letter, it constitutes a short treatise on dark contemplation and falls naturally into some dozen sections, for the most part following the spiritual exegesis of a series of Scripture texts, which are the pegs on which he hangs his teaching. Cf. Introduction, *supra*.

6. ME: whan thou comyst bi thiself. The "Boys' Latin Dictionary," (*Promptorium Parvulorum*) of A.D. 1440 gives, for "by thyself," *seorsum*. When in the Gospel the Lord invites his disciples—"Come apart into a deserted place and rest awhile," the Latin Vulgate has *Venite seorsum in deserto loco et requiescite pusillum* (Mk 6:31). As Guigo II says: "He who is not alone cannot be silent. And he who is not silent cannot hear you when you speak to him. . . . Let all my world be silent in your presence, Lord, so that I may hear what the Lord God may say in my heart" (Meditation I, *Ladder of Monks*, p. 104). One main source of distraction and dissipation is to be thinking of what I am to do at the end of my prayer. Presence demands concentration on the moment. Cf. the methodology prescribed at the beginning of the "Letter on Prayer," *supra*.

7. The personal prayers of those who exercise themselves in the dark contemplation of the *Cloud* "rise directly to God. . . . And if words are used—and this happens rarely—they are very few indeed; in fact, the fewer the better" (*ed. cit.*, ch. 37, p. 192). But there, as here, he allows for words "which break out because of devotion in your spirit to speak to God as to men" (ch. 48, p. 212). Perhaps the source is Hugh of St. Victor, *De modo orandi*, who proposes three kinds of petitionary prayer: supplication (*oratio*), request (*postulatio*), and insinuation (*insinuatio*). Examples of insinuation are Mary's request at Cana, "They have no wine," or Mary of Bethany's "If you had been here, Lord, my brother would not have died" (Jn 11:32). The third kind of supplication Hugh calls "pure prayer, when out of abundance of devotion, the spirit is so ardent that, when it turns to make its requests to God, it forgets what it is going to ask for, out of the greatness of its love" (P.L. 176, 979–81). The same point is dealt with at length in ch. 7 of the *Cloud* (*ed. cit.*, pp. 133–34). Hugh of St. Victor anticipates: "The heart's de-

255

votion alone could suffice as far as God is concerned, unless the prayer takes on a form of words, simply that the spirit of the one praying may be kindled to greater devotion" (P.L. 176, 982).

8. "When you are praying do not speak at length, like the heathens. They think that they will be heard because of their many words. Do not be like them. For your Father knows what your need is before you ask him" (Mt 5:7).

9. The author has already made the point in ch. 37 of the *Cloud* that contemplatives "have more regard for the Church's prayer than for any other"; and distinguishes there between "specyal preiers" and "thoo preiers that ben ordeynid of Holy Chirche." St. Thomas makes the same distinction: "Common prayer is that offered to God through the Church's ministers in the person of the whole faithful people of God. Special prayer (*oratio singularis*) is that offered by the individual person who prays either for himself or for others" (*Summa Theol.* 2–2ae, 83, 12). Hugh of St. Victor gives a list of Psalms that correspond to the various "affections of piety" (in which all the power of praying resides)—love, praise, joy, humility, etc. (*loc. cit.*, ch. 7: P.L. 176, 985–86).

10. ME: nothing leve in thi worching minde bot a nakid entent streching into God: The *Cloud*'s confident rendering of the classic term for the effort of will proper to dark contemplation, "extension." Its origin is not in the Neoplatonic *ascensio mentis* but in Pauline vocabulary, as the Apostle strives to describe his desire for assimilation to the crucified and risen Jesus— "stretching forth myself (*extendens me ipsum*) to those things that are ahead, I press toward . . . the heavenly vocation in Christ Jesus" (Phil 3:13–14). Cf. Introduction, *supra*.

11. ME: Lat (that) beleve be thi grounde. This is the first time the author, either here or in the *Cloud*, nominates faith directly as the springboard of the contemplative search for God. It is opposed, of course, to the power— the subtlety—of reasoning. It corresponds, in his understanding of the Dionysian ascent, to "what we see *in faith*," sc. the God who transcends all things. Cf. "Hidden Theology," *supra*, as the following sentence indicates.

12. ME: This nakid entent, freely fastenid and groundid in verray beleve. It is Gregory the Great who reminds us that "our first gateway to the knowledge of the omnipotent God is faith"; the second stage in the ascent is in the soul's self; and finally to that which is above itself (*Homiliarum in Ezechielem* II, 5, 8: P.L. 76, 989).

13. The movement, as Thomas Gallus stresses in his *Explanation of the Ecclesiastical Hierarchy*, ch. 2 (R52 rl), is that the soul may diligently know itself; and then that it should rise from the knowledge of itself, which is the image of God, as from a mirror to the truth of what it images. The most familiar analogue may well be *Benjamin Minor*, chs. 71–72, where Richard of St. Victor first stresses the difficulty of coming to the contemplative knowledge of God—"if you cannot know yourself, how can you presume to grasp the things which are above you?" So man's spirit (*animus rationalis*) is the mirror for seeing God, "since it is made in his image and likeness. This

is what we believe, and therefore as long as we walk by faith and not by sight (2 Cor 5:7), as long as we see through a glass darkly (1 Cor 13:12) we cannot find a more authentic vision" (P.L. 196, 51).

14. Cf. 1 Cor 6:17, "He who cleaves to God is one spirit with him." A detailed description of the dissipation is given in the *Cloud* (*ed. cit.*, ch. 7, pp. 131–34). The antidote is recollection and what is called introversion. St. Gregory says: "The first step is for the mind to gather itself to itself, then to consider itself within itself, and thirdly to rise above itself and submit itself with diligent attention to the contemplation of its Maker . . . so the soul, stripped of sense-images, is the object of its own thought" (P.L. 76, 989–90).

15. "We shall say much and yet shall want words, but the sum of our words is, he is in all things" (Eccl 43:29). "For in him we live and move and have our being. . . . Certain people adhered to him [Paul] and believed; among whom was also Dionysius the Areopagite . . . " (Acts 17:28, 34). "All things shall be subjected to him . . . that God may be all in all" (1 Cor 15:28). "He is above all things and all things subsist in him" (Col 1:17). Ps. Denis, *The Divine Names* iv, i: "The existent God is, by the nature of his power, super-essentially above all existence; he is the substantial Cause and Creator of Being, Existence, Substance and Nature . . . the Existence of those that have any kind of existence . . . the Essence of existence in things that exist" (Rolt, *Dionysius the Areopagite*). Hugh of St. Victor, in his commentary on the Heavenly Hierarchy of Denis, writes: "All things that subsist participate in his being. The one and the same divine nature, existing in itself, is the principle and the essence of all things, from which they take their essence and in which they subsist, with regard to effect, powers and operations" (V, in IV 1) (P.L. 175, 1008).

16. Julian of Norwich has the same *caveat;* the Divine Immanence does not mean any form of Pantheism: "God, who is our Maker, dwells in our soul . . . and our soul, that is made, dwells in God in substance. Of which substance, by God, we are what we are. And I saw no difference between God and our substance, but as it were all God. And yet my understanding took it that our substance is in God; that is to say, that God is God, and our substance is a creature in God" (*Revelations*, ch. 54).

17. "God is not only his own essence but also his own being . . . for if the being of a thing is different from its essence, this must be because its being is caused by something outside itself or by its own essential principles. It cannot be said that God is caused by another, because he is the first efficient cause" (*Summa Theol.* 1a, 3, 4).

18. *Divine Names* V, 5: "He who is pre-existent is the Beginning and the Cause of all Eternity and time and of anything that has any kind of being. All things participate in him, nor does he depart from anything that exists. He is before all things, and all things have their maintenance in him, and, in short, if anything exists under any form whatever, it is in the pre-Existent that it exists" (Rolt, *Dionysius the Areopagite*, p. 136).

19. Hugh of St. Victor, after stating that God is present in all things, by

his essence and his power, adds: "We say that God is also in some creatures by the grace of indwelling (per inhabitantem gratiam). . . . He is also in his creature, that is, in Christ, by personal union. . . . Those in whom he dwells by the grace of indwelling, have him in them as in a vessel: because he fills them with virtues as a vase is filled with whatever is contained in it" (*Allegoriae in Novum Testamentum* V: P.L. 175, 858).

20. "This ascent is called blind, or a knowing through unknowing; so that when all operations of imagination, reason, intellect or understanding are done away with, the mind has immediate experience through the union of most ardent love, which the understanding is not able to grasp; and what is more, all speculative knowledge is wholly in ignorance of it" (Hugo de Balma, *Mystica Theologica* III, IV, in *S. Bonaventurae Opera Omnia* tom. viii [Paris; Vives, 1866], pp. 39–40).

21. "In the extension itself, insofar as the intellect mingles with the affection in that far there is impurity; and insofar as the eye of the intellect is wholly blinded, in that far the eye of the affection in its extension is freed and elevated" (ibid., p. 43).

22. This extended apologia, it is generally thought, is too personal and vehement to be considered a merely conventional defence of the *docta ignorantia*. Cf. Introduction, *supra*. However, Hugo de Balma insists almost as strongly—with oblique reference to the divine wisdom confounding the wise of this world (1 Cor 1:25)—that a simple old woman or a village yokel can attain to the perfection of dark contemplation with the proper purgative and illuminative preparation. His language is much the same as the Cloud author's here. Citing a verse from Ecclesiasticus (24:10) that "wisdom, by its own power has trodden on the necks of the high and the mighty" (*omnium superborum sublimium colla propria virtute calcavit*), he comments: "No matter how famous or how scholarly (*clericus*) a person might be in outshining all others, he will never succeed in touching the hem of wisdom's garment (that wisdom which is high above mind), unless he prepares himself for the unitive way through the way of the little child, the purgative—always supposing that he has committed mortal sin: sorrowing and sighing that he has provoked the wrath of him who holds together all wisdom and all good. It is necessary for the proud and the haughty to be brought down to the humility of the little children learning their A.B.C." (loc. cit., p. 43).

23. St. Thomas, in his discussion on how the soul endowed with intelligence (*anima intellectiva*) knows itself, states: "The knowledge through which we know the nature of the soul belongs to us because the light of our intellect is derived from the divine truth, which contains the reasons of all things." And he goes on to quote St. Augustine (*De Trinitate* 9, 6) "We gaze upon inviolable truth, according to which, insofar as we can, we define not what man's mind is, but what it ought to be in terms of the eternal reasons." "For this knowledge," St. Thomas continues, "there is required diligent and subtle investigation" (*diligens et subtilis inquisitio*) (*Summa Theol.* 1a, 77, 1).

24. One might immediately conclude that the author was being heavily ironical, but for this phrase "with help of grace." It is perfectly possible that

the addressee is studying monastic theology in the Carthusian cloister. Cf. Introduction, *supra*.

25. The language here is reminiscent of a similar consideration in the *Cloud*, *ed. cit.*, ch. 16, p. 155: that to ponder the qualities of human nature is at best an inquiry into its sinfulness.

26. The author describes the purgative way for contemplatives, beginning from his customary point, sacramental confession, which here as elsewhere is a *conditio sine qua non*, not only for the exercise described in the "Letter on Prayer" and in the *Cloud* (e.g., ch. 15, p. 152 and ch. 28, p. 176), but also for true discernment, cf. Introduction, *supra*.

27. Hugo de Balma's sentiments are very similar. The soul is as it were born again through humiliation, in order to be united to him who is the supreme majesty and the indefectible God, through the unitive treacle (*glutinum*) of most ardent love. And if there are to be thoughts concerning the passion of the Lord, the purpose is that through the wound in his side we might come to touch the divinity lying hid within, through the experience of love (*loc. cit.*, I, 1 and 2, p. 5). Cf. Introduction, *supra*.

28. Cf. St. Augustine, *Enarratio in Psalmum 85*, 9: "Let God be your physician. Seek safety from him; not healing from without, but let him be salvation itself. Do not desire any other salvation besides himself—as we have it in the psalm: 'say to my soul, I am your salvation' " (P.L. 37, 1085).

29. Cf. Mt 9:20–21. The author is citing from memory and conflates two verses. The actual text says that "the woman touched the edge of his garment. And then she said to herself: If I can only touch his garment, I shall be healed."

30. ME: step up than stifly and taast of that triacle. The word goes back to the Greek *thēriakē*, remedy against snake bite. The figurative use occurs in religious and scriptural contexts. For Lydgate, the holy name of Jesus is a triacle; and in Piers Plowman (B text, Passus I, 46) we have: "For trewthe telleth that loue is triacle of heuene."

31. "That wisdom . . . by which the minds of God's lovers desire no temporal gain nor any of his gifts—neither grace, virtue nor glory, but him alone who is the principle of all; reaching out to obtain with shining affection and insatiable desires and to touch him alone with unitive aspirations, to be united with him" (Hugo de Balma, *loc. cit.*, III, 1, p. 21).

32. This is the point made at the beginning of Denis's *Hidden Theology*, says Hugo de Balma—"Ascend in ignorance" (*Consurge ignote*): "This is a necessary condition to this most elevated apprehension, that in the elevation itself all speculative knowledge is void; and it is essential that it be left aside, if the spirit is to come to the knowledge above mind" (*loc. cit.*, p. 43).

33. ME: the coriouste of any of my wittis, bodely or goostly. As P.H. indicates, the distinction is that of the "Hidden Theology," I: "all those things outside yourself which can be known by any of your five bodily senses; all those things within you which can be known by your spiritual senses" (*supra*). On the latter, she has a curious note (139/22–23): "The five 'goostly wittes' or spiritual senses were (1) Common Sense, uniting the var-

ious things entering the mind through the five 'bodely wittes'; (2) Imagination, retaining the images of various qualities; (3) Fancy, retaining and combining images; (4) Estimation, a natural instinct of what is beneficial or hurtful; (5) Memory." No source is given for this list. It is clear, however, that our author is speaking of the spiritual senses in the traditional sense. Hugo de Balma, commenting on the *sensibilia* of the *Theologica Mystica*, lists the *sensus interiores* as responding to *dulcis* (sweetness to the taste), *olfactibilis* (sweet-smelling), *pulchri* (beautiful to the sight), *melodiosi* (melodious to the ear), and *suavis* (smooth to the touch) (*loc. cit.*, p. 40).

34. A summary of the metaphysical statement with which the letter opens; "the first point of your spirit" is the characteristic or even the "fine point" of one's being where the creature is still one with the creator—"He is your being, and in turn you are what you are." Julian of Norwich says that our "kind" is in God's substance, and this "kind" is his first gift to us (*Revelations*, chs. 56–57).

35. Prv 3:9–10. In the Vulgate, the second phrase of v. 9 reads: *et de primitiis omnium frugum tuarum da ei*—"and give *him* (the Lord) the first of all your fruits." In the sapiential books, any thought of material plenty is usually followed by a thought for the poor. Cf., e.g., Eccl 4:1, 14:13. So the Lord himself says, "When you make a feast, invite the poor . . . " and goes on to tell the parable of the Supper—Lk 14:13. Here, however, it is possible that there is conflation between this text and Tob 4:7: *Ex substantia tua fac eleemosynam*—"Give alms out of your substance and do not turn away your face from any poor person."

36. ME:The text that Salamon spake to his son bodely: i.e., as devoid of any real significance, "unspiritually" is the first meaning of the adverb, as O.E.D. points out. The "ghostly understanding," here, as when he cites further from Proverbs, is the "moral sense." Cf. *infra*.

37. As is said in "Hidden Theology," it is by "purifying yourself . . . of everything that can be known according to its own proper form in the intellect . . . that you shall be carried up in your affection" (ch. 1, *supra*, and note 28). Hugo de Balma comments: "The intellect is contaminated, that is, darkened, because as long as it is infected with speculative knowledge . . . it is rendered opaque as by a lowering cloud" (*loc. cit.*, 111, 4, p. 45).

38. The teaching of the great commandment—"You shall love your neighbour as yourself," and of the corporal and spiritual works of mercy— the one taken from the great parable of the Judgment (Mt 25:35–36), the other traditional—"to convert the sinner, to instruct the ignorant, to counsel the doubtful, to comfort the sorrowful, to bear wrongs patiently, to forgive injuries, and to pray for the living and the dead."

39. There are similarities between the author's teaching here and that of Julian of Norwich in ch. 57 of her long text. The first gift is our kind, which is wholly in God; and from kind, God "makes diversities—different qualities—flowing out of him to work his will." These other gifts are faith, the commandments, and the virtues of nature and grace, as well as the sacraments.

40. William of St. Thierry, following Gregory of Nyssa, says: "See, O man, the dignity of your nature, how precious you are within; by your inner dignity you are born into royal dispositions" (*De Natura corporis et animae* II: P.L. 180, 717). Julian adds (*loc. cit.*): "Of this high nobility virtues come to our soul according to measure, in the time when it is knit to our body."

41. ME: the first poynte and the pricke of thi beholdyng, what so ever it be, is thi nakid being.

42. Hugo de Balma, speaking of the Illuminative Way, says: "Just as the rational spirit is more noble than all inferior creatures, so the divine clemency shows itself in a more noble way in that spirit through the rays of goodness emitted" (*loc. cit.*, II, 1, p. 9).

43. A very elaborate and drawn-out *argumentatio perfectissima*, involving syllogistic hypotheses, with an *inclusio* that is an exact repetition of the same sentence: "And so it is . . . "

And so it is your being alone that is the first of your fruits. [*proposition*]

For if you draw out . . . substance of your being. [*reason*]

It is as though you said . . . specific qualities of your being. [*confirmation of the reason*]

And then—this is more . . . fellow-Christians.

And so you may see that the ultimate target . . . [*embellishment*]

And so it is your being alone which is the first of your fruits. [*conclusion*]

44. The "memento of the living" in the canon of the Mass so familiar to the author reads: "Lord, be mindful of your servants . . . who offer you this sacrifice of praise, for themselves and for all their own, for the redemption of their souls, for the hope of their safety and salvation."

45.

ME: *For as all men weren lost in Adam,* for he fel fro this onyng affeccyon, *and as alle that with werk* acordyng to here clepyng *wol witnes here will of saluacion,* ben sauid and schul be by the vertew of the *passion of only Crist,* offring himself up in veriest sacrifice, al that he was in general and not in specyal withoutyn special beholdyng to any o man in this liif, bot generaly and in comon for al: right so a verey and a parfite sacrificer of himself thus by a comon entent unto alle *doth that in him is* to knit *alle men* to God as effectively as himself is.

For as alle men weren lost in Adam and alle men that with werke wil witnes their wille of saluation ben sauyd and scholen be by vertewe of the passion of only Crist—not in the maner bot as it were in the same maner—a soule that is parfitely affecte in this werk and onyd thus to God in spirit, as the preof of this werk witnessith, doth that in it is to maak alle men as parfite in this werk as itself is (*Cloud, ed. cit.*, ch. 25; cf. pp. 171–72 and notes).

The obvious question is whether the author is here citing what he wrote in the *Cloud*, or unconsciously using the same phraseology for the same doctrine. He never refers to his other writings except the "Letter on Prayer," which was written for the same recipient. He does cite its title along with "other different places in my own writings" (cf. *infra*). The two passages are sufficiently different and similar to allow for citation from memory.

46. Cf. Is 53:10: "and the Lord was pleased to bruise him in infirmity; if

he shall lay down his life for sin, he shall see a long-lived seed . . . by his knowledge shall this my just servant justify many." 1 Jn 3:16: "In this we have known the charity of God, because he has laid down his life for us; and we ought to lay down our lives for the brethren." Jn 15:13: "Greater love than this no-one has, than that a man lay down his life for his friends."

47. The scriptural allusion is to the Eucharistic discourse in Jn 6, 27:31–39; 41:48–52, 58–59, etc.

48. This paragraph is a brilliant example of the rhetorical figure *expolitio*, "a dwelling on and refining of the same topic, by repeating it in a variety of ways, and by descanting upon it, varying words and treatment." Cf. *A Book of Showings to the Anchoress Julian of Norwich*, Part II, Appendix, p. 740. The whole is also an *argumentatio perfectissima*, the "ready reason," following on the testimony of Scripture and the example of Christ.

49. ME: There is no name, ne felyng ne beholdyng more ne so moche accordyng unto everlastyngnes the whiche is God, as is that the whiche may be had, seen and felt in the blinde and the lonely beholdyng of this worde *is*. At the beginning of ch. v of the *Divine Names*, whose subject is "Existence," the author writes: "Now we must proceed to the name of 'Being' which is truly applied by the divine science to him that truly Is . . . not to reveal the super-essential being in its super-essential nature—for this is unutterable, nor can we know it or in anywise express it, and it is beyond even the Unity" (Rolt, *Dionysius the Areopagite*, p. 131).

50. In his discourse on the purgative preparation for Dionysian contemplation, Hugo de Balma, after observing that "God in himself is unnameable, but we name him in his effects and praise his magnificence through them," says that the divine goodness is made manifest in the diffusion of his graces, which can be summed up in five words, "Good, Beautiful, Lord, Sweet, Merciful" (*Mystical Theology* I, ii, p. 7). So here we have "Good or Faire, Lord or sweet, merciful," followed by variations on the traditional "Might, Wisdom and Goodness." We notice that both authors not only have the same names, but they have them in the same order. De Balma repeats them in a short prayer: "Good, most fair Lord, sweet, merciful, have mercy on this sinner, whom you have redeemed with your precious blood" (ibid.).

51. Cf. the final sentences of "Hidden Theology": "nor is there any way by which reason or understanding may attain to him; there is no name, no knowing of him, nor to sum up is there either affirmation or negation of him . . . his unintelligible transcendence is, in an unintelligible way, above all affirmation and negation" (ch. V, *supra*). "The sacred writers call it nameless while they celebrate it by every name" (*Divine Names*, ch. I, 5: Rolt, *Dionysius the Areopagite*, p. 61).

52. "The most wonderful speculation of them all must be set aside: not because they are not good and noble, but . . . there is no speculative contemplation which has the power of transforming, but only the extensive love which deifies" (Hugo de Balma, *loc. cit.*, III, IV, p. 42).

53. "Human souls and all other creatures possess from the same source their existence and their blessedness, and exist and are blessed only because

they possess their existence and their blessedness from the pre-Existent, and are blessed in him" (*Divine Names*, ch. V, 8). Our author's use of the word "blessed" (ME: blisful) makes it almost certain that this is his direct source.

54. "For, as has often been said, he contains beforehand and created all things in One Act, being present to all and everywhere, both in the particular individual and in the universal whole, and going out into all things yet remaining in himself" (ibid., V, 8: Rolt, *Diomysius the Areopagite*, p. 143). A similar statement in the *Cloud* makes no reference to the supposition that anyone other than God is "from without beginning" (*ed. cit.*, ch. 67, p. 250).

55. ME: fillid with the fulheed of loue and of vertuous leuyng in God. The crux here is that three important MSS read "lykyng" for "leuyng." P.H.'s defense of "leuyng," which she translates as "living," is at first sight convincing, "virtuous living in God" being a pious stock phrase. It is, however, out of the context of the author's spiritual exegesis, whereas the "powerful faith" is a wholly licit translation, since the first meaning of virtuous is "manly," "courageous"—O.E.D. Cf. E. Colledge, *The Mediaeval Mystics of England*, p. 168.

56. After summarizing the spiritual (tropological or moral) exegesis of the first part of his text from Proverbs (3:10a), the author proceeds to the anagogical or mystical meaning of the second half of the verse (10b). ME: Thi grape-stockes (*torcularia*) scholen rebounde ful of wyne. The three words—"wine-presses," "run over," and "wine"—are given exact and extended meanings, which underline the skill of the interpreter in choosing as well as glossing his text to draw out the deeper spiritual meanings, with an impeccable sense of tradition. "Give and it shall be given to you: good measure and pressed down and shaken together and running over" (Lk 6:38).

57. "The soul drinks wine when it relishes the savor (that is, the wisdom) of the Godhead (*divinitatis saporem*) and is so inebriated by this cup that it forgets all earthly things and clings to those that are above" (Richard of St. Victor, *Explicatio in Cantica Canticorum*, ch. 32: P.L. 196, 487).

58. ME: this schal be done sudenly, listely and gracyously. "Contemplation is when the mind is in some sort lifted up to God and held above itself, so that it tastes the joys of everlasting sweetness" (The *Ladder* II, p. 82). The same author, speaking of the soul at prayer, says: "The Lord breaks in on the middle of its prayer and runs to meet it in all haste" (ibid., VII, p. 87).

59. Walter Hilton, following St. Bernard, cites Heb 1:14 in the last chapter of *Scale* II: "Wot you not well that all holy spirits are ministers sent of Jesus for those who will receive the heritage of health?" (*Sermo I in festo S. Michaelis:* P.L. 183, 447ff.). "All this ghostly working of words and of reasons brought to the mind, and such fair likenesses, are made by the ministry of angels, when the light of grace abundantly shineth in a clean soul. It may not be told by tongue the feelings, the lightenings, the graces and the comforts in special that clean souls perceive through favorable fellowship of blessed angels" (*Scale* II, ch. 46, p. 461).

60. Cf. Ps 122:2: "As the eyes of the handmaid are on the hands of her

mistress, so are our eyes on the Lord our God, until he have mercy upon us."

61. The summit of contemplation is always the sole and direct work of God himself. For the Dionysian, this *culmen contemplationis* is the spark (*scintilla*) of the *apex affectus* (the summit of the affection) or the *spiritualis intelligentia*, which the *Cloud* author translates as "the sovereign point of the spirit." It is, says Thomas Gallus, "the supreme and the pure participation in the divine goodness, which flows from the Truth into its image, ineffably separated off from all that is beneath it; and as it passes in some way into the divine life it is, in a manner unknowable, deified" (from the prologue to his second and third Commentaries on the Canticle of Canticles). There is another description of this dark illumination and unitive operation of the spirit in the *Cloud, ed. cit.*, ch. 26, p. 174. On these passages and others, cf. Introduction, *supra*.

62. The literal English of the author's Latin of Prv 3:13–14, 21–26, would run as follows:

3:13: Blessed the man who finds wisdom and is rich in prudence.

14: The purchasing thereof is better than the merchandise of silver and gold. The fruits of it are the first and the purest. (The Douai version translates and punctuates differently: " . . . of silver, and her fruit than the chiefest and the purest gold.")

21: My son, keep this law and this counsel. (Vulgate: "My son, do not let these things depart from your eyes: keep the law and counsel.")

22: And there shall be life to your soul and grace to your mouth.

23: Then you shall walk confidently in your way, and your foot shall not stumble.

24: If you sleep, you shall not fear: you shall rest, and your sleep shall be sweet.

25: Do not be afraid of sudden terror, nor of the power of the wicked rushing upon you.

26: For the Lord will be at your side, and will guard your footstep so that you be not taken.

63. In the *Benjamin Major* (II, X) of Richard of St. Victor, gold stands for the understanding (P.L. 196, 88).

64. ME: worching in oure kyndely wittis benethe us, withinne us or even with us. In the *Cloud*, the author says that in the lower part of the contemplative life, "a man is within himself and on a par with himself" (*ed. cit.*, ch. 8, pp. 137–38).

65. The source here is the *De Consideratione* (II, 2–3) of St. Bernard, where he describes contemplation as that spiritual wondering gaze at anything which is true and certain (*verus certusque intuitus animi*), and consideration as the concentration of the spirit investigating the truth of things that are below, on a level with, and above us (P.L. 181, 745–46).

66. ME: high goostly wisdom, sodenly and frely riftid of the spirit inly in itself and unformid, ful fer fre fantasie, impossible to be streinid or to

falle under the worching of naturele witte. The rhetorical figure *expolitio* ("a dwelling on and refining of the same topic, by repeating it in a variety of ways") is used to describe yet again the high point of the contemplative act. "Riftid" is the translation of *eructavit* in the messianic and epithalamic Psalm 44 (Vulgate): "My heart has brought forth a good word, I speak my poems to the king."

67. ME: Bot feynid foly formyd in fantome, as fer fro the verrey sothfastnes. The whole passage spills over with rhetorical colors.

68. A further description, by *expolitio*, of the contemplative experience. The author uses the same comparison between the darkness of a midwinter's night and the brightness of midsummer day in the *Cloud*, *ed. cit.*, ch. 4, p. 127. There is probably an allusion to 2 Pt 1:19: " . . . attend to the word until the day dawns, and the morning star rises in your hearts." Cf. the frequent naming of the prevenient Christ in Wisdom literature as *sol intelligentiae, iustitiae.*

69. In particular, the ten commandments of Exodus (ch. 20ff.). Cf. Mt 5:18ff.

70. In "Inward Stirrings," the perfection of virtue, which is charity, is said to consist of "two side branches of love"; and in the *Cloud*, the author uses the same term, "the lower branch of love" (*ed. cit.*, ch. 24, p. 170).

71. "This humble stirring of love . . . is nothing else but a good will that is directed to God . . . the substance of all perfection" (*Cloud*, *ed. cit.*, ch. 69, pp. 214–15).

72. Rom 13:10.

73. In this sentence we have the threefold repetition, "lyuely" . . . "liif" . . . "leuyng," the rhetorical figure *traductio*. Its purpose is hermeneutical: Love is the interior life-force—"with thy whole heart, and with thy whole soul, and with thy whole mind" in the new law—Mt 22:37—and in the old—Dt 6:5. The "lovely (law) and the lively (counsel)" are interchangeable. There is also the figure *similiter cadens* ("when in the same period two or more words appear in the same case, and with like terminations"—Caplan, *Cicero*, p. 299) with "trewest techyng, bodely beryng, forme of leuing." In the *Cloud*, the author goes so far as to say that "if a man were practiced in this exercise, it would give him true decorum of body and soul . . . make him truly attractive" (*ed. cit.*, ch. 54, p. 224). This is the courtly-love belief that "handsome is" and "handsome does" go together.

74. Mt 22:40.

75. ME: then schal thou goo tristely, groundid in grace, the gide of thi goostly way; the Vulgate Latin being *Tunc ambulabis fiducialiter in via tua.* The author's translation echoes his reference to hope in the "Letter on Prayer," *supra.*

76. "Leaving behind human wisdom (with its vanities and illusions, its various opinions and diverse errors), and its careful investigation into useless erudition, (*curiositate scientiae inutilis*) the pious soul mounts by means of love to the fountain of all desires" (Hugo de Balma, *loc. cit.*, *Prologue*, p. 2).

77. The author is repeating the teaching of the *Cloud*, *ed. cit.*, ch. 9, pp.

140–41. Thomas Gallus says that during the time of contemplation or the anagogical study of the Scriptures, or during the celebration of the Eucharist, the lightest fancies (*fantasiae levissimae*) are to be excluded. He describes *fantasia* as "that which is offered by the work of the imagination for the reason's consideration." The reason is because these thoughts draw the mind away from "superintellectual business," no matter how good in themselves they might be (*Explanation* of the *Ecclesiastical Hierarchy*, c. 3).

78. ME: the fel fende, the fals woreld and the freel flessche. The adjectives, though doubtless chosen for alliteration, are used in "Discernment of Spirits," *supra*.

79. "All the devils are furious when you undertake this exercise" (*Cloud*, *ed. cit.*, ch. 3, p. 120). "We pray within our room, with the door closed (Mt 6:6) when we withdraw our hearts from the tumult of all our thoughts and cares and offer our prayers secretly and intimately to our Lord. . . . We are to pray in absolute silence, not simply to avoid distracting our brethren who are praying around us, with our chattering and noise; but also to hide from our enemy, who lies in wait for us, particularly when we pray" (Cassian, *Collationes* 2, 9, *S.C.* 54, pp. 71–72).

80. In "the primal state of man's soul, as it was before sin . . . all [your stirrings] would reach out to the preeminent and supreme object of your will and desire, which is God" (*Cloud*, *ed. cit.*, ch. 4, p. 122). Cf. Jb 19:25–26 (Vulgate): " . . . in the last day I shall rise out of the earth . . . and in my flesh I shall see my God."

81. Like the blind beggar of Jericho: "Jesus, son of David, have mercy on me . . . what do you wish that I do to you? . . . receive your sight; your faith has made you whole" (Lk 18:35–42).

82. "Some men he tempteth also, and mainly solitary men and women, by dreads and ugliness and quakings and shakings" (Hilton, *Scale* I, ch. 38). His source is Eccl 4:18–21—ch. 39 *loc. cit.*, pp. 84–91. Cassian notes that solitaries "wage open war upon the demon in the solitude of the desert" (*Couationes* 18, 6: P.L. 49, 1101). "The love of Jhesu and the ghostly sight of him as he will show him," says Walter Hilton, "shall save thee from all perils . . . from thieves and robbers the which I call unclean spirits, that though they spoil thee and beat thee through divers temptations, thy life shall aye be safe" (*Scale* II, ch. 21, p. 308).

83. ME: thof he stire any of his mighty lemys to rise and to renne in apon thee. St. Bernard speaks of the devil's *satellites*, and the Latin is transliterated in modern English. Our author, however, translates as *seriauntes*—sergeants. Cf. "Discernment of Spirits," *supra*.

84. The five senses are given concrete illustration in a vignette of the pains of hell, attributed to St. Gregory. "Fire unquenchable, cold insuperable, worm that never dies, stink insufferable, darkness so thick it can be felt, scourges of devils' beating, ghastly sight of fiends, despair of all good things—so it shall be in hell" (*Speculum Christiani*, ed. G. Holmstedt, Early English Text Society 182 [London, 1933], p. 720).

85. Julian of Norwich, when the devil tempted her, "in all this time

trusted to be saved and kept by the mercy of God" (*Revelations*, ch. 67). In the *Lives of the Fathers* it is told how the devil leapt and tore at the Abbot Pachomius. But he disappeared when the old man made the sign of the cross. Pachomius "knew all the wiles of the enemy and . . . thought nothing of his illusions" (P.L. 73, 240).

86. "Other enemies there are, as unclean spirits, that are busy with sleights and wiles for to deceive others" (Hilton, *Scale* II, ch. 22, p. 311). Augustine, *Enarr. in Psalmum* 9, 16: "Their foot has been taken in the trap which they hid: the hidden trap is the guileful thought. The foot of the soul is crooked desire (*cupiditas aut libido*). When it is straight, it is called love or charity (*dilectio vel caritas*). The soul then is moved by love as to the place whither it goes . . . not a spatial place, but delight" (P.L. 36, 124). ME: bi the whiche thou gost to God. This is the anagogical or mystical meaning: *quo tendas anagogia*.

87. ME: mightily, wisely, and goodly—the classical trinitarian attributes—almighty for the Father, wise for the Son, goodly for the Holy Spirit. The triadic structure persists in the three verbs "sukour, kepe, and defende," also in "love, trust . . . fele," and "wylen, forsake and kepyng." This rhetorical passage ends with the figure *compar*, "a combination of cola (rhythmical phrases) with a virtually equal number of syllables": Lo frende, thus shal oure Lorde and our love/ mightely, wisely and goodly/ sokoure, kepe and defende/ all thoo that for love trist/ that thei fele in hym/ wylen utterly forsake/ the kepyng of hemself. The material aspect of this self-abandonment is treated in the *Cloud, ed. cit.*, ch. 23, p. 167.

88. "Blessed is the rich man who has not gone after gold . . . who is he and we will praise him, for he has done wonderful things in his life? He has been tried and made perfect" (Ecclus 31:9–10). "May Christ dwell in your hearts by faith, being rooted and founded in love" (Eph 3:17). "Friend, go up higher . . . he that humbles himself shall be exalted" (Lk 14:10–11). "O God, be merciful to me a sinner . . . he that humbles himself shall be exalted" (18:13–14). "Humble yourself under the mighty hand of God" (1 Pt 5:6). Cf. also Wis 7:21–22, 25–26; Col 2:3; Ecclus 44:29: "We shall say much and yet want words; and the sum of our words is, He is all." Cf. Rom 3:22, 11:36; 1 Cor 8:6, 12:6, 15:28; Col 1:16–17; Eph 4:6. "The supreme Godhead is called omnipotent because it is potent over all things, and rules with unalloyed sovereignty over the world it governs; and because it is the object of desire and yearning for all, and casts on all its voluntary yoke and sweet travail of all powerful and indestructible desire for its goodness" (*Divine Names* X; Rolt, *Dionysius the Areopagite*, p. 169).

ME: verely mekyd in ful noughting of itself. Cf. Julian, *Revelations*, ch. 5: "No soul can be in rest until it is naughted of everything that is made. When the soul is willingly naughted, for love, so as to have him who is All, then is she able to receive ghostly rest."

89. "Christ Jesus thought it not robbery to be equal with God. . . . He humbled himself . . . for which cause God has exalted him" (Phil 2:8–9). "Thy almighty word leapt down from thy royal throne" (Wis 18:15). "God

has chosen the things that are contemptible, and things that are not" (1 Cor 1:28). "We must be transported wholly out of ourselves and given to God. For it is better to belong to God and not to ourselves, since thus will the Divine Bounty be bestowed . . . for in it are hid all the treasures of wisdom and knowledge" (*Divine Names* IV; Rolt, *Dionysius the Areopagite*, pp. 147–48). "The third grade of contemplation, ecstasy, is reached when the person forsakes himself and is above himself, though not outside himself; it is a loving ascent when the soul reaches out towards the superintellectual radiance of the divine light with the co-operation of dynamic powers. These powers, we may say, are humility and purity" (Thomas Gallus, *De septem gradibus contemplationis*, in *S. Bonaventurae Opera Omnia, ed. cit.*, tom. XII, p. 183).

90. Cf. the *Cloud, ed. cit.*, ch. 18, where the expression is certainly less violent. It also appears to be more general: "They [sc. relatives and friends] reprove him [the contemplative] sharply, saying that what he is doing is nothing" (p. 159). Conceivably, the author is here answering an accusation that he is preaching a form of quietism or false abandonment, of which his contemporaries on the continent of Europe were similarly accused: that the soul which is preparing itself for the transforming union must despoil itself of all activity to a point of excessive passivity. Cf. *Abandon*, in *DSp.* I, 40.

91. ME: thof al you thenk hem passe the cours and the comoun dome of your reason. In the next paragraph, the author is going to cite Richard of St. Victor (though not by name) in his defense. He appears to use the same source here: The things that belong to the sixth kind of contemplation are beyond reason because we cannot establish them by experience or investigate them fully by any reasoning: such as, that the Son is co-eternal with the Father. Cf. *Benjamin Major* IV, 3: P.L. 196, 137.

92. One of the author's "olde Faders" is certainly St. Bernard, who has written: "Contemplation happens through the condescension of the Word of God to human nature by grace, and the exaltation of human nature to the Word himself through divine love. . . . The incarnation happened through the fruitfulness of divine grace. It is the same with contemplation: It cannot happen by means of the human will, but only by the divine gift" (*Sermones de diversis* 87: P.L. 183, 704).

93. Gregory follows Augustine in interpreting the narrative of the two wives of Jacob, Lia and Rachel: "one the temporal life in which we work, the other the eternal, in which we shall contemplate the delights of God" (*Contra Faustum* 22, 52: P.L. 42, 434). "Rachel is beautiful but barren, Lia blear-eyed but fruitful, in that when the mind seeks the repose of contemplation, it sees more but is less productive" (*Moralia in Job*, 6, 37, 61: P.L. 75, 764). Bernard follows in their wake; cf. *Sermones in Cantica* 41, 5: P.L. 183, 987. The allegory takes a new turn with Richard of St. Victor's *Benjamin Minor*. "As soon as Benjamin is born, Rachel dies" (ch. 74). "By Benjamin we understand the grace of contemplation" (ch. 67). "By Rachel we understand reason" (ibid.); cf. *supra*.

94. "Rachel departs from this life, because the mind, when carried above

itself, exceeds all the limits of human reason. All human reason, when raised above itself in rapture, is overwhelmed by that ray of divine light on which it fixes its gaze. What else is the death of Rachel than the eclipse of reason?" (ibid., ch. 73).

95. The author in the *Cloud* declares his reluctance to cite St. Denis to support his views, "or any other doctor either" (*ed. cit.*, ch. 70, p. 256). This is presumably the reason he does not name names here.

96. "How often Benjamin is overcome by ecstasy of mind, how frequently taken out of himself into a state of rapture, astounded, and undoubtedly fulfilling what is written of him: *Benjamin adolescentulus in mentis excessu*" (*Benjamin Minor*, ch. 85: P.L. 196, 61). This verse from Psalm 67:28 opens Richard's *Benjamin Minor*, P.L. 196, 1. Our author does not quote it in his version. Cf. *supra*.

97. There is possibly association by reminiscence here from the young child, Contemplation, born of Reason, to the story of Solomon's wisdom: the child who was overlaid, the woman willing to see the child slaughtered, and the great figure of contemplative wisdom, Solomon, giving judgment (3 Kgs 3:16–28).

98. The well-known schoolboy martyrs Justus and Pastor of Alcalá de Henares in Spain during the persecution under the Emperor Dacian in A.D. 304. According to the Acts of their martyrdom, Justus, aged thirteen, and Pastor, only seven, were actually in the public school of Alcalá when they heard that the Roman governor was rounding up the Christians for martyrdom. Without more ado, they threw down their slates, rushed to the marketplace and demanded to be executed with the rest. Their fame spread through Roman territories, and St. Paulinus of Nola had his little son buried close to them. They are the patrons of Alcalá and feature in the Roman Martyrology for August 6. Cf. *Butler's Lives of the Saints*, ed. Thurston and Attwater (London, 1933), p. 73.

99. Taken almost verbatim from the *Cloud*, ed. cit., ch. 29, pp. 177–78: "It often happens that some who have been wicked and habitual sinners come more quickly to the perfection of this exercise than those who have not. This is a miracle of mercy from our Lord, who gives his grace in this special way, to the wonder of all the world. But truly, I look forward to the delight of judgment day, when God and all his gifts shall be seen clearly." Cf. 2 Thess 1:10: "He shall come to be glorified in his saints, and made wonderful."

100. Walter Hilton also speaks of "thus louely noughtning itself and thus heily allyng its God." Cf. *Scale* II, ch. 27: "This is a good darkness and a rich nought that bringeth a soul to so much goodly ease and so still softness. I trow David meant of this night or of this nought when he said thus: *Ad nichilum redactus sum et nescivi* (Ps 72:10). That is, I was noughted and I wist not. That is: the grace of our Lord Jhesu sent into mine heart hath slain in me and brought to nought all the love of the world, and I wist not how" (Underhill *ed. cit.*, p. 343).

101. The reference is to St. Paul in 2 Cor 11:1–9: " . . . caught up into

paradise and heard secret words . . . for such a one will I glory, but for myself I will not glory save in my infirmities . . . my grace is sufficient for you, for power is made perfect in infirmity. Gladly therefore, will I glory in my weakness, that the power of Christ may dwell in me . . . when I am weak, then am I powerful."

102. "There will always be someone to speak something against us contemplatives," says the author in the *Cloud* (*ed. cit.*, ch. 23, p. 167) and adds: "Whoever is doubtful of this, either the devil is in his heart and robs him [the ME is the same here as in the *Cloud*: outher the devil is in his brest and revith hym] of his faith . . . "

103. The author, in drawing this section of his letter to a close—he has once more cited the last verse of his quotation from Prv 3:26—takes up again the theme of sleep as the image of dark contemplation in a *conclusio*, "a brief argument in which is deduced the necessary consequences of what is said and done" (Caplan, *Cicero*, p. 331); here by the comparison between bodily and ghostly sleep. It is noteworthy that the author anticipates the teaching of John of the Cross: ". . . that we may attain to this possession of the union of God, wherein all things of the world shall be put aside and renounced, and all the natural affections and appetites be mortified, and all the operations of the soul, from being natural, become divine" (*Living Flame of Love*, Stanza 1, p. 69, trans. Allison Peers, *Works of St. John of the Cross*, vol. II, [London, 1947]).

104. ME: thou hast ben yit hedirtoward over wise in thi wittys.

105. The same point is made in an objective and abstract fashion in ch. 6 of the *Cloud* (*ed. cit.*, p. 130). Here it is part of the game between master and pupil.

106. "Perfect obedience has no laws, nor is it bound by any limits" (*Liber de praecepto et dispensatione* 6: P.L. 182, 868).

107. ME: I coveite souereinte of thee; and trewly so I do, and I wol have it. The Latin term is *praelatura, praelatus*—"souereyn goostly." St. Bernard uses *praelatus* and *spiritualis pater* synonymously: "Whoever openly or tacitly works to have his spiritual father (*spiritualis pater*) bid him do what he himself wants to do deceives himself if he flatters himself that he is being obedient. He does not obey his spiritual sovereign (*praelato*); rather his sovereign obeys him" (*De diversis, Sermo* 35: P.L. 183, 636).

108. ME: in height of kunnyng,/or yit of worching/ or degree of levyng.

109. One who claimed such a gift of speech was Richard Methley in his *Scola Amoris Languidi*. "In the name of Jesus," he says, "I write in new tongues."

110. The allusion is to 1 Cor 2:4–16—the hidden wisdom of God.

111. The Pseudo-Dionysius illustrates what he means by ecstatic or unitive love by citing Paul: "I live, now not I, but it is Christ that lives in me" (Gal 2:20); *Divine Names* IV, 13; Rolt, *Dionysius the Areopagite*, p. 106. Thomas Gallus, in his *Explanation* of this passage, says: "As my soul governs me in the natural order, and orders me towards every act, interior and ex-

terior, so this eternal power of Christ, with whom I am made one, vivifies me and orders me towards all things. But no matter how we try to express the sum of these words, we must take it for granted that the power of this apostolic experience can never be worthily expressed, either in writing, word or thought."

112. "This humble stirring of love . . . is nothing else than a good will directed to God. . . . This good will is the substance of all perfection" (*Cloud, ed. cit.*, ch. 49, pp. 214–15). St. Bernard says that the good will, which alone makes the soul good, has four grades—*voluntas recta, valida, devota, plena*. The fourth we can desire in this life. The third enables us to run in the way of God's commandments (*De diversis, Sermo* 124: P.L. 183, 745–46).

113. Cf. the *Cloud, ed. cit.*, ch. 12, p. 147, where the author offers us Richard of St. Victor's definition of virtue (an ordered and controlled affection that has God alone for its object), and says that if we possess humility and charity, we possess all virtues.

114. In the *Cloud*, the author discusses at great length the virtues of humility (*ed. cit.*, chs. 12ff.) and charity (chs. 24ff.). In the letter "Inward Stirrings," the perfection of virtue and love of God and the brethren constitute the crown of life, with wisdom and discernment. Cf. *supra*. In the *Pursuit of Wisdom*, the author examines the whole range of purgative and illuminative powers that prepare the soul to receive discernment and contemplative wisdom. Fear of the Lord and hope leading to reverent affection are the subject matter of the *Letter on Prayer*.

115. The dark contemplation of the *Cloud* is given in several synonyms, some of which may be identified as the author's "owne writyng." The reverent affection is "the fruyte departid fro the tre," i.e., the ripe and not the unripe fruit (*supra*).

116. ME: This is the cloude of unknowyng. This refers to the book, as well as to the contemplative exercise. Cf. Introduction, *supra*.

117. ME: this is that priuy loue put in purete of spirit. This appears to be the author's favorite definition of what is at once an exercise, an impulse, a contemplative grace, and the divine operation. So in the *Cloud* we have "the purity and depth of spiritual feeling," "the spiritual knot of burning love in spiritual oneness," "that which is hid in the depths of the spirit," "in the purity and depths of the spirit," "what is hidden in your heart" (*ed. cit.*, ch. 47, pp. 210–11); "the devout stirring of love which dwells in purity of spirit," "this simple, devout, zealous stirring of love" (ch. 48, pp. 213–14).

118. The *Benjamin Major* of Richard of St. Victor. Its other title is *De gratia contemplationis occasione accepta ab Arca Moysis*. At the end of the treatise, Richard gives us a recapitulation, which he calls *Allegories of the Tabernacle of the Covenant*. There he says that the great candlestick is the bearer of the light, and discretion is the light of the interior man. Devout meditation belongs to the candlestick, as does diligent meditation; sacred reading (*lectio sacra*) to the table of the sanctuary, and devout prayer (*devota oratio*) to the

inner altar. And the ark is contemplation. "It is deservedly named the ark of sanctification (Ps 131:8), for it prefigures the consummation of our justification" (P.L. 196, 19ff.).

119. The author is doubtless referring to his translation of the *Mystical Theology* as well as to its content. Cf. Col 2:3: "In him are hid all the treasures of wisdom and knowledge."

120. Here we have another reference to the "Hidden Theology," as we read in the prefatory prayer: " . . . to those utterly unknown and sovereign-shining heights of your mysterious, inspired utterances where all the secrets of divine knowledge are concealed and hidden under the sovereign-shining darkness of wisest silence" (*supra*).

121. Cf. *Hidden Theology*, ch. III: "When the ascent is complete, there will be no words at all, but all will be made one with the Ineffable."

122. So the *Cloud, ed. cit.*, chs. 37 and 38: "Their personal prayers . . . if words are used—and this happens rarely—they are very few indeed." "It is written that a short prayer pierces heaven" (pp. 192, 193).

123. Lk 9:23.

124. St. Bernard uses the same formula—the figure that introduces the spiritual sense: "It is as if he said: he who wants me, must despise himself. He who wishes to do my will, must break his own" (*Festo S. Andreae Apostoli, Sermo* 2, 5: P.L. 183, 511). Bernard exposes the moral sense; our author carries his interpretation through to the anagogical sense—"the bliss of heaven and the summit of perfection."

125. The reference is to the Christological hymn in Phil 2:3–13, with its reference to the preexistent Christ: "In humility, let each esteem others better than themselves . . . let this mind be in you which was in Christ Jesus, who, being in the form of God . . . emptied himself . . . humbled himself, becoming obedient unto death . . . for which cause God has exalted him. Wherefore . . . work out your salvation with fear and trembling. For it is God who works in you both to will and to accomplish, according to his good will."

126. The Fourth Lateran Council declared against Joachim de Flores that, in Christ's prayer, "I would that they might be one in us as we are one" (Jn 17:22), "one" is to be understood, as far as the faithful are concerned, as the union of love in grace, but for the divine persons, as the union of identity in nature; just as when Christ says "Be perfect as your heavenly Father is perfect" (Mt 5:48), it is as if he said "Be perfect by the perfection of grace as your heavenly Father is perfect by the perfection of nature" (*Denzinger-Schönmetzer*, 806).

127. ME: For criste yede before be kinde/ and we comyn after by grace/ His kynde is more worthi then grace/ and grace is more worthi then oure kinde. The author uses the figures *compar*—cola with virtually the same number of syllables; *membrum*—a sentence member, brief and complete that does not express the entire thought, but is in turn supplemented by another; *chiasmus*—inversion: kynde . . . grace, grace . . . kynde.

128. Cf. the *Cloud, ed. cit.*, ch. 26, pp. 173–74.

129. "Not by the works of justice we have done but by his mercy has he saved us" (Tit. 3:5); "It is not of him that wills nor of him that runs, but of God that shows mercy" (Rom 9:16).

130. "Give glory to God who has anticipated you, and prompted and initiated your doing" (St. Bernard, *De gratia et libero arbitrio* I, i: P.L. 182, 1001). "To wish and to fear and to love is the gift God gave us in our natural condition that we might be creatures; to will the good, to fear God and to love him, this is the gift by the visitation of grace, that we might be God's creatures" (Ibid.).

131. "The third grace is more special, for it is not given to all men, but only to those who open the gates of their hearts, and make their free will ready to receive it. This grace is a gift of the Holy Spirit which moves men to do good works. God gives it to man that through it he may gain reward. For without it nothing we do is meritorious. It consists of three elements: the first is the free gift that moves the free will; the second is the consent of that will; the third is God who creates and gives the grace. This grace is a token of God's special love for those to whom he sends it. It makes a man patient in his anger, enables him to endure meekly the loss of worldly goods, of worldly friends, bodily harm, sickness and penance for his past sins . . . " (*A Ladder of Four Rungs: Middle English Text*, in Hodgson, *Hid divinite*, pp. 105ff.).

132. Here again the author has dealt with this matter theoretically in the *Cloud* (*ed. cit.*, ch. 73, pp. 260–61), following Richard of St. Victor.

133. Guigo II likewise appeals to the experience of his correspondent, at the beginning of his letter on the contemplative life: "So I decided to send you my thoughts on the spiritual exercises proper to cloistered monks, so that you who have come to know more about these matters by your experience than I have by theorizing about them may pass judgment on my thoughts and amend them" (*Ladder*, p. 81). Cf. *Cloud, ed. cit.*, ch. 33, p. 182.

134. Here our author is surprisingly close to St. Bernard as the latter sets out four degrees of love in his short treatise on love for God (*De diligendo Deo*). First, man loves himself for his own sake. "And when he sees that he cannot subsist of himself he begins to seek God by faith as necessary to him, and to love him. So secondly, he comes to love God, but for his own and not for God's sake. But when he begins out of necessity to cultivate his God and frequent his company by reading, meditation and prayer (*legendo, cogitando, orando*) and by obedience, then God gradually and sensibly becomes known to him. Having tasted how sweet the Lord is, he ascends to the third degree, where he loves God for God's sake rather than for his own. And there he stays; for no one can say how perfectly anyone achieves the fourth grade in this life—loving God for his sake alone. For in some marvellous way he forgets himself, falls away from himself and clings to God, becoming one in spirit with him" (ch. XV, 39: P.L. 182, 998). Cf. Introduction, *supra*.

135. The reference is doubtless to Col 3:10: "Putting on the new Adam, him who is renewed into knowledge, according to the image of the One who

created him." Julian of Norwich says that "God is our clothing, our love, that wraps us and winds us about" (*Revelations*, ch. 5).

136. "My flesh and my heart have failed, but God is my heart and my portion forever" (Ps 72:26).

137. "He that loves, knows God, for God is love. By this has the love of God appeared toward us, because God has sent his only begotten Son into the world that we may live by him. In this is love: not as though we had loved God, but because he has first loved us, and sent his Son to be a propitiation for our sins" (1 Jn 4:8–10).

138. "Here we can see and appreciate the wonderful nobility of this wisdom, and why it is called in Denis' definition 'truly divine' (*divinissima*). For the soul must, so to say, despoil itself of itself (*quasi seipsam exspoliare*) and follow, as it were step by step, the divine love conferred by God on the affection; and by means of this divine ascent which occurs through the touch of love, it must leave behind with the intellect its habitual knowledge" (De Balma, *loc. cit.*, III, 4, p. 41). Cf. Introduction, *supra*.

139. This contemplative sorrow is described in detail in the *Cloud*. Cf. *ed. cit.*, chs. 43–44, pp. 201–05, and notes.

140. "Somehow or other to lose yourself, as though you did not exist, not to experience yourself in any way at all, to be wiped out almost, this is heavenly dwelling, not human affection. And if a mortal soul is carried off and admitted to such an experience for a moment, then the envy of an evil world threatens, the body of this death threatens the needs of the flesh; and what is more violent than these, fraternal charity withdraws. Alas, the soul is compelled to return into itself and to cry out in its misery: Unhappy man that I am, who will deliver me from the body of this death?" (*De diligendo Deo* X, 27: P.L. 182, 990).

141. ME: not for to unbe, for that were woodnes and dispite unto God. Cf. *Cloud* PH 84/21: "not to unbe, for that were deuelles woodnes and dispite unto God."

142. This, says Thomas Gallus, is human nature's natural condition. The soul's dark awareness of itself is not only due to the relics of original sin (cf. the *Cloud*, *ed. cit.*, ch. 12); it is its mortal dwelling ("the earthly house of this habitation, in which we groan, desiring to be clothed, where we walk by faith and not by sight"—2 Cor 5:1–7).

143. "His place is in peace, and his abode in Sion" (Ps 75:3). "Love is this mountain, the high mount of God. . . . When will flesh and blood achieve it? When, forgetful of itself, overwhelmed with divine love, it makes of itself a lost cause, and enters wholly into God" (*De diligendo Deo*, ibid.). There is a vivid description of the sort of experience in the *Cloud*, *ed. cit.*, ch. 25, pp. 174–75.

144. Cf. the similar affective invocation of the name of Jesus in the *Cloud*, *ed. cit.*, ch. 4, p. 125.

145. Cf. "Letter on Prayer": "the high mount of perfection, that is to say, the perfect love of God" (*supra*).

146. Cf. Hilton, *Scale II*, ch. 33: "And therefore he that will seek God within, he shall forget . . . thinking of his own soul and think in that unmade kind that is Jhesu . . . upon this manner shall the soul do when grace toucheth it" (Underhill, p. 377).

147. For a more detailed treatment, cf. *Cloud, ed. cit.*, chs. 8 and 9, pp. 137–40.

148. Cf. Hilton, *Scale II*, ch. 32: "He seeth Him, not what He is, nor . . . as He is, but that He is . . . not blindly and nakedly and unsavorly, as doth a clerk that seeth Him by his clergy only through might of his naked reason" (Underhill, p. 370).

149. "Many souls beginning and profiting have many great favours and much sweetness in devotion . . . yet they have not perfect love nor spiritual knowing of God. For wit thou well, feel a soul never so much fervour . . . as long as his thinking and his beholding of God is most in imagination and not in understanding, he cometh not yet to perfect love nor to contemplation" (ibid., ch. 30, p. 358).

150. Rom 12:15: "Rejoice with them that rejoice; weep with them that weep." "Their meditations are, so to speak, sudden awarenesses and obscure feelings of their own wretchedness, or of God's goodness . . ." (*Cloud, ed. cit.*, ch. 36, p. 190).

151. ME: It is a merveilous householde, goostlines. The scriptural references abound: the house of God—"House of God and gate of heavens," Gn 28:17; the (spiritual) temple—*domus Dei*—Ps 25:8, 35:9, 48:17, 68:10; the Church (Kingdom)—1 Pt 2:5; Heaven—Jn 14:2; Is 38:20.

152. "There may be many sundry ways and divers works leading sundry souls to contemplation. . . . Nevertheless there is no gate but one; for what exercise it be that a soul have, but if he may come by that exercise to this knowing and to a meek feeling of himself and that is that he be mortified and dead to the world as in his love . . . hath not fully contemplation. And if he will come by any other gate, he is but a thief and breaker of the wall" (Hilton, *Scale II*, ch. 27: Underhill, p. 341).

153. "I am the door. If anyone enter through me he shall be saved; and whether he goes out or enters he will find pasture (Jn 10:9). But he who does not enter through the door, but climbs over another way, he is a thief and a robber" (10:1).

154. Augustine (*In Joannis Evangelium* xlv) says that Christ is the "One gateway of faith: the Christ born of the Virgin, who has suffered, is risen and ascended to heaven" (P.L. 34, 1722). Cf. Lk 23:39–43. As the author insists in the *Cloud*, "the second degree of the active life, and the first of the contemplative life, consists in good spiritual meditations on a man's own wretchedness, on the passion of Christ" (*ed. cit.*, ch. 21, p. 164). He also teaches that imagination is brought under the control of reason by "continual meditation on . . . our wretched state and on the passion and humanity of our Lord God" (ch. 64, p. 247). Thomas Gallus, in his first commentary on the Canticle of Canticles observes that the soul is kept in readiness for

dark contemplation by holding the crucified Christ before the eyes of the heart, and by meditating continually on his most blessed passion. Cf. B. Pez, *Commentarium in Cantica Thomae Abbatis Vercellensis*, p. 674.

155. Augustine distinguishes the coming in and going out according to the contemplative and active lives: "I could say that we enter when we think on something, and go out when we perform some work outside. And since Christ dwells in our hearts by faith (Eph 3:17), to enter through Christ is to perform deeds of faith before men" (*In Joannis Evangelium* xlv: P.L. 34, 1727). For our author, as we have seen, "satisfying meditations" themselves belong to the active life, to the Christ who is "the humble doer," and who "is man and God" (ibid.: P.L. 34, 1727).

156. "Whoever enters through this door, ought to humble himself so that he can enter with the proper dispositions" (*ut sano capite possit intrare*). "He that does not humble but exalts himself, wants to enter through the wall." P.H. cites Richard of St. Victor, who alludes to Jn 10:9—"they go out and enter and find [spiritual pasture]—*Benjamin Major* II, 16: P.L. 196, 95.

157. These iniquities of the "devil's contemplatives" are carefully described in the *Cloud, ed. cit.*, chs. 50–55: "They prop themselves up on every side with many humble-sounding words and gestures of devotion" (ch. 54, p. 225). He follows Augustine in identifying "the thief and the robber" not only as the hypocrite of the Gospel but as the heretic. Augustine names Sabellius, Arius, and Photinus (*loc. cit.*, xlv, 2–5: P.L. 34, 1720–21).

158. ME: the comoun plein wey of cristen men. Augustine in his sermon xlv constantly returns to the presentation of Christ as the Way. Our author here employs the rhetorical figure *frequentatio*—"when the points scattered throughout the whole cause are collected in one place so as to make the speech more impressive or sharp or accusatory" (Caplan, *Cicero*, p. 361).

159. ME: til the grete rust of his boistous bodelynes be in grete party rubbid away. Cf. Hilton, *Scale II*, ch. 28: "Our Lord Jhesus, seeing what thing is behovable to a froward soul, suffereth it to be travailed and teased by sundry temptations, and for to be well examined through ghostly tribulations until all the rust of uncleanness might be burnt out of it" (Underhill, p. 348).

160. Though the author and his spiritual contemporaries might agree that all Christians are called to perfection in the sense defined by Gregory the Great: "Perfection is to love everyone as oneself, to know the truth about God, and to consider others better than oneself," it is rather, as Richard of St. Victor writes, in the anchorholds and the monasteries where the soldiers and athletes of Christ are to be found: "rich in the perfection of the virtues and in the fulness of grace" (*Explicatio in Cantica Canticorum*, ch. xxii: P.L. 196, 470–72).

161. It is clear that the author's frame of reference is the "two lives" as he treats of them in the *Cloud, ed. cit.*, ch. 8, pp. 136–39. The work of salvation is essentially meditation, so he writes: "It would be a wrong thing for a man engaged on meditation . . . to turn his mind to outward corporal works (sc. the lower part of the active life)."

162. The author deals with the same point and in the same way, but again impersonally, toward the end of the *Cloud, ed. cit.*, ch. 72, pp. 259–60.

163. ME: Have pees with thi perte, whether that thou have. Thee nedeth not to pleyne thee; for thei ben bothe precious.

164. The reference is, as the author makes clear in the *Cloud, ed. cit.*, ch. 17, to Lk 10:38–43, the traditional interpretation of the story of Martha and Mary. Cf. also *Cloud, ed. cit.*, Introduction, pp. 66–68.

165. Jn 15:5. Cf. Rom 8:26; Phil 2:13; Tit 3:5; 1 Cor 12:3.

166. What our author says in this excursus on "the higher part of the active life [which] is the same as the lower part of the contemplative life" (*Cloud, ed. cit.*, ch. 8, p. 137) has much in common with the ME version of the *Scala Claustralium*; here, for instance: "How is it possible to think properly, and to avoid meditating upon false and idle topics, overstepping the bounds set by our holy fathers, unless we are first directed in these matters . . . ? Again what use is it to anyone if he sees in his meditation what is to be done unless the help of prayer and the grace of God enable him to achieve it? For . . . we can do nothing without him. It is he who achieves our works in us, and yet not entirely without us" (1 Cor 3:9: *Ladder of Monks*, pp. 93–94).

167. Wharton (*Anglia Sacra* [London, 1691], I, p. 640) tells the story of the election of the Bishop of Ely in 1302. It was first annulled by the Archbishop of Canterbury on the grounds of his insufficient learning. But the election was ratified when the bishop himself appealed to the pope and was summoned to Rome to defend himself *coram Pontifice*. Cf. Pantin *The English Church in the Fourteenth Century*, pp. 19 and 51.

168. "God is like a partner performing half his works. He acts with us like a partner who wants to make a profit. He gives his grace and we give our works . . . but like miserable cheats we defraud him. We think that the gain is all ours. . . . So be like a true partner to God and let him have his share" (*Ladder of Monks*, pp. 48–49).

169. "The third grace is more special, for it is not given to all men, but only to them who open the gates of their hearts. . . . This grace has three elements: the first, itself a grace freely given, moving the free will; the second, the will assenting; the third, God creating and giving this grace . . . it is the sign of God's special love . . . it opens the way to joy" (ibid., p. 49).

170. "If God works in us the thought of the good, the willing and the doing of it, these three, he achieves the first without us, the second with us, and the third through us. If he anticipates us by planting in our hearts the good thought, and even joins us to himself through consent by changing the evil will . . . the consent and the work, even if not from us, do not occur without us" (St. Bernard, *De Gratia et Libero Arbitrio* XIV, 46: P.L. 182, 1026).

171. "Prayer when it is fervent wins contemplation. . . . There is no limit to God's power, and his merciful love surpasses all his other works; and sometimes . . . he forces the hard-hearted and reluctant to comply of

their own free will . . . when he enters where he has not been invited, when he dwells in the soul that has not sought him" (*Ladder of Monks*, p. 95).

172. " . . . when he gives himself to us, we do right nought but suffer him and assent to him; for that is the most that we do, that we assent wilfully to his gracious working in us" (Hilton, *Scale II*, ch. 34, p. 385).

173. In the first chapter of the *Cloud*, the author categorizes four forms or degrees of Christian living, the first of which is "living in the company of your worldly friends," and the fourth, the higher part of contemplative life (*ed. cit.*, pp. 115–16).

174. This paragraph may indicate that the neophyte has recently entered or is still a novice with the Carthusians or some other contemplative community. In any case he is still finding the exercise difficult, as is said in the last paragraph of the Letter. The author may also have in mind that others besides his immediate dirigé will read his letter.

175. The grace is described in the ME version of the *Ladder*: "There is a more special grace . . . offered only to man to take if he wishes . . . this grace always stands at the gates of our heart" (Apoc 3:20). It is the justifying grace; and the translator quotes Augustine: "He who created you without your help will not justify you without your help," and "this is always ready for me, if it finds me ready" (pp. 46–49).

176. Much of the *Cloud* is concerned with the nature of dark contemplation and with the attitudes and dispositions that foster it; and in particular the answering of doubts and objections to the exercise of dark contemplation and the life-style demanded by it: cf. the chapter titles, *ed. cit.*, pp. 105–13. Here he is offering the subjective signs, dealt with briefly in the last chapter of the *Cloud* (pp. 263–65), which will enable the individual to decide whether he is being called to and chosen for this kind of contemplation.

177. Augustine, commenting on the verse of Ps 37:10—"All my desire is before you, Lord": "Your desire is your prayer; and if your desire is continual, so is your prayer. . . . If you do not wish to cease praying, never cease desiring. If your desire is continual, so is your voice. You become silent only if you stop loving. . . . The cold of charity is the silence of the heart; its heat is the cry of the heart. If charity never falls away, neither does your heart's cry" (P.L. 36, 404).

178. The author describes the call to contemplation in the first chapter of the *Cloud*: "And so with his great grace he kindled your desire, and fastened to it a leash of longing, and with this led you into a more special state and degree of life" (*ed. cit.*, p. 116). But first, in the prologue, he insists that his book is only for one "who is doing all that he can, and has been for a long time past to fit himself for the contemplative life by the virtues and exercises of the active life"—the common entrance of Christians (pp. 101–02).

179. ME: the windowes of the bodily wittys. Cf. the *Cloud*, *ed. cit.*, ch. 2, p. 119, and ch. 48, p. 214. "Listening is a kind of reading, and that is why we are accustomed to say that we have read not only those books which we

have read to ourselves or aloud to others but those also which our mentors have read to us" (*Ladder*, p. 93).

180. The author is describing that traditional "reminiscence of God" (*mnēmē tou theou*) taught by the Greek Fathers and cherished by the monastic writers of the West as the *memoria Christi* or the *sensus Christi;* Ignatius Loyola equiparated it with the grace of devotion, which he described as "a certain facility for finding God in all things." Allied to this is the aphorism of the *Imitation of Christ*, which sums up the monastic teaching on single-mindedness: "Simplicity seeks God; purity finds him." Cf. J. Walsh, "*Application of the Senses*," *Supplement to the Way* 27 (Spring 1976): 61.

181. The author in this paragraph is using the highly effective rhetorical figure *expeditio*, "when we have enumerated several ways by which something could have been achieved, and all are then discarded except the one on which we are insisting" (Caplan, *Cicero*, p. 329).

182. The contemplative has to stand in desire all his life long, says the author when he first speaks about this work, this matter, in the *Cloud* (*ed. cit.*, ch. 2, p. 118); and at the very end (ch. 75, p. 266) he quotes St. Augustine: "The whole of the life of good Christian men is nothing else but holy desires."

183. In ch. 54 of the *Cloud*, the author says that one practiced in this exercise is "truly attractive to all men and women who look upon him" (*ed. cit.*, p. 224).

184. Cf. Jer 11:16: "The Lord called thy name a plentiful olive tree, fair, fruitful and beautiful; at the noise of the word a great fire was kindled in it."

185. "For the word of the cross, to them that perish, is foolishness, but to them that are saved, that is, to us, it is the power of God . . . unto the Gentiles foolishness, but to them that are called . . . Christ the power of God and the wisdom of God" (1 Cor 1:18–25).

186. The author is describing what the great monks called *sancta simplicitas:* "Holy simplicity is an unchanging will in the pursuit of a changeless good. In essence, simplicity is the will substantially turned towards God, asking the Lord for one thing alone and seeking that fervently, without any ambition to become many-sided by worldly complexity" (William of St. Thierry, cited in J. LeClercq, *The Love of Learning and the Desire for God*, p. 254).

187. ME: thi list is likyng to pleye with a childe. Previous editors have indicated MSS contamination, though this is the reading of the three best. One scribe inserts the name of Jesus before "a childe." McCann, *Cloud*, p. 230, refers to the image of the Father playing with the child—the *Cloud*'s version of the *ludus amoris* (*ed. cit.*, ch. 46, p. 209 and note); P.H. would paraphrase "thy delight is pleasure in playing with a child," and cites Mk 10:14–15, "Suffer the little children . . . " (*ed. cit.*, p. 213).

188. The long paragraph from "But if it happens that this attraction . . . " to " . . . you are not to be too despondent about this . . . " is formed from a single sentence with a protracted series of subordinate clauses that list the

various items of evidence leading to the conclusion, "do not be too despondent." The author makes emphatic use of the figures personification and *expolitio*.

189. Cf. the ME "Exposition of Psalm 91," attributed to Walter Hilton: "When the just man is conscious that grace is in some way withdrawn, and he is deprived of devotion and compunction, when his sweet affections and his special consolations seem to be lost . . . he does not despair. . . . He knows well that grace is withdrawn from him in one way, but it is given to him in another, as God wills—not so sweetly, not so perceptibly as it was given, but more secretly, more powerfully, more divinely" (*Of the Knowledge of Ourselves and of God*, ed. J. Walsh and E. Colledge [London: Mowbray, 1961], pp. 17–18).

190. ME: schipping over fro bodelines to goostlines. The image of the ship is drawn with great vividness in "Inward Stirrings," *supra*.

191. The *Scala Claustralium* sums up the medieval tradition in the *ludus amoris*, the game of love between the spouse and the contemplative soul that is the sustained allegory of the Canticle of Canticles. "I sought him whom my soul loves": "And so he withdraws himself . . . so that when he is absent he may be desired the more, that being desired he may be sought more eagerly, that having long been sought he may at last be found" (*Ladder*, pp. 91, 32–33).

192. Julian of Norwich tells us graphically how she experienced this alternation of consolation and desolation: "I was left to myself, feeling the heaviness and weariness of life. But soon our Lord gave me the comfort and rest of soul. . . . I experienced the pain and then the liking, and now the one and now the other" (*Revelations*, ch. 15).

193. The author speaks of other and traditional reasons for the withdrawal of the felt presence of God in the last chapter of the *Cloud* (*ed. cit.*, ch. 75, pp. 264–65): in order that the contemplative apprentice might not become too familiar with it; to prevent him from thinking that he can have it when he wishes; because of carelessness; to enlarge his experience; to make him care more for it. Heb 10:37: "He that is to come, will come and will not delay."

194. "It is truly your beloved who visits you, but he comes invisibly, secretly, incomprehensibly . . . not to fulfil your desires but to capture your affection: to proffer some first-fruits of his love. At the same time you will in the meantime be consoled for his absence, when, lest you languish, you are unceasingly refreshed by his visitation" (Hugh of St. Victor, *De Arrha Animae:* P.L. 176, 970). Cf. *Ladder*, pp. 90–91.

195. "There are many kinds of experience which are comparable with bodily feelings such as hearing beautiful singing, feeling consoling warmth, seeing light. This is none of it spiritual experience. . . . At their best and truest, they are only outward signs of the inward grace which is felt in the powers of the soul" (*Exposition of Psalm 91, ed. cit.*, p. 83).

196. In the *Cloud*, the author has already made the distinction between the substance of perfection—the good will directed to God, and the acci-

A LETTER OF PRIVATE DIRECTION

dentals—all the sweetnesses and consolations, sensible and spiritual (*ed. cit.*, ch. 49, p. 215 and note 321). Here in "Private Direction" (*supra*, p. 15), he has defined the perfection of man's soul as "the union made in perfect charity between God and itself."

197. "The heart has become chaste, God is now loved for his own sake; no other prize is sought. God himself is the prize. If the heart loved anything else, the love would not be chaste" (St. Augustine on Psalm 72, 26—*Deus cordis mei et pars mea Deus meus*).

198. The author is speaking here of the moment of rapture—the consummation of the contemplative ascent. So Hugo de Balma, *Mystica Theologia*, III, 4: "Thus by the Divine Mercy, after the mind has aspired through long periods of time to be fastened more closely to its Beloved by the knot of burning love, for a short time and according to the capacity of the person, as it must be in rapture, what happens is that the blessed vision is granted." And again: "At the beginning of the exercise, the sovereign point of the loving power (*affectus apex*) rises only with difficulty; but through the excess of love carrying it above itself, it soon ascends without difficulty, and when it will" (*ed. cit.*, pp. 44–45).

199. "The spirit must first leave all consideration and love of sensible things, and the contemplation of all intelligible things. For the loving power must ascend in all purity without defilement from the intellect, to him whom it recognizes in its striving as the fulfilment of its desires, so that it may be more intimately united with him" (ibid., p. 44).

200. "During this time [of rapture] when you are striving by grace to reach a point to which you cannot come by nature, that is to say, to be made one with God in spirit and in love and in oneness of wills . . . it can be said that during this time God and yourself are not two but one in spirit . . . you or any other who experience the perfection of this work, because of this oneness may truly be called a God" (*Cloud, ed. cit.*, ch. 67, p. 249). Here our author is more pronouncedly metaphysical in expression than in this passage from the *Cloud*, but it adds little. Doubtless, his metaphysics are those of St. Thomas (since he quotes him later on), who teaches (1) that God's existence is, in a certain sense, self-evident—*Deum esse est per se notum secundum se*, and this would be particularly true (in the circumstances envisaged here) of God as the beatitude of man; (2) that God is the same as his essence or nature. Cf. *Summa Theol.*, 1a, 2, 1, and 1a, 3, 3.

201. The author is equally influenced by St. Augustine, perhaps in his commentary on Ps 49:2: "He who justifies, deifies, because by justifying he makes them children of God (Jn 1:12). If we are made sons of God, we are made gods: but this is by grace which adopts, not by nature which generates. There is one and only Son of God. . . . The rest who become gods do so by grace." "We know that when he appears we shall be like him, for we shall see him as he is (1 Jn 3:2). The only-begotten is like by birth, we are like by seeing. We are not 'like' in the same way that he is 'like' " (*Enarr. in psalmum* XLIX: P.L. 36, 565).

202. In this penultimate section he returns to a short consideration of

"the worthiness of thi clepyng" with which he had begun the *Cloud* (*ed. cit.*, ch. 2, pp. 117–18). De Balma is even more specific: "Let him recall in particular that to him, and not to everyone, the Father of all consolation has called him by his divine mercy to the Institute of the Carthusian Order . . . into the desert, to the solitude of contemplation . . . which he himself chose when he was led into the desert and fasted for forty days and nights" (De Balma, *Mystical Theology, ed. cit.*, I, 2, p. 6).

203. St. Thomas in his *Expositio in Joannis evangelium*, 16, 2, cites Augustine: "How could he [Christ] not send the One who had come upon him at baptism and remained with him—him from whom, we know, he could not be separated? What then does it mean, 'If I do not go, the Paraclete will not come to you?', except 'as long as you persist in knowing Christ according to the flesh, you cannot receive the Spirit?' " The citation is from Augustine's *In Joannis Evangelii*, 94, 4: P.L. 75, 1869.

204. "The doctor" could be either Augustine or Aquinas, who continues: "When Christ left them bodily, not only the Holy Spirit was present to them spiritually, but also the Father and the Son." He then cites Gregory the Great (*Moralia in Job*, 8 24, 41: P.L. 75, 826): "It is as if he said: 'If I do not take my body away from your physical gaze, I cannot lead your minds invisibly by the Spirit's consolation.' " And Thomas also says: "It was appropriate for Christ to ascend to heaven, so that, no longer knowing him according to the flesh, we might be joined to him spiritually, and thus become able to receive the gifts of the Holy Spirit" (*Summa Theol.* 2a–2ae, 82, 3ad 2). Augustine says elsewhere: "It seems to me that the disciples had been preoccupied with Christ in his human form, and, like men tend to be, were fixed in their human affections for the man. He wished them to have a godly affection for him and from being fleshly to become spiritual" (*Sermones de tempore*, 270, 2: P.L. 38, 1238).

205. St. Bernard: "They loved him with their bodies and not with their minds, they loved him with all their heart and not with all their soul. 'It is to your profit that I go' " (*Sermones in Cantica*, 20, 5: P.L. 183, 869). Hilton, *Scale I*, ch. 36: "For as long as he was with them, they loved him very much, but it was fleshly, in his manhood, and therefore it was to their profit that he should withdraw the bodily form from their sight, that the Holy Spirit might come to them and touch them to love and to know in him more spiritually" (Underhill, p. 83).

206. Aristotle, *Metaphysics*, 1, 1. The ancient Latin translation begins: *Omnis homo naturaliter scire desiderat.*

207. In the highest mansion of the soul—the three hierarchies represented by Seraphim, Cherubim, and Thrones—the rational creature is illuminated and carried by grace alone. "There are two feet, two hands, two ears, two nostrils, two eyes: the feet operate in the first mansion, and the hands in the second; the nostrils, eyes and ears of the spiritual understanding in the third; but there is only one palate of the heart, the taste of the loving power (affectus palatum)" (Thomas Gallus, in his *Commentary on Isaiah* 6, 1–4).

A LETTER OF PRIVATE DIRECTION

208. 1 Cor 8:1: "Knowledge puffs up, love builds up." St. Bernard; *"Scientia inflat.* First of all, I want the soul to know itself, for that is what reason demands of profit and order. . . . Profit, because such knowledge does not inflate; it humiliates, and this is a preparation for building up. . . . As long as I look at myself, my eye dwells on bitterness. But if I look up and raise my eyes to the help of the divine mercy, soon the joyful vision of God tempers the bitter vision of myself. So knowledge of the self is a step towards knowing God. And from his image, which is renewed in you, he himself will be seen" (*Sermones in Cantica* 36, 5–6: P.L. 183, 969–70).

209. A late MS, Ampleforth 42 (1677 A.D.), has the following colophon: "And therefore go forth with meekness and fervent desire in this work, which begins in this life and never shall have an end in the life everlasting; to which I beseech almighty Jesus to bring all those whom he has bought with his precious blood, Amen" (cf. McCann, *Cloud*, p. 239). The *Cloud* itself has a formal *envoi* (*ed. cit.*, ch. 75, p. 266) as do the other two letters (cf. *supra*), and even *Discernment of Spirits*. No editor has commented on the absence of a satisfactory ending to "Private Direction." One can only conjecture that the letter was never sent or that it had a covering letter or that the envoi has been lost, etc.

Appendix:
Introduction to an English Carthusian Manuscript

Introduction: Bodleian Library Douce MS 262[1]

This manuscript is not only significant testimony to the dissemination of and the common practice of Dionysian spirituality in English Charterhouses in the century or so preceding the dissolution of the monasteries in the England of Henry VIII.[2] It also gives eloquent witness to that love of learning and desire for God which lies at the heart of the Carthusian vocation. But most of all, it is a worthy memorial to the fifteen monks of the London community who, under the leadership of their Prior, St. John Houghton,[3] gave their lives for the unity of the Church in England.

Maurice Chauncy, who was a young monk in the "House of the Salutation of the Blessed Virgin Mary" at the time of Prior Houghton's death, uses a time-honored image to describe the latter's continual contemplative devotion. He is speaking of Houghton's grief when called to administrative office in the community:

> Oh, what grief assailed him, what abundant tears, what sighs he sent forth, what bodily distress overcame him, who thus altogether against his will, is constrained to leave his beloved solitude and silence! Lia, with her uncomely countenance, pleased him not; he preferred his first love . . . delighted in solitude, where the sweet whispering of his Beloved could reach him in secret.[4]

Chauncy also mentions the saint's "peculiar gift of tears." Not only would he weep when celebrating Mass, but "even in the refectory, so inebriated was he with a richness of divine love and devotion as to be unable to contain himself . . . he would hasten to his cell, which had so often witnessed his devout compunction, and entering into it, weep copiously."[5]

Finally, we may mention how the saint and martyr prepared his community for likely passion and death. He suggested that they should make a Triduum of prayer together. He recommended that on the first day, all should make a general confession, gave the power of plenary absolution to every priest, and leave to everyone to make his confession to whomso he would. On the second day, he preached on love, patience, and the need to cling to God in adversity, and initiated a ceremony of reconciliation, kneeling at the feet of the brother next to him in choir, and begging his pardon and forgiveness. On the third day, a community Mass of the Holy Spirit was celebrated. Chauncy writes:

> During the Mass it pleased the Almighty and merciful God to work wonderful and ineffable things. . . . In that conventual Mass, after the Elevation, a whisper as of light air, faintly sounding outwardly to the senses but operating intensely within, was observed and heard by many with their bodily ears, and felt and drawn in by all with the ears of their hearts. The whole community stood in astonishment, hearing the voice and experiencing its wonderful and sweet operation in the heart, not knowing whence it came or whither it went. But all rejoiced in that most holy breathing, and well understood that God was indeed in that place.[6]

St. John Houghton was still alive during his disembowelment, and as the executioner seized his heart, he cried out, "Good Jesu, what wiltst thou do with my heart?" He was forty-eight years of age.

The Parkminster MS[7]

Those to suffer next from the London Charterhouse after their Prior were BB. Sebastian Newdigate, Humphrey Middlemore, the Vicar, temporarily appointed to take on the duties of Prior, and the Procurator, William Exmewe. The three of them were incarcerated in a filthy prison, bound and fastened tightly with iron chains around neck and thigh, standing erect against post and pillar without any relaxation of any sort. Bl. William Exmewe's distinctive early sixteenth-century hand is still clearly recognizable in the Parkminster MS, as the copyist of *The Dyuyne Cloude of Unknowyng* and the *Pistle of Priuate Counsell*, which carries the following colophon in a rather later sixteenth-century hand. It is the *affidavit* of Maurice Chauncy. "This book which comes from the House of the Salutation of the most blessed Virgin Mary, of the Carthusian Order near London, was written out by St. Wille Exmewe. Signed, M. Chauncy." In all probability, the MS was copied from our Douce 262, since some of the textual readings are found in no other MSS copies of the *Cloud* except these two.[8] Exmewe was another spiritual hero of Chauncy, and he was anxious that the Prior of the Grand Chartreuse, for whom he composed the *Historia*, should know that the Blessed William was an Oxford graduate. Writing of the virtues of the brethren he says:

> I will not be silent about one who thought most humbly of himself, namely Fr. William Exmewe. He was a mere youth of twenty-eight, of very good family, very clever and well-versed in Greek and Latin literature.
>
> When obedience forced him to undertake the office of Procurator, an immense grief afflicted his humble heart, for he feared to lose the precious pearl he had found, and after savoring the spiritual sweetness and quiet of solitude, he had lost all taste for the fleshpots and the freedoms of the slave.[9]

The Love of Letters

Yet these MSS are but two among many tokens of the intense and zealous literary activity energizing the mystical spirituality of these English Charterhouses on the eve of the Reformation.[10] James Grenehalgh, apparently the director of the scriptorium of the house at Sheen, and certainly the best-known medieval English textual critic, is on record as the annotator of a score of MSS and printed books,[11] while his brethren, from Sheen in London to Mount Grace in Yorkshire, are the transcribers of the *Ancrene Riwle*, Margery Kempe's biography, the *Revelations* of Julian of Norwich, and many of the genuine and spurious works of Walter Hilton and Richard Rolle. They are also translators: from the Middle English into Latin and from Latin into English.[12] An abundance of these MSS are still extant in the great libraries of England and some few in private hands, and more are still being discovered on the continent of Europe.[13] All this is extraordinary testimony to the industry, high spirituality, and literary labors of the English Carthusians, and also of their great competence in matters contemplative, and knowledge of the Dionysian scene and its literature.

Guigo the Venerable, fifth Prior of the Grande Chartreuse, and scribe of the *Consuetudines*, in listing the utensils which each Carthusian cell must contain, had written:

> 2. For writing, a writer's stool (*scriptorium*), pens, chalk, two pumice-stones, two ink-horns, a pen-knife, two razors (*novaculas sive rasoria*) for scraping parchment, a stylus for pricking it, a lead weight, a ruler, a

wooden tablet for ruling lines (*postem ad regulandum*), tablets, a writing-stylus (*graphium*) . . . and we are to teach all whom we receive to write, insofar as this is possible.

Guigo continues:

3.   In addition, each one is to have two books at a time from the librarian (*armario*), and he is to be told to look after them with the greatest care and diligence, lest they be soiled by smoke, dust, or any other dirtiness. Indeed, books should be looked after with the same sort of heedfulness as though they were the eternal food of our souls; it should be our desire that they be made with the utmost devotion, so that we may achieve with our hands what we cannot do with our voices—preach the word of God.
4.   For as many books as we write, so many heralds of the truth we make for ourselves, or so it would seem. And thus we may hope that God will reward us for all those who are saved from their errors or make progress in the Catholic truth by means of our books; or are pierced to the heart for their sins and vices, or are fired with longing for their heavenly home.[14]

Certainly, under the leadership of John Houghton, this compunction which is the fruit of monastic prayer filled the House of the Salutation of the Most Blessed Virgin Mary, to prepare sixteen of their number for martyrdom.

The Latin texts of MS Douce 262

On the twenty folios (ff 119a–139b) between *The Dyuyne Cloude of Unknowyng* (ff 2a–118b) and the final work, *The Pystelle of Privat Councelle*, are four works, three in Latin and one, the shortest of all, in English. Their titles in translation read as follows:

f.119a   The Explanation of a passage from the book of the Blessed Dionysius on *The Mystical Theology*[15]
(This piece is an extract from Hugo de Balma's *Viae Syon Lugent*[16])
f.128a   The Seven Degrees of Contemplation.[17]
(This is wrongly attributed in the MS to St. Bonaventure. Its author is in fact Thomas Gallus.[18])
f.132b   "When a solle begynyth to fele grace . . . "[19]
(This short piece has no title in the MS, nor is it given an author. It has not been identified.[20])
f.134a   A very short directory on the Ascent of the Mind to God, ac-

cording to the *Life of Perfection* of Br. Henry Herp of the Order of Friars Minor.[21]
(This is a paraphrased synopsis of part of Harphius' *Mystical Theology*. The original is in Flemish.[22])

The context of the extract from De Balma's *Mystical Theology* is the last part in his long chapter on the Unitive Way. He first declares what it is (*Via Unitiva quae sit*), using a famous quotation from the seventh chapter of Denis's *Divine Names:* the wisdom that, in the words of the great "O" antiphon, proceeds from the mouth of the most high, reaches out from end to end mightily, ordering all things sweetly.[23] Finally, he takes the key text from the Introduction of Denis's *Mystical Theology*—the explanation of that which every Dionysian believed to be the method of contemplative prayer taught to St. Timothy by St. Denis of France, St. Paul's disciple.[24]
    De Balma analyzes this text. There are two steps in the experience of the mystical theology: the experience of the progress to assimilation with the divine, and second, the experience of its achievement. The first is an experience of love alone, so that every other faculty of knowing—sense, imagination, understanding, intellect—is totally stripped of activity; equally the objects of all these faculties are to be ignored, even the personification of divine love, which is the Third Person of the Blessed Trinity, the eternal begetting of the Word, or the processions of the Persons. The Supreme Spirit is never preeminently comprehended by such speculative contemplation:

> They [the pagan philosophers] considered that the highest knowing power was in the intellect, whereas there is another which surpasses the intellect no less than the intellect outstrips the lower reason and the reason the imagination. This is the supreme power of the affection— the spark given off by the higher reason, which is alone capable of union with the Holy Spirit.[25]

The main problem in the ascent is the inordinate independence of the intellect as it strives to superimpose itself on the affect, which is being raised to God by the ardor of its love. The author of the *Cloud* and other commentators on the *Mystical Theology* of the Pseudo-Denis prescribe the device of the "cloud of forgetting."[26] De Balma employs an image from Thomas Gallus that John of the Cross in his turn will employ—the shearing away of all intellectual activity. Other common images are derived from Scripture: the blinding of the intellectual eye from the Canticle, the bursting of bonds from Psalm 115, the self-stripping and despoilment (*kenōsis*) of the Christological hymn in Philippians, and the silence of the Word from the eighteenth chapter of Wisdom. All this is because of the innate tendency of the understanding to a reflexive comprehension of each and every object of the affect, including the God who is love. As the *Cloud* author insists, the exercise is painful to begin with,[27] and more arduous for some than for others. But with practice, as De Balma says, eventually "without hindrance the loving power is carried up on the wings of its ardent affections, and enjoys such liberty that as often as it wills it is brought up into a most ardent union with God. And so in its prayer, by the desire of the affections in the mind's loving power, and insofar as may be here below, it prays with such attention as though it saw him face to face."[28]

The seven degrees (or fruits) *of contemplation* is an attempt to describe more affectively the various aspects of De Balma's analysis of the infused contemplative process toward felt union, and the experience of the union itself. In the first grade, *ignis*, "burning ardor," we have a description, it would seem, of what we would now call the transition from acquired to infused and formally passive contemplation. The soul at prayer, in the full ardor of her loving desire to see God, is suddenly inflamed by a purifying love, in which she is offered as the perfect victim of this purifying love that is poured out in her heart. The second grade, the *unctio* or anointing, is the sweetness of the divine love diffused through the entire soul to strengthen and educate it. The third grade is ecstasy—*extasis* or *excessus mentis*, in which a man is lifted beyond the externals of the self: an inchoative ecstasy, in which the soul is now trained to run in the way of the active virtues, humility and purity. It means the suspension not only of the exterior senses, but also of the natural understanding and of all active mental operations, under the influence of infused grace. It does not however conform to any classical definition of ecstasy,[29] for the soul has not yet "gone out of herself," but intellect and affection are both in some way separated from the self.

In the fourth grade, *speculatio*—gazing, the soul, after being simplified and purified in her "superior part" by the contemplation of the eternal verities and the desire for union with the Good and the True, is poised at the extreme limits of her natural operations. Here the affection is content to rest and to be drawn upward, since the soul has already been brought into joyful contact in the supreme point of her affective power with the divine goodness;[30] but for the time, the knowing power must remain docile and silent, since there is no face-to-face vision here below. The *degustatio* or "spiritual relish" of the fifth grade confers an experiential knowledge of the divine *suavitas*—"taste and see that the Lord is sweet." This leads inevitably to the mental passivity—*quies*—which describes the total openness of the spiritual intelligence, insofar as this can be experienced here below. It is the effect of the visitation of wisdom such as is described by the *Cloud* author in "Private Direction," the union of the perfection of faith and holy love: "the high wisdom of the Godhead descending through grace into a man's soul, knitting it and uniting it in spiritual wisdom and discernment . . . [so that he] is filled in his spiritual exercises with this loving simplicity."[31]

The seventh and final grade, the ultimate term of unitive contemplation here below, is glory. It is the union of the perfection of faith, in all its loving submission, with the divine ecstatic love—such as that between the infant Christ and his mother at Bethlehem. "How shall I describe this glory?" writes Gallus, at the end of the treatise: "It is none else but he who was nurtured at the Virgin's breast, whom her white arms fondled as she dandled him on her lap, and embraced with her purest love: Our Lord Jesus Christ who is blessed without ages. Amen."[32]

Henry Herp was born in East Flanders at the beginning of the fifteenth century. His writings show that he imbibed the teaching of Thomas à Kempis and others on the *Devotio Moderna;* but he is revealed also as a close student of John Van Ruysbroeck and is known generally as his heir. The MS tradition of his main work, *The Mystical Theology,* is very tangled, and a great deal of the other writings ascribed to him are synopses and extracts from it. It is clear that he knew and was influenced by the works both of Thomas Gallus and Hugo de Balma. He distinguishes two contemplative ways, the scholastic and the mystic. The first represents a slow ascent by means of the exercise of the moral virtues, and the dictum of St. Paul at the beginning of Romans: "The invisible things of God are clearly seen from the creation of the world, being understood by the things that are made; his eternal power also and his divinity."[33] The mystic contemplation is, however, easier, quicker, and more endowed with spiritual riches. It begins from charity, and its active component is aspiration rather than meditation—the ejaculations traditional since the time of Augustine, and so dear to the heart of the Carthusian followers of the Pseudo-Denis. Yet if you take the mystic way, you will spend half a year considering the love of the Lord in his Passion, in somewhat the same way as St. Bernard recommends in his sermon for Wednesday of Holy Week: the following of Christ in his inestimable love, his wonderful humility, and his steadfast patience.[34] At the same time, these preliminary meditations are necessary as scaffolding. As soon as the edifice is up and the keystone in place they can be dispensed with and the aspirations take over, which express the soul's love and its fervent desire to be united with God.[35]

Finally, the piece beginning "When a solle begynyth to fele grace . . ." is a short narrative of what happens to those who submit themselves to the affective contemplative process, over and above the philosophical disquisitions and theological ruminations drawn out in the other treatises of this MS. The object of this negative or mystic way, which all the Dionysian authors revere so much as the hidden doctrine of the Apostle Paul, over and again turns out to be the experience and praise of God's ineffable love for the creatures made in the image and likeness of his Eternal Son the Incarnate Word, who communicates this healing, redemptive, and unitive grace. It is, teaches the *Cloud* author, the lower part of the contemplative life, which first of all "consists in good spiritual meditations and earnest consideration of a man's own wretched state, with sorrow and contrition."[36] This is the state out of which the contemplative apprentice was led when he was "lost in Adam," when a loving God "with his great grace kindled your desire and fastened to it a leash of longing."[37] This is the higher part of the active life when the soul, illumined by grace, is filled with the remembrance of Christ's Passion, the kindness and the wonderful works of God.[38] When the author of the *Cloud* speaks of the meditations of those called to anagogical contemplation—as is the soul which is summarily described here—he writes of "sudden awarenesses . . . of God's goodness . . . of sudden intuitions without previous cause, and single words bursting forth from the depths of the spirit."[39] So it is in this brief treatise, when the soul "feels God in himself and himself in God."[40] When this author re-echoes many of the sentiments and the very phraseology of the *Cloud* author, we are assured that "knowing by unknowing" for these late medieval Dionysians is not so much the metaphysical exercise described in the negative naming of God, which is largely the Neoplatonist, pre-Christian contemplation, but the act of love that is the knowledge of pure faith,[41] rooted in and grounded on the love of Christ, which surpasses all knowledge and yet fills us with all the fulness of God.[42] "You wounded my heart with your Word, my God, and I loved you."

APPENDIX

Notes

1. The Oxford University Library was restored by Sir Thomas Bodley at the end of the sixteenth century. The distinguished antiquarian Francis Douce (1757–1834) bequeathed his collection of MSS to this library.

2. It is surmised that the language and handwriting of *When a solle begynyth to fele grace* belongs to the late fourteenth century, while the *Pystelle of Privat Councelle* was transcribed by Andrew Boorde, who entered the London Charterhouse about 1510. Cf. P.H., *The Cloud*, XVI. All nine English Charterhouses had been suppressed by 1539, including London.

3. John Houghton, along with two fellow Carthusian Priors, Sts. Robert Lawrence of Beauvale in Nottinghamshire and Augustine Webster of Axholme in Lincolnshire, were the protomartyrs of the English Reformation. They were hanged, drawn, and quartered on Tyburn hill May 4, 1535, two months before Sts. John Fisher and Thomas More suffered, for refusing to acknowledge the king as the only Supreme Head on earth of the Church in England, a charge that the Act of Supremacy had made high treason. They were canonized by Pope Paul VI on October 25, 1970.

4. Maurice Chauncy, *Historia aliquot nostri saeculi martyrum* (*The History of the sufferings of eighteen Carthusians of England*), p. 6. Chauncy grieved for the rest of his life that as a young monk he had allowed himself to be seduced into taking the oath of the king's supremacy. Later he founded a house for exiled English Carthusians in Bruges, known as Sheen Anglorum, named after the suppressed Carthusian House on the Thames in southwest London. The typology of Lia and Rachel as images of the active and contemplative lives is given in "Pursuit of Wisdom." Cf. *supra*.

5. Ibid., p. 11.

6. Ibid., p. 51.

7. This MS is now lodged at the modern Charterhouse of St. Hugh of Lincoln at Parkminster in the county of Sussex. P.H. *The Cloud*, pp. xviii–xix.

8. Cf. Michael G. Sargent, "The Transmission by the English Carthusians of Some Late Medieval Spiritual Writings," p. 238.

9. Chauncy, *History*, p. 35.

10. Sargent, "Transmission by the English Carthusians," *passim*.

11. Ibid., p. 229.

12. The most influential translation from Latin into Middle English was that by Nicholas Love, Prior of Mount Grace, of the *Meditationes Vitae Jesu Christi*, for centuries attributed to St. Bonaventure. Love entitled his translation of it *The Mirror of the Blessed Life of Jesus Christ*. I have written at some length on Richard Methley's translation of the *Cloud of Unknowing* into Latin in a previous volume in this series.

13. Sargent, "Transmission by the English Carthusians," *passim*.

14. *Consuetudines*, ch. xxviii: P.L. 153, 694–96.

15. *Expositio super quaedam verba libri Beati Dionisii de Mystica Theologia.* The MS does not identify the author. De Balma, a French Carthusian, died

295

APPENDIX

in 1340. His work was soon attributed to St. Bonaventure—Carthusian authors in the main remained anonymous. The definitive edition (Quarrachi) of Bonaventure's works restored it to Hugo in 1895. Cf. *The Cloud, ed. cit.*, Introduction, pp. 19–20. We have translated this extract from the MS, and present it below.

16. As we note elsewhere, the treatise is named from its opening phrase, a citation from the Lamentations of Jeremiah (1:4). It is often entitled both *The Mystical Theology* and *The Threefold Way* (*De Triplici Via*)—purgative, illuminative, and unitive. Cf. *The Cloud, ed. cit.*, pp. 19–23.

17. *De Septem Gradibus Contemplationis.*

18. This work was finally rejected as pseudo-Bonaventuran by the Quarrachi editor in 1898. Cf. also Théry, "Thomas Gallus et Egide d'Assise," pp. 180–90.

19. It is presented in modern English "When a soul begins to feel grace working in him . . ."

20. N. R. Ker, the Oxford palaeographer, thought that the handwriting and language of this text indicate that it was written in the late fourteenth century—earlier than all the rest.

21. *Directorium quoddam brevissimum mentis in Deum ad consequendam Vitae Perfectionem fratris Henrici Herpe Ordinis Minorum.*

22. Henry Herp was first one of the Brothers of the Common Life, and rector of their community at Delft in 1445. He joined the Franciscans of the Observance while in Rome in 1450, and died in 1477.

23. He cites the entire antiphon, "*O Sapientia . . . veni ad docendum nos viam prudentiae*" (come and teach us the way of discernment). This is from chapter III, part I, p. 21. (I cite from Peltier's edition of the *Opera Omnia* of St. Bonaventure, tom VIII.)

24. Cf. *supra.*

25. Cf. *infra.* This is a citation by De Balma from *Vercellensis.*

26. Cf. *The Cloud, ed. cit.*, ch. 5, p. 128.

27. Cf. ibid., ch. 71, p. 259.

28. *Infra.*

29. Cf. J. Lemaître, s.v. *l'extase*, in "Contemplation chez les orientaux Chrétiens," D.Sp.II, 1863.

30. The Latin here reads: *Superessentialis et superintellectualis bonitas, unitam sibi ineffabiliter affectionem et superfervide ipsum desiderantem et se sursum impingentem occurrens hilariter excipit . . .*

31. *Supra*, V.

32. The colophon in the MS reads: *Finit tractatus Sancti Bonaventura de septem gradibus contemplacionis. Deo gracias.*

33. Rom 1:20.

34. *Sermo de Passione Domini*, P.L. 183, 263–70.

35. M. Viller, "Harphius ou Bourcelli?" *La prima collatio de la Theologia Mystica*, RAM 3 (1922): 155–62.

36. *The Cloud, ed. cit.*, ch. 8, p. 137.

37. Ibid., ch. 1, p. 116.
38. Ibid., ch. 8, p. 136.
39. Ibid., chs. 36–39.
40. Ibid., ch. 40, p. 198.
41. Cf. J. Krynen, "La pratique et la théorie de l'amour sans connaissance dans le *Viae Sion Lugent* de Hugues de Balma," *RAM* 40 (1964): 161–83.
42. Eph 3:17–19.

Text: MS Douce 262 ff. 132v–134r.

"When a solle begynyth to fele grace . . . "

When a soul begins to feel grace working in him, he weeps in sorrow for his sins.[1] There comes to his mind the great unkindness he has done to God,[2] and what peril his soul is in.[3] He weeps and wails for his offense, and in great sorrow and lamentation he cries and calls upon God for his mercy.[4] As he continues in this state, he decides to enter Religion, or at least to go to Confession;[5] and there he purifies himself by contrition and doing penance, until he is cleansed from all the rust of sin.[6] Soon he feels himself eased in body and soul, and rescued from remorse of conscience, which is the greatest pain on earth.[7] Then straightway he experiences great sweetness in reading and prayer and in listening to sermons.[8] He thinks that this exceeds all worldly consolation; and he draws great comfort from that which was hitherto very tedious and painful to him.[9] Then he is prompt and ready to do all the things that will please God,[10] and to avoid those things that will displease him.[11] Next, he learns meekness, fear, and love, intent on turning his will and his prayer to God's will.[12]

As he continues in this way, God sees the good will and desire of his soul,[13] and draws him nearer to himself, with sweet stirring of love and compassion.[14] And where before he wept and sorrowed for his sins and his unkindness, now he weeps out of love and compassion.[15] Nothing brings him comfort or joy except the remembrance of Christ's Passion and the joys of heaven.[16] And so, as he perseveres in purity of conscience, in prayer and meditation, suddenly God sends into his soul an ardent love and desire, with such fervor that all physical strength leaves him, and his corruptible body falls to earth.[17] He thinks no more on joy or pain or sin, or of the Passion of Christ or of our Lady,[18] or of anything in heaven, in hell, or on earth, but only on God:[19] not what God is in nature or in his qualities, but that God is; and this is all his desire.[20] Out of the abundance of love that is in his heart, his mouth speaks: "Heart, heart, heart," or "God, God, God."[21] Then is his soul still and at rest. He feels God in himself and himself in God.[22] So glad is the soul and body then that it is a wonder that the heart of the man does not burst out and leap from his mouth and into God, for love.[23]

At other times, before the soul is rapt into God, he seeks in the first fire of love through the streets of heaven[24] for the One his heart desires among the saints and angels.[25] He has no care for their company and joy, for his mind is not set on them, nor on any other thing, as I said before, but only on God.[26] And when in this way he has sought and found his Love,[27] he runs with a meek and ardent desire to be at home with him.[28] And yet he does not go into Our Lord now and at once, but moves to and fro about him with a most ardent love, and stands piteously by with his desire of God, so as to enter into his heart.[29] But God pretends to be ruthless and discourteous, as one who takes no heed of his lover and keeps him at a distance. Nevertheless the poor soul abides in his longing desire, trusting to have what he came for. Then God, his countenance full of love,[30] takes the soul and sets him in the midst of his heart.[31] Then all the world and, I think, all heaven and hell besides cannot express the joy that the soul feels in his Lord and Love.[32] Amen.

This high thing is quickly lost by sin and negligence.[33]

Notes

1. All the late medieval Carthusians—Guigo the Angelic, Hugo de Balma, Guigues du Pont, Ludolph of Saxony, the author of the *Cloud*, begin their treatment of contemplation and the contemplative life as does the anonymous author here: cf. for Guigo, *The Ladder of Monks*, ME version, cited in the *Cloud*, ed. cit., p. 116, n. 15; for de Balma, *De modo purgativo*, p. 5.i; for Guigues and Ludolph, *Proemium*—God invites sinners to pardon and sorrow—Rigollot I, p. 1; those called to the contemplative life are penitents. For the *Cloud* author, "Mary [Magdalen] stands for all sinners called to the contemplative life" (ch. 16, pp. 154–56).

2. "Unkindness: Unnatural conduct; absence of natural affection or consideration for others." N.E.D. s.v.

The contemporary *Layfolks' Catechism* has: "If he does not keep the commandments, he does to God more unkindness than any brother may do to another." De Balma says that every capital sin shows contempt by the creature for the Creator (I, 1, p. 4).

3. Ludolph offers seven reasons why the sinner should ponder the life of

APPENDIX

Christ. The last is that this will rescue him from the dangers of this mortal life (*Proemium* 8: Rigollot I, p. 2; cf. *Cloud, ed. cit.*, ch. 2, p. 118).

4. The *Cloud* author uses similar language about contemplative sorrow and the lump of sin, which is "none other than yourself." "He is nearly out of his mind with sorrow, so much so that he weeps and wails and denounces and heaps curses on himself" (*ed. cit.*, ch. 44, p. 204).

5. The author with his "leastwise" is doubtless thinking of those sinners who are already religious; while the *Cloud* author repeatedly insists that anyone entering on contemplative prayer must consider sacramental confession an integral and necessary part of the process and preparation (cf. *Cloud, ed. cit.*, index, p. 279, s.v. n. 1).

6. "the rust of sin": an image common to all these authors. De Balma develops it: "For just as scouring works on iron, so that with each scrubbing something of the rust on it is removed; so every sigh and groan removes something of the rust of sin, which is left behind after it has been treated by grace" (ch. I, 2, p. 5). For the *Cloud* author's use of the image, cf. ch. 15, p. 152.

7. Walter Hilton describes the beginning of conversion, that a man's "thought is most upon his sins, with great compunction and sorrow of heart, great weepings and many tears . . . asking mercy and forgiveness of God for them. . . . And though he shrive him never so cleanly, yet shall he feel biting and remorse of conscience . . . and he can hardly have any rest" (*Scale I*, Underwood, p. 77).

8. The Illuminative Way—substantially the *lectio divina*—"follows immediately on the purgative. It is through the groans and tears that the soul, washed clean from the rust of sin, is immediately prepared for the reception of the divine beams" (De Balma, II, 1, p. 8). The *Cloud* author here appears to follow Gregory the Great, in his *Moralia* II, 1: "Holy Scripture brings before the eyes of our mind a kind of mirror." We need God's word when we are blinded by habitual sin, to see our blemishes (ch. 35, pp. 187–89; but cf. de Balma, *op. cit.* II, 1, p. 8).

9. Walter Hilton says that some men, after giving themselves to praying, reading, and other good works, are likely at first to say "Ho! I will no more of this, for I have had enough" (*Scale II*, ch. 18, p. 292).

10. Cf. "The Letter on Prayer"—ME: For deuocioun is not ellis, as Seinte Thomas the doctour seith, bot a rediness of man's wile to do thoo thinges that longen to the servis of God . . . Methink that Seinte Bernard acordeth . . . where he seith that alle thinges should be done swiftlich and gladlich. Cf. *supra*.

11. Cf. *The Ladder* for the common definition of the prayer integral to the contemplative process: "Prayer is the devoted heart's turning to God to drive away evil and to obtain what is good" (p. 82).

12. The *Cloud* author, offering us Richard of St. Victor's definition of virtue in the context of contemplative prayer, says that meekness and love are good examples, since whoever has these two has them all (*ed. cit.*, ch.

APPENDIX

12, p. 147). In "Prayer" the author tells his dirigé to begin his prayer in the atmosphere of fear of the Lord (cf. *supra*).

13. The good will directed to God "is the substance of all perfection. All sweetnesses and consolations . . . are accidentals of this good will." Cf. *Cloud, ed. cit.*, ch. 49, p. 215. On desire, cf., e.g., ch. 75, pp. 265–66.

14. For St. Bernard's aphorism, "You would not have sought me, had you not found me," cf. Dumontier, *St. Bernard et la Bible*, p. 43, n. 2.

15. The gift of tears, the "sorrow that is full of holy desire . . . a strong and profound spiritual sorrow," is the sorrow that makes all other sorrows seem to be a sort of pretense. So the *Cloud, ed. cit.*, ch. 44, pp. 203–05.

16. De Balma writes of the qualities of the Lord who becomes the spouse of the sinner and speaks to him with accents of love ("Your voice is sweet and your face beautiful," Sg 2:14): "Good, most beautiful Lord, sweet and abounding in mercy, you have redeemed me with your precious blood" (ch. I, 2, p. 7).

17. Daniel, the "man of desires" (10:11) says: "Lord, at the sight of you, my joints are loosed and no strength remains in me" (Vulgate 10:16). The "soon" and the "suddenly" of the contemplative tradition as it ponders the *maranatha* at the end of the Apocalypse, Guigo writes in his *Ladder:* "The Lord . . . does not wait until the longing soul has said all its say, but breaks in upon the middle of its prayer, runs to meet it in all haste . . . by making it die to itself, he gives it new life in a wonderful way" (VII, p. 87).

18. Here the soul begins the anagogical contemplation " . . . in this exercise it is of little or no profit to think of the kindness or the worthiness of God, or of our Lady . . . or even of the joys of heaven" (*Cloud, ed. cit.*, ch. 5, p. 129). Cf. "Private Direction," *supra*.

19. "Insofar as there is anything in your mind except God alone, in that you are further from God" (*Cloud, ed. cit.*, ch. 5, p. 129).

20. The burden of the "Letter of Private Direction"; cf. *supra*.

21. Cf. Mt 12:34 (Vulgate): *Ex abundantia cordis, os loquitur*. Here are the short prayers, "words of one syllable," the prayer proper to anagogical contemplation, which pierce the palace of heaven, bursting out of the depths of the spirit (*Cloud, ed. cit.*, chs. 37–40).

22. Cf. Prv 3:24 (Vulgate): "You will be at rest and your sleep will be sweet"; the text the author interprets anagogically in "Private Direction" (cf. *supra*, V, "In this loving union of God and your soul, your sleep shall be very sweet, for it shall be a spiritual nourishment and inward strength . . . ")

23. Cf. Ps 44:1 (Vulgate): *Eructavit cor meum verbum bonum; dico ego opera mea Regi*—"My heart has burst forth with a good word. I will tell of my doings to the King." "It bursts on the ears of almighty God." *Cloud, ed. cit.*, ch. 37, p. 193.

24. Guigues du Pont speaks of the fiery and loving devotions (*ignitas devotiones*), which the fervent heart (*pia mens*) sends upward to God even as do the angels. Cf. Grausem, "De Contemplatione," p. 275. John of Fécamp

APPENDIX

speaks in similar accents, as does our unknown author, in a disquisition on heaven, "in which the soul, full of devotion, animated by extreme love for Christ, sighs for him . . . and the firm and stable city of God . . . Thy streets, O Jerusalem, will be paved with gems and with pure gold" (cited in Le Clercq, *Love of Learning*, pp. 76–83).

25. The author of the piece conflates the reference to the scriptural anagogy of Apoc 21:10–13, with an allusion to the Song of Songs, where the bride is searching for her spouse in the streets of the city of Jerusalem, leaving behind "those who keep the city" (3:1–5).

26. "I have found him whom my soul loves, I will not let him go until I have brought him into my mother's house." This is the "affective impulse of the love of God for himself alone" (*Cloud, ed. cit.*, ch. 8, p. 138).

27. Cf. Sg, 3:4.

28. ME: with a mek and a fervant desyr homly to hym. "Homely" is perhaps the favorite word of the late medieval English Spirituals, and Julian is the most prominent as she describes her concluding revelation of the Divine Indwelling, which was, she says, confirmatory of all the rest. "In us is his homeliest home and his endless dwelling" (ch. 67). The first example of the word "homeliness" in the N.E.D. is from Rolle: "Festerand barnes with hamlynes" (cherishing children familiarly). Cf. ME: "in the tyme of this werke schal alle be iliche hamly unto hym for he schal fele than no cause bot only God" (*Cloud, ed. cit.*, ch. 25). Perhaps one of the author's most beautiful passages is in "The Pursuit of Wisdom," on "how love rises in the affection"; cf. *supra*).

29. This sentence and the next are a brief allusion to the traditional game of love. The *Cloud* author suggests that the contemplative should play the wretch and the coward, so that God will "take you up, cherish you, and dry your spiritual eyes," like a father with his infant son (*ed. cit.*, ch. 32, p. 181). The waiting on God, to be called to the work of contemplation, is dealt with comprehensively in "Private Direction" and its spiritual exegesis, "I am the door of the sheepfold" (Jn 10; cf. *supra*).

So the soul confesses its love to the spouse in Hugh of St. Victor's *De Arrha Animae:* "I confess my woes to you, Lord God. How is it that you have not left me, Sweetness of my life and Light of my eyes? You wish that I may love you, and how shall I love you? How much I should love you, and who am I to love you? . . . Oh, how much is there in me for which I should blush in his presence? Oh, would that I could be hidden from his eyes, if only for a moment, so that I could wash away all my stains, and so come into his presence immaculate and without spot!" (P.L. 176, 967–69).

30. "Truly he is your beloved who visits you. He comes stealing in, incomprehensible, invisible. He comes to touch you, not to be seen by you" (ibid.).

31. Julian begins the account of her sixteenth revelation with this image of mutual indwelling: "And then our good Lord opened my ghostly eye, and showed me my soul in the midst of my heart . . . large as it were an

301

APPENDIX

endless citadel and also as it were a blessed kingdom. In the midst of that city is our Lord Jesus true God and true man" (ch. 68).

32. "Contemplation is when the mind is in some sort lifted up to God and held above itself, so that it tastes the joys of everlasting sweetness." Guigo's definition in *The Ladder*, p. 82.

33. So *The Ladder:* "He will leave you at once and give his favors to others if you play him false" (XI, pp. 91–92).

Appendix Text: MS Douce 262: ff 119r–127r.

Exposicio super quedam verba libri beati Dionisij De Mistica Theologia

Here is a commentary on an extract from the *Mystical Theology* of the Blessed Denys. It concerns the wisdom received directly from God by the great priest and apostle Paul, and handed on to Denys the Areopagite, who in his turn wrote it down for Timothy, the disciple of truth, in anagogical and obscure style, as follows:[1]

My friend Timothy, in these dark contemplations you must abandon with an intense effort your senses and intellectual operations, and all the objects of sense and understanding, and all existent and nonexistent things, and insofar as possible, ascend, without knowing, to union with him who is above every substance and all knowledge. For it is by passing beyond yourself, purified from all that might hold you back or limit you, that you will be carried up to the sovereign-substantial radiance of the divine darkness. See to it that none of those who are uninstructed hear of these things.[2]

In these words of the Apostle Paul and his disciple are contained supreme wisdom, the height of all perfection insofar as it can be attained during this earthly pilgrimage, and all the profound teaching of the books of Denys the Areopagite.[3] When this perfection is comprehensively known, whatever is above understanding in the Dionysian writings is acquired with an ease beyond all calculation. This ascent, which is called ascent by unknowing, is nothing else than to be impelled directly by the ardor of love, without any creaturely image, without any thought going before, without any accompanying impulse from the understanding; so that it is the affection alone which hits the target. In the actual exercise itself, the speculative knowing power must not be exercised in any way or attain to any knowledge.

According to the Canticle of Canticles, this affection is the eye in which, as it is written, the Spouse is wounded by the Bride, and he

302

himself bears witness to it when he says: "You have wounded my heart, my sister, my bride, you have wounded my heart with one of your eyes."[4] This ascent to union alone is called unknowing, or knowing through unknowing. When all the activity of the imagination and of the intellect or understanding is done away with, the union of most passionate love is directly felt,[5] one which the understanding cannot reach. And what is more, all speculative knowledge is ignorant of it.

So the blessed Denys says that it incomparably exceeds all other forms of knowing: "Wisdom is the most divine knowledge of God which is known by unknowing."[6] It is far more lucid and much more informative than all other kinds of learning, knowledge, and apprehension, for not only does it raise the affection above itself and perfectly unite the creature in loving ecstasy to the most high Spouse, but also it so elevates the understanding that it is flooded with the light of all discernment and knowledge which streams from the divine rays, and far more perfectly than can happen by the exercise of any natural ability.

So the Blessed Denys says: "We praise this sovereign wisdom which is irrational, mindless, and foolish, because it is the cause of mind and reason, and of all wisdom and prudence; it is all counsel, and is the source of all knowledge and prudence; in it are hidden all the treasures of wisdom and knowledge."[7] By wisdom and knowledge Denys here means everything that can be achieved by the power both of loving and of knowing.[8]

He calls this wisdom irrational: because reason cannot apprehend it, nor does it employ rational investigation. He also calls it mindless: that is, without mind and without intellect; for in its operation this wisdom does not use the intellect, nor is the power of the intellect enough to reach this highest knowledge. He also calls it foolish: for this wisdom rises up in the affection without any use of the understanding at all. It cannot in any way be grasped by the understanding.

This wisdom is perfectly expressed in the words of Denys cited at the beginning. In his philosophical system, which transcends all reflection, Denys calls contemplation "mystical": that is, when the intellectual power knows by means of the loving power which has gone before it, and not vice-versa. And this is the truest and most certain knowledge, far removed from all error and opinion and deception in the imagination.[9] In this mystical knowledge, where the loving power is in control, the command is to abandon both the senses and the intellect, root and branch: first, those very powers of appre-

APPENDIX

hending, where he says: "the senses and the intellectual operations"; second, the objects of those powers, where he says: "the objects of sense and intellect." "Existent and nonexistent things" must also be abandoned. By existent things are to be understood the eternal exemplars in the divine mind to which whatever is exemplified in the lower order of creatures must correspond.[10] By nonexistent things are meant those which have no exemplification in creatures: as when we consider the Trinity and the procession of the Persons. For we do not find in creatures any example of someone giving birth to another who is the same as himself, each a substance truly existing; nor any example of the love which joins those who love, itself existing substantial and equal to the lovers themselves. Therefore this contemplation, the best among all speculative contemplations, is to be abandoned; not because it is not good and noble, but because in the human mind there is a higher apprehension by which alone the supreme Spirit is preeminently grasped; and this alone is said to be the best part which Mary chose.[11] (There is another kind of contemplation which Rachel typifies; and yet another, typified by Leah, exercised by the senses on creatures[12]). The reason is because the more like to God the mind becomes in its operations, and the higher it ascends in reaching heavenly things, the more like to them it becomes, and the more intimately transformed into God; and also because there is no contemplative speculation which has this power of transformation, but only the love which extends and deifies.[13] It is this alone which grasps divine things; intellectual contemplation cannot reach them, but merely moves toward them, catching a glimpse of them from afar. In the *Divine Names*, it is said: "It is necessary to understand that our mind has a knowing power by means of which it gazes on invisible things; but union passes beyond mind's nature, and by this it is joined to that which is above itself. It is by this unitive power that divine things are to be understood, not on the level of our own powers but when we are wholly outside ourselves and wholly deified."[14]

Because it is difficult to abandon all those things, we are directed to shear them away by contrition and a strong effort of the mind.[15] For the soul must, as it were, despoil itself of itself;[16] and the affection must follow, so to speak, step by step the love given from on high; and by means of this divine elevation the intellect itself, leaving its habitual knowledge at the touch of love, is informed with the most godlike qualities.[17] So it is that the whole of this wisdom is contained in ardent desire; and it is here that we are ordered to eradicate and abandon every being and the exercise of the knowing power.[18] For sometimes the knowing power has a great share in divine things, particularly when it is illuminated by the more godlike truths.[19] But the mind has another power, much more exalted than this, by whose impulses it is set on fire and raised to a higher wisdom. This is because the affective appetite itself is brought into play, and also through the ardor of him who is raising it:[20] for he has the primacy over the rational spirit above all graces, habitual and infused, both by reason of the importunate attraction he exercises and the dignity he possesses.

So it is that the worthy doctor, the *Commentator Vercellensis*,[21] writes of the author of the *Mystical Theology*:

> He has handed on another and incomparably more profound way of knowing God, one which is above the intellect and beyond substance, which pagan philosophy did not apprehend.[22] They never sought it out, nor did they dream of its existence, nor did they detect the presence of this power which is diffused throughout the soul. For they considered that the highest knowing power was in the intellect;[23] whereas there is another which surpasses the intellect no less than the intellect outstrips the lower reason, and reason the imagination. This is the supreme power of the will—the spark given off by the higher reason, which is alone capable of union with the Holy Spirit, that is, with the divine.[24]

For this reason, since the work of the entire intellect is suspended in this incomparable way, the mind's sovereign affection must be cut off from everything; not only must the activity proceeding from the sensible and knowing powers be eliminated, but also the objects of those powers, sensible and intelligible things.

After he has dealt with what has to be abandoned, the next point logically concerns the unitive ascent itself. First he notes the dispositions of him who makes the exercise, when he writes "without knowing"; and then the upward nature of the extension, when he says, "be lifted up"; and finally he indicates with precision the sole object of the ascent, when he says, "to union with him."[25] But since we have said that all apprehension is outside this mystical ascent, then there must be absence of knowing while it is taking place: that is, the intellect itself must be wholly cut off.[26] For in this ascent it always desires to grasp the object toward which the affection is tending. So there is a very great conflict during the ascent, because of the intense attachment of the intellect to the affection.[27] And this attachment has to be rejected at the cost of great labor; for the intellect's apprehension is by means of the imagination and fancy, or by circumscribed definition, or in some other way that is limiting. Therefore the affection must leave the intellect behind by its upward swiftness. This, then, is a necessary condition for the highest knowledge: that in the journey upward all speculative knowledge must be evacuated. For he himself is unknown to the intellect, which must be left behind if we desire to come to the knowledge which is above mind. In this ascent, whenever the intellect joins itself to the affection, to that extent there will be impurity. It is only insofar as the eye of the intellect is totally blinded—and this can only happen by great travail and labor—that the eye of the affection, in its extensions, is lifted up to an incomparably greater freedom and height.[28]

This can be seen by means of a bodily example. Just as in the action of breathing, inhalation and exhalation proceed from within without any deliberation, so the affection, when it is set on fire, of its own accord reaches above the intellect toward that with which it desires to be more perfectly united. Its action is completely separated from all understanding by a distance which corresponds to the prompt help it receives from above;[29] so that it ascends by the wonderful speed of its impulses[30] (they are swifter than thought), and by the dilating and importuning ardor of the impulses themselves, just like breathing in and out. And the intellect is repudiated and rejected like a good-for-nothing beggar, though it clamors to take part with its own activity of speculative knowledge in an exercise which cannot be expressed or properly explained in words, according to *Mystical Theology:* "But now in the upward movement from the lowest to the highest, the higher one reaches in the ascent, the less grows the number of words. And when the ascent is complete, there will be no words at all, and all will be made one with that which cannot be spoken."[31]

For uncreated Wisdom desired to reserve to itself alone the teaching of this wisdom, in order that every mortal creature might know that there is a teacher in heaven who manifests true wisdom only to his chosen scholars, by his heavenly touches and the beams of his radiance;[32] and also to confound the wise of this world, since a simple old woman or a village yokel, as long as they prepare themselves in the way prescribed, can arrive at this ascent of wisdom, to which no natural philosophy nor human industry can attain.[33]

Denys then adds a rule for this ascent: "Ascend without knowing to union with him"; that is, with the most High who is above mind and thought. And the reason has already been given in part; for neither grace nor glory nor release from pain nor anything else is demanded by those desires of this upward-striving ascent, but only he with whom alone, for whose sake alone, the mind aspires to union when it treads down those other clamorous desires.[34] And he is attained and perceived by the grasp of the affection, which strains toward him above every human mind and thought.

All this wisdom comes to fulfilment only by the shearing away of all intellectual activity; when the loving power, in its sovereign point, desires nothing else than to be united to God alone. And because this is very difficult, he adds: "so far as is possible"—to the furthest possible extent; saying with the Psalm: "Lord, you have burst my bonds; I offer you the sacrifice of praise."[35] Because when by God's help the obstacles mentioned before, the sensible and intelligible objects, and particularly the intrusion of the knowing power which always wants to grasp what the affection is seeking, the fetters, that is, which bind this unitive extension are completely broken; then without hindrance the loving power is carried up on the wings of its ardent affections, and enjoys such liberty that, as often as it wills,[36] it is brought up into a most ardent union with God. And so in its prayer, by the desire of the affections in the mind's loving power, and insofar as may be here below, it prays with such attention as though it saw him face to face.[37]

Sometimes the mind is so lifted above itself by this impulse and ascent that it seems to be entirely outside the body.[38] And so Denys adds: "as far as is possible," because no mind can experience these things except by the divine visitation, as is said in the *Divine Names*, "To that unknowing of the sovereign-substantial, which is above reason, intellect and substance itself, we must ascribe the sovereign-substantial knowledge; gazing upward only insofar as it descends to us through the rays of the divine oracles."[39] This is the same as saying that the knowledge through unknowing is the teaching of God alone. And hence, the more of this divine instruction the affection receives, which is the heavenly infusion by whose means the mind and heart enjoy loving converse with the Beloved, the more intimately God himself penetrates the mind; so that he who is true Wisdom is known more clearly through these divine beams.

Next Denys says, "and by passing beyond yourself," because unitive Wisdom does not merely urge that the creature be completely blotted out, but it also spiritually mortifies the intellect, and subjects it to the divine influence alone. Of this passing beyond oneself, the Apostle said to the Corinthians: "If we be transported in mind, it is to God."[40]

Through this constant passing above itself, by the fire of love, the soul achieves a more efficacious separation and purification,[41] and through its burning extensions which consume the rust, advances more efficaciously than before, when it begins to ascend through this wisdom. For just as there is a twofold purification in material things, by water and fire, so it is in spiritual things: The purgative way purifies by means of sorrow, of frequent acts of attrition and tears; but purification through the ascent of burning love is much more efficacious. So it is by this excess of ardor that the mind is much more easily set free from all that holds it back, that is, from all worldly pleasure, and is purified from all extraneous affections.[42] And when all the obstacles are thus removed and its bonds broken, it is carried up in the most agile way to the shining of the divine incomprehensibility.[43]

This, then, is the order of the mind's ascent: first it must leave all consideration and love of sensible objects, and the contemplation of all intelligible things. For the loving power must ascend in all its purity, without intellectual defilement, to him whom it recognizes in its striving as being alone the quiet harbor of its desire, so that it may be more intimately united with him. Through this ascent of long-lasting, upward-striving impulses the affection is extended more and more; and, as it were, by a shower of burning sparks,[44] the mind is more surely purged and because it finds rest elsewhere from the love of fleshly things, of necessity it becomes detached without complaint from the flesh, much more than before. From now on the loving power becomes more agile, because its impulses are pure; and as often as it will, without being pestered by the intellect, it is carried along by most ardent love.

So Denys says at first: "ascend in unknowing," and later, "you will be carried up." He means that in the beginning of this exercise of the mystical ascent, the sovereign point of the loving power ascends only with difficulty.[45] But through the passing beyond and above the self, and the more effective purification, it now rises without difficulty and when it will, and is made weightless by the wonderful agility of its impulses.[46] And so, though in this upward movement nature and love are running together,[47] at the same time, once the obstacles are removed and greater graces are being infused from above, the ardor of love is incomparably more effective than the vigor of the affection in arousing the natural facility and agility of its impulses.[48]

And this is the meaning of "when all things are done away with," and so forth. For there are two things in particular which must be abandoned: that which holds back and that which limits. The first refers to the loving power: insofar as it is affected by any created thing, it is necessarily joined to it, and in consequence held back;[49] so that it is made less agile in the ascent to the divine. But we must abandon not only what holds us back but everything which limits us. The limited is that which is known in its proper form, as having definite being; and all the speculation and contemplation of it must be removed.[50] For just as what holds one back defiles the affection, in that the affection is taking pleasure in a creature viler than itself, so through the other the intellect is defiled, that is, darkened. For as long as it is filled with human speculative knowledge, the intellect, in comparison with that wisdom which comes from the sovereign-shining rays of God's light, is, as it were, covered with a dark cloud.

So this last word refers not only to a more agile ascent, but to the highest knowledge of the understanding itself. For according to the wisdom of the blessed Denys, that alone is true knowledge of divine things which is conferred by the experiential comprehension of the upward-striving ascent. And so by the divine mercy and according to the competence of the person making the exercise, when the mind has aspired through long periods of time to fasten the beloved to itself more closely by bonds of more ardent love, for a short time and according to its capacity, as it must be in rapture, then it is that the blessed vision is granted.[51] This happens especially when a person is cleansed from what holds him back or limits him, and he "is carried up to the radiance of the divine darkness," that is, to the light of the divine incomprehensibility, here called darkness. So Denys writes in his letter to Timothy: "The divine cloud is inaccessible light in which God is said to dwell; for he is invisible because of his surpassing brightness."[52] This wisdom is immediately present before the knowledge of the rapture. And to him who has long aspired to it, these words are spoken by his Beloved: "Friend, come up higher."

So it is said first: "Ascend," and then "you will be carried up": because in the actual ascent to unitive wisdom both nature and grace are at work. But in this supreme ascension of the intelligence, it is the elevating grace alone which is activated, and this in the most immediate way: that is with regard to the raising up which is rapture, insofar as the mind is so lifted up in the body that the senses are left behind. For in this last elevation of the higher reason, both the intelligence or the knowing power, as well as the loving power, have the final consummation of their activity, though they are still acted upon.

Afterward it is said, "Let no one who is uninstructed hear of these things," and so forth. Denys says: When we speak of holy things we are to treat them as holy, according to the sacred tradition; and these

APPENDIX

things are to be taken away from the profanation or the derision of the uninstructed.

Notes

1. The words *anagogia* and *anagogicus* carry a double meaning in medieval spiritual literature: first, it is the ultimate spiritual sense of Holy Scripture. Richard of St. Victor says it is a foresight of the heavenly realities revealed and hoped for (P.L. 196, 200). Then there are two kinds of contemplation (speculatio) depending on the etymological derivation of *speculatio:* i.e., whether it is derived from specul*um* or specul*a* (a high-place, a watch-tower). So we have *speculatio aenigmatica* and *speculatio anagogica*. The former is St. Paul's *speculum in aenigmate*, contemplation of God through a mirror dimly, by means of analogies, resemblances, and images; the other is when the mind is led upward, without any signs or causes and cleansed of all images, and simply carried into its infinite Origin. Cf. Garnier, P.L. 205, 765.

2. "with an intense effort," *forti contritione*. The text is of course Sarracenus's. The printed text of Hugh (p. 39.i.) here reads *concertatione*.

3. Thomas Gallus distinguishes between all the other named works of Dionysius: the two *Hierarchies*, the *Divine Names*, and two others that have not been found—*Outlines of Theology* and *Symbolic Theology*, as well as a few letters and the *Mystical Theology*, "which contains an incomparably more profound way of knowing God" (Théry, pp. 13–14).

4. Sg, 4:9. The same text is used in "Inward Stirrings," nn. 60–63.

5. *Haec consurrectio sola ignorata vel cognitio per ignorantiam dicitur . . . per unionem ardentissimi amoris id sentiat. . . . Hugo's Latin is often clumsy.

6. The citation is from the *Divine Names*, ch. 7. Cf. *Cloud, ed. cit.*, ch. 70, p. 256.

7. The quotation from *Divine Names* itself cites Col 2:3.

8. Gallus writes, in the *Prologue* to his *Explanatio*, "This wisdom, that is, of knowing God in this way, is acquired by a most ardent love of God and a powerful reaching out of the spirit towards the contemplation of eternal wisdom" (Théry, p. 17).

9. There is a similar phrase in "Private Direction"; cf. *infra*.

10. "The existent things are those which come forth into being from the Word by creation" (Théry, p. 40).

11. Lk 10:42. Cf. *Cloud, ed. cit.*, pp. 163–65.

12. Cf. *Cloud, ed. cit.*, p. 161.

13. Ibid., ch. 67, pp. 249–50, where the author expands his own thoughts of Deification. In the "Letter on Prayer," he uses the telling phrase "the marriage which is made between God and the soul" (cf. *supra*).

14. The *Divine Names*, ch. 7. For the Dionysian union or unitive power (*henōsis*), Gallus speaks of *synderesis* or the apex of the affection or loving power. The *Cloud* author is probably the simplest and clearest of all the

310

APPENDIX

Dionysians in his description of the operation of this loving power that can make God comprehensible to the human mind and heart. Cf. *Cloud, ed. cit.*, ch. 4, pp. 122–23.

15. . . . *ideo contricione et forti conatu mentis ista resecari iubentur.* The vocabulary is from Sarracenus's translation of the *Divine Names*, ch. 1.

16. The scriptural source is (Vulgate) Col 3:9: "Despoil yourselves of the old man with his deeds, and put on the new, the one that is renewed in knowledge by means of the image of the One who created him."

17. "Through the sovereign-point of the affection (*affectionem principalem*) and the elevation of the intelligence, you will be brought into ineffable oneness with him, God, who is above all substance and knowing" (Théry, pp. 41–42).

18. . . . *omne ens et officium intellectualis virtutis extirpari et derelinqui precipitur.*

19. The language here is reminiscent of Richard's distinction between the fifth and sixth grades of contemplation. Cf. *Benjamin Maior* IV (P.L. 196, 135ff.).

20. "This love is so powerful that it not only draws a man out of himself to God, but it draws God out of himself to man" (Théry, p. 18).

21. Cf. *supra*, and *Cloud, ed. cit.*, pp. 43–47.

22. *Vercellensis* writes "the pagan philosopher," and in another place *philosophers;* while elsewhere he names him as Aristotle. De Balma has written, it appears, *gentilis prophetia* (the gentile prophecy or divination). Cf. p. 41, i.

23. Gallus's text here reads: "They thought the highest knowing power was the intellect"; both de Balma and our text read " . . . was *in* the intellect" (*inesse intellectui*).

24. "*sc. principalis affectio, et ipsa est scintilla synderesis, quae sola est unibilis spiritui divino.*" For these various names for the sovereign-point of the spirit, cf. *supra*.

25. Sc. the *aphairesis*—the abandonment, the movement upward by way of unknowing—*agnōsia*, the union with the Transcendent—*henōsis*. Cf. *supra*.

26. "Here it is necessary to cut off (*resecari*) the operations of the intelligence in that they cannot make any headway." So Gallus, in his *Explanation* of the *Divine Names*, ch. 1.

27. Thomas Gallus says that intellect and affection at first help one another in the upward striving, like Peter and John running to the empty tomb. Then John, who represents the intellect, gets there first, but he cannot enter the sepulchre but must wait for Peter, who is the affection, to go in first. Ibid.

28. In another place, Gallus writes: "The best way of seeking God is to be enabled to reach out above the sovereign point of the intellect until the apex of the mind is separated from every being, and comes to understand the sovereign-substantial which transcends all existence, and by

311

APPENDIX

entire unknowing which transcends unknowing comes to know the unknowable."

29. Again the idea here is that of Gallus, who says that the Divine Goodness goes out to greet with joy the one who desires to meet him with an overpowering fervor, and draws him up to union (*Divine Names, loc. cit.*, cf. ch. 2, pp. 89–90).

30. Again, it is the *Cloud* author who expatiates on those impulses that have an extraordinary velocity (*mira velocitas*). Cf. ch. 4, p. 122.

31. Cf. Théry, pp. 89–90.

32. For similar language and descriptions, cf. "Private Direction" V, n. 61, and the *Cloud*, ch. 26, pp. 174–75.

33. Cf. "Private Direction" VI, *supra*.

34. Gallus says that to see the truths of wisdom is very difficult indeed; for one needs to ascend to the almost inaccessible summit of a very high mountain (Théry, p. 40).

35. Ps 115:16–17.

36. The symbol of the eagle flying above the rest of the symbolized faculties in Ezeckiel's vision is similar to that of the *scintilla synderesis*, the purest part of the affective faculty, the sovereign point of the affect (*scintilla apicis affectualis . . . principalis et pura participatio divinae bonitatis*), which passes into the divine life and is somehow deified.

37. Richard of St. Victor, speaking of the sixth grade of contemplation and the *excessus mentis*, says that the mind in this state is so greatly expanded or dilated (*humana intelligentia ex dilatationis suae magnitudine quandoque accipit*) that it is beside itself; and though it does not cease to be itself, seems to be no longer human, but more than human. For it gazes on the glory of the Lord and is transformed into his likeness (2 Cor 3). *Benjamin Maior* V, 9: P.L. 196, 178–79.

38. This appears to be rapture as described by Walter Hilton in his English version of the *Stimulus Amoris* of James of Milan—*The Goad of Love*. "It is being ravished from the use of your bodily wits, so that all kinds of phantasms of bodily likeness are withdrawn from your soul, and your mind overpasses the common and reasonable manner of knowing in this life" (*ed. cit.*, p. 154).

39. *Divine Names*, ch. 1. For Gallus, following Richard of St. Victor, "the sovereign-substantial knowledge" is here the infused contemplation of the Blessed Trinity.

40. 2 Cor 5:13.

41. The purification, says Gallus, is from the interior imaginary phantasies—what Coleridge called "imagination and fancy"—and also from rational and intellectual impulses, so that we are finally left only with "sharp darts of longing love," as the *Cloud* author says.

42. Gallus, in his *Explanation* on the *Ecclesiastical Hierarchy*, when speaking of the preparation for Holy Communion, is not only concerned with purification from sins and the roots of sin, but also with intellectual abstrac-

312

APPENDIX

tion from all imaginary and discursive elements for receiving Christ with the best possible dispositions.

43. Cf. Théry, p. 44.

44. The exercise of the *Cloud* is described as "a sudden impulse, one that comes without warning, speedily flying up to God as the spark flies up from the burning coal" (ch. 4, p. 126).

45. "By the long labor of Moses, and the delay in the revelation to him, we are to understand those who cannot come to the perfection of this spiritual exercise unless long labor precedes it" (*Cloud, ed. cit.*, ch. 71, p. 259).

46. Cf. *supra*, n. 30.

47. Cf. *supra*, n. 37

48. The *Cloud* author remarks that it belongs to human nature never to be without these impulses, one of which is equal to the smallest particle of time (ch. 4, pp. 124–26).

49. Temporal cares, says Gallus, are the restraining force or any action that is an obstacle to the soul's receptivity. Cf. Théry, p. 43.

50. Here is one of these phrases where the *Cloud* author seems to be translating directly from the text of de Balma, whose Latin reads: *Absolutum enim dicitur omne quod sua propria forma cognoscitur habens esse distinctum.* ME: "al thing that may be knowen by the propre fourme in thi knowyng." Cf. *supra*.

51. The *Cloud* author is more sophisticated than de Balma in identifying the various states of suspension and rapture. Cf. *ed. cit.*, ch. 71, pp. 257–59.

52. The citation is the *incipit* of the fifth letter of the pseudo-Dionysius. The fictional (?) addressee is not Timothy but Dorotheus the deacon. The Latin text of Sarracenus reads: *Divina caligo est inaccessibile lumen in quo habitare Deus dicitur. Et invisibilis quidem existens propter excedentem claritatem* (de Balma writes *invisibile*). The scriptural reference is given in Gallus's *Expositio* on the Letter: "The apostle says that the Lord dwells in inaccessible light" (1 Tim 6:16). Cf. Walsh, "The Expositions of Thomas Gallus on the Pseudo-Dionysian letters," p. 215.

Bibliography

Adam Scot (of Dryburgh). *De Quadripertito Exercitio Cellae.* P.L. 153, 785ff.

Pawsey, H., Dom. "Adam of Dryburgh," in *Pre-Reformation English Spirituality.*

Allison Peers, E., ed. and trans. *The Complete Works of St. Teresa of Avila.* 3 vols. New York/London: Sheed and Ward, 1946.

—. *The Complete Works of John of the Cross.* London: Burns and Oates, 1953.

Augustine of Hippo, St. *In Joannis Evangelium.* P.L. 35, 1379–1976; *In Epistolam S. Joannis ad Parthos.* P.L. 35, 1977–2062; *Enarrationes in Psalmos.* P.L. 36 and 37; *Sermones de Tempore.* P.L. 38; *Epistolae.* P.L. 3; *De Civitate Dei.* P.L. 41; *De Gratia et Libero Arbitrio.* P.P. 44, 881–912; *De Confessionibus.*

Aux Sources de la vie Cartusienne. Grande Chartreuse, 1960.

Barbet, J. *Thomas Gallus: Commentaires du Cantique de Cantiques.* Paris: Vrin, 1967.

Bernard of Clairvaux, St. *Sermones super Cantica.* P.L. 183, 785–1198; *Sermones de diversis.* P.L. 183, 537–763; *Sermones: In Circumcisione.* P.L. 183, 131–42; *In Assumptione B.M.V.* P.L. 183, 415–30; *In festo S. Michaelis.* P.L. 183, 447–54; *In festo S. Andreae Apostoli.* P.L. 183, 503–44; *In Psalmum Qui Habitat.* P.L. 185–254; *De Gratia et Libero Arbitrio.* Ed. J. Le Clercq, H.M. Rochais; *De Diligendo Deo* Romae: Traditiones Cistercienses, 1963; *Tractatus de Caritate,* P.L. 184.

Bonaventure, St. *Opera Omnia* tom. 1. Paris: Vives, 1860.

BIBLIOGRAPHY

—. *Itinerarium mentis in Deum.* Ed. E. Cousins. *The Soul's Journey into God.* New York: Paulist Press, 1978.
Bruno, St. *Epistolae.* In *Lettres des Premiers Chartreux,* S.C. 88, 1962.
Butler, C. *Western Mysticism.* London: Constable, 1951.
Benedict, St. Rule of, in D. Parry, ed., *Households of God.* London: Darton, Longman and Todd, 1980.
Butler-Bowdon, *The Book of Margery Kempe.* London: Jonathan Cape, 1936.

Caplan, H., ed. *Cicero ad C. Herrennium de ratione dicendi.* London: Loeb Classical Library, 1954.
Carleton Brown, F. *Religious Lyrics of the XVth Century.* Oxford: Oxford University Press.
Chatillon, F. "Hic, ibi, interim." *RAM* 25 (1949).
Chaucer, G. *The Canterbury Tales: Complete Works,* ed. F. N. Robinson. Oxford: n.d.
Chauncy, Maurice, Dom. *The History of the Sufferings of Eighteen Carthusians of England.* London: Burns and Oates, 1890.
Chénu, M-D., O.P., *Introduction à l'etude de S. Thomas D'Aquin.* Paris: Vrin, 1950.
Chévalier, P., ed. *Dionysiaca.* Paris: Desclée, 1937.
Clay, R. M. *The Hermits and Anchorites of England.* London: Methuen, 1913.
Colledge, E., *Mediaeval Mystics of England.* London: John Murray, 1960.
—. "English Religious Literature" and "Piers Plowman." In *Pre-Reformation English Spirituality.* Ed. J. Walsh. New York: Kenedy, 1964.
—. *Julian of Norwich: Showings.* New York: Paulist Press, 1978.
—. *Julian of Norwich: Showings* (crit. ed.). 2 vols. Toronto: Pontifical Institute of Mediaeval Studies, 1978.
—, and J. Walsh, eds. *The Ladder of Monks and Twelve Meditations of Guigo II.* New York: Image Books, 1978.

Daniélou, J., S.J., *Platonisme et Théologie Mystique.* Paris: Aubier, 1944.
Déchanet, J.M., O.S.B. *Guillaume de St. Thiery.* Paris: Beauchesne, 1978.
—. "John Scotus Erigena." In *Pre-Reformation English Spirituality,* ed. J. Walsh. London: Burns and Oates, 1964.
De Lubac, Henri, S.J. *Exégèse Médiévale.* toms I et II. Paris: Aubier, 1959.

BIBLIOGRAPHY

Denzinger, H., and A. Schönmetzer. *Enchiridion Symbolorum*. Freiburg-im-Breisgau: Herder, 1967.
Dickens, A. G. *Clifford Letters of the Sixteenth Century*. Surtees Society, 172, 1957.
Dumontier, P. *S. Bernard et la Bible*. Paris: Desclee, 1953.

Gardner, J. E. G. *The Cell of Self-Knowledge*. London, 1921.
Gilbert of Hoyland. *Sermones in Cantica*. P.L. 184.
Glossa Ordinaria. In Vetere Testamento. P.L. 113.
—. *In Novo Testamento*. P.L. 114.
Grausem, J. P. *Le* De Contemplatione *de Guigues du Pont. RAM* X, July 1929.
Gregory the Great, St. *Moralia in Job*. P.L. 75.
—. *Dialogi*. P.L.
—. *Homiliarum in Ezechielem*. P.L. 76.
Guigo I. *Consuetudines Cartusianae*. P.L. 153, 631–758.
Guigo II. *Epistolae in vita contemplativa*, S.C.

Hilton, Walter. *The Scale of Perfection I and II.* Ed. and trans. E. Underhill. London: Watkins, 1923.
—. *The Goad of Love*. Ed. and trans. C. Kirchberger. London: Faber and Faber, 1952.
—. *Expositions on Psalms 90 and 91*. Ed. and trans. J. Walsh and E. Colledge. London: Mowbray, 1961.
Hodgson, Phyllis, ed. *The Cloud of Unknowing and the Book of Privy Counselling*. London/New York: Early English Text Society, 1944.
—. *Deonise Hid Diuinite and Other Treatises on Contemplative Prayer related to 'The Cloud of Unknowing.'* London/New York: Early English Text Society, 1955.
Hope Allan, Emily. *Writings ascribed to Richard Rolle*. London: Oxford University Press, 1927.
Horstman, C. *Richard Rolle of Hampole and his Followers*. London: Sonnenschein, 1895.
Hugh of Folieto. *Claustrum Animae*. P.L. 176, 1017–1184.
Hugh of St. Victor. *Expositio in Hierarchia Caelesti S. Dionysii*. P.L. 175, 923–1154.
—. *Homilia in Ecclesiasten*. P.L. 175, 173–616.
—. *Allegoriae in Novum Testamentum*. P.L. 175, 751–922.
—. *De Modo Orandi*. P.L. 176, 977–86.
—. *De Meditando*. P.L. 176, 993–96.
—. *De Arca Noë Morali*. P.L. 176, 618–80.
—. *De Arrha Animae*. P.L. 176, 951–68.

316

BIBLIOGRAPHY

Hugo De Balma. *Mystica Theologia*. In *S. Bonaventurae, Opera Omnia I*. Romae: Vives, 1866.

Ignatius of Loyola, St. *The Spiritual Exercises in Spanish & English*. Ed. J. Rickaby. London: Burns and Oates, 1915.
—. The *Spiritual Exercises*. Ed. J. Puhl. Chicago: Loyola University Press, 1957.

John Cassian, St. *Collationes I, II* ed.
—. *Institutiones I*. Ed. J. M. Guy, S.C.
John Scotus Erigena. *De Predestinatione Liber*. P.L. 122, 355–440.
—. *Commentarium in Evangelium S. Joannis*. P.L. 122.
John of Toulouse. *Ricardi Canonici et Prioris S. Victoris Parisiensis Vita*. 1650.
Johnston, W. S. J., *The Mysticism of the Cloud of Unknowing*. New York, 1967.
Jones, W. *Crowns and Coronations*. London: 1883.
Julian of Norwich. *Revelations of Divine Love*. Ed. J. Walsh. London: Burns and Oates, 1961; Wheathampstead: Anthony Clarke Books, 1973.
—. *Showings*. New York: Paulist Press, 1978.
—. *Showings, Vols. I and II*. Toronto: Pontifical Institute, 1978.

Kirchberger, C., ed. and trans. *Walter Hilton: the Goad of Love*. London: Faber and Faber, 1952.
—. *The Coasts of the Country*. London: Harvill Press, 1952.
—. *Richard of St. Victor*. London: Faber and Faber, 1954.
—. *Hugh of St. Victor*. London: Faber and Faber, 195.
Knowles, D. *Medieval Mystics of England*. London: Burns & Oates, 1961.

Le Clercq, J., O.S.B. *L'Amour des lettres et le désir de Dieu*. Paris: Editions du Cerf, 1957.
—. *The Love of Learning and the Desire for God*. Trans. C. Misraeli. New York: Fordham University Press, 1960.
— et al. *Histoire de Spiritualité Chrétienne*. Paris: Aubier, 1961.
Longfellow, W. H., ed. and trans. *Dante's Divina Comedia. Il Paradiso XI*.
Ludolph of Saxony. *Vita Jesu Christi, tom I–V*. Ed. L. M. Rigollot. Paris: Palmé 1878.

McCann, J. *The Cloud of Unknowing*. London: Burns and Oates, 1934.

BIBLIOGRAPHY

Margery Kempe, The Book of. Ed. S. Meads and Emily Hope Allan. London: Early English Text Society, 1940.
Maisons de l'Ordre des Chartreux. Parkminster: Chartreuse de St. Hugues, 1919.

Nostinger, M., O.S.B. *La Nuage de l'inconnaissance, et les epitres qui s'y rattachent.* London: Solesmes, 1977.

Owst, G. R. *Literature and Pulpit in Mediaeval England.* London: Cambridge University Press, 1933.
Oxford English Dictionary. Complete text, vols I–XIV, reproduced micrographically. Oxford: Oxford University Press, 1972.

Pantin, W. A. *The English Church in the Fourteenth Century.* Cambridge University Press, 1955.
Parry, D., O.S.B., ed. *Households of God: The Rule of St. Benedict.* London: Darton, Longman and Todd, 1980.
Pepler, C., O.P. *The English Religious Heritage.* London: Blackfriars, 1958.
Pez, B. *Commentarium in Cantica Thomae Abbatis Vercellensis.* In *Thesaurus Anecdotorum Novissimus.* Augustine Vindelicorum, 1721.
Pfeiffer, Fr. *Meister Eckhart.* London: Evans, 1924.
Promptorium Parvulorum

Rahner, K., S.J. "Coeur de Jésus chez Origène." *RAM* 1934.
Richard of St. Victor. *Benjamin Minor seu De Preparatione Animi ad Contemplationem.* P.L. 196, 1–63; *Benjamin Maior.* P.L. 196, 64–302; *De Trinitate.* P.L. 196, 987–91; *Expositio in Cantica Canticorum.* P.L. 196, 405–21; *Adnotationes Mysticae in Psalmos.* P.L. 196, 265–400; *De Eruditione Hominis Interioris.* P.L. 196, 1229–1634; *In Apocalypsim.* P.L. 196, 683–888; *De Quattuor Gradibus Violentae Caritatis.* P.L. 196, 1207–26.
Rolt, C. E. *Dionysius the Areopagite.* New York: Macmillan, 1920.
Roques, René. *L'Univers Dionysien. Structure Hierarchique du Monde selon le Pseudo-Denys.* Paris: Aubier, 1954.
Routledge, D., O.S.B. *Cosmic Theology: The Ecclesiastical Hierarchy of Pseudo-Denys.* London: Routledge Kegan Paul, 1964.

Sargent, M. "The Transmission by the English Carthusians of some late Medieval Spiritual Writings." *The Journal of Ecclesiastical History* 27, 3 (July 1976).
Salu, M. B. *The Ancrene Riwle.* London: Burns and Oates, 1955.

BIBLIOGRAPHY

Smaragdus. *Diadema Monachorum*. P.L. 93.

Teresa of Avila, St. *The Complete Works, Vols. 1–3*. Ed and trans. E. Allison Peers. New York/London: Sheed and Ward, 1946.

Théry, G., O.P., ed. *Thomas Gallus: Grand Commentaire sur la Théologie Mystique*. Paris: R. Haloua, 1934.

—. *"Thomas Gallus, Aperçu Biographique." Archives d'Histoire litteraire du Moyen Age (AHDLMA)* XII (1939).

—. "Thomas Gallus et Égide d'Assise." *Révue Néo Scholastique* XXXVI (1934).

Thomas Aquinas, St. *Summa Theologica I–IV; Commentarium in Iam Epistolam ad Corinthios: In Divinis Nominibus S. Dionysii*. Turin/Rome: Marietti editions, n.d.

Thomas à Kempis. *Imitatio Christi*.

Thompson, E. M. *The Carthusian Order in England*. London: SPCK, 1930.

Vandenbroucke, F. *et al*. "*La Spiritualité du Moyen âge*. Paris: Aubier, 1961.

Vanneste, J., S.J., *Le Mysteére de Dieu*. Paris: Desclée, 1959.

Vitae Patrum. P.L. 73.

Walsh, J., ed. and trans. *The Cloud of Unknowing*. New York: Paulist Press, 1981.

—, and E. Colledge, ed. and trans. *Of the Knowledge of Ourselves and of God*. London: Mowbray, 1961.

—, ed. *Spirituality through the Centuries*. New York: Fordham University Press, 1963.

—, ed. *Pre-Reformation English Spirituality*. New York: Harper and Row, 1964.

—, ed. and trans. *A Letter of Private Direction*. New York: Whetstone Press, 1973.

—. "*Nuâge de l'Inconnaisance La*." *Dsp*. fasc. 1980.

—. "*The Expositions of Thomas Gallus on the Pseudo-Dionysian Letters*." *AHDLMA* 38 (1964).

—. "*Thomas Gallus et l'effort contemplatif*." *Revue d'histoire de Spiritualité (RAM)* 61 (1975).

(For published works and MSS of Gallus, see "The Ascent to Contemplative Wisdom." *The Way*, July 1969, pp 243–9. "A Letter on Prayer." *The Way* VII (1967): 156–62. "A Letter on the Discernment of Spiritual Impulses" *The Way* VII (1967): 240–48.

Index

320

INDEX

322

INDEX

Trinitate, 14–15; discretion of, 19; and Gallus (Thomas), 14–15; and humility, 213–214; *Instruction of the Interior Man*, 14; *Justus Meus*, 15; life of, 13; and moral sense, 16, 18; mystical theology of, 14–16; Pound's study of works of, 15–16; and virtue, 190–191

de Rochefort, Garnier, 199–200

Roques, René, 53

Salvation, 7, 17–18, 201

Sarracenus, John, 62–63

Scripture, 225–227

Sensible things, 80, 209, 217–218, 245

Sensuality, 21–22, 27–29

Shame, 18–19, 31–32

Silence, 134–135

Sin: of Adam, 202; aversion from, 18; forgiveness of, 197; hatred of, 30–31; temptation of spirit to, 113–114

Smaragdus, 209

Society, 5–6

Solitary life, 210–211

Solomon, 223

Sorrow, 23–24, 209, 236–237

Soul: and confession, 114; and grace, 239; nourishment of, 203; perfection of man's, 234; powers of, 21

Spirit: and confession, 114; devil, 109–112; distinguishing type of, 108; of flesh, 108–

109; knowledge of own, 112–113; lustful thoughts, 109–110; peaceful thoughts, 110–111; purity of, 114–115; temptation of, 113–114; of world, 108–109

St. Denis's Prayer, 74–75

St. John of the Cross, 52

St. Victor, 13–14

Suso, Henry, 206

Temptation, 113–114, 136–137, 244–245

Theology: apophatic, 8–9; cataphatic, 8; goal of, 202; mystical, of Richard of St. Victor, 14–16; *Mystical Theology* on, 51; negative, 79–80; positive, 8, 79–80

Thomas of St. Victor (*See* Gallus, Thomas)

Trinity, 207

Tropology, 16, 18

Union, 57–58, 163–164

Unitive love, 196

Unity, 57–58, 77–78

Unknowing, 55–57

Vandenbroucke, François, 206

Vercellensis, 66–68

Virtue, 190–191

Whiterig, John, 195

Will (*See* Affection)

William of Champeaux, 13–14

William of St. Thierry, 51–52, 205–206

Other Volumes in this Series